The Road Forward

The Road Forward

Bailo and Barclay

400 Commonwealth Drive
Warrendale, PA 15096-0001 USA
E-mail: CustomerService@sae.org
Phone: 877-606-7323 (inside USA and Canada)
724-776-4970 (outside USA)
FAX: 724-776-0790

Library of Congress Catalog Number 2021932281
http://dx.doi.org/10.4271/9781468603002

ISBN-Print 978-1-4686-0299-9
ISBN-PDF 978-1-4686-0300-2
ISBN-ePub 978-1-4686-0301-9

To purchase bulk quantities, please contact: SAE Customer Service

E-mail: CustomerService@sae.org
Phone: 877-606-7323 (inside USA and Canada)
724-776-4970 (outside USA)
Fax: 724-776-0790

Visit the SAE International Bookstore at books.sae.org

Chief Growth Officer
Frank Menchaca

Publisher
Sherry Dickinson Nigam

Development Editor
Dan Reilly

Director of Content Management
Kelli Zilko

Production and Manufacturing Associate
Erin Mendicino

Contents

“We’ve learned we can do remarkable and inspiring things—with speed—when we share a vision. As leaders, we have a responsibility to make the world a better place and do what it takes, in any crisis, to ensure we come out stronger on the other end.”

Mary Barra

Chairman and CEO

General Motors

Preface

COVID hit the automotive industry like a sledgehammer on March 13, 2020. The disruption to the industry included shuttering all production facilities and workplaces. A few designated essential workers were left, but everyone else went home.

What's happened since has been well documented: Women—especially black and Hispanic women—have been hardest hit by the pandemic and have lost their jobs or voluntarily left the workforce in numbers that far exceed men. According to the National Women's Law Center, there were nearly 2.1 million fewer women in the labor force in December 2020 than there were in February. In December alone, women accounted for *all* of net U.S. job losses.

So what can leaders do? What have we learned that we can carry forward? What have our team members learned that they will rightfully ask us to continue? How can we best prioritize diversity, equity, and inclusion to ensure that we provide support and opportunities for all of our workforce?

As Jill Greene, Vice President and General Counsel of the International Legal Regions of Faurecia, pointed out: It is not enough to simply have a diverse workforce—the goal is to have an environment where people from all segments of life feel included and valued.

Each of the 70 women in this book was asked to select one of several questions that address these issues in five categories: Change control, resilience, and work/life balance; growing our professional network and maintaining mentor and sponsor relationships; personal growth; diversity, equity, and inclusion; and sustainability.

Similar to this book's predecessor, *The Road to the Top is Not on the Map*, the answers were diverse and inspiring.

What we know is this: The automotive industry is resilient and strong. We expect our leaders and employees to be bold and thoughtful. The pandemic caused us all to reflect on what's really important for our society and future generations to thrive. Mobility is the crux of health, education, and employment.

We hope that this book will give you a toolkit for resiliency for whatever crisis you may encounter throughout your career and embolden you to forge your own path to make a difference.

We know we can't provide all of the answers, but as Lynn Antipas Tyson, Executive Director of Investor Relations for Ford Motor Co., wrote: "Leaders remove barriers to people doing what's best for themselves and the company. The past year has shown that the range of what's possible to accommodate people is much wider than most of us imagined."

Or as Helen Keller once said: "Alone we can do so little, together we can do so much."

Carla and Terry

Acknowledgments

When we worked on *The Road to the Top is Not on the Map* in 2019, we knew it was important, but we weren't sure how wide its impact would be.

It's hard to overstate how gratified and pleased we were with what happened after publication. The book became a SAE best seller, and we heard from women—and men—from across the industry who were inspired and motivated by the experiences and wisdom of the women who were part of it. The contents were discussed in ERGs and executive suites. Book clubs met to discuss it. And we were asked when there would be a second installment.

Well, here it is. *The Road Forward* contains insights of more than double the number of women that appeared in the first book. And we want to express our gratitude to everyone who made this possible.

First and foremost, we want to thank the women who took the time to provide thoughtful insights and useful advice—and amazing stories. In *Road to the Top*, we observed that rapid changes in technology, consumer preferences, and the economy demand strong and nimble leaders. Add to that, the global pandemic and the need for the best leaders to be even better has never been stronger.

The women in this book continue to be some of the best and most resilient of those leaders, and we find their openness and commitment to continually improved leadership humbling. We could not be more grateful to them.

Our co-producers, Sherry Nigam and Dan Reilly, and many others behind the scenes at SAE provided much-valued patience and guidance as we learned the process of book creation. Thank you.

We also want to thank our coworkers, who helped us refine our ideas at the beginning of this project as well as tie up loose ends as we moved along. Special thanks go to Neil Hawkins, Sc.D., President of the Erb Family Foundation, for his help and expertise in shaping the sustainability questions.

Lastly, we want to thank you, the reader. We truly want to make a difference for women in automotive and help create a way for all people—women and men—to be successful in our business. We hope you feel as inspired by the women in this book as we did.

Aruna Anand

Vice President
Business Unit Connected Car Networking
Business Area, Vehicle Networking and Information
Continental North America

Background

Aruna Anand is Vice President, Connected Car Networking business unit for the North American region of Continental's Automotive Vehicle Networking and Information business area. She was appointed to this position effective January 1, 2021. In this role, Anand is responsible for all global Connected Car Networking business activities that support customers based out of North America.

Executive Biography

Previously, Anand was responsible for leading an independently operating business unit that offers comprehensive engineering services. Continental Engineering Services harnesses the extensive know-how and creativity of its engineers, combined with access to Continental's entire technology pool, to provide innovative engineering solutions to external customers. In addition, it leverages its flexibility to transform mass production technology to apply to small series and niche applications at economic costs.

Since joining the company in 1997, Anand has held numerous leadership positions across the different business areas of the Continental Automotive group sector. She was Head of Software for Gasoline Engine and Transmissions Systems for the Electronic Controls business unit within Vitesco Technologies North America. She also led the Wireless Product Group Engineering within the Connected Car Networking business unit of Continental's Vehicle Networking and Information business area.

Anand earned her master's degree in Computer Science and Engineering from Oakland University and a bachelor's degree in Electrical and Electronics Engineering from Anna University, in Chennai, India. In 2018, she was honored with the prestigious *Automotive News* Rising Star award. Anand was also recently recognized at the Women of Color Awards Gala and received the 2017 Professional Achievement in Industry award. In 2020, she was recognized among 100 Leading Women in the North American Auto Industry by Automotive News.

Anand currently resides in Rochester, Michigan with her family.

Questions and Answers

1. Change Control, Resilience, and Work/Life Balance

What did you learn when you began to work from home or work in the office with a limited number of co-workers? What did you need to start doing and what did you need to stop?

On March 13th (a Friday!), we were asked to start working from home. Initially, we were told that it was going to be for a couple of weeks! And here we are a year later still at it. At first, it was a scramble to understand the impact on work-related topics such as access to labs, vehicles, and test equipment. Customer milestones and deliverables were not very forgiving. Our Leadership team quickly sprang into action by formulating safety protocols to help access critical infrastructure. Additionally, they also invested to ensure that technological obstacles for remote working were minimized or eliminated in many cases. These two measures allowed us to seamlessly transition from an in-person to an in-place work environment.

But what crept up on me stealthily and forcefully was the need to integrate my children's educational needs as well. I was not the only one working from home. The kids were also going full steam ahead with online schooling. Very soon, it became apparent that balance was replaced with integration. Work meetings and projects interweaved with lunch preparations and my need for quiet time. Work extended deep into the evening and the lines between home and workplace blurred and vanished. And then the stress followed. This called for a quick rethink. A clear demarcation in both the temporal and spatial dimensions was the result.

I had to think quite a bit and adapt to having teenagers at home and working a full-time job. I can only imagine the stresses and anxieties of families having to grapple with toddlers and grade-school kids at home. Therefore, I came to the realization that a lot of sensitivity is needed in managing the team and I had to calibrate my interactions and expectations of them in order to not be an additional source of stress.

An important learning that emerged out of this experience was the need to refresh the mind and manage the ennui. I was able to find a way to visit many places within Michigan. However, there was no interaction with other individuals, just the enjoyment of the natural wonders sprinkled liberally around where I live.

2. Growing Your Professional Network and Maintaining Mentor and Sponsor Relationships

How do you keep your existing relationships in this remote world? Are you maintaining face time with other execs while being remote? How do your direct reports maintain their face time with you?

The first couple of weeks I got by using just an audio device for all communication with mentors, the team, and mentees. Quite quickly and naturally, I realized the need to integrate visual cues as a necessary component for fruitful communication. And since then, I have been asking for and using video as an essential add-on in various meetings.

A vital part of relationship building (during pre-COVID times) was the impromptu conversations about work and many other non-work-related topics that I used to have with co-workers. This was an enjoyable aspect of going to work. At first, using electronic means to do so seemed unnatural and forced. We quickly hit upon the idea of allocating dedicated time to have these conversations. We soon started finding excuses to virtually assemble to celebrate anniversaries, awards, and birthdays. We intensified our feedback sessions and paid particular attention to topics that intersected with remote working.

I also made a conscious decision to connect with my mentors more often than before. Knowing that there were people around me to use as sounding boards, get second opinions, and share best practices was very comforting. And by the same token, I made it very clear to my team that I was available to help them navigate any thorny issues they needed help with. Our scheduled "impromptu no work, just talk" meetings helped immensely. All-around communication and the continued nurturing of relationships has helped me cope with and thrive during these trying times. These methods have also helped the team immeasurably, and that has been rewarding to hear and very gratifying.

3. Personal Growth

Have you developed new behaviors (exercise, diet, meditation, hobbies, etc.) that help you get through this new stress?

Balance is key and intense periods of focus on any one activity over all others is unsustainable. This point has been reinforced in spades over the past few months. Restrictions on travel and other entertainment options have only served to remind us to discover activities to help manage free time. As they say, variety is the spice of life.

I have strived to develop and sustain a regular schedule interspersed with activities to exercise the body and nurture the mind. Pilates and Yoga sessions help me relax and get ready for a hectic day of work. Additionally, I listen to discourses by learned scholars on a variety of philosophical subjects. Light-hearted entertainment in the form of stand-up comedy shows and such on streaming services rounds out the portfolio. During the late summer and early fall season, we developed a routine of going on a weekend picnic to nearby parks and lakes. Taking in the serene waters, followed by delicious home-cooked food, opened our eyes to a new form of spending time together and bonding.

There are many learnings from working remotely during this pandemic period. Some of these are business and life changing. I strongly believe that on the business front we will see a lasting impact in how we use real estate for office space and innovative communication tools for better collaboration. Already on the personal front, these past months have reinforced the realization that life is not all work, and relationships and experiences are key to a satisfying life.

4. Diversity, Equity, and Inclusion

The pandemic has hit hard for women in particular. Many are thinking about dialing back their careers or exiting altogether, which is very frightening for many companies. What should be done differently to retain women in the workplace?

With many responsibilities competing for and demanding effort and attention, it is unfortunate that some are choosing to leave the workforce. As many of the domestic challenges are overwhelmingly directed towards women, it, therefore, does not come as a surprise that they are being disproportionately affected. The recent sharp economic downturn coupled with the reduction in wages as a result of people leaving the workforce is devastating in the short term and very debilitating in the long term. This is driving many families deep into debt and crippling their ability to provide for their well-being.

Companies are losing experienced female talent and therefore need to devise creative approaches to address this issue. Ideas such as temporary part-time work, work-share programs, sabbaticals, and role rotations must be implemented. In addition to these short-term measures, companies must organically look into gender pay inequities and leadership opportunities for women. Creating a diverse and inclusive corporate environment is a necessary goal but is not something that should be a reaction to the currently simmering issues but rather a long-term endeavor.

At Continental, we have formed a gender, equity, and inclusiveness team that is staffed with influential leaders. Periodic town halls, focus meetings, and transparency into the process are key enablers for helping us build a trusted organization. This mind-set starts at the top of the corporation, and we are well on our way to executing the vision both globally and regionally.

5. Sustainability

Sustainability trends (climate change, water availability, health, etc.) are some of the strongest drivers for future changes for companies and their strategies. What are you seeing within your company? Is your firm reading the trends and adapting strategies to survive and then thrive with new growth?

Continental has rightly identified the ongoing and upcoming challenges with respect to preserving and enriching our environment and ecosystem for future generations. We are propelling the industry with many initiatives. We have a defined sustainability ambition that is aligned with international frameworks including the United Nations

Sustainable Development Goals, the United Nations Global Compact, the OECD Guidelines for Multinational Enterprises, and the United Nations Guiding Principles on Business and Human Rights with specific reference to the ILO Core Labor Conventions. We want to shape this sustainable future with our products, services, and operations and reduce adverse impacts along the value chain. Carbon Neutrality, Emissions-Free Mobility, Circular Economy (100% closed resource and product cycles), and Responsible Value Chain (100% responsible sourcing and business partnerships) are key sustainability focus areas. There are eight sustainability essentials that help us manage our vision and focus areas. Green and Safe Factories, Corporate Citizenship, Innovations, and Digitalization are some examples of the essentials.

The sustainability policy is broadcast within the company and its subsidiaries and is made transparent. The focus areas and the essentials are regularly reviewed for appropriateness and applicability.

Additionally, the bonus structure for company executives comprehends the sustainability performance as a key element, thus further reinforcing the need to understand the impact of our actions and products on the environment and baking such behaviors into the compensation framework.

Sue Bai

Chief Engineer
Automobile Technology Research
Honda Research Institute USA, Inc.

Background

Sue Bai is a chief engineer in the Automobile Technology Research division of Honda Research Institute USA, Inc.

Bai's areas of research include wireless communication for in-vehicle navigation systems, telematics system design and development, and connected and automated vehicle system research. She currently leads a team that supports Honda's transportation safety and mobility goals through connected-vehicle and vehicle-to-everything (V2X) communication systems.

Bai has held leading roles on SAE V2X technical standards committees for many years, working to improve safety and mobility for a variety of road users including vehicles, pedestrians, cyclists, and road workers. She is also the Honda technical leader for various industry-government collaborative projects including Ohio's 33 Smart Mobility Corridor that, when operational, will be the longest stretch of continuously connected highway in the world.

Bai holds Master of Science degrees in Computer Science, Electrical Engineering, and Industrial and Systems Engineering.

Questions and Answers

1. Change Control, Resilience, and Work/Life Balance

How do you and your team continue to innovate and improve?

Genuinely maintaining an open mind to new ideas—that, most times, are not the same as yours—certainly most important. But that is not all. I always challenge my team to be diligent in creating our own new value and then be active in sharing that new value with our industry partners. That is why we join committees and present at conferences—to share what we think is new value and help power new thinking by our also open-minded partners. This draws everyone closer and fuels collaboration and even more new thinking, which in turn leads to innovation. That can only happen through both sharing and listening.

2. Growing Your Professional Network and Maintaining Mentor and Sponsor Relationships

Are you continuing to grow your professional network while being remote? How?

Personally, I don't like to use the word network as it has a tendency to convey more "taking" than "giving," and innovation actually requires at least as much "sharing" as it does "listening." But, obviously, the larger and more diverse the group of people that you can have trusted exchanges with, the greater the opportunity is to share and listen, which powers more personal growth. Recently, I have taken great joy in regular exchanges with some of my friends who have retired from the industry and organizations such as NHTSA. Their perspectives on books, art, and history—especially early U.S. history—have greatly richened my thinking, especially as an immigrant to the U.S. Where we previously focused on technical issues, these days we are sharing much more comprehensive thoughts about people's lives and society overall. And I can sense their happiness and satisfaction in being able to share their experience and wisdom with me. These are the kinds of mentoring relationships that I feel are most beautiful.

3. Personal Growth

Have you developed new behaviors (exercise, diet, meditation, hobbies, etc.) that help you get through this new stress?

Over the past year, I've raised my mental strength by increasing my physical strength with yoga, which I enjoy very much. I've also been focusing on more basic things like making sure I have correct posture during my virtual meetings, and I find that to be much easier and refreshing. I've also been working on intellectual growth by pursuing my PhD in Human Factors Engineering. While it may be more common to seek further education in technology, I chose to learn more about the human perspective, which is ultimately where we are trying to create new value for people and for society through Connected and Automated Vehicle (CAV) technology.

Through that, I've learned a lot about the importance of research integrity and acknowledging the work of others, which builds more trusting relationships. And within a trusting environment, there is much less stress and the greater potential for more effective collaboration.

4. Diversity, Equity, and Inclusion

Are men engaged in the conversation around gender diversity, and if so, in what way?

Almost everyone is engaged in the conversation of diversity, including gender diversity. For Honda, we are fortunate that respect and appreciation for diverse viewpoints, regardless of origin, is integral to our most fundamental corporate philosophy known as Respect for the Individual. It dates to the beginnings of Honda and is comprised of three fundamental values: Initiative, Equality, and Trust. Equality explicitly recognizes all people as being different. As such, their unique perspectives and ideas should be equally welcomed and respected, regardless of who the person is or what level they hold in the organization. Personally, I believe I am ultimately judged on the value that I can bring to others, and I am inspired by that challenge. Even if someone would initially judge my ideas a certain way solely because of who I am, I take comfort in believing that they would quickly recognize real value if I can clearly provide that. Although it could be that I need to work harder sometimes, the reward of that hard work is that I can become stronger and more resilient. And as a result, I may be able to bring even more value to others. In the end, it comes down to viewing your uniqueness as an opportunity to further strengthen yourself personally and professionally.

5. Sustainability

What do you as a leader do to stay informed about sustainability trends that can impact the success of your company and its strategy?

As part of Honda's 2030 Vision, we will strive to become a company that leads the effort to realize a carbon-free and collision-free society. My daily work in the area of Connected and Automated Vehicle (CAV) technology development is helping build the way to a collision-free society and will soon deliver day-one benefits to enhanced fuel efficiency and carbon reduction as well. It is my passion, and I am excited about my work every day. I couldn't be more proud to help lead these efforts for my team and for Honda, as a member of our industry and society.

Donna Bell

Director, AV and Mobility Strategy
Ford Motor Company

Background

Dr. Donna Bell is Director of AV and Mobility Strategy at Ford Motor Company. Collaborating with key stakeholders, Donna establishes and communicates customer-driven strategies that increase corporate growth in autonomous technology, mobility, and new businesses.

Throughout her career at Ford, Donna has served in many engineering and leadership roles. Her leadership experiences include serving as Global Director of Technology and Features Strategy; CTO Chief of Staff; Research Operations Director at Ford's Greenfield Labs in Palo Alto, CA, where she was instrumental in promoting and delivering transformational technologies including AI, machine learning, autonomous driving technology including LiDAR, in-vehicle infotainment (IVI), and connectivity for Ford's winning portfolio; and global electrical product development quality manager.

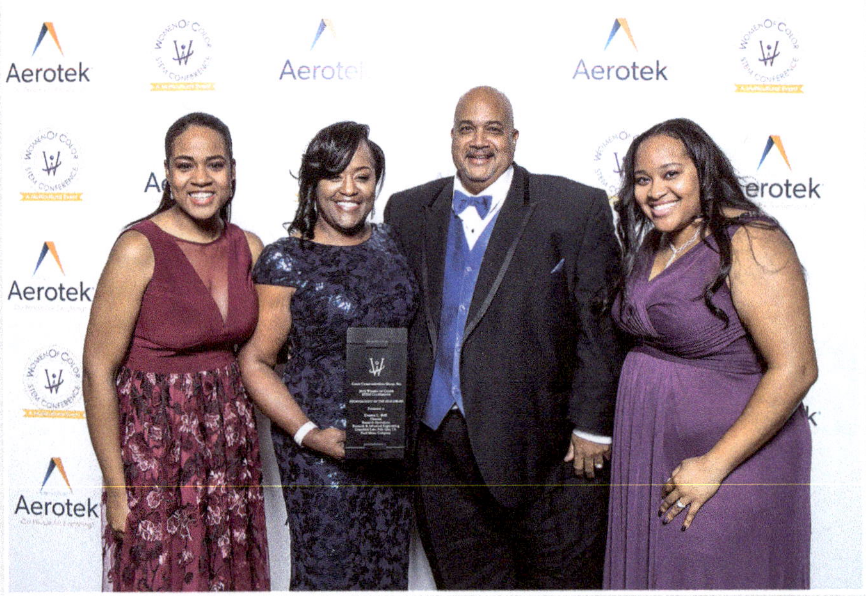

Donna Bell

Donna's involvement in the community is extensive and involves creating programs that educate and develop students in science, technology, engineering, and mathematics (STEM). She has volunteered and held multiple leadership positions in professional organizations, including the National Society of Black Engineers, Society of Women Engineers, Society of Automotive Engineers (SAE) Foundation, and the Ford African Ancestry Network. Donna has been recognized for her leadership in STEM including the highest honor of being named the 2018 Women of Color in STEM Technologist of the Year, which recognizes the exceptional achievements of distinguished multicultural women who excel in STEM.

Donna holds a Bachelor of Science degree in Electrical Engineering from Lawrence Technological University (Southfield, MI) and Master of Science degrees in Electronics and Computer Control Systems and in Engineering Management and a PhD in Industrial and Systems Engineering all from Wayne State University (Detroit, MI).

Questions and Answers

1. Change Control, Resilience, and Work/Life Balance

How has your self-motivation been to excel, learn, reach out (virtually), and manage all aspects of your new work life?

This year has been a challenge for most people around the world. The COVID pandemic, racial injustices, social unrest, and economic crisis in the U.S. have all contributed to the challenges that most have faced, myself included. Staying motivated has been essential to my well-being, with this year requiring a little more effort. Over the course of my career, I have maintained the mantra "stay focused." It means to stay focused on what matters most to me, my family, and to those around me. I have always aspired to be an executive, leading teams to greatness and exceeding the expectations of those that may underestimate me. There are many distractions that can cause me to lose focus on my goals. So, at the end of every year, I take time to reflect on my accomplishments and areas for growth in all aspects of my life: spiritual, home, work, and community. At the start of the new year, I take the time to establish my revised set of SMART goals for these areas, and I put them on a vision board. Establishing, taking action, and seeing progress toward these goals is what keeps me focused and motivated. I set the bar higher for myself every year, regularly researching ways to be better and to do better.

Donna Bell

My main motivation is my family; however, the community has a special place in my heart, as well. Now that my children are adults, I spend even more time giving back to the community, both inside and outside of Ford: volunteering, mentoring, and speaking to motivate and inspire others to be their best selves. I recently became a member of Delta Sigma Theta Sorority, Inc., an organization committed to the development of its members and to public service, with a primary focus on the black community. This membership is very special to me in that it allows an even greater impact on the community with the support of more than 300,000 women. The commitment I've made requires putting in extra time and can sometimes be a challenge in managing work-life balance, but it's what I love, and this year has been no exception. When I speak to motivate others, I normally share the following strategies for success:

- Take responsibility for your own success.
- Take an active role developing the vision for your future.
- Spend quality time on self-reflection.
- Create a plan; sharing with those that you trust will help move it forward.
- Embrace taking risks.
- Create the Vision; Stay focused; Do your best.

These strategies stay posted in a place for me to see and reflect on regularly.

2. Growing Your Professional Network and Maintaining Mentor and Sponsor Relationships

How do you keep your existing relationships in this remote world? Are you maintaining face time with other execs while being remote? How do your direct reports maintain their face time with you?

To maintain a healthy career, it is essential that you stay connected to your mentors, sponsors, and advisors. This year has forced me to think creatively about engaging with executives and leaders, both inside and outside of Ford. For existing relationships, I continue to have one-to-one sessions with my mentors, taking the lead to establish the talking points and being focused and efficient with discussions. My goal is to limit our discussions to 30 minutes, using our time wisely to ensure the greatest impact. To be the most impactful, I'm sure to have a specific topic or experience that I want to discuss with my mentor. Learning key strategies from other's experiences is a great ingredient for continuous improvement. I also leverage their knowledge to strengthen my own. Earlier this year, I had a sensitive situation where I needed some guidance. From my mentor, I was able to learn a thoughtful way to approach the situation. Even in this virtual environment, I was able to listen intently, plan thoughtfully, and take action toward a winning outcome. More recently, I approached a key leader in the company to be my sponsor. They agreed and now we meet regularly to discuss the best approaches to developing my career.

Additionally, as a leader, it is important to meet with your team members regularly throughout the week. To do that, I have planned a weekly start-up and strategy meeting with my team. I also meet with my direct reports one-to-one to address topics that they feel better discussing in a smaller setting. It is very important to me to maintain a regular cadence to build rapport with my team; in this current environment, it gets to be a challenge as the schedule of my leadership changes often and I have to adapt accordingly. In my new role, and any role for that matter, it will be important for me to establish a solution that will keep bonds strong with my team, leadership, and colleagues.

3. Personal Growth

What personal development opportunities have you taken advantage of now that you're not traveling?

This year, more than ever, has been a time for self-reflection and self-improvement. For me, self-reflection is the hardest part of my personal development journey. However, I take the time to really understand my strengths and areas of opportunity toward self-improvement. Most recently, with the guidance of one mentor and coach, I was able to reflect on my past and establish a vision for my future. It was important for me to identify the vision for my career and life. This exercise allowed me to establish a career plan that identified my skills and areas for growth. I was able to use this insight in discussions with my sponsor, which in turn exposed me to an opportunity for growth and development. Just like the coaching I receive from my mentors, I encourage my mentees to create a career plan and share it with those that can help move it forward. As opportunities arise, your sponsors and advocates will be ready to offer your name up as a suitable candidate. It has also been important for me to engage my family in my endeavors. Your family will likely be the most honest with you. I recall early on in my career my husband giving me candid and constructive feedback that allowed me to make changes in the way I showed up at work. At times, the advice was difficult to hear, but necessary if I wanted to make progress. These constructive and candid conversations were a springboard toward reaching my goals. The same holds true for your interactions with your direct line supervision: ask for feedback that will allow you to make the necessary course corrections that will in turn help move you closer to your goal.

4. Diversity, Equity, and Inclusion

There has been a lot of talk about diversity—and, in recent years, inclusion. Equity has entered the corporate conversation in a major way this year. What actions are you and your company taking? Are these methods aligned with company goals?

Diversity can be addressed from a number of different viewpoints: gender diversity, racial diversity, diversity of thought, and diversity of talent are just a few. When added to equity and inclusion, it brings on an entirely different meaning for me. To have a diverse team is one thing, but to ensure equity and inclusiveness requires a different level of leadership and attention. For me, it's personal. I serve in various capacities where I use my influence to drive change. A few examples include serving as VP of Operations for our employee resource group Ford African Ancestry Network (FAAN), where we create programs to develop our members; and as a board member for Ford's Women of Ford employee resource group dedicated to the unique needs of women of Ford, which involves bringing together employees to work on creating an environment that promotes the empowerment and development of women. Additionally, I serve as a trustee for SAE Foundation an organization whose mission is to enrich STEM experiences for all students; and as Ford's liaison to The National Action Council for Minorities in Engineering (NACME), an organization focused on developing and connecting underrepresented STEM scholars to major corporations. The recent racial tensions in the U.S. have been a catalyst in understanding the issues that exist both in corporate and community settings. Our company recently completed an internal audit aimed at understanding where internal tensions may exist. The results of the audit will be used to pinpoint key areas for opportunity in leveling the field for all of our employees. Philanthropic actions taken outside of the company also show our commitment to driving change in underrepresented and underserved communities. I am fully committed to supporting the company's vision for driving sustainable change relative to diversity, equity, and inclusion both inside and outside the company.

5. Sustainability

Sustainability trends (climate change, water availability, health, etc.) are some of the strongest drivers for future changes for companies and their strategies. What are you seeing within your company? Is your firm reading the trends and adapting strategies to survive and then thrive with new growth?

Ford's has a comprehensive Sustainability Blueprint. The most recent 2020 Sustainability report lays out Ford's vision and plans relative to our sustainability strategy and aspiration and goals that impact climate change, human rights, diversity, energy, waste, access to mobility, water usage, air emissions, and use of recycled materials over time. The steps we have taken to address the most recent COVID pandemic has proven to be most effective; providing much needed PPE to frontline workers that cannot do their jobs from home. Our philanthropic arm, Ford Fund, has allocated resources to support communities hit the hardest by COVID. The blueprint takes into account the recommendations for improvement from key experts, considering trends and insights that are considered toward our aspirations and goals. It also shows the inputs used to create value within the inner workings of the company. Any potential new employees would benefit from reviewing our sustainability plan.

Jacquelyn Birdsall

Senior Engineering Manager
Toyota

Background

Jacquelyn Birdsall is Senior Engineering Manager of the Fuel Cell Integration Group at Toyota Motor North America Research and Development. The mission of her group is to improve quality of life by developing fuel cell solutions to replace gasoline and diesel engines.

Birdsall specializes in hydrogen infrastructure, high-pressure hydrogen systems, and associated standards and regulations. She also serves as a technical spokesperson for the Toyota Mirai and has been in numerous publications including *Car and Driver* and the *Wall Street Journal.*

Prior to joining Toyota in 2012, Birdsall held several roles in the automotive industry. She has over seventeen years of experience in hydrogen, including a thirteen-month assignment at the Toyota Motor Corporation Global Headquarters in Japan, working on the 2021 Toyota Mirai.

In addition to her activities in hydrogen, Birdsall takes a personal interest in promoting STEM learning and diversity within the industry. In 2015 she was honored by the Manufacturing Institute as an Emerging Leader and by *Automotive News* as Rising Star.

Birdsall received a Bachelor of Science degree in Mechanical Engineering from Kettering University (previously General Motors Institute).

Questions and Answers

1. Change Control, Resilience, and Work/Life Balance

What did you learn when you began to work from home or work in the office with a limited number of coworkers? What did you need to start doing and what did you need to stop?

Back in March 2020, very abruptly, I had to undock my laptop, pack up my desk, and drive home. What followed was a significant disruption to the schedule my family and I had become accustomed to: five days a week in the office plus twenty percent travel to one hundred percent home.

What I first learned from this experience is the criticality of consistent, dedicated schedules. For me, the lines between work and home blurred to the detriment of my focus and productivity. We had to adjust, setting aside specific space and time for deep focus, uninterrupted conference calls, and breaks. On the other hand, I had to learn how to shut down my work cell phone and laptop to engage fully with my family. Being half present in both my work life and personal life was not a space I could operate in.

Once I reclaimed my productivity, I realized that I really missed my coworkers. I took for granted the moments in the office in between meetings when we would chat. I realized that without an in-person work environment, I would have to virtually foster our relationships and brainstorm ideas. I started to check in more and encourage team members to turn on their cameras, which was previously forbidden in the R&D office. I consider my coworkers as part of my family, and after all this time apart, I don't want us to return to the office as strangers.

2. Growing Your Professional Network and Maintaining Mentor and Sponsor Relationships

Has your company maintained learning and leadership development opportunities, culture surveys, 360 surveys, etc., to grow skills and manage the emotional intelligence of the company? Has anything shifted? What have you learned?

Moving an entire workforce from in-person to remote work required a significant shift in our communication strategy. The amount of surveys, company-wide communications, and reports from upper management increased significantly to ensure team member knowledge, morale, and productivity remained at or exceeded the pre-work from home levels.

If anything, our opportunities for development have increased over this period. Panels, presentations, and training sessions previously requiring travel and real-time attendance were amended to be available, virtually, anytime. This improves access for team members seeking additional training. Also, in R&D we have seen departments spearhead training sessions to share their projects internally.

We have also deployed new technologies to allow for frequent communication within the company through multiple means: chat, phone calls, video calls, and shared virtual work environments. Our IT department deserves a huge amount of credit for rolling out the latest and greatest for us, quickly, to enable our learning and growth opportunities remotely.

3. Personal Growth

What is the most profound impact this pandemic has had on the way you think about your job, company, family life? Will it be sticky or do you expect everything to return to the previous status quo?

The most profound impact this pandemic has had on me is how I appreciate time with my family. My parents are a flight away, which means, like many people, I have been unable to see them. I think we have often taken for granted that the people we love will always be available; therefore, we don't prioritize our time to be with them. I have also found that now, without my commute or travel, I am able to spend more quality time with those in my household—less rushed and more peaceful.

As always, I am proud to be a member of Team Toyota and witness, yet again, how the company has effectively pivoted during a difficult period and maintained the vision that together anything is possible. Our fuel cell development department continues to persistently strive towards our vision for a zero-emission future—not allowing a pandemic to impede our purpose.

Finally, we have all demonstrated our resilience and capability to manage work from home. While I do not feel that my personal work can be done from home one hundred percent of the time, I think there should be more flexibility, promoting a greater work/life balance. I cannot predict the future, but I would be surprised if we ever go back to the previous status quo.

4. Diversity, Equity, and Inclusion

Are men engaged in the conversation around gender diversity and, if so, in what way?

I am thrilled to see this question included here. There are so many wonderful men in my life and our company who are absolutely a part of this conversation and hungry to learn more about gender diversity and implicit bias.

Recently, we had a company-wide training on bystander intervention to help improve our internal culture. Without having a name for it, I had been practicing this type of communication throughout my career in hopes that my stories and perspective could help the men in my life understand where gender-based sensitivities may originate. Though these discussions were not always easy, my viewpoint has been taken with genuine consideration and led to some fascinating insights.

Within the past few years, I have noticed a transformation from being the one to push a different outlook to being sought out for my unique perspective. Particularly, diversity training has been a good catalyst for these conversations as men want to unpack the information they recently acquired with me.

While my response is focused around the enlightened men in my life, I do not think our conversation ends there. I am on my own journey to improve my capacity to reflect inwardly and identify my implicit biases. I believe that if we all take the time to listen, reflect, and educate, we will create a more inclusive industry.

5. Sustainability

Sustainability trends (climate change, water availability, health, etc.) are some of the strongest drivers for future changes for companies and their strategies. What are you seeing within your company? Is your firm reading the trends and adapting strategies to survive and then thrive with new growth?

Toyota always has been and always will be a leader in providing our customers with solutions to reduce their environmental impact. Starting with the introduction of the Prius in 1997, we have been on the frontline of sustainable technology in the transportation space. Today we have sold over 16 million electrified vehicles worldwide and estimate that, by 2025, fifty percent of our annual fleet, or 5.5 million vehicles globally, will be electrified in some form. In 2015 we launched our first-generation fuel cell electric vehicle named the "Mirai" (Japanese for "future") and, just this month, launched our second-generation Mirai.

But we aren't stopping at the tailpipe. In 2015, along with the launch of our zero-emission Mirai, we announced our Environmental Challenge 2050: six challenges aimed at achieving zero CO2 emissions and a net positive environmental impact. These challenges include eliminating emissions from vehicles, manufacturing processes, and suppliers; eliminating waste and creating recycling programs; conserving water; and protecting local habitats. Our new headquarters in Plano, Texas is an example of our sustainability goals and achieved LEED Platinum status in September 2017. Additionally, we are working aggressively to reduce our overall carbon output by entering into Virtual Power Purchase Agreements (VPPAs) and extending our zero-emission technologies beyond the light-duty market.

The technological advancements and sustainability commitments I have seen in this industry within the last ten years give me great hope. I have a vision of a day where there is no longer pollution lingering over Los Angeles, where all people have access to mobility to achieve their dreams without imposing a negative impact on the planet. I believe this is the industry to make that vision a reality, which is why I am thrilled to be a part of it and hope you are too.

Olabisi Boyle

Vice President, Product Planning and Mobility Strategy
Hyundai Motor North America

Background

Olabisi Boyle is the vice president of Product Planning and Mobility Strategy for Hyundai Motor North America. Boyle is responsible for guiding the strategic direction of Hyundai's U.S. vehicle lineup, leading long- and short-range planning, and overseeing market research, business analytics, and pricing. She also leads Hyundai's U.S. mobility strategy, including IT business solutions, connected car technology, and future innovations.

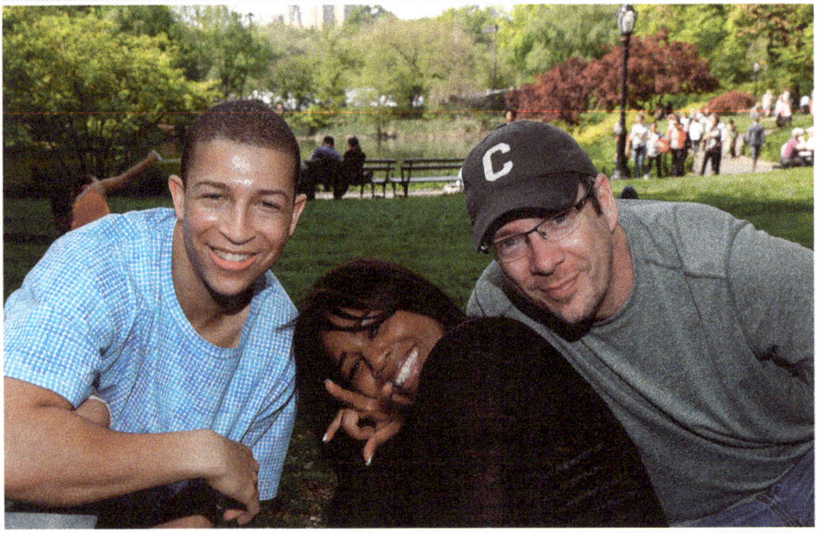

Olabisi Boyle

Previously, Boyle worked at Visa, where she was the vice president of Connected Commerce. She has also held various engineering, product strategy, and manufacturing leadership roles at Stellantis and Ford Motor Company.

Boyle has been recognized for her career accomplishments and was recently selected to the *San Francisco Business Times*' 2020 Most Influential Women in the Bay Area list, named to Automotive News' 100 Leading Women in the North American Auto Industry and was the recipient of the 2018 Women in Payments Innovation Award.

Boyle has a Bachelor of Science in industrial engineering from Columbia University, a Bachelor of Science in physics from Fordham University, and a Master of Science in mechanical engineering from Columbia University.

Questions and Answers

1. Change Control, Resilience, and Work/Life Balance

How has your self-motivation been to excel, learn, reach out (virtually), and manage all aspects of your new work life?

"Relationship wealth" at both work and home is critically important to your overall effectiveness and happiness. It is something I've always valued, but have made it an even bigger priority while managing work and life during the COVID-19 pandemic.

When you are no longer losing time to travel, there is an opportunity to actively schedule and deliberately plan to strengthen your relationships. I've used this time to authentically communicate more in depth with colleagues and teammates in group and one-on-one settings. In virtual settings, you need to be clear in describing the vision and work together through the details that will achieve it. During this time, we also need to have empathy, give people space and let them know if and WHEN they need you, you care. People are going through many different things, and we need to know we are supported as human beings.

I've also used this time to change up my routines and expectations of my team. I will go for a walk in the middle of the day and work later if I have to. I encourage my team to do the same. At home or in the office, I care more about results than I care about WHEN or WHAT time the work gets done.

2. Growing Your Professional Network and Maintaining Mentor and Sponsor Relationships

How do you keep your existing relationships in this remote world? Are you maintaining face time with other execs while being remote? How do your direct reports maintain their face time with you?

Fortunately, technology has enabled us to communicate and maintain relationships with less frequent and sometimes nonexistent face time. We hold agile leadership team meetings across the organization. I have a virtual, weekly stand-up meeting with my team, and our CEO holds a leadership team meeting every Monday morning. At each of those, it's an opportunity to connect regularly on the most pressing initiatives for that week.

For more in-depth discussions, we have monthly governance meetings where all teams meet cross-functionally on specific topics. I am regularly engaged with all the other executives on the leadership team to ensure that we are working together seamlessly to achieve the organization's broader goals.

We also have held virtual meetings with our dealer partners, and I participated in a virtual reveal for one of our all-new products.

To maintain relationships, social networking sites, like LinkedIn, allow you to stay connected amongst professionals in the automotive space or other relevant industries. I've also spent a lot of time talking to employees, mentees, friends, and family about what really matters to them. This has accelerated during the pandemic as people think more deeply about what they want to do in life and with their career.

3. Personal Growth

What is the most profound impact this pandemic has had on the way you think about your job, company, family life? Will it be sticky or do you expect everything to return to the previous status quo?

Unexpectedly, I changed jobs during the pandemic. I previously worked at Visa as the Vice President of Connected Commerce, expanding their presence in in-car payments. An opportunity came along to lead product and mobility strategy for Hyundai Motor North America that includes connected car technology and future innovations. While I knew changing jobs during a pandemic would be challenging, this was an opportunity to help lead Hyundai's transition into the future, and I couldn't pass it up.

I had not met my new boss face to face, only virtually, until I accepted the position, and we came into the office briefly before the COVID-19 cases started going back up. I am in a new position and, with mobility changing so quickly, there will be no status-quo for me. Moving forward, I think those that will have the most success will be the ones that can merge the best of the pre- and post-COVID-19 world.

I've also used this time for personal growth opportunities that weren't possible with all the time commitments for travel and other in-person activities. I've started taking Spanish and Korean language classes and have found more time for exercise, including kettlebell and swimming.

4. Diversity, Equity, and Inclusion

The pandemic has hit hard for women in particular. Many are thinking about dialing back their careers or exiting altogether, which is very frightening for many companies. What should be done differently to retain women in the workplace?

We need to have empathy for underrepresented minorities in majority-centered spaces. We have to understand their unique concerns about belonging and address pipeline issues from entry level to C-suite. Once at a company, we must proactively make efforts to ensure underrepresented minorities feel included. This is not a passive effort. We have to perform additional work to make inclusion a reality actively. The allies need to be vocal and openly supportive and respectful of new ideas and set a supportive behavior standard.

I'm fortunate that the leadership team I'm on, headed by Jose Munoz, the CEO of Hyundai Motor North America, is one of the most diverse in the automotive industry or really in any industry. Before he joined, that was not the case, but he understands the importance of diversity to our performance and backed up that commitment. He's the perfect example of how improving diversity starts at the top, and leadership at Hyundai Motor North America is demonstrating that by example.

We know there is still work to be done throughout the company in catching up to the example established by our CEO. We must actively engage all employees, regardless of gender or race, in this commitment because we know our differences will make us a better and stronger company.

5. Sustainability

What do you as a leader do to stay informed about sustainability trends that can impact the success of your company and its strategy?

A key pillar of the organization I manage is leading Hyundai Motor North America's eco-strategy and future of mobility initiatives. We are not only making, selling, and servicing cars. We are also on a journey to provide the clean, smart mobility solutions of the future.

We have significantly improved fuel efficiency and reduced emissions with each successive powertrain and vehicle generation. We started the process of electrification through the application of hybrid and plug-in hybrid powertrains. And we have, as part of our strategy, full electrification with battery-electric and fuel cell vehicles. We are employing and investing in all the technologies that will get us there. Ultimately, the goal is to enable a planet-friendly, zero-emission ecosystem.

We have an aspirational North Star set by our global company Chairman to facilitate "Progress for Humanity" and create the future we can imagine. This aspirational vision sets customers, society, innovation, and social contribution as our future direction. In our work, we look at megatrends associated with poverty, inequality, post-pandemic resilience, sustainability, economic disruption, wildfires, politics, extreme weather, global social injustice, etc. as we evaluate where we can make the biggest impact for humanity with new mobility solutions.

Susan Brennan

Chief Operations Officer
Bloom Energy

Background

Susan completed her Bachelor of Science in Microbiology from the University of Illinois, C-U and her Master of Business Administration from the University of Nebraska. Susan has more than 30 years of manufacturing experience, including energy, automotive vehicle, powertrain, and components assembly. Susan has dedicated her career to improving American manufacturing and assuring that the United States maintains a vital manufacturing footprint, especially in areas of key technological advances.

In her time as a manufacturing practitioner, she has always been a strong proponent of sustainability, starting in her first role as the Environmental and Coating Manager with Douglas and Lomason, leading the plant to the State of Iowa's first-ever Waste Minimization award to launching the all-electric Nissan Leaf in Smyrna, TN, and now the COO of Bloom Energy, in San Jose, CA, bringing clean, reliable an affordable energy #AlwaysON energy to critical infrastructure including data centers, hospitals, grocery stores, banks, and other essential services.

Throughout her career, she has maintained that jobs and the environment can have a symbiotic relationship, and that passion drives her as she pursues her role at Bloom. In addition, she has created and supported organizations that encourage young women to pursue careers in math and science as a way to support future generations of technological manufacturing in the United States.

Susan founded Southern Automotive Women's Forum, a 10-year-old 501c3 whose mission is provide professional development for women in automotive and support to young women of ages interested in STEM. The organization provides scholarships and educational programs including the All Girls Auto Know® initiative which offers free events across the southeast. Designed specifically for middle school girls, each event features a presentation, an interactive panel discussion and a hands-on activity. The Southern Automotive Women's Forum has changed the face of automotive leadership in the Southeast United States. Susan is now an ambassador for C3E, a Department of Energy program tasked with bringing more women into the energy industry and providing professional development opportunities for women currently in the energy field. Both of these organizations support Susan's passion for building and growing technical fields to be more open and accessible for highly talented and skilled women.

Susan shared the story of her career with her alma mater, the university of Illinois, giving the molecular and cellular biology commencement speech in 2019. She shared her story of how a technical degree will be a rewarding and exciting path for those who are willing to take on the challenge.

Questions and Answers

1. Change Control, Resilience, and Work/Life Balance

How do you keep team spirit with your direct reports? Are you sensing any lack of trust or more trust? What factors/actions have the most effect on trust/lack of trust?

Anyone who has worked for, with, or around me knows that I build a culture of trust. I have worked for multiple companies, in many U.S. states and in several countries. Work does not progress without trust. The challenge with something like a global pandemic or any disruption is that you cannot build trust when you are in a crisis. Trust must be built BEFORE, not during, and it won't happen after.

I believe workforces that built trust before the pandemic have MORE trust now. When communicating virtually, one can still read body language, but it is difficult. I make a very concerted effort to read Zoom body language. I watch this very diligently. A leader must pay attention to trust through not just hearing what people say but also watching their response when conveying a message. Eyes and tone become important. Watch your teams. Be genuine and be present yourself, as a leader too. People are watching.

My prediction is companies that had low employee and customer trust before the pandemic will struggle during pandemic and likely not be successful or survive.

At times of disruption, as business is seeing today, you must rely on employee judgment and engagement. If you have built trust before, these empowered people will do what they know how to do. Mistakes will be made, but the leader will emerge with a stronger, more cohesive team.

2. Growing Your Professional Network and Maintaining Mentor and Sponsor Relationships

Have your mentees been asking different questions than under usual working conditions? Have you needed to do more hand-holding? Do you see more mentees seeking career change or seeking educational opportunities? Something else?

I think this is a great question. Employees are questioning everything. I mentor many people outside of my current company. Many women I know are taking advantage of the disruption to finally make time for themselves and to be intentional about pivoting their career model and biases. Many are engaging their passions after years of debate on whether they should stay on their current path or make a change they have contemplated. I believe we will see many women make the career change.

I am of a generation that is approaching retirement. Many women I know are either actively or contemplating using retirement to start their third act and more ON, no OUT.

Younger and mid-career women are challenging their own personal assumptions around boundaries, with significant others as well as with their companies. The culture is already accepting new and different work patterns. They are using the learnings from COVID-19 to build their new work environment. Whether the post-COVID-19 workplace will accept the changes, in the long run, is still uncertain, but I believe the young women coming behind me have the energy and intelligence to build a workforce and home life that works for them, even though these changes won't be easy.

3. Personal Growth

What is the most profound impact this pandemic has had on the way you think about your job, company, family life? Will it be sticky or do you expect everything to return to the previous status quo?

The pandemic has had a significant impact on me, my family, and my team. I lead a team of essential workers, have two children who are in the education system, and had personal disruption in my self-care and health actions I have been taking such as gym workouts and other health actions.

Career—my job is intense, and the intensity of working through this time has been significant. I had to both step up and step down at the same time. As my team was deemed essential, I have a strong bias to never ask anyone to do something I would not do myself. I moved from my corporate office and back into the factories for the first 90 days of the pandemic. Unfortunately, I could not travel to all my factories, but I spent time in the ones I had access to. Even though we needed to social distance and I could not walk around and spend time with people, it was important to be on the ground and witness and participate in the response—adjusting the production line layout, restrooms, break areas, get my temperature taken with everyone else, wash my hands in the same restrooms, etc. I did not want to hear what was happening by Zoom. I wanted to hear by walking the halls and walking through the break rooms. I worked with my Ops leadership team to shoot videos and to meet with the production supervisors to ask what the teams needed. The first and most important action I made was to provide the team with official letters that included my personal phone number and signature to identify them as essential workers in case they were stopped.

The most important action a leader can take, I believe, is to build a culture that addresses psychological safety. The teams asked for the letters and I complied. To my knowledge, no one ever used them. No one was ever questioned why they were out, even when we went through curfews in the Bay Area. Listen and respond to the "ask." It is not about you. A team that feels safe and knows they are being listened to is the most effective way to run a team during calm times. It is essential to have this psychological safety during trying times.

Family life—I am a person with means and resources. That being said, my time and attention is heavily focused on my work. I had to keep energy for my family, especially for my daughter as her expectations of being a graduating senior changed radically and her preparation for her new chapter in her life changed. Going to college as a high school senior changed dramatically. It went from "where do I go" to "do I go or do I wait a year," "should I go to community college and not spend money on a four-year freshman year by Zoom," to even "does a traditional four-year degree matter anymore." The toll on my family was significant, and I did not save enough energy for my children. I am working in 2021 to adjust and be better with the time I spend with them and my patience in the support I give them. I am not a patient person by nature, and as a single parent, I am often drained. My kids are amazing, but they are human, and I need to give them the proper time and attention.

Part of my struggle with the pandemic is that I had developed a strong eating and exercise regime. I was working out 5 days a week—boxing, spinning, and hiking. I work better with structure. My structure of exercise was disrupted when gyms were closed and then I started eating poorly—because we were working on site, we brought in food. I did not have the mental energy to grocery shop and make good food, so my eating backslides to my comfort of high carbs and caffeine! I am back on the path—my gyms are outside, and I am taking time to eat better. I can't support my team and my family if I am not healthy. Simple, intuitive comment but hard to practice in "normal" times, much less times of social and business disruption.

4. Diversity, Equity, and Inclusion

The pandemic has hit hard for women in particular. Many are thinking about dialing back their careers or exiting altogether, which is very frightening for many companies. What should be done differently to retain women in the workplace?

This is a great question, and I believe it is one of the very important outcomes of the pandemic that all of us need to be thoughtful about and, most importantly, take action on.

What I saw as the most impactful consequence of the pandemic response was the "pivot" to online schooling. I work in a 24/7 manufacturing and supply chain world, and have for 30 years. The demands on people at all levels and all roles in a "hands-on" job are very challenging. The data is clear that women who work eight plus hours go home and do a significant share of the housework and childcare. When you add the need to this, the need for young mothers and mid-career mothers to homeschool their elementary and middle school children, the impact, I believe, is substantial. These are women, and men, who cannot work from home. If a decision has to be made for someone to stay home with children NOT going to school, but staying home AND too young to manage themselves, I believe the data will show it was the wife that dropped out of the workplace to take on this extra action, causing mid-career and entry-level women to step back their career progression and have a financial impact when they are in the place of building their compensation trajectory. My personal view is that the impact on single women will be both professional and financial. Career trajectories are interrupted and incomes are lost as some women must stay home with their children, potentially driving them into poverty.

In response, I believe companies will need to think differently about how to manage the needs of working parents of school-aged children while we are still in the pandemic and homeschooling. It was expected to be a short action, has now turned out to be possible a three- or four-semester outcome. Manufacturing companies and essential workers have already had to adjust to women either leaving or to women requiring schedule changes. One option in the manufacturing space is to add additional resources to the workforce pool to support the need for extra flexibility: cover the request for shorter shifts, different start times, different shift-end needs. To a production worker, the opportunity to be offered schedule flexibility is generally not conducive to the job requirement, but I believe the pandemic is forcing the debate on schedule flexibility and will result in the adoption of new work patterns that have been debated for the 30 years I have been in the business: job sharing, shift start-time staggering, etc. The short-term investment in cost will have long-term benefits in retention of key talent and in loyalty in return for working with the women.

For professional women, fortunately, the current work environment and generation are much more open to being respectful of gaps in women's resumes. In my generation, white space in your resume was a career-limiting step. Leaders and companies must be understanding and not penalize women who, a year or two from now, attempt to reenter the workforce after stepping away to address the schooling needs of their children and/or being on the caregiving end for affected family members. They should be allowed to return to the workforce at a similar level and at fair compensation, not at a penalty due to their time away. In order for this to happen, the conversation needs to occur while women are still in the workplace, not after they have left. Companies must be mindful of their professional women while they are in the workforce and let them know they will support them and explain the how. Companies should also check in with women who have stepped away. Call them every other week and check in so they know that they are valued, someone cares about them and, most importantly, is advocating for them.

Finally, I believe that companies will need to address their benefits offering, especially around mental health. The impact of mental health is already well documented, but I believe the impact will be much more significant and lasting. The cost of benefits is already a significant issue for companies, especially small and medium-sized businesses, but I know from my many years as a leader, people bring who they are outside of work into the workforce.

Companies need to urgently address their benefit offerings as employees return to work and as new hires come into the workforce. As an example, my daughter was a senior in high school when the pandemic shut down her school. Even though she is from a high socio-economic status family, she and I have personally been impacted by the drastic changes to her senior year—no prom, no yearbook signing, no girlfriend weekends to say goodbye, and an online graduation. The rituals of our culture have been changed significantly. Next my daughter started university under lockdown which meant online classes and meeting her peers via Zoom. None of the normal social events were available to help her adjust to college. And she and I are the lucky ones.

My other daughter was a junior in college and lost her internship. Although she was allowed to stay in campus housing, the lockdown meant online classes and cancellation of all the activities she enjoyed in college. Now, a senior, my daughter will likely graduate college by Zoom just as her sister did for high school.

The social impact of isolation and lack of traditional rituals on workers who have dropped from the workforce and from those who will be entering the workforce will have a long-term effect. Companies need to provide benefits and need to prepare their current leaders and managers for the shifts in the workplace post-pandemic.

This is a multivariate equation—and, and, and—address benefits AND manager/leader training AND flexible scheduling in fields where that is extremely difficult AND be prepared for entry-level employees to come in with a new set of challenges and potential skill gap from isolation at a critical time in their emotional development and preparation for the workforce AND prepare to onboard professional women who stepped out and many choose not to come back if they are not encouraged and advocated for AND, AND, AND.

Employers, I believe, will need to step away from how they lead, manage, and compensate pre-pandemic and do the preparation for the pivot in the workforce. The companies and businesses that reflect and prepare are those that will emerge in the 21st century as leaders.

5. Sustainability

What do you as a leader do to stay informed about sustainability trends that can impact the success of your company and its strategy?

As a leader in energy and as a board member of an industrial, I find it very important to stay informed about sustainability trends. I engage in a combination of multiple activities: participating in organizations that host events on sustainability topics, listen to podcasts, follow influencers who post interesting and provocative comments on topics and trends, and reading books, magazines, etc.

I am an ambassador for a group called C3E. I find the topics and forums they host keep me informed of future trends, and more importantly, I learn from the conversations and social media posting of the members. What I find to be the most helpful in staying informed is the individual and group conversations with the members of the organization.

What I find to be most impactful in today's world of "information overload" is the individual connections. Being able to pick up the phone and talk to someone about trends in the marketplace and the globe. A friend of mine is leading a forum next week on this exact topic—what are the future global trends in energy. I am fortunate that I have built the network where I can not only join and participate in the webinar but also pick up the phone and call her and have conversation and debate.

If I could only give one piece of advice around this important topic, it would be to build your "kitchen cabinet." Build strong, meaningful relationships with people in the field you are interested in and make it a two-way dialogue. Make sure you are keeping up on trends so you can reciprocate. It needs to be a dialogue, not a relationship where the person is giving you information and you are just listening.

In today's world, people who stay informed and educated and share their opinions are in high demand. Build relationships with key members in your industry but make sure it is a relationship that makes you smarter and more well informed but also gives back to the person who you are in dialogue with. Join organizations; reach out on social media; post your own opinions.

In my opinion, it is more important than ever to have a strategy on how to stay informed and be open to new ideas, and one last comment, which is very important, make sure your information set and network includes people who don't think like you and have other points of view. Be open, build a network, come to your own conclusions, and execute!

Kimberly (Kim) J. Brycz

Senior Vice President, Global Human Resources
General Motors

Background

Kimberly (Kim) J. Brycz was appointed to the position of Senior Vice President of Global Human Resources in March 2018. In this role, she leads an HR team and systems that build enterprise-wide employee engagement, develop talent, and support strategic planning at all levels.

Previously, Brycz served as Executive Director of Global Product Purchasing, where she oversaw General Motors (GM's) $80 billion annual global product spend as well as customer care and aftersales purchasing. Brycz was instrumental in transforming supplier relationships by providing strategic solutions to future sourcing and supplier engagement.

Brycz, a native of Detroit, began her GM career in 1983 with the Cadillac Motor Car Division in Detroit. Since then she has held various positions in GM's Global Purchasing organization, including the Global Purchasing lead for electrical systems, batteries and hybrids, and interiors. Prior to her most recent role, Brycz served as Executive Director of Global Purchasing, Indirect Materials, Machinery, and Equipment.

Brycz received her Bachelor of Business Administration degree from Michigan State University. In 2010 and 2015, she was named one of the "100 Leading Women in the North American Auto Industry" by *Automotive News*. She is an active leader in two of GM's employee resource groups, participating on the executive boards for the GM Asian Connections and GM Women groups. She is also a founding member of GM's Inclusion Advisory Board. Additionally, Brycz has served as the GM executive champion sponsor for Making Strides against Breast Cancer.

Questions and Answers

1. Change Control, Resilience, and Work/Life Balance

How do you and your team continue to innovate and improve?

When the COVID pandemic started, nobody realized we would be in this for an extended length of time. One of the things that we've learned as an organization was the need to utilize the muscle of agility. This means truly listening to the pain points of our employees so we can react quickly with solutions to help. We found ourselves needing to help leaders better connect with their employees in the new virtual environment with the appropriate coaching tools. Everyone has been impacted by the virus, faced isolation, or uncertainty, so providing online support to help them through these challenging times has been at the forefront of our efforts.

2. Growing Your Professional Network and Maintaining Mentor and Sponsor Relationships

Has your company maintained learning and leadership development opportunities, culture surveys, 360 surveys, etc., to grow skills and manage the emotional intelligence of the company? Has anything shifted? What have you learned?

The way we work has changed immensely in the wake of the pandemic. Yet we continue to see through our engagement surveys that the role of the frontline leader is crucial to employees feeling engaged and valued. As it relates to leadership development opportunities, we have 180-degree leadership feedback surveys as well as in-depth 360-degree assessments for our executive talent intended to upskill our leaders across our 9 leadership competencies. The main shift I think we have made is that we aren't focusing solely on event or survey methods. We spent a lot of time in 2020 getting conversation guides, short videos, and other stories out there for leaders so they can reap the benefits of learning in different ways. Our culture surveys allowed us to check in with employees and to take a step back and evaluate. We've learned our employees really value the flexibility that remote-based work provides. It shows we trust our teams and recognize their true performance. Empathy underpins so much, and through our internal listening and external benchmarking, we made that a highlight for leaders to lean in to.

3. Personal Growth

What is the most profound impact this pandemic has had the way you think about your job, company, family life? Will it be sticky or do you expect everything to return to the previous status quo?

The most profound impact of the COVID pandemic for me was realizing how important a company really is to our employees—in different ways than I saw before.

This crisis left everyone in a different place, and I found that my role was not only making sure employees were safe, but they had the tools for success on both a personal and professional level. We even revamped all of our development programs so that they could continue virtually. Our "North Star" in the human resources organization is the employee experience. Everything that we do has to be in support of their experiences, both at work and at home. COVID has blurred the lines between the two and accelerated this model in a meaningful way. Everyone has a different story or challenge outside of work, and in order to build and maintain company trust, we must see the whole person.

4. Diversity, Equity, and Inclusion

The pandemic has hit hard for women in particular. Many are thinking about dialing back their careers or exiting altogether, which is very frightening for many companies. What should be done differently to retain women in the workplace?

Certainly, the pandemic has hit hard for women and families. This has reinforced for our team the importance of more directly meeting the needs of all caregivers, including all types of families. We must continue to listen to the needs of women by engaging in personal conversations, showing empathy, and taking actionable steps to make for better experiences. Talk to them first, and don't assume anything, because everyone has their own story. Ensure that every leader is equipped with conversation tools to be able to lean in with their female employees. Flexibility means different things to each employee. Listening with empathy and developing creative solutions to support is critically important during times like this. Also, keep the development of your female talent front and center and do not take a pause because of the current situation. As a woman leader in the company, I think it's important to role model that it's okay to make time for family, exercise, and our health.

5. Sustainability

Human capital—employee talent—is one ultimate driver of business and company success. Aligning talent to sustainability trends has proven to be a winning approach for recruiting, retaining, and developing top talent because employees want to do more with their careers ... and do good while also doing well. Have you and your company moved to incorporate sustainability into your strategies for attracting, retaining, and developing your human capital?

As we drive towards the future, we are creating talent communities and engaging with talent before we have a specific job opening. We see that, increasingly, the vision and purpose of an organization is key to deciding whether they establish a career with us. We see that our vision of Zero Crashes, Zero Emissions, and Zero Congestion is incredibly appealing to our potential candidates. Keeping this vision front and center starting with our talent marketing initiatives to our onboarding activities has been instrumental to why people come to GM. Reinforcing this vision and delivering to our promise is why they stay.

Tonit Calaway

Executive Vice President, Chief Administrative Officer, General Counsel, and Secretary
BorgWarner

Background

Tonit Calaway was named Executive Vice President, Chief Administrative Officer, General Counsel, and Secretary of BorgWarner Inc. in October 2020. In this role, she oversees the global legal function, security, facilities, government affairs, sustainability, environment, and aviation. Previously, Ms. Calaway served as Executive Vice President and Chief Legal Officer and Secretary and Executive Vice President and Chief Human Resources Officer.

Before joining BorgWarner, Ms. Calaway held various positions during her 18-year career at Harley-Davidson in Milwaukee, Wisconsin. She served as President of The Harley-Davidson Foundation and Vice President of Human Resources. A securities attorney by training, Ms. Calaway rose through the legal department, serving as Associate General Counsel–Motor Company Operations, Assistant General Counsel, Chief Compliance Counsel, and Assistant Secretary.

Earlier in her career, Ms. Calaway worked for two Milwaukee-based law firms: Davis and Kuelthau, S.C. and Godfrey and Kahn, S.C. Her professional affiliations include board appointments to Froedtert Health, Inc., the Black Arts Think Tank, and the Boys and Girls Clubs of Greater Milwaukee. She is a past president of the Board of Directors of Meta House, Inc. In 2013 and 2016, *Savoy Magazine* named Ms. Calaway to its list of "Top Influential African-American Women in Corporate America," and the *Milwaukee Business Journal* named her a "Woman of Influence" in 2014. She also spoke at the Clinton Global Initiative in 2015.

Ms. Calaway is a graduate of the University of Wisconsin-Milwaukee and received her Juris doctorate from the University of Chicago Law School. She is a member of the State Bar of Wisconsin.

Questions and Answers

1. Change Control, Resilience, and Work/Life Balance

How do you keep team spirit with your direct reports? Are you sensing any lack of trust or more trust? What factors/actions have the most effect on trust/lack of trust?

Maintaining team spirit with my direct reports during this unprecedented time dealing with a pandemic has been challenging. I think it is safe to say everyone is missing the human contact. Despite this, my team has risen to EVERY single challenge that came their way. During this pandemic, my team, among other things, closed a huge acquisition and helped manage the integration of nearly 20,000 new employees. I recognized not only was my leadership team working tirelessly but so was the entire department, and we became creative in maintaining personal contact. Like many people, we changed our meetings to "Zoom" or "Webex" meetings. In addition, each member of my leadership team was tasked with hosting a virtual "game night/happy hour" event. This quickly revealed how creative and adaptable my team was—there were some innovative and competitive challenges, and they all served as great team builders through these trying times. In addition to these events, personally, I wanted to touch each and every team member and show my appreciation for their hard work. So I put my team into categories. Many of my team members have young children and are working full time while also teaching their children, which has to be daunting. I love kids and I love buying toys for kids, so each member of my team that has kids thirteen and under received age-appropriate toys, puzzles, or games from me. This was an effort to provide some joy and alleviate some stress—both for the parents and kids—even if temporary. Those team members with teenagers received a gift card from me for their teens to spend how they like. Those team members with no kids or adult kids received a gift basket with wine and cheese. Finally, for my international team members, they received a floral "pick me up" as it was harder to send gift baskets internationally. All of this was done to make sure the team felt valued and knew I appreciated the family and work challenges they were facing.

I don't believe there was ever a lack of trust in the team as we communicate frequently, we were quite busy, and there is always a general sense of camaraderie. If anything, I saw an improved sense of trust as we all adapted to working virtually and holding ourselves further accountable in our work.

2. Growing Your Professional Network and Maintaining Mentor and Sponsor Relationships

How do you keep your existing relationships in this remote world? Are you maintaining face time with other execs while being remote? How do your direct reports maintain their face time with you?

The biggest change for me in managing existing relationships is the "who" part. The pandemic coupled with the social justice and political issues has made me cull my relationships. I have decided that I would spend my limited time on those that were truly important to me whether professional or personal relationships. My integrity and my personal values trumped the importance of certain relationships. I was not afraid to stop communicating with some of those that had expressed values I couldn't personally accept. To be clear, I didn't end relationships with those that had a different point of view than mine, but I did end relationships with those I felt had extreme views that didn't appreciate the fact that I am both a woman and African American. For those relationships I maintained, they have become even more valuable. To keep the personal connection, I "Zoom", text, and call—oftentimes just to check up on them and make sure they and their families are okay. With respect to my fellow colleagues, most of our meetings changed to virtual, except for a few in-person meetings that were held in a socially-distanced, mask-mandatory manner. My meetings with my direct reports are done virtually.

3. Personal Growth

What is the most profound impact this pandemic has had the way you think about your job, company, family life? Will it be sticky or do you expect everything to return to the previous status quo?

The biggest change for me during this odd period of time when we are managing a global pandemic, social injustice issues, and a divisive political climate was determining with whom I would continue a relationship with. It's in times of adversity that you see the true character of those around you. I appreciate relationships with people whom I can debate with and disagree with and still maintain mutual respect.

4. Diversity, Equity, and Inclusion

Is the board of directors of your company diverse and representative of your workforce and/or customers? Is the leadership team? Is the workforce? If the workforce and customers aren't currently diverse, is there greater interest and commitment to making change in this regard?

I am happy and proud to be able to say yes to all these questions. Our Board of Directors is comprised of both gender and ethnic diversity as is the BorgWarner Leadership Team, 27% of our board is female and 27% of the board is racially diverse. As outlined in our 2020 Sustainability Report, three of the ten CEO Leadership Strategy Board members have international backgrounds and three are female, where two are women of color. In 2019, 33.9% of our new hires were female and 66.3% male, with our total population of female talent making up 14.1% of what we call our MIP Leadership. Our customers are geographically diverse as we are a global company. Are we perfect? No. But our company and our leadership team have made a commitment to being diverse across our organization. This commitment has been reinforced through many ways including being a CEO Action for Diversity and Inclusion™ signatory and having a culture that promotes the BorgWarner beliefs of inclusion, integrity, excellence, responsibility, and collaboration. Our internal actions are being recognized externally through Great Place to Work Certifications, recognition on the Bloomberg Gender-Equality Index and the Human Rights Campaign Corporate Equality Index for dedication to LGBTQ workplace equality. We were recently recognized by Newsweek as one of America's Most Responsible Companies. We show up and we work together to be better every day.

5. Sustainability

ESG (Environmental, Social, and Governance) expectations of investors are greatly accelerating for both equity and debt investments among the largest investment banks and pension funds. Is your company taking this investor trend seriously and adapting strategy to meet these expectations?

We are seeing an increased focus on ESG from all our stakeholders, especially our investors and customers. It's something we've always done but over the past few years, we have made a conscious effort to take a more cohesive and strategic approach to ESG to ensure we effectively manage and disclose the risks and opportunities that are most material to our business and society. Part of our sustainability strategy is "partnering with and reporting to stakeholders," including our investor stakeholders. We cover material ESG topics in our discussions with investors and have robust two-way conversations to ensure our management and disclosure of ESG topics is meeting expectations. Many of our investors have also applauded our most recent Sustainability Report in which we have increased transparency and level of reporting to a higher standard. We continue to assess and adapt our strategy to address the topics' material to our bottom line.

Denise Carlson

Vice President, North American Production Innovation Center
DENSO International America Inc.

Background

Denise Carlson is Vice President of DENSO's North American (NA) Production Innovation Center in Southfield, Michigan and is the company's first-ever executive lead of NA diversity and inclusion (D&I) initiatives. She has been at the company for 25 years, beginning as a material engineer and now in the current role of overseeing DENSO's safety, health, and environmental operations at all facilities.

In her role as Executive Lead of DENSO's NA D&I initiatives, Carlson implements strategies to make DENSO's work environment more inclusive and collaborative. Carlson has long advocated for workplace improvements, such as better work-life balance and more flexible part-time and remote working policies, which help attract and retain a more diverse, more talented workforce. After her son was born, she pushed for and developed DENSO's first-ever part-time policy for engineers. These efforts and her love for her family are the roots of her focus on service leadership.

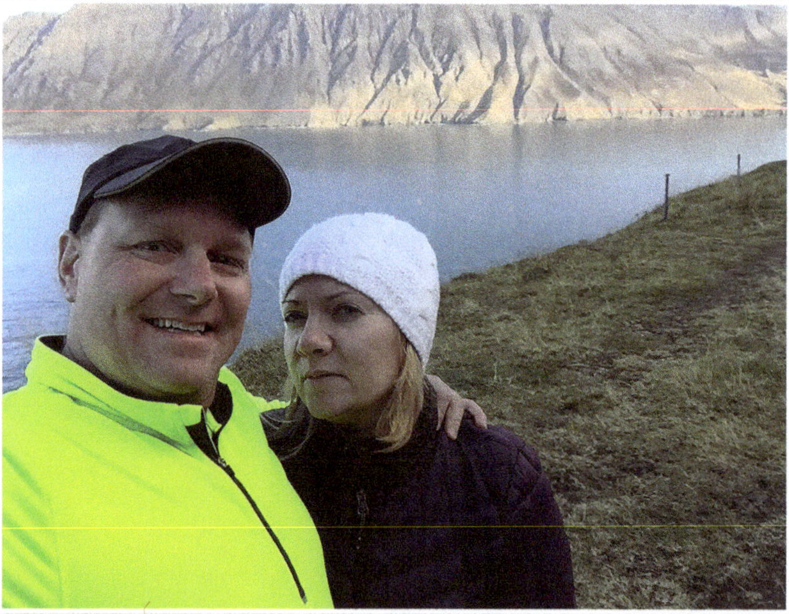

Denise Carlson

Outside of work, Carlson is a year-round mentor and coach for a FIRST Robotics High School team. Carlson also currently sits on the boards of the Michigan Science Center and the Engineering Society of Detroit, positioning her to act on her passion of building development opportunities for the next generation.

Questions and Answers

1. Change Control, Resilience, and Work/Life Balance

Many have said that there is no separation of work and home these days. What do you do to manage this for your own work? What are you doing to increase the ability of your team to create and respect boundaries?

Separation comes in many forms: physical, mental, social, and so on. Prior to the pandemic, I traveled 3~4 times per month with a few global trips scattered in throughout the year and worked at home 2~3 days per month as well. This work schedule required me to be fluid in my work/life balance, being able to work in many different settings. I initially felt that I had a slight advantage in the mindset needed to work away from the office as it seemed the entire world became remote. However, as it became apparent that we would likely not return to a fully work-from-office environment, I recognized that I would need to do even more to manage the boundaries. First, came the physical separation. I do not have a permanent office nor dedicated office space within my house. To create this physical separation, I fashioned a work station in the basement, complete with an office chair, large computer monitor, and a beloved whiteboard. Mental separation was slightly more difficult. Working at a global organization requires flexibility with timing: late night and early morning meetings. By blocking off time for personal events, from working out with my husband to zoom calls with friends allowed me to keep space. Socially, the separation was already there in light of the pandemic, and we need to find alternatives to become more social, more connected, in a limited, set amount of time.

For my team, the usage of calendars to respect and understand everyone's time is key. I ask for their flexibility if we need to hold a meeting during typical lunchtimes and trust them to arrange their schedules to be able to support. The transparency needed to work effectively is understood by all team members. Weekly team meetings along with one-on-one meetings provide a way for us all to stay connected to provide support needed as well as an opportunity to raise a hand to ask for assistance or to share concerns.

2. Growing Your Professional Network and Maintaining Mentor and Sponsor Relationships

How do you keep your existing relationships in this remote world? Are you maintaining face time with other execs while being remote? How do your direct reports maintain their face time with you?

Keeping up with existing relationships is definitely a challenge. Virtual face time within our company was nowhere near a norm prior to the pandemic. Even as a global organization, we valued "real" face time as our primary form of communication, using it to assist in overcoming any language challenges. There has been a shift from informal touchpoints and actual visits to each location towards shorter and more frequent scheduled meetings. Due to the nature of my current position, I have the opportunity for several weekly meetings in which I can share directions and have dialogue with many of the executives throughout DENSO in North America.

The contact and discussion that I have with my direct reports has expanded from a weekly meeting to include individual one-on-one time. For a smaller group directly at the site in which I call my home base, we've incorporated a more relaxed atmosphere, encouraging an in-person feel even though some of the team may be on site while others are working remotely. For the entire team, we've increased meetings from large all person meetings once per month to the same meeting once per week. This more frequent meeting has enhanced transparency and created a sense of community throughout North America.

3. Personal Growth

What is the most profound impact this pandemic has had the way you think about your job, company, family life? Will it be sticky or do you expect everything to return to the previous status quo?

During this pandemic, my youngest child, my daughter, graduated from high school. She was set to go away to college and begin her new life. However, COVID had other plans. My daughter was one of the younger generation, who had at some point and time in early spring of 2020, contracted the virus. Unfortunately, she did not have the classic symptoms, and it wasn't until three months later when she took the antigen test, that this was confirmed. We had months of visits to various specialists to identify and treat the symptoms she did experience. Thankfully, she is significantly better now and planning to take a full load of college courses during the spring of 2021, anxiously awaiting to move to her off-campus apartment later in the year. The reason I want to share this story is that it really solidified for me how life can change in an instant. Getting healthy, staying healthy, and enjoying life with loved ones has taken on a higher priority. The flexibility to work remotely has enabled me to spend more time with my husband and focus more on my health. We're able to workout together as our work schedules can be a little more in sync. My kids (aforementioned daughter and my son who is also currently at home wrapping up his last year in college remotely while working remotely) no longer ask why I'm home (because I had been traveling so much in the past) or why I'm home so early (anything before 6:30 was early). Now my son comes into my workspace (aka basement) and we can discuss how his day is going. I have the chance to spend the last year with my daughter before she goes to an apartment, likely never to return home for any significant period of time.

I believe that the remote way of work will continue. There can be a healthy balance between remote and in-person, depending on the nature of one's work and personal needs. I hope that all leaders can recognize this balance and be able to ask not only themselves but also those they work with to find the right balance for the team.

4. Diversity, Equity, and Inclusion

The pandemic has hit hard for women in particular. Many are thinking about dialing back their careers or exiting altogether, which is very frightening for many companies. What should be done differently to retain women in the workplace?

First, I'd like to recognize that this seems to be hitting women harder, but there is a larger gender balance in play that needs to be acknowledged. The pandemic has highlighted the many challenges that a dual-career household faces. It is typically understood or assumed that the women in a familial unit is the most flexible, receives the lower pay, and has a lower potential of promotion in the future. This mindset is what needs to be changed in order for long-term change in our society. In the near term, increased flexibility, which requires enhanced trust and transparency, is important. Providing increased part-time opportunities or longer sabbaticals with increased mentoring as well as active sponsorship will also assist in the retention of key personnel.

I've had the experience of going part-time when my children were younger, which actually pushed to create the first part-time policy that would allow engineers to go part-time within the company. On the other hand, when my children were older and my career led me to a path to Japan, my amazing husband left his job to support me and the family on our adventure and path forward. I firmly believe that there needs to be a balance for all persons, an opportunity to use the skills and knowledge that each individual has in a capacity that is beneficial for the individual, the organization, and society as a whole.

5. Sustainability

Sustainability trends (climate change, water availability, health, etc.) are some of the strongest drivers for future changes for companies and their strategies. What are you seeing within your company? Is your firm reading the trends and adapting strategies to survive and then thrive with new growth?

As an organization, sustainability is a key facet of our history — DENSO has made electrification systems for decades — and is a focus for us as we create our long-term strategies for future growth. We've long recognized that the world's resources aren't infinite and have made commitments to preserve them. In 2015, we created our EcoVision 2025 policy: to halve our energy consumption and double our production and use of clean and green technologies. We also strive to be a carbon neutral company by 2035, an ambitious target we intend to meet by reducing the environmental impacts of our operations, our products and energy use. Globally, we are aligning these initiatives with the United Nations Sustainable Development Goals (SDGs) and are in the process of creating our next actions for 2035 and beyond. All options are on the table as we expand beyond the traditional automotive areas into a more connected, autonomous, shared and electric future.

Mamatha Chamarthi

Chief Information Officer
Stellantis–North America and Asia Pacific

Background

Throughout her career, Mamatha Chamarthi has made it her business to turn the conventional approach to technology on its head, focusing on inspiring innovation, customer-centric business transformation, and striving for greater productivity.

Appointed Chief Information Officer, Stellantis–North America and Asia Pacific in April 2019, Chamarthi oversees the company's digital transformation initiatives in addition to all information technology applications and infrastructure. In addition to her role as CIO, Chamarthi has cross-functional program leadership responsibility for connectivity and infotainment, ensuring the company develops and delivers software solutions that exceed expectations. In this role, Chamarthi is continuing her unconventional approach to technology as she leads the company's transformation from a traditional full-line automaker to a customer-centric mobility company.

Often sought out for her unique perspectives on technology, digital transformation, diversity, and leadership, Chamarthi serves on multiple boards, including the ChampionX (CHX) Public Board, Health Alliance Plan of Michigan, Gartner Research Board, Enterprise 50, Michigan Council of Women in Technology Board, and Midwest Technology Leaders Board. She has been named to the 2020 list of "100 Leading Women in the North American Auto Industry" by *Automotive News*, 2020 CIO of the Year by Michigan CIO, a "Top 25 Finalist for Breakthrough Leaders" by *CIO* magazine, a "Premier 100 IT Leader" by *Computerworld*, and a "Technology All-Star" by the Women of Color in Technology Institute.

Previously, Chamarthi was Senior Vice President and Chief Digital Officer for ZF Friedrichshafen AG.

Questions and Answers

1. Change Control, Resilience, and Work/Life Balance

Many have said that there is no separation of work and home these days. What do you do to manage this for your own work? What are you doing to increase the ability of your team to create and respect boundaries?

The pandemic has put an interesting twist on the work-life balance for everyone. Earlier, there was a physical separation for many of us between the workplace and home, and with that separation gone, each of us had to create our own unique way of handling the separation between work and home. "Atomic Habits: An Easy & Proven Way to Build Good Habits & Break Bad Ones" is a book that conveys a poignant message of how tiny changes make a big difference. As I began to work remotely, I have started to work out six days a week, maintain a healthy diet, ensure an eight-hour sleep cycle, and meditate daily. After several years of traveling around the world, being with my family at home has created opportunities to bond and reconnect with my boys and husband. My younger son Nikhil and I are into cooking. We participated in several Airbnb experiences to learn about different cuisines, cultures, and also enjoy everything we make as a family. My older son Rahul and I are car enthusiasts and sometimes make a four-hour trip to Bloomington, Indiana to drive our cars on twisty, winding roads. My husband and I workout together six days a week. I have a better quality of sleep and overall healthier lifestyle being in one time zone and no travel.

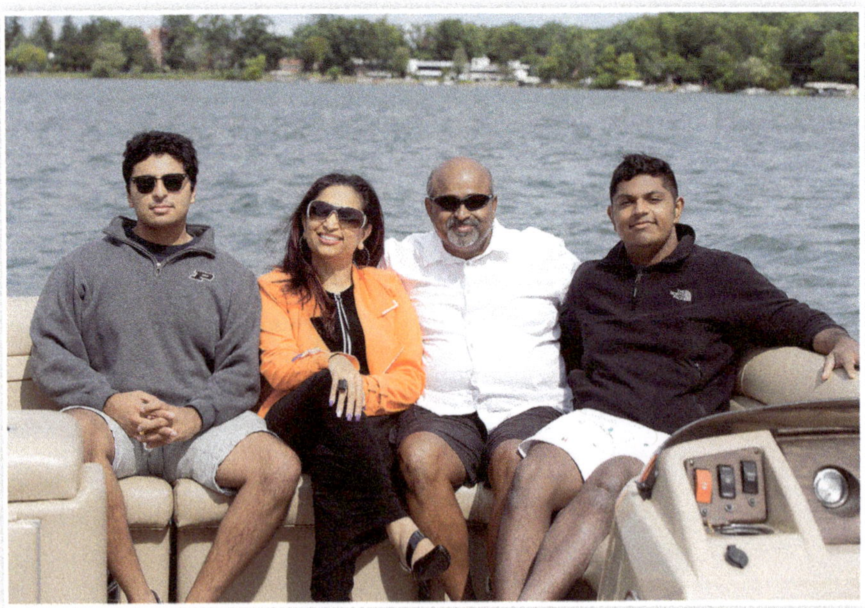

Mamatha Chamarthi

Being a leader, I also understand that not everyone has a similar personal situation. I totally believe when a person is relaxed, they are more productive at work. One of the biggest challenges I see leaders struggle with is being mindful of relaxing and unwinding from work. I don't think we can create a one-size-fits-all rule or guideline. It is all about flexibility and also making the work environment fun. Our team members "Do what we do," so it is important to be a role model and clearly articulate how I manage my day and also make sure they understand the guidelines around flexibility. For example, there is one specific boundary which my team follows when a team member is on vacation. Unless the issue is urgent, we don't reach out to them.

Intentionally compartmentalizing is also an effective way of balancing work and life. Whatever you do, be fully present—when you are talking to your team or family, looking at your phone is not being fully present. Acknowledging what is distracting you from being fully present also helps improve focusing on the topic.

2. Growing Your Professional Network and Maintaining Mentor and Sponsor Relationships

How do you keep your existing relationships in this remote world? Are you maintaining face time with other execs while being remote? How do your direct reports maintain their face time with you?

Stellantis started working remotely March 16, 2020, and we were able to seamlessly shift the company's workforce (>100,000 employees globally) to remote working. We transitioned to the Google collaboration suite a year before the crisis, which helped us manage the crisis, helped engage with our employees and continue collaborating globally. Regionally we formed crisis management task forces that virtually met on a daily basis to manage our operations and risks, along with that we looked for opportunities to engage with the communities that we operated in, accelerated our digital transformation, and continued the path towards our vision of being "a customer-centric mobility company." The biggest challenge as a leader is to engage and motivate the workforce virtually. In order to set an example for my team, I always turn on my camera for all meetings. In response, my entire staff turns their cameras on for staff meetings and have adopted the practice of using interesting virtual backgrounds, which has become a new and fun topic of discussion.

Being the Chief Information Officer, it is my responsibility to properly communicate major company news to my organization. With the implementation of remote working, I have consistently held biweekly townhall meetings. Every townhall is unique, with business updates, employee recognition, and courageous conversations that build a deeper understanding of the issues and identify and drive actions that result in social justice and equality for all of us. During each town hall, we have question-and-answer sessions, allowing employees to interact with the leadership team and get answers to their questions instantly. In a recent survey, 80 percent of our employees stated that they are very happy with the remote settings. Virtual meetings have become a great equalizer, there is increased participation from introverted employees as compared to a hybrid setting where there is a mix of employees participating remotely and in person.

I have been able to participate in many virtual conversations with other executives, including my public board and committee meetings. With the constraint of travel removed, it has created room for increased participation in a diverse range of topics. I am part of several professional organizations, some of them have been very successful in pivoting to the virtual format, while others have struggled.

The crisis also serves as an accelerator for Stellantis' transformation from a traditional full-line automaker to a customer-centric mobility company. We have established a digital steering committee that meets on a weekly basis that has made several pivotal decisions to make the customer and employee digital experiences more immersive and engaging. Each of the business leaders also sponsored building roadmaps including Key Performance Indicators (KPIs) to build the customer-centricity DNA within our company.

3. Personal Growth

What is the most profound impact this pandemic has had the way you think about your job, company, family life? Will it be sticky or do you expect everything to return to the previous status quo?

With remote working, our pace of work and decision-making has changed significantly. One example is the pace at which vaccines were developed. Consider the following facts from Nature News:

- Typhoid fever was discovered in the 1880s and the vaccine was licensed in 1990s.
- Meningitis was discovered in the 1880s and the vaccine was licensed in 1980s.
- Polio was discovered in the 1900s and the vaccine was licensed in 1950s.
- Measles was discovered in the 1950s and the vaccine was licensed in 1960s.
- Ebola was discovered in the 1970s and the vaccine was licensed in 2010s.
- COVID was discovered in the 2020 and the vaccine was licensed in 2020.

The pattern to note is the pace of decision-making has consistently improved over time, with COVID being the record-breaker by having a vaccine in the same year as discovery. Public education was remodeled in a couple of weeks. Shared economy business models took a huge hit, companies like Airbnb and Uber suffered. In the initial days of crisis, we lauded the virtual engagement with our teams, saw an uptick in productivity, and soon we started craving for that physical presence because it enabled an effective decision-making process. There is a debate in my mind on if this pace of decision-making will continue post-COVID and, if it does, will it lead to a state of emotional, physical, and mental exhaustion or will it become a new normal leading to accelerated transformation.

Within Stellantis, each of the business leaders sponsored building roadmaps including KPIs to build customer-centricity DNA within our company. As a result of COVID-19's impact on sales, we created an online immersive shopping experience for our customers, which has become a new revenue stream for the company.

What's even more remarkable is that we created and launched the online marketplace in just a couple of weeks.

Nearly every aspect of our lives have been changed by the pandemic. However, I truly believe that we, as human beings, are programmed to adjust based on environmental changes, which is clearly visible by how our community came together to fight the pandemic. Stellantis executives have reflected on the purpose and role we play in our communities. We started making masks and ventilators at our plants, millions of meals donated to hungry school children, and most importantly rethinking diversity and inclusion. In the middle of the pandemic, the George Floyd incident made us all think about how we as a society are working towards an inclusive society. With this in mind, Stellantis has taken a strong path towards renewing our commitment to diversity and inclusion, encouraging employees to participate in Courageous Conversations that raise our multicultural IQ by giving one another the opportunity to walk in the other person's shoes that helps develop respect and empathy.

4. Diversity, Equity, and Inclusion

Are men engaged in the conversation around gender diversity and, if so, in what way?

Men and women have to be equally engaged in the conversation around gender diversity and, for that matter, in creating a diverse and inclusive environment for all. The progress we have made as a society does seem glacial, given the gradual increase in women at all levels. Men continue to outnumber women at all corporate levels, including leadership roles that influence creating the supportive environment and workplace policies for gender equality at work.

Personally, there are many men leaders that I worked with that believed in the results that I delivered and promoted me into critical roles. For every woman that comes up, there are many male colleagues that have supported her too, who role model inclusive behavior.

As part of its commitment to diversity and inclusion, Stellantis supports ten business resource groups (BRGs) whose objectives include promoting a positive awareness of diverse people and issues within the company and ensuring that the company's products meet the expectations of diverse customers.

Stellantis BRGs represent a range of affinity communities that include women, working parents, veterans, people with disabilities, the LGBTQ+ community, and people of color to name just a few. We have introduced several family-friendly policies such as 12 weeks of paid leave to support new parents.

These employee-directed groups work to foster greater multicultural understanding among employees, career development of members, and engagement with diverse communities. Giving visibility to these business resource groups in my monthly town hall meetings further promotes a work culture where all employees are engaged, included, and respected. Our company's continued sponsorship of *Automotive News* Top 100 women, Society of Women Engineers, and Women of Color showcase role models to other aspiring women talent.

5. Sustainability

Human capital—employee talent—is one ultimate driver of business and company success. Aligning talent to sustainability trends has proven to be a winning approach for recruiting, retaining, and developing top talent because employees want to do more with their careers ... and do good while also doing well. Have you and your company moved to incorporate sustainability into your strategies for attracting, retaining, and developing your human capital?

My most significant accomplishment in my career is to drive digital strategy for ZF and drive innovation at scale and speed. My charter was to transform ZF into a software-centric automotive supplier with a vision of Zero Accidents and Zero Emissions. One of the critical capabilities was to establish robust software engineering capabilities that would drive the transformation. I created a global talent strategy including launching talent hubs in Poland, California, Shanghai, and India. I helped open the doors to ZF India Technology Center, which ushered in an era of change in an aggressive eight-month timeline. The center initially ramped up to 3,000 engineers by 2019. The center played a pivotal role in the development of autonomous-vehicle and electrification technologies, which amounted to 70 percent of R&D projects.

My goal at Stellantis, amidst the COVID crisis, is to in-source technical competencies from a largely outsourced model to create a competitive advantage through agility and flexibility. I am taking a multipronged approach—upskilling and reskilling existing talent using boot camp-style training—with General Assembly and Pluralsight, increasing college recruiting and internships, and launching a Global-In-House Center (GIC) to support our digital transformation. The goal is to shift 1,050 external resources to the GIC within three years. Additionally, I remain focused on attracting the best talent, by leveraging the relationships that I have built in the industry, as well as through in-house events such as Pitch Night, where we invited employees to submit ideas for connected vehicle features. More than 500 ideas were submitted, 14 were presented to our internal shark team. Subsequently, we invested in three of these ideas. Know n' Go, the first of the three ideas to hit the market, gives our customers the opportunity to use a mobile app to scan a feature in the vehicle to get a detailed description of the feature and how to use it. Thanks to the innovation of the app's inventors—two Stellantis women—we were able to enter the market with this feature in three months with our 2021 Ram 1500 TRX truck to help our customers. In helping our customers, involving our employees, and developing new features, Stellantis is working towards the key objectives to be customer-centric, be employee-centric, and continue being a leader in technology.

Françoise Colpron

President
Valeo North America

Background

Françoise Colpron is a strategic global automotive executive with more than 28 years of international experience in North and South America, Europe, and the Asia Pacific region.

She joined Valeo, a €19 billion tech company enabling autonomous driving, electrification, and digital mobility in the global automotive industry, more than 23 years ago. Today she serves as President of Valeo North America, representing 20 percent of the Valeo Group's global sales with 18,500 team members in the USA, Mexico, and Canada.

Appointed to her current position in 2008, she successfully led Valeo North America through the economic downturn and steep recovery that followed, quadrupling its sales and turning around its profitability.

Colpron serves on the Board of Directors and currently is Chair of the Original Equipment Suppliers Association (OESA). She also is on the Board of Directors for the Motor and Equipment Manufacturers Association.

In addition, Colpron serves on the Board of Directors of Sealed Air Corporation (NYSE: SEE), an innovative packaging solutions company with $4.9 billion in sales and approximately 16,500 employees serving customers in 124 countries. She also has served on the Board of Directors of Alstom, a publicly listed French company that is a world leader in integrated rail transportation systems.

Automotive News has recognized her three times as one of the "100 Leading Women in the North American Auto Industry" (2010, 2015, and 2020). *Crain's Detroit Business* named her one of the "100 Most Influential Women in Michigan" in 2016 and *DBusiness Magazine* placed her on its "Detroit 500" list of most powerful leaders in 2020.

Colpron was inducted into the French Legion of Honor, the highest French order of merit, in 2015. She holds a law degree from the University of Montreal in Montreal, Canada, and is fluent in English, French, and Spanish.

Questions and Answers

1. Change Control, Resilience, and Work/Life Balance

What did you learn when you began to work from home or work in the office with a limited number of co-workers? What did you need to start doing and what did you need to stop?

When we started to work from home, I found out how much our teams are adaptable, flexible, and resilient. I have experienced—more than ever before—how much engagement/commitment is core when it comes to facing major challenges. Working remotely did not mitigate our efficiency and productivity at all. Getting rid of commute time and all the traveling has been an immediate benefit that we all recognized—managers and teams.

It was also a good exercise for those of our managers who were reluctant at first as to the ability of our teams to work remotely and have since embraced the experience. The pandemic accelerated the acceptance of a trend and challenged us to rethink our approach regarding talent (for example, having to relocate someone versus allowing him or her to work remotely).

Our teams remained extremely engaged, despite working remotely. They also appreciate the increased work-life balance, although, in certain cases, it can be a challenge as there is less separation between work hours and family time (for example, for team members with younger children).

Virtual meetings are quite efficient, although you do not have the same spontaneity and some team members do not feel as comfortable to speak up. I learned that we collectively needed to communicate more and more often by different means and beyond our immediate teams. Working remotely and isolation can be trying for some of our team members living alone, as they no longer have the sociability of the office hours. In addition to organizing social hours on Zoom, we decided early on to make available emotional support resources.

Even though, overall, working remotely has been a successful experience, I miss the energy of our team and the more informal interactions that can only happen when sharing the same space together (for example, the interactions at the coffee machine or at the cafeteria). I believe that the future will be made of a combination of more flexibility and remote working but still some in-person time, physically in the office. In my opinion, time in person is essential to facilitate collaborative work and to foster a strong company culture, especially as we continue to hire new talent.

I believe that we will also considerably reduce the business travel going forward, and probably alternate between virtual meetings and in-person meetings to find the right balance between efficiency and the benefits of interpersonal relationships.

2. Growing Your Professional Network and Maintaining Mentor and Sponsor Relationships

Are you continuing to grow your professional network while being remote? How?

During the pandemic, I learned that you had to be intentional in reaching out to your business contacts in order to maintain your relationships and create new ones, as you do not have the same social events that create the opportunity for you. Some associations like OESA and Inforum adapted very early on to virtual events and offered useful platforms, with opportunities to interface with other industry leaders. My service on other boards and councils (whether corporate or nonprofit) also allowed me to grow my professional network, by reaching out to other board and council members directly, given that we no longer had the opportunity of the occasional hallway conversation, around a scheduled meeting. Even the format of outreach activities and community service changed. We recently held one of our annual fund-raisers for the first time in a virtual format and ended up with a much broader audience, with people from out of State. Indeed, there can also be some benefits to adopting some of these new communication platforms, and we are now thinking about a hybrid format for next year. Instead of lunch or drinks, I have been organizing regular Zooms with business contacts, around tea or a glass of wine, in order to keep in touch. It is certainly not the same, and you can have Zoom/Webex fatigue, but it is important to remain active and maintain your relationships, and even grow your network.

Ironically, I probably have had more meaningful conversations with some of my business contacts, as most of us are working from home, in a different (less formal?) setting, facing similar challenges, sharing our views for the future and best practices. Some conversations have been more personal and genuine, fostering closer relationships. Your business contact is no longer a customer or a partner, he or she is a parent, he or she has been sick or knows someone who has been sick, he or she has recently lost someone, etc. As life comes back to a "new normal," those conversations may not be mentioned again but I will certainly not forget them.

3. Personal Growth

What is the most profound impact this pandemic has had the way you think about your job, company, family life? Will it be sticky or do you expect everything to return to the previous status quo?

Now that we are all working/studying from home, "work-life integration" has become the "new normal." On the one hand, the challenge has been to respect certain boundaries, as now that everyone is working from home, the temptation can be to consider everyone "available" 24/7. On the other hand, the upside has been the opportunity to be more present at home and spend more time with my family. Even if we might not see each other all day while working from different parts of the house, we gather at dinner and catch up around a nice meal. The evening meal has always been important in our family as a time to be together and discuss our respective days. It is easier now to respect this time together since we do not commute nor travel nor have after hours events. I treasure these moments together as I know that it will not last forever;

the pandemic will soon be over, and our busy lives will likely resume. However, it has been like a golden parenthesis in time for these past few months, and I am grateful for these precious memories.

From a professional standpoint, our priority at Valeo has been (and continues to be) the health and safety of our team members and their families, and of course the continuity of the business. It was a challenging year, especially during the second quarter when our production facilities were stopped for two full months, but we decided to take a "share the pain" approach, as opposed to a short-term approach. I commend the way that the automotive industry came together as an industry during these difficult times, we all put our differences aside to share health protocols and best practices. I also commend the companies in our industry that repurposed their facilities to contribute by manufacturing personal protective equipment—and I am proud to work for one of them.

I believe that the combination of the lessons learned from this pandemic with the social topics of the moment and the accrued focus on Environmental, Social, and Governance (ESG) topics should make us better people and better companies.

4. Diversity, Equity, and Inclusion

Is the board of directors of your company diverse and representative of your workforce and/or customers? Is the leadership team? Is the workforce? If the workforce and customers aren't currently diverse, is there greater interest and commitment to making change in this regard?

Our Valeo Board of Directors is quite diverse from a gender standpoint: of the 14 Board members, 8 Board members are men and 6 are women.

In Valeo NA, our leadership team is also quite diverse, both from a gender and culture standpoint. Today, in my immediate team, we are 50% women and 6 different nationalities. In the U.S., we are now working towards having a better representation from an ethnic standpoint, in line with the communities where we do business.

In my experience, in order to be successful in your diversity initiatives, you need to ensure a diverse pipeline of candidates (in terms of recruitment and promotion) and, equally important, to provide an inclusive workplace where all talent can thrive. In this respect, the Valeo North America leadership team recently renewed its pledge to diversity and inclusion with a call to action to our team members to lead by example and to speak up when witnessing intolerance, injustice, or unfair treatment. We also took the opportunity to revamp and re-energize our diversity and inclusion council.

Earlier in my career, I also had the privilege of launching our gender diversity initiative "Valeo Women Connected." Today, it is a very active network, organizing events for women and men around the world, sponsored by our Chairman and CEO. In my experience, it is key to have the commitment from the top of your organization and to associate men so it is truly about gender diversity and inclusiveness.

As an industry, I believe that we still have opportunities for diversity, equity and inclusion. First, we need to work collectively on the pipeline of candidates starting early on by encouraging more girls and minorities to study STEM. Once they are in the workforce, we need to encourage women and minorities to take more P&L roles.

We also have to promote a more inclusive work environment, not only for women, but for all minorities.

5. Sustainability

ESG (Environmental, Social, and Governance) expectations of investors is greatly accelerating for both equity and debt investments among the largest investment banks and pension funds. Is your company taking this investor trend seriously and adapting strategy to meet these expectations?

As often indicated by our Chairman and CEO, our commitment to sustainable development is embedded in Valeo's DNA. As a technology company, Valeo offers innovative products and systems that help reduce CO2 emissions and promote the development of an intuitive, connected, and more autonomous driving experience.

At Valeo, sustainable development goes beyond our innovative products. Sustainable development at Valeo is built around four key axes: innovation, environmental eco-efficiency, diversity and human capital development, and commitment to corporate citizenship. Indeed, we actively manage our environmental performance at all of our sites to reduce resource consumption and waste emissions. We strive to promote an inclusive workplace and promote diversity and human capital development. Sustainable development is central to our purchasing policy, and we are committed to corporate citizenship in the communities in which we operate.

In February 2021, Valeo expanded its sustainability goals with its commitment to achieve carbon neutrality by 2050. Valeo also tied the variable compensation of more than 1,500 senior executives to the company's success in reducing CO2 emissions. For me, it is very important to work for a company that has purpose and that operates in a sustainable way from a governance and human capital standpoint. ESG commitment is becoming more and more important for all of our stakeholders: customers, employees, investors, communities where we do business. This trend will likely accelerate as consumers increase the demand for sustainably marketed products and as companies want to attract and retain top talent from the next generations. For example, our teenage daughter likes to research companies and their sustainability policies and ethical reputation before buying consumer goods.

In conclusion, I believe that sustainable development is the right thing to do and a business imperative if you want to be successful and create long-term value.

Lori Costew

Chief Diversity Officer and Director of People Strategy
Ford Motor Company

Background

Lori Costew is Ford Motor Company's Chief Diversity Officer and Director of People Strategy. She assumed this role in June 2019.

In this role, Lori oversees the company's corporate diversity, equity, and inclusion (DEI) efforts to cultivate a culture of belonging and advance the organization's mission and business objectives.

Lori also serves as Ford's Director of People Strategy, where she ensures Ford's talent strategy supports corporate goals and transformation efforts.

Before being appointed to this role, Lori held positions within Ford leading human resources for the organization's mobility division, as well as The Lincoln Motor Company.

Lori joined the automaker in 1993 starting at the Lima Engine Plant and, for nearly three decades, has leveraged her expertise in positions supporting marketing, United Auto Workers (UAW) negotiations, equal employment planning, and organizational development.

In addition to her leadership role at Ford, she is also an accomplished author of two award-winning novels that provide inspiration and tools against bullying and the importance of positivity. Lori has a master's degree in Human Resources from the Ohio State University and a certification in executive coaching from the Hudson Institute.

She lives in Michigan with her husband and two children. She loves to travel and is most happy with friends at a winery or when her toes are in the sand.

Questions and Answers

1. Change Control, Resilience, and Work/Life Balance

How do you and your team continue to innovate and improve?

Only the automotive industry could immediately pivot resources to design and manufacture at scale ventilators and personal protective equipment like face masks, face shields, and gowns. Project Apollo was the epitome of innovation, and the subsequent donation of 100 million employee-made face masks to at-risk communities speaks to our commitment to doing the right thing.

The Human Resources function has been central to the response in both COVID and the social justice reckoning sparked by the murder of George Floyd. We had employees in pain, and this required us to listen, really listen, to understand their experience inside and outside of Ford in order to address bias and make sustained change. Prior to COVID, Listening Sessions were held in conference rooms for employees to share their perspective with leaders. Post COVID, having a large virtual workforce in some ways made the hundreds of Listening Sessions easier; all participants were online while speaking about difficult topics from the comfort of their own home. Many employees were hungry to learn more. We leveraged our learning platform to house-curated content on multiple Diversity, Equity, and Inclusion (DEI) topics; hosted multiple external speakers; and invited our employees to share their voice via short videos and surveys.

We also embarked upon the most comprehensive, global DEI Audit ever undertaken, leveraging quantitative data, qualitative data, and deep ethnography, to truly understand the unique barriers faced by female and minority employees along their employee journey. Change does not happen through wish management. We will take what we have learned, follow human-centered design principles, and then build solutions into our systems and processes to ensure Ford is a place where every employee belongs and can thrive.

Being innovative requires leaders to "raise their gaze" by looking outside their industry or function for inspiration. Even more important, leaders must serve as coaches while trusting their team to deliver, accept, and learn quickly from mistakes and provide an environment where all voices are heard. Otherwise, growth and transformation will never happen.

2. Growing Your Professional Network and Maintaining Mentor and Sponsor Relationships

How do you keep your existing relationships in this remote world? Are you maintaining face time with other execs while being remote? How do your direct reports maintain their face time with you?

Our employees working in manufacturing and testing facilities are considered place dependent and operate under extensive protocols to maintain safety. Those of us who have roles that can be done remotely had to discover our new way of operating while working from kitchens, bedrooms, and basements.

Connection is critical, especially when decisions need to be made quickly. I'm fortunate in my 28 years at Ford to have built strong relationships across the company as well as with external partners. The trust built over time with these relationships has created a "short-hand" to enable us to handle the day to day as well as work in the white space to find solutions that address really big issues. Yet new employees have joined Ford since the pandemic began who never had the benefit of being on site to meet their colleagues and learn the organization. So extra care must be made to properly welcome and help new people learn both their job responsibilities as well as how to be effective in a large, complex company. As efficient as text, email, and group-sharing platforms can be, it's easy for misunderstandings and misinterpretations to happen. Technology can't replace talking with others.

In some ways, working remotely has resulted in a more inclusive and accepting culture. In allowing others to peer into our homes via video calls, we highlight our universal shared experiences of kids attending school virtually, dogs barking, losing Wi-Fi connectivity in the middle of a meeting, phones ringing, yards being mowed, and, my favorite smile maker, the occasional toddler running and giggling in the background. While important to keep connection by seeing colleagues on screen, camera fatigue is prevalent. I try to honor that; when a personal or professional accomplishment is to be celebrated, or I need to share major news, the meeting notice highlights to be "camera ready" so we can see faces and wave hello. Sometimes people just need to talk. I've had many 20-minute "walking meetings" outside with earbuds when I don't need to be connected to a screen. The fresh air and change of environment are great mood boosters and actually help with creativity... and sanity!

3. Personal Growth

What is the most profound impact this pandemic has had the way you think about your job, company, family life? Will it be sticky or do you expect everything to return to the previous status quo?

While the pandemic has us in the same storm, we are all in very different boats financially, socially, mentally, and physically. It's important to give and ask for grace, compassion and empathy are needed now more than ever. I have always struggled with creating boundaries, and this is exacerbated by the "always on" new way of working. Women tend to be more self-critical than men; we must remember that "NO" is a complete sentence and we don't have to always explain ourselves. Especially now, women need to give ourselves grace by reframing the negative voices in our heads to be more supportive and positive. We are doing the best we can in an environment that we never could have imagined.

I worry about the short- and long-term mental and emotional impact on all kids due to social isolation and the lack of a typical school schedule, sports, and activities. I mourn the loss of a "normal" high school senior year for my son. Yet there are some silver linings that I intend to remain sticky. After my Fitbit had me logging less than 1000 steps a day as I was glued to my laptop, my husband and I started walking in the evenings, which became a great stress reducer and bonding time. I have relished the gift of family time including eating dinner together, playing board games, and binge-watching our favorite shows.

We can look back, but we can't go back. Most corporations will not return to the previous status quo. This pandemic has forever shifted the expectations of current and future employees. Even organizations and industries that had extreme "face time'" cultures have realized work is actually getting done, and many employees are able to be more productive for a number of reasons, including greater flexibility and better use of commute time. By shifting the paradigm in where and how work is done, companies can discover more diverse candidate pools that can bring in an influx of different types of talent. However, community and connection are still critical. Organizations that offer their employees greater flexibility and craft an optimal hybrid model of in-person and virtual will attract and retain the best talent.

4. Diversity, Equity, and Inclusion

The pandemic has hit hard for women in particular. Many are thinking about dialing back their careers or exiting altogether, which is very frightening for many companies. What should be done differently to retain women in the workplace?

As a working mom of two teenagers, I have so much empathy for this topic. It was hard enough having the two full-time jobs of work and home. Now parents have the added responsibilities of being teachers, therapists, and playmates. Wellness resources are critical and can cover a broad range of needs including supporting children's education, mindfulness, and physical, mental, and emotional health.

Women make up half of the population and generally have significant input into the vast majority of purchasing decisions. If that voice is not in the room, companies can miss the mark on developing products, services, and experiences that customers want and value. Great talent can go anywhere. Smart and progressive companies provide their employees greater flexibility and create a working environment that allows everyone to be their authentic and best selves.

I like to use the analogy that a career should be viewed as a dimmer switch versus an on/off light switch. There are times when the dial is all the way up, and other times when we need to dial back to address life issues like going back to school, caregiving, or pursuing other interests. Dialing back does not mean we still can't contribute significantly. While this concept applies to both men and women, women take on a greater proportion of child and elder care responsibilities that mandate the need for additional flexibility. I am very proud to work for a company that promotes a variety of formal and informal flexibility programs. When my children were very young, my role included managing Ford's WorkLife Programs. During that time, I worked an 80% schedule. As a response to the COVID pandemic, we added an Enhanced Sabbatical Program for U.S. salaried employees that maintained all benefits and 25% pay while being off work for up to 6 months. Companies need to evaluate not just their programs but whether their culture is truly accepting to use the programs. Women are just as ambitious as men. If women are penalized or experience micro/macro aggressions for working flexibly, they may opt out. That is not good for business, our economy, or society.

5. Sustainability

Sustainability trends (climate change, water availability, health, etc.) are some of the strongest drivers for future changes for companies and their strategies. What are you seeing within your company? Is your firm reading the trends and adapting strategies to survive and then thrive with new growth?

It's a pride point for me that Bill Ford was green, before it was cool to be green. Sustainability is one of the biggest issues facing businesses today, and it has always been one of our priorities. In 2020, Ford announced our aspirational goal to become carbon neutral by 2050. This goal expands on our previous commitment to the Paris Climate Agreement. Since the Paris Agreement call for achieving carbon neutrality in the second half of this century, it was a natural next step for Ford.

Building on our commitment to address climate change, we are proud to be the only full-line U.S. automaker committed to doing our part to reduce CO2 emissions in line with the Paris Climate Agreement and working with California for stronger vehicle greenhouse gas standards. We remain committed to meeting emission reductions consistent with the California framework and continue to believe that this path is what's best for our customers, the environment, and the short- and long-term health of the auto industry.

But reaching those goals depends on us creating exciting electric vehicles that our customers want to drive. We're going to electrify our iconic nameplates—like the Mustang Mach-E and electric F-150—and our commercial vehicle strategy with the electric Transit will help our commercial partners realize their carbon neutrality goals as well. With this electrification strategy, we can prove to customers that we can build electric vehicles that are great to drive and good for the environment.

Leah Curry

President
Toyota Motor Manufacturing Indiana, Inc.
Princeton, Indiana

Background

Leah Curry is honored to serve as President of Toyota Motor Manufacturing, Indiana, Inc. (TMMI), where she leads all production and administrative functions at the manufacturing facility in Princeton, Indiana, which produces the Toyota Highlander, Highlander Hybrid, Sienna, and Sequoia.

Previously, Curry served as President of Toyota Motor Manufacturing, West Virginia, Inc. (TMMWV), a transmissions and engines manufacturing plant located in Buffalo, West Virginia.

During her 23-year career with Toyota, Curry has held several management positions at TMMI, including Vice President of Manufacturing. She has also served as General Manager of Assembly and held leadership positions in body weld, stamping, maintenance, production engineering, and new model launch.

Additionally, Curry serves on several national and regional boards, including the Manufacturing Institute, Women in Manufacturing, Deaconess Health System and The Evansville Regional Business Committee. In 2013, she received the Manufacturing Institute's STEP Ahead award that recognizes female leadership in manufacturing. Curry was twice named one of the top 100 women in automotive by *Automotive News* (2015, 2020). She studied chemistry at the University of Evansville and industrial electronics at Ivy Tech Community College in Evansville, Indiana.

Questions and Answers

1. Change Control, Resilience, and Work/Life Balance

How do you and your team continue to innovate and improve?

Continuous improvement is a pillar of Toyota's core philosophy and is part of everything we do.

In March 2020, Toyota suspended production at all vehicle and unit plants across North America in response to the COVID-19 pandemic. During the production suspension, we were still hard at work on the new model Sienna in order to be ready for launch. I'm proud of the dedication and innovative solutions our team came up with to work within the parameters we had at the time. Our teams had to get creative during the trial phase with no travel and face-to-face problem solving with design in Michigan. Working from home, virtual meetings, and improvement to IT systems to enhance communications are some examples.

This effort during the production suspension allowed us to be prepared and minimize impact, so we were ready when the time came to reopen the plant.

2. Growing Your Professional Network and Maintaining Mentor and Sponsor Relationships

Have your mentees been asking different questions than under usual working conditions? Have you needed to do more hand-holding? Do you see more mentees seeking career change or seeking educational opportunities? Something else?

At Toyota, and specifically at our plant here in Indiana, our team's response reflects our company's belief in mendomi, the Japanese word that means "to care for others like family."

The impact of this pandemic can be felt in many ways, and it is different for everyone. Conversations with mentees have evolved to understand more about their emotional needs. Our priority is to listen and offer help.

During the production suspension, many employees had to adapt to unexpected challenges whether it was working from home, adapting to new technologies, or taking on assignments and responsibilities they may not have normally worked on. These revealed opportunities for employees to learn new skills and facilitate conversations around professional development.

3. Personal Growth

What is the most profound impact this pandemic has had on the way you think about your job, company, family life? Will it be sticky or do you expect everything to return to the previous status quo?

There are many impacts due to the COVID-19 pandemic, including physical and mental health. I think it is important to show empathy because each of us is affected differently.

Something I think we have all collectively felt is the loss of connection with others. The inability to meet casually with friends and family has caused emotional strain.

The resilience of our company and employees has been remarkable during this year to overcome and continue to support each other. It is times like these that you realize, even more so than usual, that we truly are a family of people who genuinely care for each other.

4. Diversity, Equity, and Inclusion

Are men engaged in the conversation around gender diversity and, if so, in what way?

Respect for People is a core belief at Toyota. All employees, including men, are engaged in conversation around diversity and inclusion.

For example, male Toyota executives, among others, work collaboratively with cross-functional groups to lead conversations and training on diversity topics. Additionally, they lead deliberate succession and development strategies focusing on our employees.

5. Sustainability

As part of employee development, does your company encourage and support employees volunteering for local nongovernmental organizations? Do you and your company consider this an opportunity for aligning company efforts, employee leadership development, and local progress on sustainability?

Toyota's philosophy is to give back with resources, time, and talent where our employees live and work. That's why we're committed to supporting local organizations to help more people gain access to the resources they need to live better lives.

Our employees take a lot of pride in the connection we have with our communities and realize as a company, and as individuals, we can be a catalyst for change.

We have developed a 360-degree approach coupling donations and volunteer efforts that align with the company's priority focus areas. Many of our plant leaders serve on local, state, and national nonprofit boards, which is a valuable component of their community support commitment and leadership development.

Corinne Diemert

HR Director
Valeo North America

Background

Corinne Diemert joined Valeo, a €18.6B tech company enabling autonomous driving, electrification, and digital mobility in the global automotive industry 30 years ago. Today, she serves as Human Resources (HR) Director for Valeo North America, a more than $4B business with over 16,000 team members in the USA, Mexico, and Canada.

Corinne leads the HR aspects for Valeo in North America. She is a member of Valeo's North American (NA) Leadership Team and directs a diverse group of high-performance HR professionals.

Corinne builds on a multifaceted professional background, beginning her Valeo North America career in Plant Logistics and then transitioning to Program Management. Subsequently, she was appointed to Leader of Operations, launching the company's first manufacturing site in the Greater Detroit area—Valeo's Highland Park Front End Module facility. In her previous role as Vice President of Sales, Corinne's leadership contributed to the company tripling its sales over the past five years.

Corinne is Co-chair of Inforum's AutomotiveNEXT Executive Committee and Director on the board of the Michigan Chapter of the French-American Chamber of Commerce.

Corinne holds a degree in Business Administration–Material Management from Conestoga College in Guelph, Ontario (Canada).

Questions and Answers

1. Change Control, Resilience, and Work/Life Balance

How do you keep team spirit with your direct reports? Are you sensing any lack of trust or more trust? What factors/actions have the most effect on trust/lack of trust?

Like many automotive companies, Valeo teams were forced into an abrupt full remote work environment in March 2020 due to the COVID pandemic. This new work arrangement resulted in so much change in how we interact socially and in our workplace. We all understand the value of teamwork in our industry and, as leaders, had to quickly adapt our way of working to avoid losing the engagement of our teams.

I rely on two key elements to focus on in this remote work environment: Communication and Trust.

Teamwork requires communication, and our remote teams have a bigger risk of missing communication because the communication needs to be intentional. We lose the informal "passing in the hallway" communication opportunities when we are not collocated in the same building. It is up to the leaders to set the expectation for regular communication. Within our teams, we rely on daily check-ins through chat or video calls, structured team reviews on important topics, and more relaxed end-of-week group video meetings for our teams to exchange some key updates on their priorities and to even share their weekend plans. Giving team members the opportunity to share experiences helps them to get to know each other.

Trust is a key foundation of any successful team and during remote work, I give special attention to encourage close interactions and open dialogue to avoid gaps that can break down the level of trust within our teams. It is more important than ever for managers to lead by example and be available and responsive and committed to regular interactions. By keeping regular contact with our teams, it shows that we are investing in them, and even if we are remote, they are not alone.

It is actually one of the key benefits of remote work... while the spontaneous interactions for team members working in the same office may be more limited, our overall trust and communications with team members located in different buildings, states, and countries has increased and is more balanced with the global team.

We still have some work to do to develop manager's skills in terms of managing remote teams. We were forced into this new way of working without preparation, and some managers have not had the opportunity to adapt as we had not fully embraced remote working before the pandemic. Some managers lack the trust of their remote team members and team members end up feeling micromanaged. We will focus on manager development in the areas of delegation and empowerment. We actually see that the managers who struggle with leading remote teams often have low-trusting managers, so our development will need to start at the top of our organization in some cases.

2. Growing Your Professional Network and Maintaining Mentor and Sponsor Relationships

How do you keep your existing relationships in this remote world? Are you maintaining face time with other execs while being remote? How do your direct reports maintain their face time with you?

When you are working in a large corporate office and attending in-person industry events, let's face it, networking is pretty simple. You are networking as you pass colleagues in the hallway, meet at the coffee station, or meet for casual lunches by the office. Now that we are all working remotely, we must put forth special efforts to maintain these connections.

I keep my links with other executives through participation in industry groups, such as Inforum's AutomotiveNEXT Executive Committee, the French-American Chamber of Commerce Board, and OESA. These types of groups offer many virtual networking events. There are also several industry information sessions and training opportunities that provide networking opportunities.

When we were first forced into the social distancing, many corporate events were being cancelled, but as we realized in-person events will not be returning soon, the industry embraced networking in a virtual world. Now we are participating in virtual wine-tasting events, award ceremonies, and fundraising events, and all of these successful events help to build your network.

It is also important to build relationships with current colleagues and stay in touch with former colleagues and business associates. The key to building and maintaining these connections is to be intentional. You need to set aside time on your calendar to reach out to your contacts, as it may still be a while before you will be running into them at the office or in-person events.

As for my direct reports, that is pretty easy. We are constantly connecting through intentional group video exchanges or informal one-on-one video or chats. Our team members located at several different office locations actually feel a stronger connection while we are working remotely as we are all on a level playing field.

3. Personal Growth

What is the most profound impact this pandemic has had the way you think about your job, company, family life? Will it be sticky or do you expect everything to return to the previous status quo?

In a matter of weeks, the pandemic threw us into chaos where our economic security was suddenly in question, our daily routines were totally disrupted, we were isolated from family and friends, and the health of our family, community, and coworkers became a primary concern. But through the last few months, we have learned how resilient we are as an industry, a community, and as individuals.

From a professional standpoint, we quickly learned how to organize our work/home life while working remotely. It is interesting how each of us defined a new routine around what works best in terms of remote working and how we can be even more productive without leaving our homes. We have learned to be more flexible and a little less rigid on the 9-to-5 schedule and how to use virtual tools to stay connected.

At the same time, I think we may be surprised at how much we miss getting to see our coworkers on a regular basis. So while we may be enjoying the flexibility and productivity remote work offers to us, we are realizing the value of being back together in the workplace. We will likely maintain a more flexible in-person/remote work balance in the future.

From a personal standpoint, I have appreciated time at home with less travel and limited socializing gatherings. We are cooking more and enjoying family time. From a personal standpoint, I hope we maintain the slower pace, enjoying each other's company without always needing to be with a large group of people.

4. Diversity, Equity, and Inclusion

There has been a lot of talk about diversity—and, in recent years, inclusion. Equity has entered the corporate conversation in a major way this year. What actions are you and your company taking? Are these methods aligned with company goals?

Valeo drives diversity in every team worldwide. We built our global diversity policy on four pillars: gender, generation, disability, and culture, and it contributes to the quality of life of our employees. In order to help drive diversity and inclusion in our region, the NA Leadership team has revamped our Diversity and Inclusion council this year. We kicked off this initiative with our Valeo NA Leadership Team signing a letter to our team members reaffirming our commitment to apply Valeo Values (Ethics, Transparency, Empowerment, Professionalism, and Teamwork) to promote an inclusive, diverse, and ethical workplace. This letter to our employees included a call to action for our team members to take their responsibility to help us create a diverse and inclusive environment at Valeo through some key actions: lead by example, speak up, and stay connected.

Our local Diversity and Inclusion council is made up of team members from our locations across the US, different Business Groups, different functions, and representing our diversity pillars. Our council has established subcommittees to focus on five areas to help drive diversity and inclusion at Valeo: communication and messaging, metrics and KPI's, team member training, employee recruitment and retention, and community engagement. This council recommends actions to the NA leadership team for approval and implementation support.

As the NA HR Director for Valeo, my role is to drive a culture that ensures all of our team members take the commitment to collaborate and share in the responsibility on a daily basis to create a better, more inclusive workplace. We will launch a program early in 2021 to help drive our inclusive culture by encouraging peer-to-peer recognition for team members who demonstrate Valeo Values in their daily interactions. We will recognize our team members who exemplify and demonstrate our inclusive culture, not just recognize the accomplishments in terms of achieving professional objectives.

5. Sustainability

As part of employee development, does your company encourage and support employees volunteering for local nongovernmental organizations? Do you and your company consider this an opportunity for aligning company efforts, employee leadership development, and local progress on sustainability?

At Valeo, sustainability is built on four key pillars: innovation, environmental, employees, and commitment to corporate citizenship. As part of Valeo's commitment to corporate citizenship, we encourage our employees to support their local communities where we do business.

Valeo partners with several nonprofit organizations locally to offer our support to the less fortunate in our communities. We also sponsor local robotics teams and give our team members the opportunity to share their time and talent to develop the young engineers in our communities. In addition to encouraging team member involvement in company-sponsored volunteer opportunities, we offer our team members the opportunity to use company-paid time to support nonprofit organizations of their choice in our community.

Our team members value this opportunity to give back to causes that are important to them and their community. Many of our potential candidates for hire, especially the Gen Y and Z, are pleased to learn about how Valeo is involved in the community and helps our employees to get involved in volunteer activities.

Lisa Drake

Chief Operating Officer, North America
Ford Motor Company

Background

Lisa Drake is Chief Operating Officer for North America, effective May 1, 2020. She reports to Kumar Galhotra, Ford's president of Americas and International Markets Group.

In this newly created role, Drake will bring enhanced focus to product launches, warranty reduction, and material cost improvements. She also will place a renewed emphasis on returning the North America business back to a 10-percent EBIT margin through her work on cost and waste reduction.

Previously, Drake served as Vice President of Global Purchasing, responsible for all category management processes and procurement functions across direct and indirect purchasing areas as well as supplier technical assistance.

She also served as Vice President of Global Powertrain, responsible for all powertrain purchasing operations worldwide. She joined purchasing in 2013 as Director of Global Program Purchasing and also served as Director of Global Interior Purchasing, a position she held since August 2016.

Previously, Drake held various positions in Product Development for nearly 20 years. In 2004, she led the F-150 product and launch team during the construction of the state-of-the-art Dearborn Truck Plant at the Ford Rouge Center. Her other notable positions include Chief Engineer of Lincoln MKC, Assistant Chief Engineer of F-Series Super Duty, and program manager roles for Explorer and Expedition.

Drake also served as the Global Hybrid/Battery Electric Vehicle chief engineer from May 2007 to September 2010. In this position, she led the development and delivery of Fusion Hybrid, Lincoln MKZ Hybrid, and the C-Max Hybrid and Energi programs.

In addition to her work with hybrid and plug-in hybrids, Drake led the development of the Focus Electric and the Transit Connect Electric. In 2008, the Automotive Hall of Fame awarded her the Young Leadership and Excellence Award, in recognition of her contributions and leadership in the growing field of electrification.

Drake joined Ford in 1994 as a Ford College Graduate in powertrain engineering. She holds a Bachelor of Science in Mechanical Engineering from Carnegie Mellon University and a Master of Business Administration from the University of Michigan, Ann Arbor.

Questions and Answers

1. Change Control, Resilience, and Work/Life Balance

What did you learn when you began to work from home or work in the office with a limited number of co-workers? What did you need to start doing and what did you need to stop?

I learned that when faced with a common challenge, humans are a highly adaptable species. In our industry, we surprised ourselves with how fast we were able to pivot to a new way of life and, for the most part, kept our heads down and moved forward. We are indestructible as teams, we have work friendships we cherish and when we don't see each other, we miss each other and we have removed the word "impossible" from our vocabulary.

We are stronger for what we endured and are enduring, and that makes us better positioned as an automotive industry to continue forward progress.

We started to appreciate the depths of our grit and resolve in the automotive industry. We stopped at nothing.

2. Growing Your Professional Network and Maintaining Mentor and Sponsor Relationships

How do you keep your existing relationships in this remote world? Are you maintaining face time with other execs while being remote? How do your direct reports maintain their face time with you?

Working remotely has required more intentional interaction with my networks and colleagues, although we have found new forms of communication. For example, a few Ford executives live within a mile or so of me, so we have started walking together on weekends or on our "stay-cations" to just catch up more informally. Inevitably, we start to problem solve and iterate our thinking, and frankly, it becomes an incredibly rich discussion. I plan to keep this up, even as we transition some work back into the offices in the future.

In terms of direct-report team members, I have always maintained time on my calendar for one-on-ones with them even before the pandemic and remote work.

And my roles in the past have been global roles, so having virtual discussions with direct reports was commonplace. So it wasn't unusual to virtually connect—the important piece for me was always ensuring that I held consistent time on my schedule for those conversations. Even when we didn't have "agenda items," there was always something to discuss, even if it ended up being books we have recently read!

3. Personal Growth

What is the most profound impact this pandemic has had the way you think about your job, company, family life? Will it be sticky or do you expect everything to return to the previous status quo?

Without a doubt, I have started to enjoy my career and my work so much more because it feels more integrated into my life. I didn't think Ford could be a bigger part of my life than it already was, but it has entered my home in a big way now... and I have embraced that and woven the pleasure I have waking up every day to problem solve, to enjoy my colleagues and friends, and to make progress for the world into an even greater part of who I am at home. And certainly, the most profound and unforgettable moments of this year were the late evening weekend calls with dozens of volunteers (engineers, purchasing specialists, lawyers, etc.) working literally around the clock to design, source, and build PPE in our fight against COVID. The human spirit knew no bounds.

Early data suggests others have similarly found better balances in our new way of working, so as an executive, my responsibility is to make the good parts stick.

4. Diversity, Equity, and Inclusion

Are men engaged in the conversation around gender diversity and, if so, in what way?

They are most certainly engaged in our work at Ford around gender diversity, and I am very proud that we have a leadership team that has such commitment. We can't make progress without them. Our employee resource group for gender equity is called the Women of Ford, and we have a program where men can join the organization and be a part of the change. Our executive advisory board for the Women of Ford is over half male and includes our CEO, Jim Farley.

5. Sustainability

What do you as a leader do to stay informed about sustainability trends that can impact the success of your company and its strategy?

Read, read, read, and read. I make time to read quite a bit—and not just late at night or on weekends. Yes, it is ok to read during work hours. Reading materials from analysts, trade publications, internal reports, and general news and internet "rabbit-hole" surfing is critical to keep up to date in many fast-moving areas in sustainability—whether it's sustainability of talent or technology trends related to EV and mobility. Most large organizations have consolidated internal reports to which you can subscribe, so seek those out—sometimes only the top executives are on those distributions, but there is no reason you can't ask to also receive the material.

I make time to not only consume material related to automotive, but I also enjoy learning from anyone who is the "best in their business" or "GOAT," and to that end, I find the MasterClass series of videos riveting. Macrotrends are macro because they transcend industry—and you can pick up how others at the top of their disciplines are shaping their thinking based on macrotrends.

Joy Falotico

President, The Lincoln Motor Company

Background

Joy Falotico is President of The Lincoln Motor Company. She is responsible for leading the evolution of Lincoln as a world-class luxury brand and overseeing Lincoln operations globally, including product development, marketing, sales, and service. She reports to Kumar Galhotra, Ford president, Americas and International Markets Group.

Falotico also served as Ford's chief marketing officer from March 2018 until January 2021 when she assumed the dedicated role of leading Lincoln globally. Falotico has been a group vice president of Ford Motor Company since 2016. She was previously Chairman and Chief Executive Officer of Ford Motor Credit Company, with worldwide responsibility for this leading global financial services business that supports Ford dealers and customers, along with the sale of Ford and Lincoln vehicles.

Prior to this, she was Chief Operating Officer, leading Ford Credit's global operations in the Americas, Asia Pacific, Europe, and the Middle East and Africa, as well as marketing, sales and brand, business center operations, and insurance operations.

Previously, Falotico was Executive Vice President of Ford Credit marketing, sales, Americas, and strategic planning. She was responsible for marketing and sales globally and, since January 2013, business operations in North America and South America, with global strategic planning responsibilities added in January 2015.

With Ford Credit since 1989, Falotico served in a number of senior positions, including Executive Vice President of North America. She was Vice President of U.S. Sales Operations and Vice President of Global Marketing. Before that, Falotico had pan-European responsibility for customer and dealer service operations and risk management for Ford Credit Europe.

Falotico is involved in American Financial Services Association, a U.S. financing industry trade organization, previously serving on its Board of Directors and Executive Committee, and as Chair of its Vehicle Finance Division board.

Falotico was selected as *MediaPost*'s 2019 Automotive Marketer of the Year. She also was recognized by *Automotive News* as one of the "100 Leading Women in the North American Auto Industry" in 2010, 2015, and 2020. Born in 1967, she holds a bachelor's degree in Business Administration from Truman State University and a master's in Business Finance from DePaul University.

Questions and Answers

1. Change Control, Resilience, and Work/Life Balance

What did you learn when you began to work from home or work in the office with a limited number of co-workers?

The first thing I learned was that now, more than ever, communication was essential. Things changed very quickly, and we had to adapt quickly. And, from the very beginning, it seemed like we were in for a long ride even before we had the data or evidence to indicate this would be the case.

What did you need to start doing and what did you need to stop?

Immediately, we needed to implement a new cadence of communications. Without the normal body language, hallway conversations, conversing on way to/from meetings, and even the occasional glimpses in passing, we needed to increase our communications to close these gaps. In the beginning, employees were uneasy, and there was a lot of uncertainty as the pandemic accelerated. We began regular meetings, and at the beginning of these meetings, we did a "check-in" to ask if the teams were healthy and if there was any help needed. We also stopped all the extra stuff to make room for the critical decision making we had ahead of us regarding how to care for our employees, dealer partners, and our customers and, at the same time, keep the business running. In 60 days, we had a full-blown health crisis, economic crisis, and social crisis, and all three impacted our company. It was a harrowing time and a time for leadership.

2. Growing Your Professional Network and Maintaining Mentor and Sponsor Relationships

Has your company maintained learning and leadership development opportunities, culture surveys, 360 surveys, etc., to grow skills and manage the emotional intelligence of the company?

We have enhanced our online learning tools, introduced a cadence of employee survey check-ins on COVID health and safety protocols and work from home, and provided access to mental health resources in response to the impact on our employees from loss of loved ones, fear of the illness and stress of working from home with children, school disruptions, and caring for parents and others. The HR department has been on full time supporting our employees across all levels with varying needs.

Has anything shifted? What have you learned?

Everything has shifted to a new mode. Our company is deploying a bimodal work model with limited to no face-to-face engagements for the knowledge workers and strict healthy and safety protocols for essential workers. I have learned that the detailed planning, scenario planning, and willingness to try new things and pivot when necessary has been key to our success in surviving the new normal. And when you put your employees and customers first, you will win. We've seen this over and over during this crisis at Ford and Lincoln.

3. Personal Growth

What is the most profound impact this pandemic has had the way you think about your job, company, family life? Will it be sticky or do you expect everything to return to the previous status quo?

The pandemic had a profound impact on my job and I'd say on the company as well in two key areas. First is the double click on the importance of not only communicating but actively caring for your team as a leader. This was/is an unprecedented time for many leaders and caring for your team is job #1. Secondly, our employees accomplished amazing things, like PPE to help others and, to help the company. The way our employees showed up and how they persevered through adversity will stay with us for many years to come. Regarding my family life, the togetherness this has created with my immediate family being sheltered in place, and with a close group of neighbors that we have self-quarantined with to create a safe "pod." On the family front, the weekend time of playing board games and putting together puzzles with college and high-school-age girls is a bright spot from this pandemic; otherwise it surely would not have occurred. And, while the workload ramped up, our social lives came to a screeching halt, and we found refuge in our close group of neighbors, and for that I feel very blessed. And, yes, we did get a COVID puppy and he will stick with us!

4. Diversity, Equity, and Inclusion

There has been a lot of talk about diversity—and, in recent years, inclusion. Equity has entered the corporate conversation in a major way this year. What actions are you and your company taking? Are these methods aligned with company goals?

Given the social unrest, it was imperative that we expand our corporate conversation to include not only diversity and inclusion but also equality. Several actions have been taken by our company and leaders to, first, listen to our employees to promote a shared understanding of what it's like for all our employees. Further, the company has introduced several initiatives including reverse mentoring, listening sessions, inclusive leadership assessments, and external training in the neuroscience of bias, to name a few.

All these actions are aligned with our company goals and are intended to accelerate our progress in the area of diversity, equity, and inclusion so that everyone feels like they belong as a part of our company family. As a leader, I continue to learn from these initiatives.

As a female, at times I have naively thought I had a deep understanding of these issues from some of my own experiences only to find out that you never really know what another person feels until you've walked in their shoes.

5. Sustainability

Sustainability trends (climate change, water availability, health, etc.) are some of the strongest drivers for future changes for companies and their strategies. What are you seeing within your company? Is your firm reading the trends and adapting strategies to survive and then thrive with new growth?

I'm proud to say the Ford Motor Company has been on the forefront of driving for sustainability for many years, thanks to our Executive Chairman, Bill Ford. Mr. Ford was advocating for this before it was popular. Our company produces an annual report to measure our progress in delivering on our sustainability strategy to protect the planet. We have publicly stated our goals for climate change, air quality, recycled and renewable materials, human rights and raw materials, renewable energy, waste, water, and human progress by providing mobility and accessibility for all. This statement makes us accountable and drives the actions in our company to achieve these goals. We continue to adapt, expand, and advance our strategy, often charting our own course even when not popular with all our constituents. And we aren't apologetic in this regard.

Given the events of 2020, health has been a key priority at our company, and the ability to not only ensure the safety of our employees amidst the pandemic but also to quickly adapt our plants to manufacture PPE for customers and communities around the world has been a key proof point of putting people first, which is a critical element of our sustainably strategy.

I believe this is not only the right thing to do for the planet, but it is a business imperative for the company. Increasingly, customers want to know the purpose of a company and to know what it stands for, not in words, but in actions. ESG expectations are not just increasing for investors but also for our younger cohort of customers that are perhaps more environmentally conscious than prior generations.

Pamela Fletcher

Vice President, Global Innovation
General Motors Company

Background

Pamela Fletcher (Pam) has been Vice President of Global Innovation since 2018. Global Innovation is on a mission to turn high-potential innovative ideas into scalable business ventures that drive growth and transform the General Motors (GM) business model beyond traditional automotive.

Fletcher's experience is broad and global. For more than a decade, she has been in leadership roles guiding the development of GM's electric vehicle (EV) and self-driving portfolio and technologies, most recently as Vice President of Global Electric Vehicles.

Her teams were responsible for developing several of GM's most awarded vehicles, including two generations of the Chevrolet Volt, and the Chevrolet Bolt EV, the industry's first mass-market, long-range, affordable electric vehicle. Her team also led the development of Super Cruise, the industry's first hands-free highway driver assist system, as well as three generations of Cruise AVs.

Fletcher earned her bachelor's and master's degrees in Engineering. She serves as a corporate director of Coherent Inc., a NASDAQ-listed company based in Silicon Valley, and is also a board member of GM Defense LLC. She continued her education with the Executive Development Program at the Kellogg School of Management at Northwestern University, the Stanford Graduate School of Business Transformational Leadership Program, and the Harvard Women on Boards Program.

Fletcher was named to *Motor Trend*'s 2018 and 2019 "Power List" of auto industry leaders and was one of *Fast Company*'s "Most Creative People" of 2017. She serves on the Board of Advisors for the College of Engineering at the University of North Carolina Charlotte.

Questions and Answers

1. Change Control, Resilience, and Work/Life Balance

What did you learn when you began to work from home or work in the office with a limited number of co-workers? What did you need to start doing and what did you need to stop?

When COVID first became prevalent, there was so much unknown. We didn't know much about the virus, we had never worked remotely as a whole company before, and many members of the team were juggling other responsibilities each day on top of their jobs, like being a teacher or caretaker for their family. I quickly learned that there was no perfect method to the new "normal," and the best thing that we could do was to continue to check in with each other, not just on a working level, but to make sure my colleagues were okay personally, too.

In the beginning, I set up daily morning calls with my core team, just to provide a time to talk and share what each of us was experiencing, personally or professionally. For a while, we encouraged using video during meetings as much as possible so we could maintain the face-to-face human interaction we were missing from not being in the office. We had social interactions via video too, like coffee chats and happy hours. In time, we found our groove, and we got used to working remotely every day. We found the right balance of checking in and using video vs. voice calls. My team has demonstrated such amazing resilience throughout everything this year has brought, and I think many have come to appreciate the benefits working from home can bring from a work-life balance perspective.

One thing I learned is that it's important to create new boundaries for yourself while working from home. The ability to disconnect is always a challenge but is exacerbated when your home is your shelter 24/7 for family and for work. I've used this as an opportunity to be a better practitioner of being present and to reengage my love of cooking and use it as quality time with my husband.

2. Growing Your Professional Network and Maintaining Mentor and Sponsor Relationships

Has your company maintained learning and leadership development opportunities, culture surveys, 360 surveys, etc., to grow skills and manage the emotional intelligence of the company? Has anything shifted? What have you learned?

We've all had to adapt during this pandemic. We've had to put a special focus on our physical health, and our mental health, too. Increased worry, stress, and/or anxiety have affected us all at some point in the past year, and pairing those feelings with increased responsibilities at home and work, it became especially important to check in with each other. One way GM kept a pulse on employee well-being was through surveys. We used survey insights to influence the steps we took as a company as we navigated through the uncertainties. For example, we learned via surveys that employees liked working from home and that they appreciated having more flexible work options. That information influenced our company's decision to continue working from home through June 2021 and also led us to lay the groundwork for more flexible work options for the future.

GM also provided employees with more virtual resources to help them during the pandemic. For example, one GM website offers employees tools and information on mental and physical health, finances, career planning, parenting, and many other topics. It also has a chat feature that allows employees to interact with a mental health professional in real time, if needed.

Making sure our employees had access to additional, virtual resources, as well as increased work flexibility was especially important this year as we faced many unique situations.

3. Personal Growth

What is the most profound impact this pandemic has had the way you think about your job, company, family life? Will it be sticky or do you expect everything to return to the previous status quo?

There have been so many things I've learned, and learned to be thankful for, during this pandemic. For me, the pandemic reminded me of what is really important in life, and that is the love and health of my family. The pandemic emphasized for me the importance of creating good environments so I can be my best when working and when with family. Not only do I dedicate time to work, but I also dedicate time to being present, physically and mentally, to care for and enjoy my family. Despite the hardships we all faced in 2020, it was special in the sense that it allowed me to spend so much time with my family.

From a work perspective, this pandemic has really shown me the power and resiliency of the team. Despite working from different locations, and facing many challenges, we're getting more done than ever. The team has gone above and beyond, and it's been an honor to see what we've been able to accomplish.

For example, we've used this time as an opportunity to identify and assess new trends and patterns that are forming due to the circumstances driven by COVID. In GM's Global Innovation organization, we strive to solve unique pain points for our customers, and beyond, with novel solutions. In a period of a few short months, we have created a significant new business to address the many pain points created from the exponential growth of eCommerce and home delivery. We look forward to telling this story in the coming weeks.

I also have been especially proud to work for General Motors during this time because of what we've been able to do as a company. Prior to March 2020, we had never built ventilators or masks, and it was incredible to see a business of our scale rally together to create ventilators and PPE that were desperately needed in our communities.

We have created a new status quo this year, and I think elements will absolutely stick and influence the way we work moving forward.

4. Diversity, Equity, and Inclusion

There has been a lot of talk about diversity—and, in recent years, inclusion. Equity has entered the corporate conversation in a major way this year. What actions are you and your company taking? Are these methods aligned with company goals?

In 2020, GM's Chairman and CEO Mary Barra set a bold aspiration for GM to be the most inclusive company in the world, and as a company, we are taking many steps towards that goal. For example, we have overhauled our recruitment efforts to ensure we are reaching and attracting a more diverse pool of potential employees. It is very important to make sure we are giving everyone the opportunity to have a seat at the table, as well as for diverse voices to be heard.

GM has also taken steps to make sure we are providing a safe and inclusive environment that promotes equity for all of our employees. To ensure a better future, we must educate ourselves and rally behind and practice like-minded, positive behaviors. To help with this, we've increased and improved our company trainings around a number of subjects, including, racism, unconscious bias, sexual harassment, and more, that we require all employees to participate in.

GM also has a number of Employee Resource Groups, like GM African Ancestry Network, GM Latino Network, GM Plus LGBTQ + Allies, and GM Women, which provide a forum for employees to share experiences and concerns, gain professional development, and engage with their local communities. I am involved with our GM Women group and recently presented at a virtual professional development seminar, where I shared career experiences and leadership advice with hundreds of women. I believe it's important to learn from the experiences of others, and as a female leader, I want to always do my part by sharing learnings with other women so that they have insights that can help them thrive throughout their career.

5. Sustainability

Sustainability trends (climate change, water availability, health, etc.) are some of the strongest drivers for future changes for companies and their strategies. What are you seeing within your company? Is your firm reading the trends and adapting strategies to survive and then thrive with new growth?

GM's vision is to create a world with zero crashes, zero emissions, and zero congestion. One big way GM plans to achieve this vision is by accelerating our path to an all-electric future by scaling the availability of electric vehicles. For GM, vehicle emissions account for 77 percent of our carbon footprint, so battery-electric vehicles are the fastest way to reduce our impact.

While we have been actively working toward a zero-emissions future, the pandemic has pushed us to work even faster. GM recently announced that it has 30 new, global electric vehicle launches planned through 2025. This is huge, especially when I think back on my career and background in EV engineering. I led the development of the Chevrolet Volt and Bolt EV, so to see where we are heading is especially exciting. We are not only creating awesome vehicles at a major scale, but we're also making big strides toward our company vision of a world with zero emissions.

In addition to being accessible, electric vehicles also need to be affordable, which, by mid-decade, GM's Ultium battery packs are projected to cost 60 percent less than today's packs with twice the energy density. We also know we can't create an all-electric future alone, so we will be collaborating with other companies along the way to make the transition from ICE vehicles to EVs more effortless for customers. For example, we are working with charging infrastructure providers to make sure there are more chargers, so charging your EV is more convenient in the future.

Karen Folger

Vice President, Actuators—Electrical Drives
North America
Bosch

Background

Karen Folger is a global executive with extensive management, sales, and leadership expertise. In her current role at Bosch, Folger maintains Profit and Loss (P&L) responsibility for two business units with over $500 million in annual sales. She also serves as a trustee for the Bosch Community Fund, the corporate foundation for Bosch in North America.

Since joining Bosch in 1999, Folger has held a number of executive roles in the company's automotive aftermarket division, joining the Electrical Drives division in 2017. Prior to joining Bosch, Folger held senior-level sales, marketing, and operations positions for SPX Corporation and Valley Forge Technical Information Services.

In 2015, Folger was recognized by *Automotive News* as one of the "Top 100 Women in the Auto Industry." She currently serves as a board member of Inforum, a professional organization focused on creating strategic connections to help advance professional women across the automotive industry.

Folger earned a Bachelor of Science degree from Eastern Michigan University. She's married and has three adult sons.

Questions and Answers

1. Change Control, Resilience, and Work/Life Balance

Many have said that there is no separation of work and home these days—what do you do to manage this for your own work? What are you doing to increase the ability of your team to create and respect boundaries?

I had a mentor tell me once that the best work was the kind where you never felt the boundary between what you do for a living and what you do for your personal satisfaction. I'm not sure I subscribe to this theory, but during COVID, we have had the opportunity to test it.

In my case, working from home has been a good thing. No commute, no travel, a separate quiet space to work, and only my husband and dogs for company. This has allowed us to create time for our home lives. We walk the dogs early every morning and make lunch for each other—though there is rarely time to eat it together. While we often finish our days late, there is no commute to extend the day. At the same time, I am cognizant that not all our team members have this same situation. Many have children or parents in the home who require care. They may or may not have a dedicated space to work and often do not have the luxury of a perfectly quiet space for conference calls.

We have adapted to this situation with humor, flexibility, and appreciation. We recognize that what matters is getting our work done—not getting it done between the hours of 8:30 am and 6:00 pm. I often see my team online early in the morning or late at night—sometimes both. It may be that they are offline during certain hours of the day to address personal or family issues. I haven't once had a concern that someone on the team was working too few hours to achieve our objectives.

Early in the pandemic when we were first working from home, our plants were temporarily shut down and we were very focused on ensuring our supply chain would be ready for ramp-up. I was concerned that the team was working hours that were not sustainable. There was no magic to fixing the reality that many were exhausted. Together we recognized that we needed to pace ourselves for this long, challenging journey. Prioritizing our personal well-being and the health and well-being of our families was more important than our work. It never meant we accepted that we would not achieve our objectives. It meant that we needed to support one another, encourage one another, and carry the load sometimes for one another. It also meant we could laugh and appreciate the children who sometimes unexpectedly joined our conference calls. We could offer to change a meeting time or have a proxy participate to enable everyone on the team to prioritize their personal needs. Everyone managing their personal life in no way detracts from the successful performance of our team. We have recognized that every member of the team has a personal life and a unique situation that requires occasional accommodation and consistent support.

2. Growing Your Professional Network and Maintaining Mentor and Sponsor Relationships

Has your company maintained learning and leadership development opportunities, culture surveys, 360 surveys, etc., to grow skills and manage the emotional intelligence of the company? Has anything shifted? What have you learned?

While we cancelled in-person training events, we have continued to stay focused on associate feedback and development. Fostering the growth of the emotional intelligence of our company began years ago with the education and engagement of our leaders and continues as a key part of the development of our associates in our leadership programs. 360-degree surveys continue to be a key area of feedback for all leaders, and we have a program where any manager or associate has the opportunity to initiate one by working with their HR partner.

I think two things have changed during the past year: first, the digital transformation effect. We have the ability to use technology for fast feedback: mood checks in Microsoft Teams, quick surveys through SurveyMonkey, and real-time feedback through Skype chat and Slido during meetings. This has changed virtual meetings from one-way information sharing to two-way dialogues. Sometimes the result is information that the speaker can target to the interest or concern of the meeting participants, but often it also means that the participants can give each other and the speaker accolades and appreciation. This has further deepened the sense of team in a time of separation.

The second thing that has changed is the way we lead. The school of "management by walking around" does not work in this virtual world—at least not in the typical sense of stopping by desks and chatting in the halls. Our leaders throughout the organization are adapting to this, and for many, it has been a big change. Some have daily check-in meetings. Some make sure they regularly contact their direct reports as well as their extended teams to check in casually. One team even held a virtual holiday celebration with music, costumes, and other activities.

The actions of our leaders provide evidence that despite the changes, we as an organization are continuing to nurture an environment of emotional intelligence. There are many encouraging signs in this area: compassion, empathy, team spirit, and listening to understand, combined with making sure our team members are able to express their questions, concerns, and ideas without hesitation.

My personal learning has been that resilience and adaptability are critical to successful and emotionally intelligent leadership—and that every member of a team can lead with these skills.

3. Personal Growth

What is the most profound impact this pandemic has had the way you think about your job, company, family life? Will it be sticky or do you expect everything to return to the previous status quo?

Professionally, this experience has been challenging, fascinating, and rewarding all at once. I have had the opportunity to collaborate with team members and customers on very complex problems that have no easy or obvious solution. The spirit of cooperation and problem-solving is invigorating and inspirational. Our internal team has worked together across borders with a great level of creativity, commitment, and problem-solving. We have found solutions to industry challenges, we have prevented issues using diligence and scenario planning, and we have reacted to the environment around us with a spirit of "how will we do this" rather than "this can't be done." I feel genuinely humbled by the skill, professionalism, and dedication of my colleagues.

I believe one of the critical success factors for our team's ability to continue to work effectively, and maybe even more effectively than before, is that we went into the pandemic with a strong foundation. We were clear on our short-, mid-, and long-term strategy, we had well-defined and measurable objectives, established milestones, and accountable owners. Even when the pandemic caused us to re-prioritize and add new more immediate objectives, we maintained a regular focus on our strategies and the associated objectives. This consistent emphasis on what is important has kept us focused on our mission. The details of where we were working, or when, or with what technology were relevant only as enablers to achieve our mission. I am confident that this focus and alignment is what has helped us to adapt, and is what will certainly stick.

We are all changed as a result of this shared experience. We have proven to ourselves that the way we work can be much more flexible than we once thought. Maybe we don't need to work in the same physical spaces that we once thought we required. Maybe travel isn't as necessary as we thought. At Bosch, we are already working on a long-term plan that will incorporate these changed points of view.

From a personal perspective, I feel more connected to my family and community than ever. I'm grateful that our family members have remained healthy and safe. We have stayed very locked-down in order to be able to visit and provide support for my mother and to see our new grandson; consequently, we've supported many of our local businesses by utilizing their curbside and delivery services. My husband and I take an hour-long hike with our dogs every day, something that I often had to sacrifice in the past because of travel or early meetings.

Karen Folger

We've had outdoor celebrations and virtual happy hours with our children and our friends and family, and I've been able to find time for personal passions like reading, cooking, and gardening.

Sometimes it feels as if the real world has pressed pause—that's been very restorative for me.

4. Diversity, Equity, and Inclusion

There has been a lot of talk about diversity—and, in recent years, inclusion. Equity has entered the corporate conversation in a major way this year. What actions are you and your company taking? Are these methods aligned with company goals?

Bosch is a values-driven company, and diversity is a cornerstone of our Bosch values. We believe in the right of everyone to experience dignity, safety, and respect. We recognize that diversity is an asset—as well as a precondition of our global success. We're committed to creating an inclusive atmosphere where our associates feel comfortable bringing their whole self to work. For us, equity represents our strong commitment to fair treatment of all our associates.

One area where our associates have the space to embrace diversity is through our business resource groups (BRGs), such as AfricanAncestry@Bosch, LGBTQ@Bosch, Veterans@Bosch, and Women@Bosch. These groups serve as important advisors to the company to promote greater diversity, awareness, and education.

We also support diversity via our engagement in our local communities. In 2019, nearly 50 percent of all grants by the Bosch Community Fund went to organizations who target underserved student demographics. In addition, more than one-third of overall grants helped to increase access to STEM education for underrepresented populations.

As a leader, it is incumbent upon me to ensure that we are encouraging and embracing diversity and inclusion in our own team. We have a solid foundation of diversity and inclusion training, which has helped us to recognize that diversity is so much more than skin color, nationality, gender, or expressed identity. It is about the experiences and perspectives we bring to our work and our interactions with one another. The spirit of curiosity, interest in each other's histories, and points of view are what make our experiences as a team rich and rewarding. We can always do better—this starts with asking ourselves tough questions and holding ourselves accountable to the standards set forth in our company values.

5. Sustainability

Sustainability trends (climate change, water availability, health, etc.) are some of the strongest drivers for future changes for companies and their strategies. What are you seeing within your company? Is your firm reading the trends and adapting strategies to survive and then thrive with new growth?

In May of 2019, Bosch made a major commitment in this area, pledging to make all Bosch locations globally carbon neutral by the end of 2020. I'm proud to say that despite the pandemic, we have achieved this promise and were the first major industrial enterprise to achieve the ambitious goal of carbon neutrality. Our 400 locations worldwide no longer leave a carbon footprint.

To make this success possible, we've applied a four-pillar strategy: increasing energy efficiency, expanding the production of renewable energy, procuring more green electricity, and offsetting unavoidable CO2 emissions.

Now that we've met our carbon neutrality goal, we're not slowing down. In fact, we're shifting our focus to an even bigger challenge: the emissions of our entire value chain—from the goods we purchase to how our products are disposed across all of our business areas. By 2030, our goal is to reduce these emissions along our entire value chain by 15 percent.

This ambitious and voluntary commitment is consistent with the Bosch brand promise of Invented for Life. We believe that climate action, innovation, and business success all go together. Our investments underscore the deep commitment we have to our role in creating a sustainable world for future generations, as well as our commitment to the future of our business.

Elena Ford

Chief Customer Experience Officer
Ford Motor Company

Background

Elena Ford was named Chief Customer Experience Officer in October 2018. In this role, she leads the organization responsible for creating a world-class customer experience throughout the entire ownership cycle.

She's dedicated her career to understanding what drives customers' perceptions and expectations of companies and products and is leading the transformation of offline and online interactions between Ford, dealers, and customers into seamless, connected experiences that meet and exceed human needs.

In previous roles, Ms. Ford led the global rollout of Ford Signature dealership design, elevating facility standards to provide a more modern, transparent, and efficient in-store customer experience and strengthened the company's dealer relationships in every region it operates through initiatives like establishing the Dealer Advisory Group, which she continues to lead today.

She also helped develop and implement Ford's global marketing vision, as well as Ford's "Go Further" global brand promise. Her 25-year tenure with Ford has spanned marketing, global brand development, dealer strategy, financial services, and digital user experience.

Ms. Ford was twice named among the leading women in the auto industry by *Automotive News*. She currently serves on the boards of FordDirect, Percepta, the Forman School, and Fair Lane, the Home of Clara and Henry Ford. For Ford Fund, the philanthropic arm of Ford Motor Company, she champions a collaboration with First Book to increase literacy skills among young people from low-income families.

Questions and Answers

1. Change Control, Resilience, and Work/Life Balance

How do you keep team spirit with your direct reports? Are you sensing any lack of trust or more trust? What factors/actions have the most effect on trust/lack of trust?

For me, communications have had the biggest impact on maintaining team spirit and morale during this pandemic. When we began working from home in March, my direct reports and I started a new routine of having daily stand-up meetings at 5 pm from Monday to Thursday. It was an informal way to stay connected and help each other solve problems as we faced this new challenge together. And it has stuck. We now hold them twice a week, on Tuesdays and Thursdays. I find them an essential way to govern my team and check in with how they are doing. I feel more in touch with my colleagues and what they are doing than I did before.

We have also been communicating as a company more. Since March, we have held company-wide Global Town Halls every week (we recently moved them to every two weeks). Our employees love the transparency and hearing from our senior leaders directly.

At Ford, there used to be a stigma attached to working remotely and a perception that if I don't see you, you're not working. This experience has turned that notion on its head. I trust my direct reports implicitly, and if anything, they have overdelivered during this time. That is true of all Ford employees and dealers, I've been so impressed with how committed and passionate they are about doing great work and serving our customers.

2. Growing Your Professional Network and Maintaining Mentor and Sponsor Relationships

Are you continuing to grow your professional network while being remote? How?

Absolutely. You are never done learning and growing in your career. Since joining Ford 25 years ago, I've had a lot of mentors and people who have helped me along the way. I wouldn't be where I am today without them. Over the past 10 months, I've found that I've taken on the role of mentor (rather than mentee), which I've really enjoyed, especially to younger women at the company. I've also been doing more skip meetings recently around the topic of Diversity, Equity, and Inclusion (DEI), which is a huge passion of mine. I've met with young women who have been in my customer experience team for several years, but I've never spoken to them before—and I love their enthusiasm and dedication. I think it's so important that we provide younger employees with the opportunity to expand their network and have their voices heard at different levels of the company.

Another thing I did was to connect and expand our global dealer roundtable. This is a group of proactive dealer principles from all our key markets who want to have an active voice in how we run the business and service customers. When the virus first hit in China, we were able to activate this group through voluntary weekly calls so they could share information and learnings. The dealers came to really value these discussions and it was a critical channel for us to be able to share learnings and best practices as the virus spread worldwide. This knowledge was captured in our Return to Work Playbook that was an essential tool used by all our dealers to welcome customers back into their stores safely.

3. Personal Growth

What is the most profound impact this pandemic has had on the way you think about your job, company, family life? Will it be sticky or do you expect everything to return to the previous status quo?

I've found that you can lose energy working from home, and it doesn't give you the same amount of time to stop and think. I feel like there aren't any clear spots on my calendar anymore, and the rules I used to follow—like no meetings on a Friday afternoon so I could catch up on things—have gone out the window. I miss those casual conversations in the office at the coffee machine or water cooler, which were, in hindsight, incredibly productive. Whereas I previously popped my head into someone's office or caught them in the hallway, I now need to schedule a Webex meeting with them. Sitting at your desk all day (and often into the night) on conference calls can be exhausting, especially those two- to three-hour long meetings. I actually miss my commute to and from the office as it gave me time to clear my head and think. My break times now involve walking into the kitchen or living room and that doesn't give you the same mental pause you need to be creative or solve problems.

4. Diversity, Equity, and Inclusion

There has been a lot of talk about diversity—and, in recent years, inclusion. Equity has entered the corporate conversation in a major way this year. What actions are you and your company taking? Are these methods aligned with company goals?

Ford is very focused on improving diversity, equity, and inclusion (DEI) at all levels within the company. We're a values-led organization and our people come first. Being there for each other, embracing diversity of backgrounds and experiences, and letting everyone know they're cared for, supported, and respected are central to our plan for the future. Driving lasting change for racial and ethnic equality within Ford will also help us be more reflective of the customers and communities we serve.

Earlier this year, Ford completed a DEI audit of our U.S. salaried workers to truly understand the employee experience as it relates to DEI. The audit showed that Ford's maturity level falls between Compliant and Emergent on Deloitte's maturity scale, meaning we have solid intentions and some bright spots, but there is an opportunity to become more inclusive. Nearly all companies audited by Deloitte fall in this area.

We are committed to providing a work environment where everyone feels like they belong. The audit allowed us to gain deeper insights into the challenges some of our employees face, which is guiding our plan of action to drive meaningful and lasting change for equality. Ford also appointed a new Racial Equity Leader,

Angela Henderson, who is focused on reducing bias and improving the employee experience journey for everyone.

Within my CX team, we have been reviewing the DEI audit results and developing our own specific plan to address them. Some of the focus areas we're looking at include transparent processes, people leader behaviors, and the removal of microaggressions.

I'm also overseeing a workstream that is focused on addressing Dealership Diversity. A key goal of this effort is to uncover the root causes preventing us from attracting, developing, and retaining more women and ethnically diverse workers at dealerships. We are doing this by studying the HR practices at a cross-section of U.S. dealerships and using this learning to develop robust talent strategies that promote a DEI workforce and better reach growth audiences.

5. Sustainability

As part of employee development, does your company encourage and support employees volunteering for local nongovernmental organizations? Do you and your company consider this an opportunity for aligning company efforts, employee leadership development, and local progress on sustainability?

Managed by Ford Motor Company Fund, the company's philanthropic arm, the Ford Volunteer Corps is a global network of Ford employees and retirees who have contributed more than 1.7 million volunteer hours in community service projects since 2005. Ford volunteers bring skill, enthusiasm, and teamwork to nonprofits, helping to get essential jobs done while the organizations focus on serving people in need. During a typical year, thousands of Ford employees fan out into communities across six continents to participate in hands-on service projects during Ford Global Caring Month, a 30-day concentrated focus on community service that happens each September.

In light of COVID, Ford volunteers found new, safe ways to help people and strengthen communities most impacted by the virus. During September's Ford Global Caring Month, over $380,000 was donated to more than 75 employee-nominated nonprofits around the world. This year, to maintain health and safety, instead of planting gardens, cleaning and renovating shelters, or stocking shelves at food pantries, Ford employees concentrated their efforts on two activities—Gratitude Grants and Acts of Kindness (see more info below).

Personally, I champion a collaboration between Ford Fund and the nonprofit First Book aimed at increasing literacy among youth in underserved communities. By the end of this year, the initiative will have invested over $600,000 and delivered 130,000 books to students in 8 markets across the USA and Puerto Rico. In October, Ford Fund, First Book, and more than 40 Ford dealers pledged to provide 30,000 books and critically needed school supplies to educators and students hard hit by COVID in Dallas, Houston, and Phoenix. You can read more about it here. https://media.ford.com/content/fordmedia/fna/us/en/news/2020/10/22/ford-fund-elena-ford-expand-support-for-reading.pdf

GRATITUDE GRANTS

Ford Fund and Ford Volunteer Corps asked employees to nominate local nonprofits or nongovernmental organizations for a "Gratitude Grant" in recognition of the essential work they are doing to address COVID. Ford Volunteer Corps is in the process of notifying selected organizations and will be awarding a $5,000 grant to help sustain or expand each group's efforts to serve its community and meet pandemic-related needs. Nominations came in from across Europe, North and South America, Australia, China, India, South Africa, and many other countries. Grants will be distributed during November and December, supporting efforts related to hunger relief, homelessness, health and wellness, education, and more.

ACTS OF KINDNESS

The Ford Volunteer Corps received nearly 400 submissions from 15 countries for its Acts of Kindness program, which invited employees to submit a photo and description of themselves performing a good deed for a family member, friend, or neighbor. Participating employees received a 15USD gift card—in recognition of the 15th anniversary of the Ford Volunteer Corps—that could be used to support their choice of one of thousands of vetted charitable projects in more than 160 countries.

To learn more about the work of the Ford Volunteer Corps, visit www.fordfund.org/volunteer.

Julie Fream

President and Chief Executive Officer (CEO)
Original Equipment Suppliers Association (OESA)

Background

Julie is the president and CEO of the Original Equipment Suppliers Association (OESA). The association represents the voice of automotive suppliers and champions their business interests. Named to the role in 2013, Julie has a 38-year career in automotive, including roles with OEMs and suppliers in engineering, program management, manufacturing, sales, marketing, and communications.

She is currently a member of the Ford Supplier Council, General Motors Supplier Council, and the Nissan North America Supplier Council, representing the interests of the automotive supplier community.

In 2015 and again in 2020, Fream was listed among the "100 Leading Women in the Automotive Industry" by *Automotive News*. In 2016, she was recognized by *Crain's Detroit Business* as one of "Michigan's Most Influential Women."

Julie is a founding member of the Board of Directors for Beaumont Health and serves as its Vice Chair, as well as Chair of the Audit and Compliance Committee; she also serves on the boards of First Robotics Michigan and the Automotive Hall of Fame.

Fream holds a Bachelor of Science in Chemical Engineering from Michigan Technological University and an MBA from the Harvard Business School.

Questions and Answers

1. Change Control, Resilience, and Work/Life Balance

How do you and your team continue to innovate and improve?

OESA's mission is to understand and address the evolving business issues of the automotive supplier community. To deliver on this value proposition, the association must also evolve; making continuous improvement is key to OESA's sustainability.

One of OESA's greatest assets for continued improvement is having the direct and consistent feedback from OESA's 500+ member companies. Through frequent dialogue and ongoing supplier assessment, the association enjoys a unique position in the industry by learning, first-hand, the needs and concerns of the supplier community. The OESA team uses both the collective feedback of members and current industry trends to deliver timely and relevant content, thought leadership and resources.

OESA staff members are encouraged to hone their individual skills, as well. They receive an annual stipend for professional development. Additionally, they are encouraged to attend all OESA events to better understand the changing landscape of the industry.

OESA strives to constantly innovate and improve all aspects of association—with improvements specifically designed to better meet member needs. This spirit of innovation is a part of everything we do, and a critical aspect to OESA's value to the members and the broader automotive supplier community.

2. Personal Growth

What is the most profound impact this pandemic has had the way you think about your job, company, family life? Will it be sticky, or do you expect everything to return to the previous status quo?

The pandemic rocked our nation, slowed our economy, halted our businesses, and confined our daily lives. Personally, the most profound impact it has on me is the many lives lost in this battle. My heart goes out to the families and friends that have lost loved ones.

The pandemic has also impacted the way I think about my organization and family.

Prior to the pandemic, much of OESA's value was delivered during in-person events and networking sessions. Like many organizations, OESA quickly learned to be more innovative to get things done. In a matter of weeks, the team moved programming to a virtual format, and found new ways to foster customer-to-supplier and supplier-to-supplier networking and collaboration. OESA also learned to be more efficient with resources and members' time. When things go back to "normal," we will maintain these improvements. Today, OESA is more agile, and we will continue to offer a virtual option for many of our events and meetings to better accommodate members.

As for my family, time at home during the pandemic was an unforeseen blessing. It brought my children home early from college and gave our family some unexpected quality time together. While we had to make a few adjustments, such as increasing our Wi-Fi speed and setting up more home office spaces, the time together was wonderful. As my young adult "children" graduate and move on to pursue their personal paths, we will have to work harder to connect with each other as we did during our life in quarantine.

The impact of the pandemic should be a reminder to us all that things can change in an instant, and with determination, we can evolve into something greater. We should also be aware that there is no going back to the way things were and we have the unprecedented opportunity to forge new norms.

3. Growing Your Professional Network and Maintaining Mentor and Sponsor Relationships

How do you keep your existing relationships in this remote world? Are you maintaining face time with other execs while being remote? How do your direct reports maintain their face time with you?

Throughout my career in automotive, and with the collective experience of my team, OESA has established many strong relationships within the automotive community. With the demand for more information during the early months of the pandemic, the OESA team relied heavily on industry contacts to serve as essential resources for suppliers, OEMs, and government officials.

OESA increased the level of supplier engagement and networking in 2020 by conducting nearly twice as many events as the previous year; it came with a corresponding increase in member participation, as well. The OESA staff continues to stay in touch with members through frequent personal phone calls and regular check-ins.

As for face time with my team, meeting frequency and content has also changed. Prior to the pandemic, I conducted weekly staff meetings, one-on-one meetings with my direct reports, and in-person meetings with industry professionals. Albeit virtual, these meetings are more frequent, and often more insightful. Staff meetings now include time for the team to share personal experiences and offer encouragement during these challenging times. This has brought the OESA team closer as a work family, while strengthening the teams' ties in the industry.

4. Diversity, Equity, and Inclusion

There has been a lot of talk about diversity—and, in recent years, inclusion. Equity has entered the corporate conversation in a major way this year. What actions are you and your company taking? Are these methods aligned with company goals?

The importance of diversity, equity, and inclusion (DEI) has taken center stage in the United States as recent events sparked a renewed focus on racial and social justice.

For the supplier community, OESA, in partnership with the Center for Automotive Diversity, Inclusion & Advancement (CADIA), launched a new Diversity, Equity and Inclusion Council. Quarterly council discussions focus on DEI strategies and trends, sharing best practices, and learning from DEI subject matter experts. The council also features hands-on workshops, industry benchmarking surveys and community outreach initiatives. OESA is also expanding programming to build stronger relationships with minority supplier organizations and develop additional diversity matchmaker events.

Internally, we organized a team of employees to lead the charge for improving diversity, equity, and inclusion corporatewide. The team launched a DEI benchmarking survey to better understand the perceptions and needs of staff members, as well as implemented quarterly "Courageous Conversations" to discuss racial and social justice issues. These conversations give employees the opportunity to learn about their personal biases and ways to address DEI issues in a safe and constructive manner.

OESA also formalized a DEI statement to be shared at every event and council meeting, and further demonstrate the association's genuine commitment to addressing DEI issues:

"OESA fosters a respectful, diverse, and collaborative community. We are stronger together because we promote inclusion in all aspects of our industry. Please join us by embracing and honoring this commitment."

The statement also continues to generate awareness of these issues throughout the supply base.

5. Sustainability

What do you as a leader do to stay informed about sustainability trends that can impact the success of your company and its strategy?

One of the most important requirements of my job is to understand the opportunities and challenges of the supplier community. Over the course of the many conversations with our members, OESA has learned to view "sustainability" in two very distinct ways. The first connotation refers to reducing waste and minimizing the environmental and carbon footprint of an organization. These aspects of sustainability are of growing importance to all companies and industries. To support automotive suppliers as they work to become more environmentally responsible, we enhanced the OESA Environment, Health & Safety Council recently by adding "sustainability" issues and topics to the discussions. Members of the new Environment, Health, Safety & Sustainability Council (EHS&S) shares best practices and hear from subject matter experts on ways to improve sustainability throughout the supplier industry.

The second (and equally important) aspect of sustainability is how organizations must continue to evolve and innovate to sustain their presence in the marketplace. OESA continually works on the association's sustainability. Over the past year, we met with many members to discuss OESA's current value proposition and how we need to evolve to support their needs for the future. We are using this information to ensure OESA has an agile and sustainable business model, and to ensure the work of the association remains relevant to the industry in the coming years.

Kara Grasso

Vice President of Strategic Operations
DENSO International America, Inc.

Background

Kara Grasso is Vice President of Strategic Operations at DENSO's North American headquarters in Southfield, Michigan. In this role, she oversees strategic planning, business operations planning, sales strategy and systems, and new entrant customers. She also co-created and is an active member of DENSO's Women in Sales and is the Executive Champion for DENSO's African Ancestry Network.

Grasso joined DENSO in 2000 as a senior specialist within Sales, responsible for leading all Chrysler Engine Cooling Module commercial responsibilities. From 2004 to 2019, Grasso held various positions within Sales, focusing on sales of thermal, powertrain, engine electrical, body electronics, and service products. Her responsibilities include strategizing and strengthening key relationships within purchasing, engineering, cost planning, and quality departments and engaging the sales associates to create alignment between divisional and product group targets.

Prior to working at DENSO, Grasso worked at Freudenberg-NOK as a sales engineer. From 2000 to 2005, Grasso also worked as an instructor for The Dale Carnegie Course. In 2008, Grasso and her husband launch 3 franchise locations of Snap Fitness where together they manage a small team dedicated to living a healthy lifestyle. Grasso is a member of the Inforum AutomotiveNEXT executive committee as well as the Consumer Technology Association Board of Industry Leaders.

Grasso completed both her Bachelor of Science in Business-Organizational Behavior and her Bachelor of Science in Business–Human Resource Management at Miami University in Oxford, Ohio in 1998.

Questions and Answers

1. Change Control, Resilience, and Work/Life Balance

Many have said that there is no separation of work and home these days. What do you do to manage this for your own work? What are you doing to increase the ability of your team to create and respect boundaries?

Early on in the pandemic, I remember naïvely thinking that we would be home for a couple of weeks and then return back to normal. But after three months, I realized I had better make my workspace comfortable and learn how to manage a world that has blended work and life into one. Without a home office, getting a new puppy, and three daughters going to virtual school, our house was in a constant state of chaos.

To manage this chaos, I committed to creating healthy boundaries between life and work. My coach recommended that I ask my girls "what do you need from mom during the day?" This exercise was enlightening. Instead of burdensome requests for help with science or geometry, each one of them individually answered:

- ***E (16)***: *"I can do everything by myself but I like having lunch with you. You can ask questions about school. I like that you are the swim team president so you can be at everything."*
- ***L (14)***: *"I need snuggle time after dinner. I like family time at night. I don't care if you ask about my classes but you really don't need to. I can keep track of myself. Swim schedule is ok, especially since we can drive now."*
- ***N (12)***:*"I just need you to love me. You do everything right. I like to have family time and I don't like when anyone is stressed out. Let's just be happy and spend time together."*

Based on this feedback and me realizing that I was trying to "do it all," we made simple schedules posted in the kitchen, which included family lunches and downtime in the evenings—certainly a silver lining.

Within my over 50-person team, we challenged ourselves to share best practice Work-from-Home tips. It was new to all of us, so we had to be open about what was working and what wasn't. A key change point was that we would schedule break time into our calendars. After months of back-to-back meetings without healthy breaks, we knew it had to stop or else we would lose our energy and motivation to solve these complex pandemic issues. Each week, I would look at the week ahead and build in "think time," "fresh air time," "work time," and "me time." Within my calendar, these entries were open so that my team would recognize I expect the same from them.

Gradually, we all got into a groove. Although work and life have blended, I believe we have found multiple silver linings that can be considered best practices for mental health.

2. Growing Your Professional Network and Maintaining Mentor and Sponsor Relationships

Has your company maintained learning and leadership development opportunities, culture surveys, 360 surveys, etc., to grow skills and manage the emotional intelligence of the company? Has anything shifted? What have you learned?

Just prior to the shutdown, I had invested in a series of training opportunities for my direct reports and me. This nine-month training has proven to be very valuable in our new virtual world. Originally, we considered to postpone until we could meet face to face in the same conference room, but after realizing this was not going to be possible any time soon, we have met via Zoom once per month for a full-day training session.

Key teachings included *Start with Why* by Simon Sinek and *5 Dysfunctions of a Team* by Patrick Lencioni. This timeframe has proven to be the perfect occasion for us all to become more vulnerable with each other. We have worked to develop our "Personal Why" and our "Team Why" to create cohesion across multiple areas of strategic planning.

However, virtual training has been difficult due to the endless opportunities to multitask as well as the long day on one call. By keeping each other accountable to learn and grow together, the team has experienced a unique bonding. This was especially important for newer members that were not able to get to know everyone pre-pandemic. Through the virtual training, we have been able to maintain personal connections as if we were in the office setting.

3. Personal Growth

What is the most profound impact this pandemic has had the way you think about your job, company, family life? Will it be sticky or do you expect everything to return to the previous status quo?

The opportunity for personal coaching has had a profound impact on my career, especially throughout this time. My coach, Jon, has challenged me in unique ways to build my capability towards my vision. His perspective, especially during this pandemic, has opened my eyes in a new way. Each time I come into a session overwhelmed with a new "crisis" issue, I leave with a clear mind and sense that I can achieve anything.

Kara Grasso

Week after week, I have made commitments to close gaps in my management style, recognize COVID silver linings, reflect on the past year's personal and professional wins, and work through critical company issues. Through the integrity to achieve these commitments, I have been able to keep a clear path towards my vision established two years ago…"To be a world-class leader, partner, and mom while living the most fulfilling life ever imagined."

I don't expect that we will ever return to the previous status quo, so I have also challenged myself to coach my direct reports in a similar manner. Working with my leaders to create commitments both personally and professionally has allowed us to achieve some significant results throughout 2020. Each leader has grown in different ways that will certainly impact their future. While preparing my traditional "Year in Review" letter to all my associates, I was struck by how many achievements were accomplished during the most difficult of work conditions.

4. Diversity, Equity, and Inclusion

The pandemic has hit hard for women in particular. Many are thinking about dialing back their careers or exiting altogether, which is very frightening for many companies. What should be done differently to retain women in the workplace?

Like myself, many women at DENSO shared the difficulties of managing school-aged children and keeping up with household management, along with their high-pressure work responsibilities. It was interesting to read the statistics of women considering to leave their jobs in order to manage their home lives. This would be devastating to DENSO's D&I efforts to improve the inclusiveness of our work environment.

As an advisor for all D&I activities at DENSO, I knew we needed to take quick action to engage these women so that they could find solutions other than leaving the industry. The Executive team listened and immediately provided support through learning seminars, professional resources, and networks.

It was during the fall that we shared experiences across an engaged group of female associates (a) what was working and (b) where we were struggling. I shared the example of asking my own daughters what they needed from me. Other women shared how they were working to manage shared home/childcare responsibilities with their partners. The openness of these discussions helped each of us to realize that we were each experiencing similar issues and that we could lean on each other when necessary.

To continue to retain women in our industry, we must continue these efforts and update resources accordingly. We cannot lose sight of the importance of a diversified decision-making team especially as we enter the C.A.S.E. world of future mobility. The insight that women and all diverse perspectives bring to a company will improve its overall competitiveness. I have committed to use my leadership role to be a part of this growing need.

5. Sustainability

Sustainability trends (climate change, water availability, health, etc.) are some of the strongest drivers for future changes for companies and their strategies. What are you seeing within your company? Is your firm reading the trends and adapting strategies to survive and then thrive with new growth?

DENSO's vision is for a safer and eco-friendlier future with fewer accidents. This philosophy is built into all of our strategic planning efforts. We are continually working to adapt to future trends but are fortunate to have a significant baseline of diverse products and services across the vehicle.

COVID has quickly taught us how to challenge ourselves even further. How will shared vehicles survive cleanliness requirements? Will sales demand continue to increase as consumer's needs change? How will we continue to invest in expensive electrification and autonomous technologies after a difficult financial year? How do we continue to close the skill set gap towards software and data? Etcetera etcetera.

These questions along with many others are constantly considered as we work to build our future plans. Thankfully, sustainability of the environment has always been a core strength of our long 70-year history. As we work to challenge ourselves towards 2030, this past year allows us to reconsider previous plans, quickly adjust to our new world and work towards achieving our management philosophy of "Bringing hope for the future for our planet, society, and all people."

Although developed pre-pandemic, it is ironic how fitting this philosophy is in our new world. I look forward to helping to contribute to the strategies established towards our exciting future.

Denise Gray

President
LG Energy Solution Michigan Inc. Tech Center

Background

Denise Gray is President of LG Energy Solution Michigan Inc. Tech Center, the North American subsidiary of LG Chem, Korea. In this position, she leads a team that provides electrification solutions to the transportation industry.

Denise holds several board of director positions, including: LG Energy Solution Michigan Inc.; Tenneco Automotive; the Original Equipment Suppliers Association; and the Board on Energy and Environmental Systems, Washington DC.

Prior to her current role, Denise held positions in Graz, Austria, as well as California, and for General Motors where she enjoyed a 30+ year professional career. Denise spearheaded efforts in vehicle electrical, and powertrain systems controls and software, including battery systems.

Denise Gray

Questions and Answers

1. Change Control, Resilience, and Work/Life Balance

What did you learn when you began to work from home or work in the office with a limited number of co-workers? What did you need to start doing and what did you need to stop?

When I began working remotely, I learned or validated the importance of emergency preparedness, project control, and communications. I was extremely pleased with our team's dedication to the safety of our employees and ingenuity that allowed us to deliver on our commitments to customers with only essential workers on site. I learned that when the "call to action" is required, leaders "stand tall," establishing clear collaborated plans, providing direction, and ensuring transparency. Lastly, an increase in efficient communications and flexibility were required. As the pandemic information and action plans evolved, our team learned that our action plan had to continue to evolve as well, emphasizing the need for more flexibility and agility.

2. Growing Your Professional Network and Maintaining Mentor and Sponsor Relationships

Are you continuing to grow your professional network while being remote? How?

Maintaining and growing my professional network has been challenged in 2020. Industry conferences, research collaborations, technology roadmap discussions, and customer project status reviews are my typical professional networking avenues. I prefer "face-to-face" communications, especially since my network is global. Having the opportunity to communicate at the "home" location of my colleagues (especially in Europe and Asia) is most effective for me. Therefore, new approaches were required. More scheduled calls, emails, text messages, and meetings with "**video on**" were essential. I participated in more virtual conferences, seminars, and webinars to stay engaged. Nevertheless, nothing takes the place of "face-to-face" communications. I am anxiously waiting for that opportunity again.

3. Personal Growth

Have you developed new behaviors (exercise, diet, meditation, hobbies, etc.) that help you get through this new stress?

With professional and personal travel eliminated, there was a lot more "at home" time. I took the opportunity to "travel by foot" or walk more in my neighborhood. My normal work schedule from 7 a.m. to 7 p.m. offered very little "outside walking time." The walks allowed me "quiet" time for introspection and opportunities to appreciate the beauty of nature, resulting in an accounting of my abundant blessings. The walks offered the needed exercise and friendly waves to neighbors (from afar). Additionally, I created family vacation and special events photo albums for me and my family members. These physical photo albums offered joy to all recalling our amazing times together and creating plans for the next vacations. Lastly, reading inspirational books uplifted my spirit and focused my thoughts on helping others.

Denise Gray

4. Diversity, Equity, and Inclusion

The pandemic has hit hard for women in particular. Many are thinking about dialing back their careers or exiting altogether, which is very frightening for many companies. What should be done differently to retain women in the workplace?

Retaining women in the workplace requires opportunities of influence to be provided. As a wife, mother, and professional, I am always making choices that balance my positive impact on others. In addition to being a wife and mother, I chose to be "a professional" because I can make a "positive" impact for my colleagues, the company, and society. I chose to be a professional at my company because I was given equal opportunity. The pandemic has presented new challenges for women due to family health concerns. The pandemic has presented new challenges to companies due to financial stresses. When financial stresses occur and restructuring becomes a lever, there is a tendency for management to revert to their "familiar" people to take on opportunities of influence or remain at the company. Women and underrepresented employees may not be judged fairly. In these situations, the choice for women became straight-forward: continue to take care of their family and seek new companies with equal and fair opportunities.

5. Sustainability

What do you as a leader do to stay informed about sustainability trends that can impact the success of your company and its strategy?

As a leader, staying informed about sustainability trends is paramount to the success of my company and its strategies. Engagement is the key! I have been extremely fortunate to have amazing industry colleagues that invite me to participate in organizations that research and debate sustainability solutions and strategies. Some examples are: (1) National Academies of Science, Engineering, and Medicine: Board on Energy and Environmental Systems; (2) Original Equipment Suppliers Association; and (3) Society of Automotive Engineers North American International Powertrain Conference Planning Committee. These collaborative forums provide the richness of thought, technology solutions, customer data, and science-based information to formulate business strategies and sustainability solutions for the environment and society.

Jill Greene

Vice President and General Counsel,
International Legal Regions
Faurecia

Background

Jill Greene serves as Vice President and General Counsel of International Legal Regions for Faurecia, where she oversees the international legal team of counsel in Europe, North America, South America, and India. Prior to being promoted to this perimeter, Greene had successfully transformed the legal department of the $6 billion North America segment of Faurecia through initiatives focused on insourcing of legal work, law firm competitive bidding, accountability, and business partnership.

Greene joined Faurecia from Transocean, an international deepwater driller, where she headed up the U.S. Securities and Transactions Legal Department and was responsible for, among other things, leading a proxy contest and resolution over two years against dissident shareholder Carl Icahn. During this time, Greene also completed an expedited JOBS Act spin-off IPO while managing the complex SEC disclosures associated with the largest maritime disaster in the U.S. history, the Deepwater Horizon.

Greene has held various in-house positions in telecommunications, energy, and automotive sectors and received her formative training at the law firms of Baker Botts L.L.P. in Houston, Texas and Moye White in Denver, Colorado. Prior to practicing law, Greene spent nine years on the business side as a lead procurement and negotiation specialist at MCI WorldCom and Qwest Communications.

As a former collegiate basketball player, Greene now spends her free time volunteering for various youth sports initiatives. She has also been certified as a Court Appointed Special Advocate and is passionate about giving a voice to children who have been placed in the foster care system. Greene received her undergraduate degree at St. Olaf College and Juris Doctorate at the University of Denver.

Questions and Answers

1. Change Control, Resilience, and Work/Life Balance

How do you and your team continue to innovate and improve?

Innovation is core to Faurecia's competitive advantage and is one of the hardest things to do in a vacuum. While we leverage remote tools as much as possible, it is easy to fall into "multitasking," passivity, or disengagement in distanced collaboration. To replicate the live dynamic that is so critical for innovation, we are targeted and specific in our meetings. This means resisting inviting dozens, in favor of smaller groups with precise and Socratic agendas. PowerPoints are being slowly replaced with virtual whiteboards, and my team is getting used to more frequent 15-30 minute scheduled calls rather than the pre-COVID hour blocks. Disengagement on calls generally yields a text from me asking if they need a sidebar or asking them a targeted, open-ended question on the call. Most importantly, however, is recognizing and fostering an innovative mindset on the team. Now more than ever, it is critical to recognize our teams for bringing new perspectives to the table.

2. Growing Your Professional Network and Maintaining Mentor and Sponsor Relationships

How do you keep your existing relationships in this remote world? Are you maintaining face time with other execs while being remote? How do your direct reports maintain their face time with you?

In July of this year, I transitioned from a U.S.-based job to leading an international team. This has meant not just maintaining relationships but cultivating a new network from afar. I used to take a "coffee walk" each morning to connect with business partners, and clearly, now that is not possible. I have therefore reverted to discipline. Although my function is not one of sales, I have adopted a sales-lead approach to keeping in touch. I have of course established regular meetings with my team members and key internal contacts. Beyond that, I have created a lead list of people I want to connect with each week. I am paying particular attention to new employees and transfers, especially among expatriates who are likely feeling detached and lost in a foreign country locked down. My contacts are not terribly substantive (nobody wants a substantive text from a lawyer) but focus on ensuring they are feeling informed. Where possible, I pass along interesting or relevant articles from our industry. Other times, I just send side notes recognizing their work or just asking if I can connect them with any resource. I've also added virtual coffees to my international team meetings—voluntary time to discuss topics ranging from our country's most goofy holiday tradition to Festivus-style airing of grievances session (sorry, Seinfeld fan). This year we added a Microsoft Teams site dedicated to our favorite family recipes. It has brought our distant team closer with minimal administrative hassle.

3. Personal Growth

What is the most profound impact this pandemic has had the way you think about your job, company, family life? Will it be sticky or do you expect everything to return to the previous status quo?

The most profound impact this pandemic has had on my life is in again learning that we must adapt and embrace change. We have all had some form of disappointment during the pandemic—whether it be a cancelled sports or academic activity, missing family visits, stretching our professional responsibilities, or experiencing financial, social, or personal loss. Through these changes and disappointments, we are also, now more than ever, called upon to trust one another. We must trust that work is being done when we cannot physically be present to see the time spent. We must trust that those who come into the office are making responsible decisions to minimize the spread of COVID. We must trust that the extra hours spent addressing the avalanche of work that came with COVID be recognized and rewarded. These are all sticky and have fundamentally changed the way we interact and face new challenges. I do not expect that we will return to the status quo. On the negative side, I think these changes will further drive separation between the high performers and those who just "get by." Those who thrive with hands-on attention will fall behind unless they find a way to connect proactively. However, positively, we have an entirely new generation of professionals who have adapted to working alone, with minimal guidance and with extreme changes. Those who adapt will make fantastic executives. I am also happy that many are rethinking the stigma around working from home—hopefully, this will yield more opportunities in nontraditional work arrangements, job sharing, and flex schedules.

4. Diversity, Equity, and Inclusion

There has been a lot of talk about diversity—and, in recent years, inclusion. Equity has entered the corporate conversation in a major way this year. What actions are you and your company taking? Are these methods aligned with company goals?

Are men engaged in the conversation around gender diversity and, if so, in what way?

Diversity went from aspiration to action this year. Faurecia redoubled its efforts by implementing unconscious bias training, naming a vice president to lead supplier diversity development and selection initiatives, establishing meaningful discussion platforms and seminars on diversity topics, and, of course, focusing on identifying, hiring, and retaining top talent across diverse groups. Our Diversity and Inclusion Group is actively led by the president of our Faurecia Clarion Electronics segment and includes active participants from all of our business segments, plants, and operating geographies. I could continue a laundry list of actions, but one of the things I am most proud to see is the engagement of our male employees in these various actions. It is not enough to simply have a diverse workforce—our goal is to have an environment where people from all segments of life feel included and valued. An example of this positivity at work is when we had more male executives than female sign up to be speed mentors at our International Women's Day speed mentoring event.

I am optimistic at the sheer numbers who have stepped up to work toward inclusive solutions.

5. Sustainability

Sustainability trends (climate change, water availability, health, etc.) are some of the strongest drivers for future changes for companies and their strategies. What are you seeing within your company? Is your firm reading the trends and adapting strategies to survive and then thrive with new growth?

The automotive industry is quietly undergoing a revolutionary change in the area of sustainability. The traditional automotive manufacturers are anything but traditional these days and are driving toward innovations to meet customer demands for sustainability. We see it in all segments of our business: from basic changes like finding renewable materials for our seating and interior systems to recycling metals to more complex innovations for exhaust and battery systems. Sustainability touches every aspect of our manufacturing process.

We recently announced a global commitment and timeline to become carbon neutral by 2030. Our roadmap to sustainability will be deployed in stages.

- By 2025, we will be carbon neutral for our internal emissions while reducing energy consumption by 15%.
- By 2030, we want to be carbon neutral for our controlled emissions—purchases, freight, travel, waste, and recycling.
- By 2050, we aim to be carbon neutral for our total emissions, including total emissions from the cars we equip.

To reach our goals, we are partnering with scientists and experts. We will use less, use better, and use longer. We embark on this journey with our customers, suppliers, partners, and all Faurecians around the world.

Britta Gross

Managing Director, Mobility
RMI

Background

Britta Gross is the managing director of RMI's mobility practice area, focused on the market-driven strategies and technologies required to accelerate towards carbon-free mobility solutions. Ms. Gross was formerly the director of Advanced Vehicle Commercialization at General Motors, responsible for the energy strategies, partnerships, and policies required to enable the commercialization of battery electric and hydrogen fuel cell electric vehicles (EVs). Britta is also currently a commissioner for the Orlando Utilities Commission, Orlando's electric and water utility.

She has an Electrical Engineering degree from Louisiana State University (LSU) and studied language arts at the University of Wurzburg in Germany. She holds and has held numerous board seats, including the North American Council for Freight Efficiency, MobilityData, Plug In America, the Electric Drive Transportation Association, and the Alliance for Transportation Electrification, and served as a Governor's appointee on both the Massachusetts Zero Emission Vehicle Commission and the Maryland Electric Vehicle and Infrastructure Council. Ms. Gross has received numerous industry awards including *Automotive News*' "Electrifying 100" and the *GreenBiz* "Verge 25" award, has testified in front of the Senate Committee on Energy and Natural Resources, and speaks regularly to national audiences on topics related to alternative fuels in transportation.

Questions and Answers

1. Change Control, Resilience, and Work/Life Balance

What did you learn when you began to work from home or work in the office with a limited number of co-workers? What did you need to start doing and what did you need to stop?

One of the unexpected benefits of being in a leadership position in this year which was like no other is that my focus had to be on keeping my team healthy and productive—which turned out to have therapeutic benefits for me as well. We were all having to deal with different issues: the overwhelming uncertainty about how long the lockdowns would last, how long we'd be working from home, not having the right equipment at home, kids running around the home "office," others living alone, or medically at-risk employees fearful of catching COVID. Almost immediately, we instituted short team check-in calls every other day to provide a space to talk about issues, concerns, share tips, advice, and, in a sense, just replace the watercooler talk that had disappeared overnight. Some were struggling more than others, and I found it was important, especially in the early days of COVID, to be very intentional about asking how each person felt and to be sure each team member knew they had license to take the time they needed to find new ways to cope. As we move into 2021, the team is in good spirits and a new realization has set in—that we (and I) can actually operate successfully as a remote team. Not that we would choose to work from home five days a week, but since our mobility work is so connected to reducing vehicle emissions, it escapes no one that eliminating some of our commutes going forward is one key area of opportunity that we'd like to see incorporated into our own strategy and more broadly into the strategies of corporations nationally.

2. Growing Your Professional Network and Maintaining Mentor and Sponsor Relationships

How do you keep your existing relationships in this remote world? Are you maintaining face time with other execs while being remote? How do your direct reports maintain their face time with you?

There's no question that work without travel, conferences, speeches, and events has turned work into a more monotonous and mundane experience. There's just you and the laptop. No more bumping into old or new colleagues and striking up spontaneous conversations. And since I had just transitioned six months prior to COVID from my corporate career in the auto industry to my new venture at a Non-Governmental Organization (NGO), maintaining my old ties with the automotive industry and forming new bonds with other NGOs was a real concern for me. However, because of our intense efforts at the institute this past year to reset our priorities and actions relative to 2030 climate goals, this has been a particularly good year to focus on planning and lining up partners for our work so that we can all hit the road running in this next year. It's clear that the USA (the largest global emitter of carbon from transportation) just hasn't made enough progress eliminating emissions over the past ten years, and at this point, extraordinary efforts are going to be required over the next ten years at an unprecedented scale—none of which are possible without government, industry, corporate America, and NGOs working in concert. I've been busy sharing this premise in key speeches at this year's numerous virtual conferences and as an excuse (an opportunity) to reconnect with old colleagues and to establish the new partnerships we'll need in order to execute on urgently-needed projects for 2021. And the good news is that because no one has been traveling this year, it's my experience that it's been much easier to reach folks at their desks!

3. Personal Growth

What is the most profound impact this pandemic has had on the way you think about your job, company, family life? Will it be sticky or do you expect everything to return to the previous status quo?

I feel we've been living in a Petri dish for most of 2020—a real-life biologic study to not only witness but participate in an experiment to see how many jobs can be done from home, what the air quality looks like when all cars and trucks are removed from the roads, and what happens when urban centers close streets to cars and instead open the streets to outdoor dining and safe bike lanes. I'm hoping some of the best practices and insights we've learned over the past year will stick with us—and that this year wasn't completely for naught. As a case in point, I'm ready to embrace remote working for both myself and my team and to encourage employers nationwide to adopt some form of reduced commuting policy for those employees who actually can work from home. Without experiencing it and seeing the positive results firsthand, I don't think I would have dared propose such a broad work-from-home strategy that we can implement to meaningfully reduce vehicle emissions in the U.S. by 2030. And I think this year has also shown us how precious our health is and how vulnerable we all are to airborne viruses—and pollutants. The stunning pictures taken around the world comparing the air quality of urban centers pre-COVID and during the COVID lockdowns when the streets were emptied of cars and trucks really drove home the point that we can control this outcome—we have to transition to cleaner mobility solutions and we have to clean up the air around us.

Britta Gross

4. Diversity, Equity, and Inclusion

There has been a lot of talk about diversity—and, in recent years, inclusion. Equity has entered the corporate conversation in a major way this year. What actions are you and your company taking? Are these methods aligned with company goals?

NGOs in the energy and transportation space do indeed have a challenge relative to diversity and inclusion, where both the majority of leaders and the workforce often tend to be white and have similar educational backgrounds and experiences. This lack of diversity can lead to a uniformity in the ideas and actions that are proposed when tackling the increasingly complex issues we face at the intersection of transportation and energy. And access to clean mobility and cleaner air in our cities can no longer be just an afterthought—we need to change our systems to ensure the solutions benefit everyone, especially those who often bear the brunt of unequal access to mobility and disproportionate exposure to tailpipe emissions in our cities. Well over a year ago, RMI decided to attack this problem head on. Among many other steps we've taken, we recognized that we had to be so much more intentional about hiring differently than before, and we are now in the midst of a major hiring effort to attract a large group of more diverse thinkers and those who bring a broader set of experiences and educational backgrounds to the institute. This major hiring step comes at a critical time for the institute, as we are planning for the growth needed to respond to our bolder vision for climate action leading up to 2030. A cornerstone of RMI's Mobility 2030 vision is "The End of the Urban Tailpipe"—a recognition that we have to prioritize the elimination of carbon and other tailpipe emissions from our urban landscapes as the singular area of highest near-term impact in the mobility transformation. Our more diverse workforce will help ensure that we can transform mobility to be both clean and in such a way that all sectors of our society benefit from these changes.

5. Sustainability

Sustainability trends (climate change, water availability, health, etc.) are some of the strongest drivers for future changes for companies and their strategies. What are you seeing within your company? Is your firm reading the trends and adapting strategies to survive and then thrive with new growth?

The urgency of addressing climate change and all of the co-benefits that come with it—improved air quality, health, an explosion in clean technology, and new, high-paying jobs—is now front and center at RMI. Beginning over a year ago, we stepped back to consider our institute's role in addressing climate change and asked ourselves whether we were placing our resources on the efforts that matter most and reflect the urgency of addressing climate change. The result is that every program at the institute, including the Mobility program, is now aligned to a 1.5°C target, and there is a heightened sense of urgency relative to all the things that need to be accomplished by 2030.

What does this all mean for us? It means that 25% of the cars and trucks we drive need to be electric by 2030, and we need to reduce the miles we drive by 20%. I would argue that getting one in four of us into an electric vehicle over the next 10 years is very doable. After all, EVs are inherently better vehicles to drive, they require less maintenance, and are cheaper to fuel with electricity; there are many (many!) more EV models coming to the market in the next two years, and more than half of all Americans live in single-family homes with access to an electrical outlet for convenient vehicle charging at night and have more than two vehicles in the household—making this transition to EVs is not only doable but likely. But although the transition to electric vehicles is almost certainly inevitable for all the reasons given above, the pace of EV adoption today is not yet in line with climate goals and the progress we urgently need to make by 2030.

If you need further evidence that climate change poses real risks, including to the economy, just note how the financial sector, including BlackRock, Goldman Sachs, and others, are beginning to shift away from carbon-intensive investments and towards clean energy solutions. Note also that the transportation industry is facing an existential crisis. China is leading the world in EV production today and aims to become the world's global battery and EV manufacturer. To remain globally competitive, the U.S. has to lead in battery technology and EV manufacturing. Because we work so closely with industry and business, we see firsthand the risk and the opportunity this represents across the mobility sector. We're now seeing billions of dollars being invested in domestic battery production and EV manufacturing—from startups like Tesla to legacy manufacturers like GM. And we're seeing major fleets like FedEx, UPS, Amazon, Lyft, and Uber announcing significant 2030 electrification goals. RMI and the true leaders of the automotive industry, business, and governments are seeing the threat of climate change and are adapting strategies to survive and then thrive over this next "decisive" decade of action.

Joan Hart

VP Program and Engineering Excellence
ZF

Background

Joan Hart is Vice President of Program Management and Engineering Excellence for ZF, a €33B global leader with 150,000 employees worldwide. ZF is a global leader in driveline and chassis technology as well as active and passive safety technology.

Hart has led engineering, program management, and continuous improvement activities for more than 30 years. Since joining ZF in 2005, she has held leadership roles in business excellence, value management, cost engineering, and program management for several divisions and at the corporate level. Hart started her career at Honeywell Aerospace, which included research and development for astronaut life support and fuel cells for transportation. Her work has been featured in conferences including the American Institute of Chemical Engineers, the International Conference on Environmental Systems, and the Partnership for a New Generation of Vehicles.

Joan holds B.S. and M.S. degrees in Chemical Engineering from Michigan Technological University and the University of Virginia and an MBA from Loyola Marymount University. She is an ASQ-Certified Six Sigma Black Belt and a PMI-Certified Project Management Professional. Her volunteer work includes InForum AutomotiveNEXT, "We Build Character," and the Coalition of Minority Engineering Societies. Joan and her husband live in Michigan and have four sons.

Questions and Answers

1. Change Control, Resilience, and Work/Life Balance

How do you and your team continue to innovate and improve?

I lead governance and excellence for program management, engineering, and product development at the corporate level. My scope involves engaging with many functions, all divisions, and all regions. Excellence requires innovation and continuous improvement for products, processes, and tools. The pandemic required us to reinvent the way we work including being flexible and supportive on how and when work gets done. This was enabled by accelerating the use of virtual tools and increasing the digitalization of the tools our product developers use.

During the initial phase of the crisis response, we needed to create a system that was resilient to local changes within each country. To achieve this, we reprioritized work, shifted people to match priorities, and balanced these priorities continually. Of course, there was a learning curve as the pandemic and restrictions on travel moved from China to European countries and eventually to the United States. But over time, we found that subsequent lockdowns were less disruptive than the initial ones, due largely to the fact that we had adjusted to some degree to the new level of flexibility and remote working that would be required for the foreseeable future.

Working from home (WFH) drove the need for my team and for me to adapt, learn, and grow. Previously, we had occasional face-to-face meetings and regular online meetings. Early in 2020, a new suite of virtual tools was in the pilot phase at ZF. The crisis created a significant and urgent pull, which accelerated our use of these tools. Innovation took off as we looked for more ways to use virtual tools to replace in-person meetings. We learned that virtual formats provide useful benefits for engagement that might not otherwise be possible in person. For example, even if you don't currently have the floor, you can share your ideas in chat to make sure they are captured. This democratizes the process by allowing everyone to have a voice. We've also used breakout rooms to have "virtual coffee breaks" during workshops or conferences or "espresso with" virtual conferences to provide opportunities for employees to engage with leaders on transformation topics.

Of course, WFH means more than virtual team calls. Everyone's lives have changed dramatically. Managing a demanding work schedule while ensuring family members have what they need to adjust to disruptions from the pandemic creates challenges more intense than ever before. For many, this means not only finding areas within the home to work and for children to attend remote school, but also being there for family members emotionally and, in some cases, managing very young children without the support of daycare. As leaders, this requires flexibility, rethinking how and when work gets done, and respecting new boundaries needed to manage family life. For example, I have one person on my team with young twins. He'll block his calendar at certain times of the day and then later reach out for synchronization calls after the twins are sleeping. The important thing is he delivers what's needed. I am grateful to and inspired by my team for showing the needed resiliency and flexibility to thrive in the disruptions we've endured.

Overall, we've used the crisis to reinvent the way we work, allowing for more inclusiveness through broader employee engagement and finding flexible ways to get work done. This intensifies our creativity in solving problems and addressing opportunities. We are extending what we've learned to further digitalize our product developer tools.

2. Growing Your Professional Network and Maintaining Mentor and Sponsor Relationships

Has your company maintained learning and leadership development opportunities, culture surveys, 360 surveys, etc., to grow skills and manage the emotional intelligence of the company? Has anything shifted? What have you learned?

Emotional intelligence (EQ) requires the ability to help others and ourselves adapt to disruptions with openness, resiliency, and commitment. The pandemic dramatically changed the way we worked and challenged everyone's EQ in new ways, including adapting to a new virtual environment almost instantaneously. Supportive leadership was needed to encourage teams to quickly become proficient in using new tools and keep them motivated without overwhelming everyone. ZF leveraged virtual learning tools for developing employees and leaders at all levels. This required consistent communications to build awareness of available learning options. After it became clear we'd be working virtually for a prolonged period, ZF initiated weekly email communications on a virtual leadership theme containing playlists with short videos and/or self-paced learning modules, articles, or other learning offerings. In parallel, a blog was initiated to get a more interactive dialogue going. Later, it was possible to register for a virtual team room meeting to exchange in real-time dialogue with leaders called "Espresso with...." Themes ranged from Remote Working: Setting Yourself and Your Teams Up for Success, to Virtual Collaboration and Communication, Leading Change, Resilience, and Managing Difficult Situations.

There are always silver linings in adapting to change. I'd like to point out two. First, the virtual learning and collaboration format works well and will remain even after the pandemic. We are adapting most of our learning content to a virtual format. Once we can return to in-person learning opportunities, a blended learning approach can be used where appropriate. Overall, this model leads to a more applied approach—training followed by immediate application of the learning—often in a team environment. Second, we've challenged and strengthened our EQ capabilities, this is essential to thrive as we face future disruptions. I am grateful for everyone's ability to pivot and reinvent.

3. Personal Growth

Have you developed new behaviors (exercise, diet, meditation, hobbies, etc.) that help you get through this new stress?

With less time spent on business travel, I've been able to focus more on opportunities I've always enjoyed along with some new ones. I am committed to lifelong learning. I like to read or listen to books, listen to podcasts and talk with others about ideas and current events. The pandemic kicked this behavior into a higher gear. I try to keep up on the pandemic and what it means from not only a health perspective but also how it affects the global community overall. The pandemic also changed my mix of responsibilities due to my boss's retirement. I have invested time digging deep into each topic, getting to know the teams, and building strategies. Collectively, these new functional excellence areas relate to preparedness for current and emerging transformation including product lifecycle management, product cybersecurity, functional safety, engineering quality, Automotive Software Process Improvement Capability Assessment (ASPICE), and product carbon footprint.

In addition to keeping up with the world and keeping up with new work topics, it is important to save enough time and energy for my family and myself. Our family has been blessed with more time together. We've had more family dinners, cooking together (trying new and family traditional recipes), game nights, and movie nights. We've had video calls with family members or friends we can't get together with in person.

Now more than ever, it's important to stay as balanced as possible. Growing up in Michigan's beautiful Upper Peninsula, I spent a lot of time outdoors. I had a paper route and every day for four years, I delivered newspapers walking through all kinds of weather, including many rainy and snowy days. I learned there is no such thing as "bad" weather. I still enjoy being outdoors and especially enjoy going on hikes or walks. It is also a great time for talks with my husband or sons. When my husband and I walk, we often share air pods and listen to podcasts together. I also like to listen to books either outdoors or indoors. The latest book I've listened to is *Who Cares Wins* by Lily Cole. It's a fascinating read that illustrates the dire need to address the climate crisis together with an optimistic approach including how we all can act to improve sustainability.

4. Diversity, Equity, and Inclusion

Are men engaged in the conversation around gender diversity, and if so, in what way?

ZF has people of all genders steering our diversity, equity, and inclusion strategies, focused not only on gender diversity but also on all aspects of diversity. One of ZF's key mantras regarding diversity hits this point: "Diversity is a fact, let's live it!" We have active diversity resource groups (grassroots) and councils (sponsored by ZF). Focused topics include Awareness and Communications, Events and Initiatives, Training, Success and Research, and Partnerships and Resources. One popular training topic is "Unconscious Bias." We've created an adaptable approach that lives on throughout the year. Having an adaptable approach means creating multiple on-ramps for conversations about diversity. Our internal communication platform includes communities and blogs focused on Diversity topics such as "Diversity@ZF" and "Women@ZF."

I have been fortunate throughout my career to work in companies where the importance of inclusion is well understood. I seek to pay this forward by being a multiplier to embed a mindset of inclusion. Overall, we are at our best when the focus is on working together to provide value through collaborative interactions based on trust and respect.

My wish for the future is that no inclusion strategy would be necessary. It would be clear that including each person is vital to an organization's success (business, government, academics, etc.). Employees would be hired with the intent to maximize their contributions to the company's success. The environment would be inclusive where everyone has a sense of belonging. Each person would be respected for the gifts and capabilities they bring to the table, with nothing standing in the way of their ability to contribute. All voices would be respected. Addressing unconscious bias is a great place to start. I know my wish already exists in many places and am optimistic that, with focused intent, full realization is not far away. The challenge is to go from inclusion existing on some days for some people to making it the norm—every day for everyone.

5. Sustainability

Sustainability trends (climate change, water availability, health, etc.) are some of the strongest drivers for future changes for companies and their strategies. What are you seeing within your company? Is your firm reading the trends and adapting strategies to survive and then thrive with new growth?

ZF's sustainability strategy recognizes that our corporate responsibility requires a global, collaborative approach. Our definition of sustainability draws from the work of international human and economic development: meeting the needs of the present without compromising the ability of future generations to meet their needs. Sustainability is embedded in ZF's corporate goal statement: "Enable **clean**, safe, comfortable, and affordable mobility for everyone, everywhere." In the product world, this means being on the leading edge of the shift from internal combustion engines to electric mobility in all forms. In addition to products, for CO2 reduction, we are also evaluating employee commuting and business trips, as well as the impact of our supply chain. A science-based target approach is being taken. Our target is to cut our 2018 plant emissions in half by 2030 and to be completely carbon neutral by 2040. ZF has formalized our commitment by joining the United Nations Global Compact in 2012. Additionally, the World Benchmarking Alliance identified ZF Friedrichshafen AG as one of 2,000 companies critical to achieving the United Nations Sustainable Development Goals by 2030.

ZF's fitness and corporate resilience depends on a strong foundation of sustainability. Consistent with the 2019 Business Roundtable's recognition of the need to serve multiple stakeholders, ZF recognizes sustainability is a basic expectation of many stakeholders: our employees; our customers, including stability of the supply chain; our regulatory environment; and ZF's overall environmental, social, and governmental (ESG) performance. Investors and financial stakeholders are prioritizing and auditing ESG ratings, which are relevant to credit ratings and access to financing. Accordingly, ZF has installed a cross-functional Sustainability Steering Committee to govern policy, procedures, target setting, and reporting.

Ecological and economic interests do not have to be mutually exclusive, they can stimulate each other positively. In fact, traditional cost-driven procurement and reporting requirements can have a negative impact due to the lack of a global-level playing field. Market-based instruments enable companies to enter into free competition for the best technologies to achieve climate targets.

I believe urgent and unwavering attention is needed to protect the habitability of our planet. The health of our planet is interconnected with many dimensions of health, whether it is public health or financial health. There is a lot of important work going on to understand what's needed to improve sustainability globally. For example, Lily Cole's book (*Who Cares Wins* mentioned above) gives hope and optimism for sustainable solutions.

Reflecting on the pandemic, we know some of our behaviors will not go back to the way they were before COVID—this includes unsustainable behaviors. We've also seen glimmers of the positive results possible due to mass behavior changes during the pandemic such as cleaner water in Venice and better air quality in many places. We need to sustain these positive changes. We all know what disruption looks like now and what effective responses look like. Driving effective sustainability responses is the key target of the electric mobility, wind power, and other clean technologies ZF is working on. Furthermore, it's worth appreciating the important role mobility has played for sustainability and health, for example, transporting the vaccines. Transportation and mobility aren't just about profits; they have real-world impact that broadly benefits society.

Lottie Holland

Head of Diversity, Inclusion, and Engagement
Stellantis–North America

Background

Lottie Holland was named Head of Diversity, Inclusion, and Engagement, Stellantis–North America in May 2020. She is responsible for driving the company's diversity and inclusion objectives, with a focus on improving its pipeline of diverse talent, and building an inclusive work culture where all employees and perspectives are respected and valued.

Previously, she served as the director of MOPAR Purchasing and Supplier Operations, leading a team sourcing service components and accessories for many Stellantis products. She's held leadership positions in Supplier Diversity, Exterior Vision Purchasing, and Product Development Purchasing.

Holland also served as co-lead of the Fiat Chrysler African Ancestry Network, one of 11 Business Resource Groups representing a range of employee affinity communities.

Holland holds a Bachelor of Science Degree in Packaging Engineering from Michigan State University and a Master of Business Administration from Wayne State University. She holds professional certificates in Project Management, Supply Management, and Supplier Diversity.

In 2016, Holland was selected by *Crain's Detroit Business* as a "Top 40 under 40," in 2017 by *Diversity MBA* as a "Top 100 under 50," and in 2018 as a "Top Champion for Diversity" by *Diversity Plus Magazine.*

She was born in Detroit.

Questions and Answers

1. Change Control, Resilience, and Work/Life Balance

Many have said that there is no separation of work and home these days. What do you do to manage this for your own work? What are you doing to increase the ability of your team to create and respect boundaries?

It was imperative from the start to establish a normal routine that included preparing to go to work. I still follow my traditional morning routine of waking up at 5:00 am to start my day. I also follow my calendar religiously; I block time throughout the day to stay productive and organized. I encourage my team members to block out and protect time on their calendars as well, allowing them to create schedules that work well for them independently. Since we can see each other's calendars, we can schedule meetings around these times. We discuss priorities daily and focus on alignment for that day's deliverables. This ensures that the team operates efficiently. Additionally, we avoid sending team correspondence late in the evening or, if we find it necessary to do so, we let our coworkers know if a matter is something that can be addressed later. Ultimately, as I learned from a former boss, the aim is for more work/life optimization rather than a complete balance; there will be occasions where work will have priority over personal issues, and vice versa—the key is knowing when the flip should occur.

2. Growing Your Professional Network and Maintaining Mentor and Sponsor Relationships

How do you keep your existing relationships in this remote world? Are you maintaining face time with other execs while being remote? How do your direct reports maintain their face time with you?

Virtual conferencing has played a vital role in helping me to remain connected with my counterparts. I use platforms such as Google Meet and Zoom to schedule touchpoints with my colleagues where we're able to exchange pertinent updates and keep each other informed about our own lives outside of work. I establish new relationships and fortify current ones by attending as many virtual networking events and conferences as possible. To maintain continuous contact with my team members, I schedule weekly one-on-one and staff meetings. During these meetings, I encourage the team to use the video feature, and we make time for non-work-related small talk and sometimes even engage in a virtual game to get to know each other better. And while I know it may not be popular, I attend all meetings with my camera on; this simple action allows me to connect with others whose cameras are on and looking to establish this connection. My team members have become accustomed to having this face time with me, which helps keep that relationship remote working can sometimes diminish. Another step I have taken is amplifying my online presence, specifically on LinkedIn, committing to at least thirty minutes daily to maintain visibility and relevancy within my professional network.

3. Personal Growth

What is the most profound impact this pandemic has had the way you think about your job, company, family life? Will it be sticky or do you expect everything to return to the previous status quo?

This pandemic profoundly impacts every area of my life; it has forced a reset that was imperative for my personal growth and will leave an indelible imprint on the way I operate in the future. Pre-pandemic, I was like many people, I consistently had an activity or an appointment of some sort that took up every minute of my day. I lacked appreciation for the simpler things like taking a walk every evening in my subdivision and talking to neighbors I have lived near for ten years but never had the opportunity to engage with personally or hosting virtual gatherings with friends and family so we could socialize and enjoy one another. This pandemic has been devastating, but through it, we've learned that anything is possible. We continue to meet company objectives while educating our children from our dining room tables, we worship in our living rooms, we exercise in our basements, and, oh yes, we even listen to music and dance in our bedrooms—thanks, Club Quarantine! It has definitely been an eye-opening experience. All of what I previously considered necessary, I have now come to discover was not; it was my faith, family, relationships, and community that were most important.

Lottie Holland

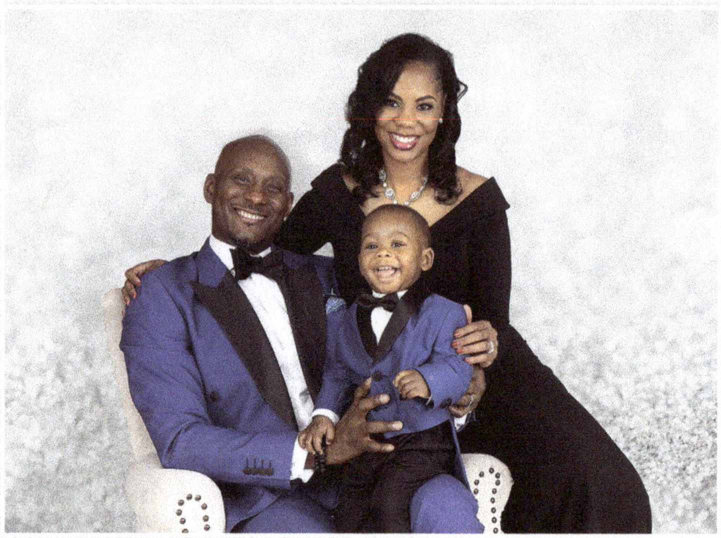

Lottie Holland

4. Diversity, Equity, and Inclusion

There has been a lot of talk about diversity—and, in recent years, inclusion. Equity has entered the corporate conversation in a major way this year. What actions are you and your company taking? Are these methods aligned with company goals?

In what we consider a conscious and continuous effort to affirm diversity, we have historically and will continue to focus our sights on increasing our diverse representation and creating a more inclusive work environment. This year, we launched a platform entitled "Courageous Conversations," which allows our employees to share their lived experiences in a safe and engaging environment. We are confident these conversations will help drive more empathy and understanding of our differences among team members in North America and globally. Topics such as the Black Lives Matter movement, racial inequities, the disproportionate effect of COVID on people of color, privilege, bias, and equity have produced discussions that are insightful, educational, and relevant. Our leadership team has identified employee-specific needs regarding race, gender, sexual orientation, disability, and other socioemotional areas in alignment with our company's goals. Our new four-year Diversity and Inclusion strategy incorporates several equity actions that align with our goal of increasing the representation of minorities and women at leadership levels, including two leadership development programs specifically for black and multicultural team members. We've also created an enterprise-wide mentorship program targeting diverse talent, in addition to conducting quarterly reviews of diverse talent with succession planning requirements.

5. Sustainability

As part of employee development, does your company encourage and support employees volunteering for local nongovernmental organizations? Do you and your company consider this an opportunity for aligning company efforts, employee leadership development, and local progress on sustainability?

Stellantis believes that volunteerism is a civic responsibility; it has a dynamic effect on the community and allows a deeper personal connection and brand presence in the areas where we live and work. We've created a culture of volunteerism through our company-coordinated volunteer program, Motor Citizens, where every Stellantis employee is allocated eighteen hours per year to spend volunteering at the nonprofit organization of their choosing. Our PR and External Affairs teams do a great job of sharing information on numerous community partnerships and engagements, allowing our team members to review and align their targeted volunteerism efforts with Stellantis's objectives, delivering the most significant impact. Through these efforts, we have discovered that company-supported volunteering boosts employee morale, improves our culture, and enhances our brands' perception; it is also a significant contributor to attracting and retaining top talent as employees place a high value on social responsibility. I firmly believe that communities benefit when our employees volunteer, but our employees can also benefit. Volunteering helps them develop their communication, critical thinking, and problem-solving skills, which is an all-around win for everyone and contributes to the company's continued success.

Karen Ideno

Group Vice President
Toyota Financial Services

Background

Karen Ideno is Group Vice President at Toyota Financial Services (TFS), overseeing the company's private-label business. In this role, she is responsible for Mazda Financial Services' sales and marketing activities. Ideno began her career at TFS in marketing, where she grew the department through the development of the TFS brand, the launch of several new products, and the creation of the company's corporate social responsibility function.

Ideno subsequently oversaw the company's corporate communications and government affairs functions. In 2013, she was promoted to Vice President of Product, Marketing and Brand, Remarketing, and Business Analytics.

Ideno is a national trustee of Boys and Girls Clubs of America, the executive sponsor of the North American Advisory Council for Women Influencing and Impacting Toyota, and served as executive sponsor of Toyota Asian American Society in Alliance. She was recognized as one of the 100 Leading Women by *Automotive News* and honored by the Greater Dallas Asian American Chamber of Commerce for her leadership in advancing diversity and inclusion in the workforce.

Ideno earned her MBA in Finance and Marketing from Pepperdine University, and her BA in Political Science from the University of California, Los Angeles.

Questions and Answers

1. Change Control, Resilience, and Work/Life Balance

How do you and your team continue to innovate and improve?

In 2019, we aggressively scheduled Mazda Financial Services to debut on April 1, 2020, wholly unaware at that time that the COVID pandemic would present a massive, unanticipated challenge to our plans. When the reality of the pandemic became clear to us in early 2020, we knew we had to quickly innovate to create new ways of working in order to launch this entirely new business on time.

Our ability to execute never would have been possible without the team's resilience and their willingness to rise to the occasion during a crisis. Our entire enterprise came together to support new ways of working. We quickly improved our ability to work from home, and we found ways to increase communications even when we were remote. I encouraged our team to adopt innovative solutions even if they required extra initial effort to put in place.

Thanks to these efforts, we were able to achieve unprecedented operational efficiencies. We introduced a series of virtual meetings with dealers, which were critically important to us as a new organization working with dealers who were unfamiliar with us. We created an entirely new process for social-distanced wholesale transitions. Our continuous improvement, or "kaizen," of processes to obtain necessary documents from our dealer partners were so revolutionary that the team won a Toyota company-wide internal award recognizing their best practices. This was the first time that the captive finance company had ever achieved this level of recognition for process improvement from our parent organization.

I'm extremely proud of all the efforts the team put forth which allowed us to launch Mazda Financial Services right on schedule, despite the challenges presented by the pandemic.

2. Growing Your Professional Network and Maintaining Mentor and Sponsor Relationships

Have your mentees been asking different questions than under usual working conditions? Have you needed to do more hand-holding? Do you see more mentees seeking career change or seeking educational opportunities? Something else?

During the COVID pandemic, since I haven't been traveling, I've committed even more time to being available to serving as a mentor and sponsor. Mentoring matters because it helps grow individual capabilities and exposes team members to new ideas and perspectives. And that's true for both the mentor and mentee. When executed properly, both mentor and mentee learn and grow as a result of the interactions.

Currently, I'm seeing mentees seeking more career advice than before the pandemic. I believe remote work is a major contributor to this. I'm noticing that several female leaders who approach me for mentoring are struggling with the lack of in-person connections that happen at the office. On top of that, many are also now supporting their children who are engaged in virtual studies. Both of these add complexity and challenges to normal working conditions.

And it's imperative that we support these women to help them achieve their career goals. Women are already underrepresented in the automotive industry, and we need to ensure we don't lose those who have already chosen the field for their career path.

So, during this unusual situation, it's important that we take time to reflect on the challenges that have been exacerbated by the pandemic, especially in creating a lack of exposure and the potential to limit new experiences. As a mentor and sponsor, I want to ensure that we're facilitating opportunities for those who need and deserve them. I want to support my mentees and even inspire them to take risks and explore new career paths at Toyota. And I believe this can only be done by being deliberate and intentional in choosing to support the next generation of women leaders. And that requires all leaders, both men and women, to be sure to engage and influence their entire teams, keeping sure that no high performers are being left behind.

3. Personal Growth

What is the most profound impact this pandemic has had the way you think about your job, company, family life? Will it be sticky or do you expect everything to return to the previous status quo?

Toyota's call to action has been "Start Your Impossible," which encourages us to consider that anything may be possible given sufficient determination. That philosophy guided me during the challenging and exciting launch of our new business to support private label financing. This entrepreneurial effort required me to overcome preconceived notions about how we should do things because the pandemic forced me to address problems in new ways. And I also realized how important Toyota's core tenet "Respect for People" is to the company and to me as a leader. While the pandemic has been truly awful, it's also sparked so much compassion across our organization and demonstrated our resiliency, and that, in turn, has been a bonding experience.

In 2020 our work and personal lives collided as our office closed and we had to carve out new home offices. Although I greatly miss the day-to-day personal interactions at the office, we've discovered different ways of working, and those have turned out better than expected. Looking ahead, I think we'll see more flexibility and recognize that people and organizations can benefit when they're able to work in the environments most suited to their needs.

Finally, the pandemic has reinforced the importance of family as a critical support network for each of us. I now try to take advantage of this opportunity to spend more time with my family and share even small moments together. That doesn't mean I don't have new worries too. As a mother, I'm concerned about my son who is attending college as a freshman in another state, and the dangers of living on campus during COVID. I feel for all the parents out there who are struggling with letting their children live their best lives while also trying to keep them safe.

In the end, I'm certain we'll never return to how things were in every respect. And that's probably a good thing. We'll continue to challenge the status quo, and I'll encourage team members to help us discover innovative approaches and new ways of thinking.

4. Diversity, Equity, and Inclusion

The pandemic has hit hard for women in particular. Many are thinking about dialing back their careers or exiting altogether, which is very frightening for many companies. What should be done differently to retain women in the workplace?

At the heart of Toyota, we are inspired and challenged to approach everything we do with a diversity and inclusion mindset—to acknowledge, respect, and value our diverse contributions. We realize that, in order to be competitive, we require diversity of thought and representation. Therefore, it's imperative that we ensure successful leadership development and sponsorship programs that promote the advancement of women. We've made great strides in encouraging more women to pursue careers in the automotive industry. We must continue to build on this progress and not pull back during this critical moment in time when women are considering exiting the workforce. That means, even as we are mindful of our fiscal responsibilities during these uncertain times, we need to continue to invest in the programs that help women succeed in their careers.

That means continued investment in training, promoting mentorship programs, and ensuring women have the exposure to fellow leaders. For example, despite the costs associated with the program, Toyota will continue to deliver the Toyota North American Women's Conference in 2021. It's the company's premier female talent development and networking opportunity.

Additionally, companies like Toyota benefit from employee resource groups. At Toyota, we call these Business Partnering Groups in recognition of the benefits they provide both our team members and the business overall. They are critically important to cultivating an inclusive workforce, offering a voice and perspective for all team members, and providing support and advocacy for women within Toyota. I serve as Executive Sponsor for the Toyota North American Advisory Council of Women Influencing and Impacting Toyota (WIIT), which connects team members to one another and provides a valuable network for feedback, development, and general support.

5. Sustainability

As part of employee development, does your company encourage and support employees volunteering for local nongovernmental organizations? Do you and your company consider this an opportunity for aligning company efforts, employee leadership development, and local progress on sustainability?

As a mobility company, Toyota is innovating, continuously improving, and thinking boldly to build a better, smarter, and more sustainable future. That future is built by our team members who are involved in countless worthy causes at both local and national levels. I'm proud to have led the creation of the community relations function at Toyota Financial Services. And, since that time, we have demonstrated our commitment to create positive social impact by encouraging and supporting our team member volunteerism.

Through expanded partnerships with allies in the community, such as the Boys and Girls Clubs of America, Girl Scouts of the USA, and Junior Achievement, we are supporting the next generation of leaders. We promote youth development programs focused on financial literacy education, workforce readiness skills development, and STEAM experiences. To demonstrate how important this is to our organization, Toyota leaders are encouraged to get involved at the Board level, supporting nonprofits in areas of interest to them. I'm proud to serve as a National Trustee Board Member of the Boys and Girls Clubs of America

Not only do the nonprofits benefit from these relationships, but Toyota benefits as well. Team members who volunteer build new skills that enhance their ability to manage projects, speak in public, and lead others. Our capability to develop our team members while doing good for the community has been a key reason that Toyota Financial Services has been recognized by Points of Light Foundation as a member of the Civic 50, which recognizes the most community-minded companies in the nation.

Jennifer Johnson

President and Chief Executive Officer
Kendrick Plastics

Background

Jennifer's passion and energy leads Kendrick as a premier full-service interior supplier. She has over 20 years of industry experience starting in design engineering and product launch through finance, strategy, and general management. Prior to joining Kendrick, Jennifer spent her career with companies like Johnson Controls, Intertec Systems, and Yanfeng Automotive Interiors. Jennifer has a Bachelor of Science degree in Mechanical Engineering from Kettering University and a Master of Business Administration from the University of Michigan.

Questions and Answers

1. Change Control, Resilience, and Work/Life Balance

What did you learn when you began to work from home or work in the office with a limited number of co-workers? What did you need to start doing and what did you need to stop? How do you and your team continue to innovate and improve?

Kendrick Plastics, a tier-one and tier-two interior trim supplier, was formed in late December 2019 through the carve-out of a manufacturing operations site of Yanfeng Automotive Interiors. Heading into 2020, I was charged to lead the start of Kendrick Plastics, transitioning the business from a manufacturing site of a multinational corporation to a stand-alone full-service engineering and manufacturing company. Regardless of a looming pandemic, my 2020 agenda was already full of high expectations. My top priorities were to continue to manufacture high-quality products for our customers while separating the business operations from the previous owner and building out the company's management team.

When the pandemic hit, Kendrick was only a ten-week-old company. We were faced with a production shutdown and a public health crisis impacting our employees, our customers, and our suppliers. Like most leaders, my level of responsibility grew exponentially overnight. Above everything else, risk management became the focus, juggling financial risks, deploying new employee health and safety measures, and monitoring supply chain continuity. For the remainder of 2020, I would remain committed to building Kendrick while managing the ever-changing environment and risks brought about by the COVID pandemic.

Central to our success during the pandemic was a newly organized leadership team, a transition to technology-based collaboration tools, and increased company-wide communications. Without a doubt, Kendrick thrived during 2020 due to the extraordinary efforts of employees. The leadership team remained agile and put employee's health and safety first as the pandemic unfolded, and our successes can be attributed to this mindset.

When COVID spread rapidly in the Midwest USA, the team transitioned to a technology-based collaboration tool to keep communications and productivity moving.

In stages of fully remote work, the management team met briefly each morning over video as a team check-in. Use of electronic topic-specific channels, group chats, and video meetings replaced the in-office conversations, face-to-face meetings, and "watercooler" exchanges. We kept topics light as often as possible, celebrating employee's newborn babies and welcoming the continuous stream of new hires that onboarded remotely.

We increased communications by supplementing physical communication postings with text messages and electronic postings sent as often as required and at a minimum on a weekly basis. We scrapped in-person business briefings and replaced them with group video town hall meetings, utilizing large digital screens and small groups of the operations teams working on site. We hosted an outdoor Employee Recognition BBQ in the summer months and, in turn, canceled the traditional indoor holiday luncheon in December.

At the end of the 2020, I am proud that Kendrick was fortunate enough to both survive and thrive during the first year of the COVID pandemic. Without a doubt, it was the dedication and hard work of the management team and employees that delivered the results; from designing and implementing Kendrick CARES (pandemic company playbook) to implementing a new Enterprise Resource Planning (ERP) system and launching our first website, and more. Knowing this, I have full confidence that the Kendrick team will successfully tackle challenges that we might face in the future.

2. Growing Your Professional Network and Maintaining Mentor and Sponsor Relationships

How do you keep your existing relationships in this remote world? Are you maintaining face time with other execs while being remote? How do your direct reports maintain their face time with you?

The obvious shift in professional networking during the pandemic is the inability to meet and connect face to face. I do miss opportunities to meet industry contemporaries, customers, and mentees in person and remain hopeful that days of socializing in person will return in the future. In the meantime, I am an advocate of using video capabilities in all internal meetings and events as well as external meetings and events. From my personal experience, speaking with people over video is the next best alternative to in-person connection. Through the pandemic, I have connected via video with Board members, customers, suppliers, employees, and industry peers, as well as friends and family, on a regular basis. Video connection is the best approach to maintaining relationships as we continue to prioritize our health through social distancing.

To reach and connect with my broader network, I lean on professional social media outlets and keep my news and network curated to my professional needs. Social media has proven to me to be an effective method to share and stay abreast of advances and opportunities automotive industry and industry segments as well as specific organizations.

As far as face time with employees, I maintain an open-door policy that applies to the current pandemic season as well. Most of my connections with employees are either still face to face with a safe distance or through video-on discussions. We utilize our technology platform freely and video call each other whenever needed as an alternative to walking into each other's office. We speak and see each other with a nonscheduled approach as we would if we were working in the same physical vicinity. While we do adhere to meetings as needed, those scheduled times to connect are best for larger agenda items that we might be working through collaboratively.

In addition, I am deliberate about being readily accessible and responsive to my team and customers, regardless of the communication mode. Pandemic or not, my direct reports and I maintain our relationships simply by consistent connection via text, phone calls, and video calls alike throughout each day.

3. Personal Growth

What is the most profound impact this pandemic has had the way you think about your job, company, family life? Will it be sticky or do you expect everything to return to the previous status quo?

The pandemic has emphasized the importance of clear communication and consistent decision-making as critical during times of uncertainty. At Kendrick, our priority during the pandemic was the health and safety of our employees. Our decision-making consistently demonstrated this priority. Our employees were well informed on what they could expect while in the workplace. We increased communications significantly, using video and text, sometimes sending informative COVID-related communications multiple times per week. As the pandemic evolved, we maintained a weekly communication to best inform employees on how their decisions impacted their safety. Our goal was to provide safety and security to our employees during a time of uncertainty.

Frequent communication and consistent decision-making also provided stability and security in my family. Married with three daughters, my family's flow of school, work, socializing, and activities was abruptly paused by the pandemic with no clear plan of returning to normal. In response, my husband reinstated a flow for us that would keep each family member growing and moving forward despite the pandemic.

We met weekly as a family to plan how each person would spend the following week to stay active socially, physically, intellectually, and spiritually. Week in and week out, we checked in with each other and maintained an undivided focus on meeting each other's needs in all four categories. Our goal was to maintain a healthy, balanced life and open lines of communication to minimize focus on the loss and uncertainty of the pandemic.

4. Diversity, Equity, and Inclusion

The pandemic has hit hard for women in particular. Many are thinking about dialing back their careers or exiting altogether, which is very frightening for many companies. What should be done differently to retain women in the workplace?

As the pandemic set in, many working people were loaded with the additional stressors to care for and educating children from home and/or putting greater effort into caring for their aging parents or family members. Anyone who is both employed and maintaining a domestic caregiver role is more than likely overloaded during the pandemic. While this applies to both men and women, often women maintain primary caregiver roles in their family.

There are strategies to retain talented women and men who also bear the primary caregiver role. A top priority would be to normalize the pandemic-induced accommodations of personal and professional life integration for the long run. It is well known that companies that prioritize results and flexibility over in-office face time retain superior talent. Companies can also seek pay parity, allowing employees to be compensated fairly for similar positions. According to research, a gender wage gap continues to put women at a disadvantage compared to men. Pay parity may offer enough economic upside for women to remain in the workforce. Last, standard healthcare and professional services hours are not accommodating to people who work during daytime hours and maintain caregiver duties. I believe a fundamental shift that offers more flexible hours in healthcare services and professional services would in turn provide more access to workplace talent who also maintain domestic caregiver duties.

5. Sustainability

What do you as a leader do to stay informed about sustainability trends that can impact the success of your company and its strategy?

I measure sustainability through the impact our business has on the health and safety of our team members and their families as well as the contributions to the communities in which we operate. I keep informed of sustainability trends by staying current on state and federal regulations and protocols, utilizing industry-specific resources, and gathering insights from the local business community. As a fundamental effort, we actively work to maintain our environmental and health and safety certifications. Much of our environmental efforts come from our quest to meet and exceed these required certifications.

Considering the COVID pandemic of 2020, the health and safety category rapidly responded by driving the formation of an internal pandemic response team. We work continuously to maintain our knowledge of the ever-changing COVID environment. We meet regularly and maintain an active conversation, sharing news, insights, and changes in protocol to ensure our organization is staying current and is a leader in health and safety. We look to our peers and industry resources to inform ourselves on trends and efforts that apply to our organization. At the outset of the COVID pandemic, we leaned heavily on the Lear Corporation Safe Work Playbook as a guidepost to best protect our employees and their families once we returned to work. Operating in West Michigan, we enjoy a rich business community that actively collaborates for greater health and safety outcomes for all of our employees and local communities.

Karen King

Global Director of IT Engineering Applications Management
Yazaki North America, Inc.

Background

Karen King is Global Director of Information Technology (IT) at Yazaki North America, Inc. In this role, she is responsible for global engineering systems that enable the design and manufacturing of products for today's feature-rich vehicles. Karen's 22 years at Yazaki North America, Inc., a global leader in vehicle power, data, and display solutions, have provided her with a well-rounded view of the automotive industry.

Karen joined Yazaki in 1999 as IT Manager, where she gained a solid understanding of the enterprise systems and end-to-end data flow from OEMs to manufacturing. This experience provided a well-rounded view of all business functions and has opened many doors for her successful career.

In 2004, Karen advanced to Senior Manager of Commodity Purchasing. In this role, she set strategies and negotiated agreements for components and raw materials. Her success in leadership within purchasing positioned her to take on the next challenge at an enterprise level. For the succeeding five years, she worked on a special assignment to deploy a major Enterprise Resource Planning system throughout North America, transforming many of the company's key business processes. As Yazaki evolved toward integrated process management, a more transparent and effective governance was necessary. Karen worked to establish a Center of Excellence organization to set corporate-level objectives, project priorities, and best practices, which is still in place today.

In 2012, Karen had an opportunity to move into Engineering. As Senior Manager of Engineering Services, she formed a Data Management Organization to centralize part registration and technical document management. This led to expanded responsibilities over other service areas, including 3D printing/additive manufacturing, engineering training, and engineering software support.

Since 2015 to now, Karen's focus has been on leading the development and deployment of Yazaki's next-generation engineering systems that are providing a data-centric integration to every aspect of the wire harness design process. She rejoined IT in 2018 as Director of Engineering Applications, where she leads a high-performance team located across the world, delivering advanced technologies and customized solutions.

Prior to joining Yazaki, Karen was the Director of Alumni at Madonna University, where she earned a Bachelor of Science degree in Marketing and a Master of Science degree in Business Administration Leadership Studies. She has been actively participating in Inforum events for the past 15 years and has served on the AutomotiveNEXT Executive Committee for 3 years. She also inspires young women to strive for careers in technology fields through her affiliation with the Michigan Council of Women in Technology Foundation.

Questions and Answers

1. Change Control, Resilience, and Work/Life Balance

What did you learn when you began to work from home or work in the office with a limited number of co-workers? What did you need to start doing and what did you need to stop?

It was late February 2020 and I was on a business trip in Europe to meet face to face with my new Portuguese and German team members. We were consolidating IT operations between North America and Europe, and I acquired a new team of direct reports across the pond. I remember vividly sitting in the hotel lobby in Porto, Portugal watching CNN and seeing the COVID pandemic unfold throughout the world. When I moved on to Cologne, Germany, I was greeted by thousands of people in costume dancing, singing, and partying on the streets celebrating the "crazy days" of Carnival, a week-long street festival that takes place annually during Lent. I thought to myself, they certainly don't' seem to be worried about the virus here, but I was. I retreated to my hotel room each night after work and proceeded cautiously that week until I could make it back home to Detroit. Meanwhile, in the background, my company was putting together a COVID task force developing policies and protocols to protect its employees. I was required to quarantine after returning from Europe. Little did I know this would mean working from home indefinitely.

I admit I wasn't ready for such an abrupt change to my work life. I struggled with productivity at first. I realized the room in my home that I called an office wasn't nearly as functional as I needed it to be. After some minor modifications, such as a new chair and a larger monitor, I was able to buckle down and effectively do my job. In the weeks that followed, governments implemented stay-at-home orders. I passed the time by working longer and longer hours. My morning began with a 7:00 am video conference call with my boss, the Head of IT, and my peer management team. This meant getting up early to prepare myself as though I was going into the office, complete with hair, makeup, and work-appropriate attire. I navigated from one virtual meeting to the next, day after day striving to keep open and frequent communication with my direct reports and project teams. Often my workday started and ended with it being dark outside. I had severe eye strain from sharing at a monitor 12+ hours a day.

By springtime when the weather was getting nicer, I realized this lifestyle was not healthy or stainable. My husband and I had many discussions about how we would need to learn to live with the virus instead of shutting ourselves away from it. We spent our time gardening and improving our landscape. We sat outside in the evenings at our firepit and learned to really enjoy our home and our yard.

My colleagues and I agreed to set boundaries for work time and personal time. I strived to close the lid of my laptop in the early evening to enable me to focus on connecting with my extended family and friends and often hosted virtual cocktail hours. The past ten months have been challenging both professionally and personally. One of the most important things I learned was to take time to pause and assess the things within my span of control. While I couldn't control the spread of COVID, I could learn to live amongst it and could effectively make adjustments along with way to control the balance of my professional and personal life.

2. Growing Your Professional Network and Maintaining Mentor and Sponsor Relationships

How do you keep your existing relationships in this remote world? Are you maintaining face time with other execs while being remote? How do your direct reports maintain their face time with you?

We are in a strange time where many of us are working from home for the first time after decades, accustomed to the cultural norm of in-person office interactions. From work meetings to social hours with friends, relationship building now occurs by phone, video, and online chat. I admit, I thrive on in-person interaction and have always felt more connected with the people I see in the office on a daily basis, even though I have always had some remote direct reports. But with the pandemic, moving all of my human interactions at work to a virtual setting has forced me to reevaluate my strategy for building work relationships.

I had to quickly embrace video conferencing. Not only becoming proficient in using the technology (knowing when to mute/unmute the call and how to share my screen) but letting people see where I work within my home. I have artwork on the walls behind me that people notice and ask about. I had to adjust the height of my laptop and ensure ample lighting in the room so that people can see me clearly and see the facial expressions, which bring authenticity to the meeting. Expression and nonverbal communication are more important than the words you are saying.

Next, I purposefully scheduled daily check-in meetings (quick, less than 10 minutes) to say hi and to see how the team members were coping. With the lockdown orders in place, I realized some team members were feeling lonely and isolated while others were facing utter chaos with a house full of family members. Since we couldn't gather around the coffee machine or go out for lunch, I found it important to engage in small talk during our video check-in meetings to stay connected. This often included seeing kids pop into the meeting or an appearance by the family dog—a great diversion to the crazy workday. Taking the time to check in and engage in some back and forth banter allowed for the other person to open up and talk through challenges they were having.

The rhythm of my weekly team meetings also changed a bit when we went completely virtual. I require all participants to have their cameras turned on during the meetings. When people are on camera, they aren't on their phones or sending emails. They stay engaged. I set an agenda and share it with the attendees before or at the beginning of the meeting. It's easy for meetings to get off course, especially in this stressful time. I find the quicker I can start the meeting the less likely it is for people's minds to wander or for the participants to get off-topic. It also shows respect for people's time. This weekly meeting is a way to store up issues and minimize the back and forth email that takes place during the week and handle it all in one meeting.

When working virtually, I find it takes extra effort to keep co-workers and direct reports feeling committed to their team. They need feedback on their work; they need to know they are contributing to a common goal and that they are valued. The pandemic has forced the industry and most companies to go through significant changes. It is critical to keep your team informed about how the company is doing. People need to know what's happening in other parts of the company and how they themselves fit in and are contributing to the bigger picture. Get everyone involved in important events and projects.

It's surreal to comprehend that in a matter of weeks, most people in the U.S. and across the world have been cut off from in-person human interaction. Just because physical interaction is limited doesn't mean we can't build strong social relationships virtually. We are social creatures and must stay dedicated to maintaining relationships. For some, this current virtual lifestyle is temporary, and, in time, we will resume normal social norms. For others, the virtual workplace will become the norm. In both cases, I believe we will come out a lot stronger.

3. Personal Growth

What is the most profound impact this pandemic has had the way you think about your job, company, family life? Will it be sticky or do you expect everything to return to the previous status quo?

When I reflect back on the impact of the pandemic, it is more than a health crisis, it's an economic one as well. The spread of coronavirus across the globe forced manufacturing to shut down, disrupted the supply chains, and quarantined workforces. We saw the automotive sector being financially crippled not just by lack of production but by lack of consumers buying new cars. With large sections of the country under stay-at-home orders and people feeling concerned about their jobs, it's not surprising to see the auto sales number drop.

At Yazaki, our President and CEO, Bo Andersson, indicated, "extraordinary moments require extraordinary responses." In March and April, we went from some of our best days to our worst days in corporate history due to financial losses resulting from the pandemic. We worked tirelessly on reducing costs and improving cash flow. Never in my 20+ years working at this company did I have to make as many difficult decisions in such a short time period, including cutting salaries of management, furloughing nonessential workers, and renegotiating contracts with our suppliers. Daily we were identifying and executing necessary corrective actions that would have once taken months to complete. Today, the company is emerging with positive free cash flow, is avoiding line stoppages, continues to elevate quality, and is stabilizing profit globally.

For me personally, the rate of change happening around me was often overwhelming. It felt like the world was on fire. I was faced with making critical business decisions that needed answers within hours but felt like it deserved more time. Directives from the C-suite needed to be cascaded throughout the organization in a way that ensured transparency, urgency, and clear understanding. To say the situation was stressful is an understatement. I was balancing the health and safety of my family, the uncertainly if I would have a job, and the intensity and pace of work within my team to keep the company moving forward.

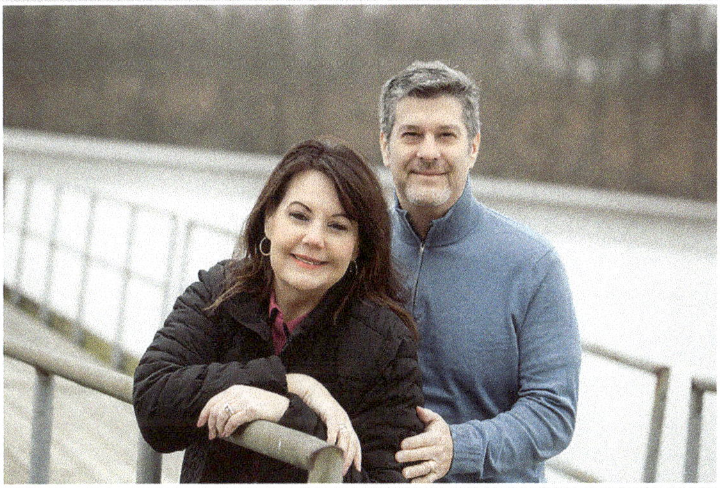

Karen King

It has been tough, yet I learned to handle the stress well and remain optimistic. How did I do it? Wine. Lots of wine. I am joking, of course. Humor, in fact, is a natural stress management tool. But in addition to laughter, I try hard to focus on the things that are in my control, such as simple handwashing and mask-wearing to keep me and my family healthy. To avoid the feeling of isolation, I maintained personal and professional connections virtually through video conferencing technology. I talked to my family, friends, and co-workers every day to talk about concerns and stay optimistic for the future.

Another factor in managing stress was my decision to actively change negative thoughts. What we think influences how we feel. When things were difficult, I would take a moment to seek positive and new stimuli such as listening to music, playing with my cats, doing some meditative breathing, or going for a walk in my garden. Ultimately, I believe the right mindset during this pandemic, or any other stressful situation, comes down to positive thinking, optimism, and resilience to pull one through tough times.

4. Diversity, Equity, and Inclusion

There has been a lot of talk about diversity—and, in recent years, inclusion. Equity has entered the corporate conversation in a major way this year. What actions are you and your company taking? Are these methods aligned with company goals?

As common goals of diversity, equity, and inclusion become even more widespread, many companies have the daunting task of figuring out what works. As business leaders, we know we need a workforce diverse in age, gender, skill set, and culture for our businesses to thrive. But this can often be challenging when a company, like mine, does not have an official program in place to recruit, develop, or retain a diverse or inclusive workforce. At Yazaki, our C-suite is focused on hiring the best person for the job, not on finding a person who fits some preconceived notions of who should have the job. Emphasis is put on upfront analysis of the position. HR professionals coach hiring managers to evaluate what is missing from their organization and what is needed. By evaluating job descriptions, managers identify which skill sets are most necessary and hire for those with an open mind.

So how do we, as women, thrive in companies, like Yazaki, that don't have DE&I targets aligned with company goals? I believe the answer is to focus on professional development to build the necessary skills, experience, and professional network to be the best person for the job. I have always taken the stand that one's development plan needs to be owned by oneself. Most companies, including Yazaki, have endless opportunities for developing new skills. I encourage my direct reports and mentees to accept new and challenging work assignments, to volunteer to be on special projects, to build their network outside of their department, and to take advantage of the corporate training opportunities. Often, we need to have the courage to move out of our comfort zone in order to grow.

While Yazaki may appear short-sighted in its diversity hiring policies and corporate strategies, its executives continue to be committed to building a pipeline of talented and diverse candidates through their long history of participation in professional organizations like Inforum, AutomotiveNEXT, Michigan Council for Women in Technology, Society of Women Engineers, and IEEE Women in Engineering. While the overall number of women in top business roles is still painfully low in the automotive industry, change is happening. Recently, six women were hired into executive-level positions at Yazaki because, as our President and CEO indicated, they were the best people for the job.

5. Sustainability

Sustainability trends (climate change, water availability, health, etc.) are some of the strongest drivers for future changes for companies and their strategies. What are you seeing within your company? Is your firm reading the trends and adapting strategies to survive and then thrive with new growth?

With growing concerns of climate change and environmental degradation, sustainability has become a strategic priority for most automotive organizations. Yazaki is no different. As a global leader in vehicle power and data solutions for automotive applications, Yazaki is broadly on par or ahead of regulations in sustainability due to a centralized governance body to oversee objectives across global operations. Having this central approach allows Yazaki to weave sustainability strategies across functions and processes, including R&D, design, operations, supply chain, sales, and IT.

In my area, information technology (IT) is a key enabler toward meeting business targets by connecting innovation and sustainability. Sustainability strategies need to be supported by an infrastructure of advanced technologies that can measure and monitor progress through well-defined KPIs. At Yazaki, IT is providing solutions for data analytics to transform information into insights. My team implements complex systems to support product design and manufacturing through simulation, automated processes, AI-based decision-making assistance, and communication technology to collaborate globally. IT organizations are driving transformative change in how business is approaching sustainability.

Another sustainability trend in information technology is migration toward a greener cloud. Yazaki, like many companies, has been moving to cloud computing in efforts to reduce on-premise energy consumption in data centers around the world. We have found that moving large services to a hosted cloud provider, such as Microsoft, has changed our carbon footprint dramatically. IT plays an important role in driving the achievement of sustainability strategies by selecting carbon-thoughtful cloud providers, taking advantage of shared infrastructure, and retiring legacy systems and data centers. The right combination of technology, data, innovation, and progressive leaders in companies are the underpinnings of this new wave of sustainability.

Heather Klish

President of Dura Automotive

Background

Heather is an authentic leader who has helped turn around underperforming businesses and meaningfully change cultures. She started her career as a co-op student at General Motors. Later at American Axle and Manufacturing Inc., she found her passion for manufacturing and lean implementation. She has since held various vice presidential roles (VP) at several automotive and off-highway companies including Borg Warner, AxleTech and Acument Global Technologies. She is now President of Dura Automotive.

Heather graduated from Kettering University as valedictorian with a BSME and earned a patent for her design work as a GM co-op student. She also holds an MS in Mechanical Engineering and an MBA from the Massachusetts Institute of Technology, which she completed as a Leaders for Global Operations fellow. She is a 2020 recipient of the *Automotive News* Top 100 Leading Women Award and was recognized by the National Association of Manufacturers as a Top 100 Woman in Manufacturing. She and her husband, Braden, have three young children.

Questions and Answers

1. Change Control, Resilience, and Work/Life Balance

What did you learn when you began to work from home or work in the office with a limited number of co-workers? What did you need to start doing and what did you need to stop?

I learned that telecommuting has its pros and cons, but overall it has brought new balance and flexibility to my life, particularly as a working mom. One of the cons is that I am working more hours, starting the day much earlier and often working more in the evenings and on weekends. It's very easy to sit down at the computer when your home office is always waiting for you where you left off. But on the flip side, I greatly appreciate the extra time I have gained by eliminating a commute and that I can take a quick walk around the block or throw in a load of laundry between meetings. I started using video call capability almost exclusively and found that I am now virtually face to face with my international colleagues more than I ever could be while traveling. I also found that most perceptions about employees being distracted or unproductive were proven to be false.

2. Growing Your Professional Network and Maintaining Mentor and Sponsor Relationships

How do you keep your existing relationships in this remote world? Are you maintaining face time with other execs while being remote? How do your direct reports maintain their face time with you?

Virtual interaction can never fully replace physical face-to-face interaction, but it can be a great substitute and in some ways superior. As people are grounded, there is no longer the challenge of scheduling around various traveling executives. Schedules are more consistent and predictable. The accepted form of communication is phone or video conferencing by scheduling time on each other's calendar. In some ways that makes people MORE accessible than they were before, especially with international colleagues who you might only see a few times a year. Now I "see" them virtually every week or numerous times a week. My direct reports and I rely on regular one-on-one video conferences where we have each other's undivided attention. My team interaction has a cadence of weekly staff meetings, and each person has a one-on-one, all done with video. We use instant messaging regularly for ad hoc discussions. Since we are all at a computer most of the day, it's very easy and almost immediate to access anyone in the company at any time our overlapping time zones allow.

3. Personal Growth

What is the most profound impact this pandemic has had the way you think about your job, company, family life? Will it be sticky or do you expect everything to return to the previous status quo?

As a mom of three young children, I have found the extra family time during the pandemic and working remotely as a priceless gift. I have also realized how efficient and effective remote working can be, not just for me, but for all types of people globally. I am so grateful to have worked at a company that allowed me to work remotely, and I do not take that for granted. I know that I am not alone as a working parent who has realized how effective they can be as a remote worker and even remote leader, and I know that many people will no longer be willing to work for a company that doesn't offer flexibility in this arena. I hope that I can support my teams with the appropriate flexibility in the future because I know that many people will not be willing to go back to the status quo. It is certainly something that will be valuable to me as an employee.

4. Diversity, Equity, and Inclusion

The pandemic has hit hard for women in particular. Many are thinking about dialing back their careers or exiting altogether, which is very frightening for many companies. What should be done differently to retain women in the workplace?

I was one of the working moms who seriously considered taking a break from working amidst this pandemic, given that schools shut down and my three children were in Kindergarten, 3rd, and 4th grades. I learned quickly in the spring that I was not capable of teaching my kids in a way that they deserved, and us moms will do anything for our kids including sacrificing our own careers. I explored a lot of alternatives and one of them was quitting my job. Employers need to realize that every family situation presents unique challenges, and we should assume that most people have some responsibilities whether it be children, parents, or otherwise. Flexibility is essential. You never know what people are going through, and it's very easy to think everyone's situation mirrors your own. Managers should open the discussion with their employees and create a welcoming environment where teammates are comfortable sharing about their personal situations when appropriate. HR policies that formalize a flexible schedule also really help the guilt or peer pressure people feel when they need to telecommute or work flexible hours.

5. Sustainability

Sustainability trends (climate change, water availability, health, etc.) are some of the strongest drivers for future changes for companies and their strategies. What are you seeing within your company? Is your firm reading the trends and adapting strategies to survive and then thrive with new growth?

Yes, my company is very serious about rapidly adapting to the mobility trends, particularly around electrification. We are evaluating our spending, R&D, talent, and technology against market and customer data and taking actions to ensure that we lead from a technology standpoint as the electrification shift occurs.

Elizabeth Krear

Chief Engineer, Model Responsible Jeep Gladiator
Stellantis—North America

Background

Elizabeth Krear has been in the auto industry for over 30 years. She's been responsible for some of Stellantis most important products, including the Ram 1500 and Jeep Gladiator. Her current responsibilities include overseeing all aspects of the Jeep Gladiator program as the Chief Engineer.

In 2020, *Automotive News* named Krear to the prestigious list of the 100 Leading Women in the North American Auto Industry.

Krear earned a Bachelor of Science and a Master of Science degree in Mechanical Engineering from Wayne State University. Additionally, she has a Master of Business Administration from Michigan State University.

She is an active member of the Women's Alliance Business Resource Group at Stellantis, which is one of 11 employee groups representing a range of affinity communities. She also serves as Industry Advisor to Wayne State University Mechanical Engineering department.

Questions and Answers

1. Change Control, Resilience, and Work/Life Balance

How do you keep team spirit with your direct reports? Are you sensing any lack of trust or more trust? What factors/actions have the most effect on trust/lack of trust?

When the pandemic started, my team was experiencing the peak of team spirit. We had just launched the iconic Jeep Gladiator, a truck that has been anticipated for almost 30 years. In January 2020, the Jeep Gladiator was named North American Truck of the Year, which was such a great honor to the team. Everyone was talking about the truck, and this gave the team the opportunity to showcase their hard work to colleagues, friends, and family.

In February, I was asked to present the Jeep Gladiator at an SAE Dinner, and I brought my team to participate in the presentation. Our host was ecstatic and said it was among the best dinner presentations his chapter has ever had. I felt so much pride to watch the team enthusiastically present their hard work in front of an eager audience. The next week, we all received our stay-at-home orders.

So how did we build this team spirit and maintain it during the pandemic?

Team spirit requires trust. The best way to build trust on a team is to demonstrate that we have each other's backs and to maintain a work environment that supports each other's strengths—individual strengths that must come together for the team to thrive. As a leader, my job is to make sure that everyone on the team knows their contributions are valued and that they feel safe to ask for help.

Although these are basic ingredients to empower employees, these alone are not enough. I am a firm believer that true trust comes from team-building experiences inside and outside of work. Whether it's a pizza party during launch at the plant or drinks after an important milestone, these events allow the team to take a moment to get to know each other on a personal level, which naturally expands into trust at work.

I took this a step further and made sure that the team was able to bond not only with each other but also with the product. A highlight for all was when my team traveled in a Jeep Gladiator caravan to Rocks and Valleys. The purpose was to bond as a team on an intense off-road course and demonstrate the amazing "Go Anywhere" capability of the product we work on. As team members maneuvered the course, some got stuck in mud, others drenched in water, but between the team coaching and the Gladiator's capability, we all made it through.

For the time being, we kindle the foundation through virtual events where we share highs and lows and reminisce about great times together and plan our next adventures together.

2. Growing Your Professional Network and Maintaining Mentor and Sponsor Relationships

Are you continuing to grow your professional network while being remote? How?

Surprisingly, I am growing my professional network while working remotely. I have always been just too busy to spend time on social media. However, with the pandemic, I have taken the time to reach out a bit more on sites like Facebook and LinkedIn. Although the former is a social site and the latter a business site, they both serve to make connections. I have always believed that if you make enough connections, and are sincere and open with your communication, eventually something serendipitous happens. I have connected with high school friends, college friends, colleagues, and retirees, all of whom I know I can call on, and they know they can call on me.

I also had the honor of being named to the 2020 *Automotive News* 100 Leading Women in the North American Auto Industry list. This opened my world to be inspired by so many amazing women as we shared stories, advice, and shared visions about the future during the virtual Leading Women's Conference. Although we were not able to meet face to face, we had a virtual celebration and exchanged contact information so that we can continue to keep in touch and support each other in the future.

I am an active board member in the Stellantis Women's Alliance. This year we did not let our remote work status prevent us from holding our Women's Summit. During Q4 we held 12 virtual events, all with the intent to provide women with a platform to learn from industry gurus, grow their network within Stellantis, and recognize their potential.

Finally, it is also important to nurture your existing network, especially your mentors and sponsors. Sometimes after a long day online, the last thing you want to do is to send one more email. But it's important to respectfully force yourself to reach out to the people that have and will continue to help you succeed. I've made the mistake of thinking "oh I don't want to bother them" later to find out I missed out on an opportunity. Always remember you have just as much to offer them as they have to offer you.

3. Personal Growth

What is the most profound impact this pandemic has had the way you think about your job, company, family life? Will it be sticky or do you expect everything to return to the previous status quo?

Job: Engineers are survivors; we will always find a way to get the job done. We launched all our products including the historic first-ever Desert Rated Jeep, the Mojave Jeep Gladiator, as well as introduced a new fuel-efficient diesel engine into the Jeep Gladiator during the pandemic. We followed the social-distancing rules and found creative ways to work safely; some engineers set up laboratories in their garages. I believe, now more than ever, it's vital never to underestimate what the engineering team can deliver. They are the reason our world continues to innovate and advance in technology.

Company: The company is strong and was quick to make decisions that protected our most important commodity—our people. In turn, our people stepped up at all levels and in all areas—they were resilient. Our IT department worked behind the scenes for everyone to transition from the office to home seamlessly—that was impressive. Manufacturing personnel showed up in the middle of the pandemic to assemble our vehicles—that's dedication! Our company is amazing!

Family: The pandemic had a silver lining for my husband, Tad, and me. It brought our 23-year-old daughter Niki home from Chicago (She's an investment banker), and it brought our 21-year-old son Alex home from MSU (he's a Marketing major). We all found corners in the house to work and study; we also found time to cook together, play music, recreate, socialize, do puzzles, and safely provide meals for and visit my parents. To have time together as adults was priceless.

Elizabeth Krear

The Future: I believe we will go back to on-site work, and when we do, we will find the perfect balance of remote working and flexible work schedules. There are efficiencies on both sides. But 100% remote working is not sustainable for our future. People's talents flourish when shared. Colleagues are motivated and inspired by each other, and new employees learn by listening and watching.

4. Diversity, Equity, and Inclusion

There has been a lot of talk about diversity—and, in recent years, inclusion. Equity has entered the corporate conversation in a major way this year. What actions are you and your company taking? Are these methods aligned with company goals?

Our CEO, in an end-of-year virtual town hall, proclaimed that diversity and inclusion is a top priority of his. Our company's merger with PSA Groupe to form Stellantis will be the fifth merger I have experienced in my career and probably the most important with regard to diversity.

No longer are we an American company with employees that primarily live and work in North America. We are a global company and industry with cultural diversity. Just prior to the pandemic, our Engineering organization reorganized to a global structure. The timing was perfect to create an environment of inclusion. When the world went virtual, and traveling came to a halt, it really no longer mattered where you live. We are all on an equal playing field, working comfortably from our home offices. A 6:00 am meeting no longer feels like an invasion. In fact, I have more communication with my colleagues in Australia and China than ever before.

Looking closer at diversity, a topic that is very important to me is promoting STEM fields for women.

Although the landscape of women in this industry has changed, there is still work to do. When I first started with the company 30 years ago, I was typically the only woman at the table. Today, my Gladiator team is comprised of about 30% women. I experienced firsthand the value that diversity brings to the success of a team. We need to continue to make progress at all management levels within the corporation. So how do we do it?

- Retention: Our company recently announced that we will provide 12 weeks paid maternity and paternity leave. This is an enormous step forward to help retain women.

- Mentorship and Sponsorship: We have several formal mentoring programs to help guide and advise engineers. That said, my big break came from another woman who advocated for me, and in turn, I consciously advocate for both men and women. This relationship is what I call a sponsorship.

- Inclusion through engagement with Business Resource Groups and other diverse affiliations: I am an active board member on the Stellantis Women's Alliance BRG. The mission is to foster an environment to enable women to develop and become leaders at both work and in the community. We have over 800 members and offer inspirational programs monthly. I also helped establish a Society of Women Engineers Cohort at Stellantis. We provide 200 free memberships to our employees. The group is governed by some of our brightest young engineers and running strong for three years now.

- Community and Education Outreach: I am excited about an initiative I will be starting next year with my Alma Mater, Wayne State University—a Women Engineering Leadership Society, whose mission is to work with the student organizations to plan strategies for promoting women's initiatives in the college as well as outreach programs in the local community. It is important for all of us to "give back" through programs like these.

5. Sustainability

Sustainability trends (climate change, water availability, health, etc.) are some of the strongest drivers for future changes for companies and their strategies. What are you seeing within your company? Is your firm reading the trends and adapting strategies to survive and then thrive with new growth?

I mentioned that one of the silver linings to the pandemic was that it brought my kids home. During the weeks, we spent together adjusting to our new lifestyle, we also talked a lot about the world around us. I learned that my kids' generation, the next leaders of our world, are absolutely engaged in conversations relative to climate change. This reinforced for me the changes we need and are making in the auto industry relative to our carbon footprint, noise pollution, and safety.

So how does one take the most capable off-road vehicle in the world and make it better? With electrification. The sister to the Jeep Gladiator, the Jeep Wrangler, just introduced the 4xe. According to the brand, "Forging a whole new path to the future, the Jeep Wrangler 4xe has all the legendary capability and open-air freedom the Jeep Brand is known for, now with a plug-in electric boost with an estimated 50 MPGe." Jeep is committed to offering hybrid or electric variants across the entire lineup.

My son spent some time backpacking in Colorado during the pandemic. He talked about how he unplugged in the Rocky Mountains, there was no TV and minimal cell signal. One of the little things that stood out for him was how quiet everything was, which allowed him to absorb the beauty of nature that surrounded him. In addition to the benefits electric propulsion systems have on emissions, they also greatly reduce noise pollution.

As a mother, I worry about my kids' safety when they take off in their cars. As a daughter with aging parents still driving, I worry even more! The strides the auto industry is making in safety and autonomous driving is incredible. Earlier in my career, I was the manager of the Safety Impact Development Engineering team. This allowed me to experience firsthand how the structural design of a vehicle and airbag technology works together to protect our precious cargo. Equally as important are the prevention technologies that have become mainstream: lane departure warning, lane keep assist, and forward collision warning and avoidance, to name a few. Our vehicles are safer and smarter than ever before and on a path to full autonomous capability.

Jessica LaFond

Head of Vehicle Programs
Stellantis

Background

Jessica LaFond is a high-energy leader whose drive to exceed expectations has rewarded her with many high-profile assignments.

Holder of two engineering degrees and an MBA from three distinguished universities—Lehigh University, University of Michigan, and Michigan State University—she has followed a dynamic career path at Stellantis that culminated recently with her appointment as global Head of Vehicle Programs.

LaFond is well prepared for her new position, having filled jobs that run the gamut of vehicle development. These include a stint in system integration and director-level responsibility for all exhaust, air induction, cooling, and fuel systems in North American vehicle programs.

Her trajectory at Stellantis took a sharp upward turn in 2008 when she was given responsibility for the high-volume Jeep Cherokee SUV. LaFond's early success leading vehicle programs inspired Stellantis management to hand her the job of launching the all-new Chrysler Pacifica and Chrysler Pacifica Hybrid—cornerstones of the Company's minivan-segment dominance.

LaFond has 25 years of automotive engineering experience and 12 years in software development. But among her strengths, she cites managing cross-functional teams in challenging environments and helping those teams exceed their goals.

Married to husband, Phil, LaFond enjoys the outdoors—especially horseback riding with her teenage daughter, Marie.

Questions and Answers

1. Change Control, Resilience, and Work/Life Balance

Many have said that there is no separation of work and home these days. What do you do to manage this for your own work? What are you doing to increase the ability of your team to create and respect boundaries?

When we were all sent home at the start of the initial lockdown, I felt like I jumped on a high-speed train with everyone working around the clock to succeed. I'd always thought I had no separation between work and home, but within a few weeks in the COVID environment, my suspicions were confirmed. I was good at managing some balance in the morning with a quick workout before starting my day, but my evenings just went right up until I fell asleep. To regain balance, I started adding evening blocks to my calendar to exercise and spend time with my family. After a few weeks of this new pattern, others adapted around the time blocks. I encouraged those on my team to create their own boundaries. Children or no children, married or single, each person needs their own balance. And the best way to encourage others is to do it yourself. I remind people that perfect balance doesn't exist, nor the work we do ever feels easy. As a leader, you must create your own balance, know when to be rigid about that boundary, and know when the boundary has to bend. I have reminded many people this year that they need to give themselves permission to define what works for them.

2. Growing Your Professional Network and Maintaining Mentor and Sponsor Relationships

Have your mentees been asking different questions than under usual working conditions? Have you needed to do more hand-holding? Do you see more mentees seeking career change or seeking educational opportunities? Something else?

This year has strengthened some of us and made others question ourselves more often. One thing is certain, mentoring has changed for me this year. The one thing that has disappeared are the impromptu requests for counsel that arose if someone walked by my office and saw that I was alone. Since my door was always open, many would stop by for a quick discussion or a word of advice. Such casual mentoring is almost gone. In contrast, the more formal requests and speaking-event types of mentoring have increased. People are wondering if others are handling the world of high remote working in the same way they are choosing to react. The most common thing I am asked is advice about when to speak out. I have been advising those that I mentor to find their voice. "Be brave and dare to share your ideas. It is easy to get lost behind the screen and not be seen. Be brave enough to grab the screen and sketch an idea like you would have done in the office with a whiteboard and a marker." I've noticed many are struggling by holding themselves back and I've been encouraging them to jump in, speak up and sketch the future.

3. Personal Growth

What is the most profound impact this pandemic has had the way you think about your job, company, family life? Will it be sticky or do you expect everything to return to the previous status quo?

The world has pivoted and we have all grown during this challenging time. As a result, going back to the way it was would actually cause us to miss the opportunity and fail to acknowledge the efficiency and effectiveness we have created in certain areas. There is no question that many things are done so much better face to face. However, the concept of wondering what someone is doing who is working remotely has completely vanished. I recall that many I worked with thought working remotely was a way to take an easy day. Now that everyone has been forced to work remotely, they realize those who work hard, do indeed work hard, and those who don't, simply do not. In addition, when working remotely, there is an incredible focus to produce output that should be exploited One size will no longer fit all. I would sum it up in the following thought. My job used to start by going to the office. Now my job starts wherever I am, and I move to the best location to accomplish the task.

4. Diversity, Equity, and Inclusion

The pandemic has hit hard for women in particular. Many are thinking about dialing back their careers or exiting altogether, which is very frightening for many companies. What should be done differently to retain women in the workplace?

Everyone was hit hard when the pandemic dawned, and we all found ourselves turning our homes into offices and classrooms. Some who are cohabiting with older parents found themselves caring for three generations around the clock. To say this stressed us out would be an understatement. Given how long we have been addressing this new lifestyle, women are at risk of choosing a different path and putting their careers on hold. What I believe we should do differently is embrace the flexibility that remote working offers all of us, especially women who are caring for young families. The best way to address this can often be by focusing on project deliverables. This would enable women (or truly any worker) to get the work done based on their own life challenges. At the end of the day, *when* you did the work is not the measure of success. Getting the work done right and on time is what matters. I believe we should be encouraging women to stay in the workforce and encouraging the current generation of leaders to emphasize this switch. Measure what matters—the quality of the work.

5. Sustainability

Human capital—employee talent—is one ultimate driver of business and company success. Aligning talent to sustainability trends has proven to be a winning approach for recruiting, retaining, and developing top talent because employees want to do more with their careers ... and do good while also doing well. Have you and your company moved to incorporate sustainability into your strategies for attracting, retaining, and developing your human capital?

Seeking the right talent and acquiring the right talent will help propel us forward. As we look to sustainability, it is clear that the automotive world of engine power and metal forming has transformed a world with an increasing emphasis on software and electrification. As we envision cars of the future, they have become computers on wheels that people are interacting with on a much more personal level. They have become different devices in their personal toolkits. Imagine where this will take our conventional skills. We will develop proficiencies we do not even fully understand we need. This means our talent needs are changing. We are actively looking at the trends in the industry and encouraging activity in two different directions: (1) encouraging those who want to grow in a different aspect of our business to seek training both on and off the job and (2) seeking new talent from industries outside of our own. This is a disruptive time in the automotive world, and paying attention to the trends around us are key to our agility and our ability to adapt.

Rebecca Liebert

Executive Vice President
PPG

Background

Rebecca Liebert is Executive Vice President of PPG. She joined the company in June 2018 and leads PPG's industrial segment, which includes the automotive OEM, industrial coatings, packaging and specialty chemicals, and monomers businesses. She also oversees the company's Asia Pacific region, mobility initiatives, and has functional responsibility for global procurement.

In her most recent role with Honeywell UOP, Liebert served as President and Chief Executive Officer. Honeywell UOP is a leading international supplier and technology licensor for the petroleum refining, gas processing, petrochemical production, and major manufacturing industries. During her career with Honeywell, she had also served as Senior Vice President and General Manager of Catalyst Absorbents and Specialties, UOP; Senior Vice President and General Manager of Gas Processing and Hydrogen; and Vice President and General Manager of Electronics Materials. Prior to joining Honeywell, Liebert served as President of Reynolds Food Packaging and Alcoa KAMA.

Liebert began her career as a development engineer with Nova Chemicals. She held positions of increasing responsibility at Nova Chemicals, including Global Business Development Leader/Sales and Distribution Manager, Commercial Leader of Styrenic Polymers, and then Business Director of Solid Polystyrene and High-Performance Polystyrene.

Liebert currently serves on the Board of Directors for Corteva Agriscience.

Liebert earned a Bachelor of Science degree in Chemical Engineering from the University of Kentucky, a Master of Business Administration (MBA) degree from the

Kellogg School of Management, Northwestern University, and a PhD in Chemical Engineering from Carnegie Mellon University.

Questions and Answers

1. Change Control, Resilience, and Work/Life Balance

Many have said that there is no separation of work and home these days. What do you do to manage this for your own work? What are you doing to increase the ability of your team to create and respect boundaries?

Work/life balance has always been a challenge, and in today's work environment, it is even more difficult. Early in my career, I had difficulty finding balance and always felt as if I was letting someone down. I began to approach things differently with the objective of achieving work/life integration. I guess that was a more natural approach for me, as growing up on a farm in Eastern Kentucky, I learned farm work was part of our daily life. You had to integrate the two for maximum success. I also learned at a young age on the farm the three "Ps"—Planning, Project Management, and *not* Procrastinating. I learned to plan my days and weeks with detail and consistency. I have transferred that planning mentality to my professional life by deploying a management operating system and consistent cadence of activities. This includes regular meetings with leaders in my organizations, consistency in reporting and analysis, and remaining in front of potential issues. Ultimately, this consistency and cadence allows our teams to prepare accordingly.

As PPG is a global company with a global workforce, it is important to respectfully schedule meetings to accommodate our global customers and business colleagues. This means a daily schedule requires flexibility, making it imperative to maintain a management operating system and cadence that reserves personal time. Remember to take time for YOU! Make time to take a walk, clear your head, think strategically, and invest in your health.

Video conferencing technology has made it easier to "connect" with people. Seeing teams and individuals face to face in a virtual setting can provide clues to how they are balancing their work/life integration. I recommend using those video tools as frequently as possible, because in today's connected world, leading your team in consistent ways is an important leadership trait.

Our people at PPG are the engine that makes our company run. As leaders, we must drive engagement. Studies show that an engaged team is directly correlated to top-performing companies that create higher shareholder returns.

2. Growing Your Professional Network and Maintaining Mentor and Sponsor Relationships

Has your company maintained learning and leadership development opportunities, culture surveys, 360 surveys, etc. to grow skills and manage the emotional intelligence of the company? Has anything shifted? What have you learned?

When the global pandemic hit, we realized we had to make decisions and act quickly, perhaps with less than 100% of the data. Given my responsibilities for PPG's

Asia-Pacific region and the automotive OEM business—which operates a manufacturing facility in Wuhan, China—our business began managing challenges related to COVID very early in 2020. We had to establish a playbook on how we were going to keep our people safe while we continued to operate our manufacturing and laboratory facilities. As I read various resources about managing during a crisis, one of the quotes that resonated with me was from Winston Churchill—"Never let a good crisis go to waste." I knew it was time to be proactive and implement adaptable and agile ways of working, especially in our manufacturing environments, as demand swings were quite dramatic. We led with frequent and open communications using a varied set of leaders in the business—shared success stories, asked for ideas for engagement, and provided the tools necessary to be successful. We knew that engagement in a virtual world is quite possibly more important than in a typical business environment. We took our leadership and individual contributor trainings into virtual and interactive formats, using Microsoft Teams, and deployed them globally. We measured our progress by continuing our employee engagement survey and deploying a communications effectiveness survey. Our engagement survey results tell us where we have opportunities to improve, but we certainly received positive feedback for how we responded to the COVID crisis with continual, proactive communication.

3. Personal Growth

Are you challenging yourself to learn more about a new technology or take courses? If so, what did you study and how do you think this will benefit you? Have you learned anything about yourself in these studies?

Those who know me would likely say I have always been interested in learning—from my early experiences on our family farm where I learned practical chemistry and mechanical engineering skills; to formal education in science, math, and engineering; to learning new technologies throughout my career. Today, digital technologies are playing a bigger, central role in the business of the future. Whether it is incorporating digital tools to enable customers to order and pay, developing and designing new products, planning and procuring materials, or connecting with our people, every process can be improved with digital tools. That said, we can't just put digital tools on stale processes. Therefore, part of what we have been focused on at PPG is introducing new ways of working—i.e., redesigning our processes for the future. With these upgraded processes digitally enabled, we can truly raise the bar for our customers, employees, and shareholders.

4. Diversity, Equity, and Inclusion

There has been a lot of talk about diversity—and, in recent years, inclusion. Equity has entered the corporate conversation in a major way this year. What actions are you and your company taking? Are these methods aligned with company goals?

In 2020, as protests erupted worldwide after George Floyd's death in the custody of Minneapolis police officers, companies and individuals realized that to make real change, we all had to lean into the conversation and seek to understand in a more purposeful way, and PPG was no different. As such, PPG leaders quickly set up open communication channels and sharing sessions, some of which included industry experts, to discuss diversity, equity, and inclusion (DE&I). Our goal, as individuals and as an organization, is to ensure our workforce is inclusive of all backgrounds and reflects the communities in which we live and work. At PPG, we know that a diverse workforce—representing wide-ranging nationalities, cultures, languages, religions, ethnicities, and professional and educational experiences—allows us to meet challenges quickly, creatively, and effectively. As an organization, we also have delivered financial support to various organizations supporting diversity, equity, and inclusion. In fact, after Mr. Floyd's death, the PPG Foundation moved to swiftly donate to organizations that address racial inequities. We also expanded how our employees can make personal contributions addressing injustices and increased our community impact in the regions we operate.

For me personally, growing up in Eastern Kentucky and attending the University of Kentucky, I felt a need to give back to the community that helped make me who I am today. That is why I established the Rebecca Burchett Liebert Dean of the College of Engineering fund that will provide scholarship support to undergraduate students from Eastern Kentucky—with an emphasis on supporting female students and those who would strengthen UK's commitment to diversity and inclusion.

5. Sustainability

Sustainability trends (climate change, water availability, health, etc.) are some of the strongest drivers for future changes for companies and their strategies. What are you seeing within your company? Is your firm reading the trends and adapting strategies to survive and then thrive with new growth?

At PPG, our approach to sustainability is grounded in our vision of delivering lasting value for our stakeholders and customers by operating with integrity, working safely, respecting the contributions of our people, preserving the environment, and supporting the communities where we operate. We remain steadfast in our commitment to developing innovative products and solutions that create value for our customers, to empowering our people to grow and succeed, to operating safely and effectively, and to delivering value to our shareholders—growing sales and earnings to consistently deliver superior returns.

Our customers demand we deliver ever-more sustainable products. In fact, within the automotive industry, many leaders are incentivized on sustainability goals, and so it is important that we adapt to meet these changing priorities. When a customer recently wanted to electrocoat (e-coat) rather than spray paint only part of its large truck fender frames, our team at PPG didn't get hung up on the solution. Instead, we designed a process where the frames are hung in such a way that only those areas that need to be e-coated are dipped into the coating tank. The solution minimizes waste, improves ergonomics, and eliminates volatile organic compounds (VOCs) associated with spray-on paint. For these painting processes, it also reduces annual energy consumption by 1,300 gigawatt hours, water use by 5 million gallons (18,927 cubic meters), and wastewater by 1 million gallons (3,785 cubic meters) due to increased throughput.

As Simon Sinek expounds, sustainability contributes to our corporate purpose—We protect and beautify the world—our golden circle, our Why! Starting every day with "Why" allows us to wake up inspired, helps us feel safe in our roles as innovative creators of value, and leaves us fulfilled when we return home. For these reasons and many more, we need to focus our culture and communications on this higher purpose. Why we do what we do is all the more relevant in a challenging business environment.

Lynn Longo

Senior Vice President of Connected Car,
Digital Cockpit
Harman International Industries Inc.

Background

Lynn Longo is the senior vice president and head of the Digital Cockpit business unit at Harman. She has over 20 years of automotive engineering and technology experience, with the majority of that time spent serving in key global leadership roles. As Head of the Digital Cockpit business, Lynn leverages her extensive understanding of automotive product strategy, development, and delivery to drive innovation and bring solutions to the market that create seamless, safe, and connected consumer driving experiences.

Prior to joining Harman, Lynn was the executive director and chief information officer of Connected Ecosystem Integration at General Motors (GM) where she led the technical integration of GM's connected vehicle ecosystem via adaptable, flexible platforms. Before that, she held three leadership positions in two different joint ventures in China (Shanghai OnStar Telematics Service Co., Ltd. and SAIC General Motors)—marking her as the first international senior executive to hold three distinct roles simultaneously. Prior to her international assignment in China, Lynn spent more than three years working for GM Europe leading a global team of engineers.

Lynn Longo

Lynn holds a Bachelor of Science from Michigan State University and a Master of Science in Information Technology Management from Carnegie Mellon University.

Questions and Answers

1. Change Control, Resilience, and Work/Life Balance

What did you learn when you began to work from home or work in the office with a limited number of coworkers? What did you need to start doing and what did you need to stop?

Overall, I was impressed with how the Harman team was able to pivot over such a short period of time. We were able to implement work from home (WFH) capabilities, organize no-contact exchanges of equipment and vehicles, and recover any efficiency lost in a 60-day time frame. If asked, I never would have predicted it was possible—so the team has done the impossible—and I'm quite impressed.

I've learned that we, as a company, put a lot of emphasis on face-to-face interactions, and while that remains important, the possibilities of more remote engagements are now just that—a possibility. We're more focused on long-term solutions to the WFH question, so it doesn't just feel like a patch effort.

2. Growing Your Professional Network and Maintaining Mentor and Sponsor Relationships

How do you keep your existing relationships in this remote world? Are you maintaining face time with other execs while being remote? How do your direct reports maintain their face time with you?

One-on-one (1:1) interactions have changed immensely as well—for the better. During the time I would have spent commuting or travelling between offices, I'm now using that time to interact 1:1 with employees or attend weekly staff meetings. I've been more dedicated to my 1:1 meetings since this all started, and that's a small gift. It's also been a great opportunity to engage more directly and personally with coworkers, since working from home has provided a window to our own personal lives, breaking down formal barriers. The entire company has been able to meet my black lab puppy, whether via a quick introduction on calls or a more informal (and not always unwelcome) barking interruption during 1:1s.

3. Personal Growth

What is the most profound impact this pandemic has had the way you think about your job, company, family life? Will it be sticky or do you expect everything to return to the previous status quo?

Overall, I think this period has really underlined the importance of safety in whatever we do, create, or sell. Safety is, and (now clearer than ever) always will be, Harman's number one priority. I've seen throughout this period how we've all constantly strived to make decisions that ensure the safety of our coworkers, direct reports, and even the wider community, and I'm grateful for that.

4. Diversity, Equity, and Inclusion

Is the board of directors of your company diverse and representative of your workforce and/or customers? Is the leadership team? Is the workforce? If the workforce and customers aren't currently diverse, is there greater interest and commitment to making change in this regard?

As leaders at Harman, we feel we've created an environment where everyone can bring their best selves to work by making sure everyone has a space to be heard.

I lead the largest, most engineering-heavy unit within HARMAN's Connected Car Division, responsible for driving innovative product strategy, design, development, and deployment in a highly disrupted global automotive market. It's fast paced and demands contribution from everyone. To cultivate that, it requires a diverse team within a company that represents everyone within a diverse population.

I personally find it very important for us leaders to advocate for gender empowerment in the automotive and technology industries. That's why I'm an active member of the Harman Women's Network, dedicated to accelerating careers for women, and Chairs the Technology Next Industry Group, where I lead professional development programs for technology professionals. I recently participated as a speaker at the Michigan Council of Women in Technology's Annual Gala. Additionally, I've served as a thought leader with Ladies Who Tech Shanghai and GM's "We for She" events.

These types of forums and active groups within our company are where leaders can really force the conversation to inspire and champion women in an empowering and effective way. At Harman, we're motivating women to embark on careers they are passionate about, without limitations.

5. Sustainability

Sustainability trends (climate change, water availability, health, etc.) are some of the strongest drivers for future changes for companies and their strategies. What are you seeing within your company? Is your firm reading the trends and adapting strategies to survive and then thrive with new growth?

As we look to emerge even stronger on the other side of the pandemic, Harman is evolving with the times.

This is already a particularly transformative period and the most disruptive time in the auto industry. But I had no idea what disruption meant until this pandemic! What we're seeing is an auto industry changing at a rate we've never seen before, in addition to navigating an international health crisis.

Traditionally the auto industry moves fairly slowly, and really what we're seeing right now is fast-paced innovative decisions being made daily. I don't think we'll ever go back to what yesterday looks like, as resiliency in handling the unpredictable everyday has become the new norm.

We will continue at this speed and urgency as we push for greater sustainability and remain close and informed by sustainability trends around the world. We know and believe in the importance of this for humanity and the future of our companies.

Lisa Lortie

Global Director, Propulsion Systems Testing and Analysis
Stellantis

Background

Lisa Lortie is the Global Director of Propulsion Systems Testing and Analysis at Stellantis. She is responsible for a team of more than 1,400 technical staff and manages 10 global testing sites that provide standardized and optimized solutions to support the Propulsion Systems organization. In this role, Lisa is responsible to ensure compliance with regulatory and safety requirements.

Her career covers more than 24 years dedicated to powertrain components and systems and includes experience in design and release, development, manufacturing, and program management with increasing responsibility.

Lortie recognized her love of engineering at a young age with parents who encouraged her education and finding her own path. They fostered her love of math and science and supported her taking courses such as machine shop.

She earned both a Bachelor of Applied Science in Mechanical Engineering and her Master of Business Administration from the University of Windsor.

Lortie was named one of the "Top 100 Leading Women in the North American Auto Industry" by *Automotive News* in 2020, is a member of the Society of Women Engineers, and promotes STEM careers to young women in the community. She also supports an organization dedicated to advancing children's rights and equality for girls.

Questions and Answers

1. Change Control, Resilience, and Work/Life Balance

What did you learn when you began to work from home or work in the office with a limited number of co-workers? What did you need to start doing and what did you need to stop?

When I first started working from home, it was very intense, with long days and endless meetings. My staff works in the engineering labs and were some of the last to leave the offices when the pandemic started, and some of the first to return. We needed to ensure safe entry and workspaces for each returning employee, and this was a thorough and long process, resulting in very long workdays. This was a stressful time for my team, and I was dedicated to making the return to work safe and comfortable for them.

With a son at home getting accustomed to virtual learning and fending for himself in the kitchen, and me with back-to-back video conferences, I realized there were some things I needed to do for myself to keep from burning out and to be there for my son. I started blocking off a lunch break on my calendar and spending that time with my son, checking in on his morning progress. I also recognized the importance of fresh air and exercise and made sure on most days to take at least a short break to step outside and stretch my legs. Exercise was difficult to fit in before the pandemic, and I had blamed it on a long commute. Now without the commute, I had filled that time with more meetings and work and recognized that needed to change, so I made time most days to work out. This has been good physically and mentally during this stressful time.

When most of my North American team returned to the office, I ensured I was also in at least once a week for some socially distanced presence to maintain the human connection. Unfortunately, with a global team and restricted travel, I haven't been able to be engaged in person in the other regions. However, I have kept communications open with regular Town Halls, staff meetings, and weekly one-on-ones with my direct staff and some of their teams. Communication has been the critical element during this period and that may have looked a little different for each team member, so considerable effort was put into ensuring messages were passed along and that I was available for the team.

I recognized my team also needed flexibility for their changed work lives for homeschooling, child care, more people in the house, etc. Communication was again the key to understanding everyone's personal needs. I have never been one to open up greatly about my personal life at work. However, in order to understand what others needed, I opened up about some of my situations to ease the conversation. This resulted in my team opening up, which helps me understand what my team needed from me.

For a lot of us working from home, it has been difficult to separate work and home, so I consciously had to stop responding to non-urgent emails during evening downtime. I did this for myself and my team so they didn't feel the need to respond. I also acknowledged the overload of back-to-back virtual meetings and minimized the number of recurring meetings, calling them only when necessary. Lastly, I stopped having every meeting rigid to an agenda in order to have some socialization and comaraderie with the team. This short banter, or a couple of laughs, was often the highlight of my day, and I hope for them, too.

2. Growing Your Professional Network and Maintaining Mentor and Sponsor Relationships

Has your company maintained learning and leadership development opportunities, culture surveys, 360 surveys, etc. to grow skills and manage the emotional intelligence of the company? Has anything shifted? What have you learned?

I am very proud of how Stellantis has not only maintained learning and leadership development opportunities but increased and adapted them during this trying time. The Product Development organization underwent a significant reorganization last January, just at the start of the global pandemic. As work turned remote and virtual, so did the courses. Each month a new executive leadership course with a new theme was rolled out, followed by interactive discussions led by HR on relevant topics. The topics were focused on global leadership. However, with most teams virtual, there were a lot of tools that could be used or adapted for remote teams. Additionally, Stellantis's Women's Alliance, a business resource group that I am involved with, quickly pivoted their planned Leadership Summit for the course of the year with interesting and relevant speakers to a new virtual format. The team that coordinated this shift was quick to adapt, resulting in a very successful series of discussions and panels.

In addition to leadership courses, there was a significant increase in the amount of technical courses available online, both live and recorded. This came at a critical time with our technology rapidly changing to electrified propulsion systems and the necessity of broader training. The virtual format gave many an opportunity to participate at their own pace and during the times they were available.

It was also important for me during this time to maintain mentoring relationships and develop new ones. During remote working situations, personal connections are essential, and mentoring relationships allow for a safe zone to discuss personal topics and challenges. These conversations certainly changed during remote work, and I found the individuals I mentor asking questions and discussing situations not previously encountered by both of us.

Through all of this I have learned that we are resilient and adaptable, and even if virtual and probably more so, the human connection is crucial.

3. Personal Growth

What is the most profound impact this pandemic has had on the way you think about your job, company, family life? Will it be sticky or do you expect everything to return to the previous status quo?

This pandemic has definitely had an impact on the way I think about various parts of my life. Relative to my job, I recognize how much I value the personal interactions

I have with people—the smiles in the hallways, the short chats, and the more casual part of the workday. This has become more difficult with the social distancing and wearing of masks and not being able to see a smile, so being more verbal has been important. I care about the people I work with and am very loyal to my team. I worked hard to ensure the return to work for them was safe and anticipate the day when we can again interact how we used to.

I am very proud of how Stellantis handled the pandemic. First and foremost was always the safety of our employees. This safety mentality also extended to shifting to mask and ventilator production—and this happened so quickly, it was amazing! Despite the challenges we faced, we were still able to unveil new products, launch many vehicles, continue investments, and report record financial results. This would not have been possible without our leadership as well as everyone continuing to work in new environments and deliver results.

Regarding family life, I realized how important it is to set reasonable work boundaries and understand what are your "non-negotiables." Each day is different and there is no perfect work-life balance solution. I also realized that I will do anything to keep my family and friends safe and how precious these relationships are. During the pandemic, like a lot of people, I took the time to reconnect with friends and extended family and nurture relationships. This has been one big positive to having extra time at home.

I don't think everything will return to the status quo. I think the negative stigma associated with working from home will be reduced as it is evident how much was accomplished with most of the workforce virtual. I also think there will be much more use of technology going forward, which will decrease travel and enable a more flexible workday.

4. Diversity, Equity, and Inclusion

There has been a lot of talk about diversity—and, in recent years, inclusion. Equity has entered the corporate conversation in a major way this year. What actions are you and your company taking? Are these methods aligned with company goals?

Diversity and Inclusion have always been part of Stellantis, and previously Chrysler. We have many Business Resource Groups (BRGs) available to join, and members can be those that identify with the group as well as allies. These groups include African Ancestry, Women's Alliance, Asians, Diversabilities, First Nations, Gay and Lesbian Alliance, Latins, Middle Eastern, Veterans, and a newly formed Working Parents Network.

The conversation on diversity and inclusion has certainly increased over the past few years, with regular discussions at town halls at every level of the organization. Organizational town halls have highlighted different BRGs and their activities, and there have been displays, dancing, and food at other events. This gives those not involved an appreciation for both cultures and challenges. I am a member of several BRGs and have learned a lot from my fellow colleagues.

After the death of George Floyd, Stellantis had an immediate response with a personal and heartfelt letter from our CEO, Mike Manley. The letter centered on the tragedy as well as the importance of diversity and inclusion everywhere, including Stellantis. Following this, the BRGs planned a unity walk in honor of George Floyd, and a recent North American COO Town Hall had a panel of leaders discussing the importance of diversity and inclusion.

Diversity and Inclusion is part of Stellantis's Code of Conduct, and there is associated mandatory training. There are also additional resources of recordings and articles available. This year Stellantis started "Courageous Conversations," and I volunteered and led several of these. The conversations are with a random group of about 12 people that have signed up. We watch a short video together related to diversity and inclusion and discuss it, as well as our own personal experiences. Each of the groups that I have participated in has had a unique conversation, but each person was there to learn and grow, and it has been a very positive experience. I consider myself an inclusive person but also recognize we all have internal biases, and I am looking to become more aware of these, as well as to more deeply understand issues that others face that I haven't previously considered. I truly think this is where change begins.

5. Sustainability

As part of employee development, does your company encourage and support employees volunteering for local nongovernmental organizations? Do you and your company consider this an opportunity for aligning company efforts, employee leadership development, and local progress on sustainability?

There is a strong commitment to sustainability at Stellantis at every level of the organization. This is a result of our corporate culture of integrity, respect for others, and commitment to community service. For example, Stellantis has a community service program called Motor Citizens, which allows employees time during their workday to volunteer in the local community. This can be painting houses, building bicycles, packing food, organizing charity races, and many more opportunities. Not only is this activity encouraged, it is part of our goals every year to participate. Every level of the organization participates throughout the year, and progress to goals is tracked publicly within the organizations. These types of activities are a chance for employees to give back to the communities where they work and live. I find these activities both humbling and rewarding. They also give me an opportunity to interact with others at Stellantis that I may not have otherwise and to get to know team members on a more personal level.

Stellantis's commitment to others has been very prevalent during the pandemic. Crisis committees were formed. Assembly lines were quickly converted to make masks, face shields, and ventilators. Other areas were transformed to repair respirators, and Stellantis continues to donate personal protective equipment to those in need. In Latin America, Stellantis was instrumental in the installation of field hospitals—donating space, equipping the hospitals, and helping with the setup. The way that our company, and individuals within the company, stepped up to help during this unprecedented time speaks volumes.

Sustainability is also considered in our product design, portfolio, and required infrastructure. This year we unveiled the new generation Fiat 500 full electric vehicle (BEV). This is monumental and a very exciting launch in our company. In order to support this shift to electrification, while recognizing challenges with energy consumption, Stellantis also announced a partnership to launch the first vehicle-to-grid project, which focuses on renewable energy.

From the small things, like packing food, to the more strategic initiatives, there is a commitment to sustainability. Personally, these impacts that we make as individuals and as a company make me both proud and fulfilled.

Stacy Lynett

CIO, Global Product Development and Quality
General Motors

Background

Stacy Lynett is Chief Information Officer (CIO) of Global Product Development and Quality at General Motors. Since entering this role in 2019, Lynett has led the technology strategy for the company's Global Product Development and Quality organizations, focusing on priorities such as high-performance computing power, virtual vehicle development, new open-source software, and other advances.

In her previous role as CIO of Global Corporate Functions, she was an integral part of the in-sourcing of most of GM's IT expertise, which improved first-response capabilities for troubleshooting and streamlined job application operations. To achieve this, she oversaw the launch of an operations center in Austin, Texas. The team secures GM's cyber environment through application monitoring, change and release management, and enterprise-wide patching. Lynett implemented a "SolveIt" initiative for employees to tackle some of the biggest challenges facing GM in a SWAT-like environment.

Lynett is an advocate for women in the industry. In 2018, she was recognized by *Crain's Detroit Business* as a "Notable Woman in Tech." She works to recruit women into STEM fields at regional colleges and through visits and presentations at junior high schools. She is also a supporter of the national nonprofit Girls Who Code.

Questions and Answers

1. Change Control, Resilience, and Work/Life Balance

What did you learn when you began to work from home or work in the office with a limited number of co-workers? What did you need to start doing and what did you need to stop?

The pandemic changed the way that we worked individually, as well as the team dynamics. The ability we had to use a common workroom to solve a problem, or design and innovate, was moved to a virtual world where tools and communication became even more critical. The transition required that all leaders and team members increase their verbal communication in workgroups. It was important that each person's opinions were heard, so we applied legacy facilitation techniques such as "round robin" to ensure each member had a chance to provide their insight or we increased the number of open-ended questions to encourage debate. These small changes to the meeting structure helped increase engagement and remind everyone that our "one team" behavior was still critical. Daily "stand-up" meetings were used to validate that everyone was being productive but also to check in that each person was emotionally connected. Beyond the day-to-day work, it was important that all leaders engaged with each team member on a personal level. Everyone had a unique situation and understanding that allowed us to customize how we could help them be the best at work and at home. We learned the importance of caring about each other and listening to each other, a lesson we have to keep with us beyond the pandemic.

2. Growing Your Professional Network and Maintaining Mentor and Sponsor Relationships

Have your mentees been asking different questions than under usual working conditions? Have you needed to do more hand-holding? Do you see more mentees seeking career change or seeking educational opportunities? Something else?

Mentoring is always an important role as an executive, but it became even more important during the pandemic. Combining remote with the increase in home and personal responsibilities challenges all of us. Many team members had to balance multiple children learning remotely, parents that needed support for suppliers or food delivery, and the health of family members. During this time, my mentee questions transitioned from "how do I get to the next level" to "how do I maintain my position and potential." In my experience, my mentees were as productive, if not more productive, during the pandemic, but because their work and personal lives were more intertwined, they were concerned with the perception. I found that when we discussed what was working and what was accomplished, they quickly realized their continued contribution, and this allowed the conversation to return to future opportunities. I think that it is important as we continue in a unique work environment that team members continue to move their careers forward including adding responsibilities, learning new technologies, seeking opportunities for extended assignments with employee resource groups, and transitioning to new positions. Rotations are an important growth component of any career, and the pandemic or working location should not limit this opportunity. During the remote work environment, my team on-boarded nearly 70 new college hires. While it was different, it was effective. A new role for an experienced hire can be just as effective, so my coaching to my mentees was to continue with their development and growth plans. Agile leadership is more than just learning new technology, it is also learning how to work differently when required, and the pandemic gave us an opportunity to demonstrate this skill.

3. Personal Growth

Have you developed new behaviors (exercise, diet, meditation, hobbies, etc.) that help you get through this new stress?

The pandemic certainly changed my schedule! I had historically had a very consistent routine that included my daily commute and focus in the office followed by my set gym schedule on my way home from work, which forced a discipline that I valued. I did not realize the value of that schedule until it was turned upside down. Like so many of us, I had to adjust to remote work and move other key routines, like fitness, to my home. While we're fortunate to be able to do work and exercise at home, there's no doubt that combining activities with the family environment created stress. To rebuild some normalcy, I added back the structure of the commute and gym to my new environment. I established a dedicated workspace at home and would even "pack my lunch" to take to work in the house! I also adopted the same schedule I had for my workouts at the gym to our home gym. I "reserved" that time on my schedule and in my plan so that my husband knew I was going to be using the equipment and could schedule around that as well. It helped me by bringing back the separation to mentally focus on the different elements of my life. I recognized during the pandemic that we all needed to establish routines and schedules that focused on bringing our "best self" to all parts of our lives...work, wellness, and family.

4. Diversity, Equity, and Inclusion

There has been a lot of talk about diversity—and, in recent years, inclusion. Equity has entered the corporate conversation in a major way this year. What actions are you and your company taking? Are these methods aligned with company goals?

Diversity and inclusion have always been important in our organization. General Motors has a very strong set of Employee Resource Groups that help to foster community, sharing, and growth. In the spring of 2020, the George Floyd incident raised the visibility of the inclusion challenges in our country, and our company responded quickly. Our Chairman and CEO, Mary Barra, spoke up—committing GM to the goal of becoming the most inclusive company in the world and welcomed other companies to follow. She initiated an Inclusion Advisory Board of leaders within and outside of the company to drive how GM would pursue that goal, and grow its citizenship. In the summer, the company rolled out a new core behavior to our seven existing cultural behaviors—Be Inclusive. This was a clear message to all employees that inclusion was the only way we would win as a company. The focus was to welcome ideas from all team members regardless of their level in the organization, their gender, race, or heritage. But beyond that, it also set an expectation that we would have difficult and sometimes awkward conversations about inclusion so we could move forward together as a team. The simple addition of a new behavior does not change everything, but it clearly provides a reminder for us to lead in an inclusive manner in every situation, every day.

5. Sustainability

Human capital—employee talent—is one ultimate driver of business and company success. Aligning talent to sustainability trends has proven to be a winning approach for recruiting, retaining, and developing top talent because employees want to do more with their careers ... and do good while also doing well. Have you and your company moved to incorporate sustainability into your strategies for attracting, retaining, and developing your human capital?

General Motors has a clear vision for our future—Zero Crashes, Zero Emissions, Zero Congestion. We call it our "Zero Zero Zero" vision, and it helps define a direction for the entire organization. Sustainability comes in many forms for companies, and we lead in several areas with our Chief Sustainability Officer focusing on plant and office transformation to be one of the most environmentally sustainable companies on the planet. This is critical, but our overall vision for zero emissions really resonates with the team and future team members on the company's true commitment to the future of the planet. It is not just something we do; it is who we are and what our products will help deliver. In 2020, we took the opportunity from the pandemic to accelerate Electric Vehicles (EV) development. In 2020, GM released details of its all-new Ultium battery platform, the key to our commitment to launch more than 20 EVs over the next few years. Two of the first examples of this technology will be the upcoming Cadillac Lyriq and the all-new Hummer EV, the world's first all-electric super truck. This accelerated technology development has big implications for talent. GM announced recently our plan to add 3,000 tech jobs—in areas like IT, AI, data science, and other disciplines. In the industry, the talent war for technology expertise continues. We believe that the next generation of technologists want to solve more than just technology problems, they want to change the world. Our "Zero Zero Zero" vision does just that, it commits to changing transportation for this generation and generations to come.

Alisyn Malek

Executive Director
Commission on the Future of Mobility

Background

Alisyn Malek is Executive Director for the Commission on the Future of Mobility, which aims to reshape the transportation policy globally across environmental, safety, and economic opportunity considerations to achieve stronger outcomes.

Prior to this role, her unparalleled understanding of how automotive and innovative technologies work together inspired her to co-found May Mobility, building an autonomous vehicle (AV) transportation solution that would solve urban transportation challenges ahead of the competition. As COO, she grew the company from laboratory concept to operations in three states and a strong pipeline for growth in less than three years creating the finance, marketing, sales, customer support, and field operations teams. Alisyn started her career as an engineer working on electric vehicle charging technology at General Motors before moving to their corporate venture arm, leading investments across electrification, connected vehicles, mobility, and autonomy.

She was recognized as an *Automotive News* All Star in 2019 and a top ten female innovator to watch by Smithsonian in 2018 and named a top automotive professional under 35 to watch by LinkedIn in 2015 for her work in cutting-edge product development and corporate venture.

Questions and Answers

1. Change Control, Resilience, and Work/Life Balance

How has your self-motivation been to excel, learn, reach out (virtually), and manage all aspects of your new work life?

When I was 8 years old, I was a bit precocious. It was Christmas time, and my older sister and I were so very curious as to what *Santa* might bring us that we started hunting the house. We searched high and low and eventually found the gifts. My mom found out about our successful snooping, and as a firm believer in *Christmas Magic*, with a 6-month-old baby to preserve that magic for, she set some consequences. I still remember the key lesson she hoped to impart, "those who don't believe don't receive."

As part of our consequences for snooping out the gifts, instead of getting to play with our new toys on Christmas morning, we would go with our dad to volunteer with Meals-on-Wheels, delivering meals to those who did not have family to celebrate the holiday with. My older sister and I loaded into the truck with our dad and went to get our assignment. We picked up 10 meals and set out on our way. When we stopped at the first house, all three of us went up and knocked on the door. As the elderly woman came to the door, the smile that lit up on her face washed all my eight-year-old devastation away. My sister and I had found the true *Christmas Magic*, in helping to uplift others, even when we were so down. From there, we could not wait to get to the next house, and the house after that, to continue spreading joy. However, I learned a valuable lesson that when I am feeling down and out, looking outward to help others will always help get me out of that funk.

2020 was a year for finding low spots and funks. Between the pandemic and trying to switch careers at the start of it to managing lingering health issues brought on by years of stress, I personally had some very low moments. In my lowest of moments, I had the opportunity to help my network. Some people were out of work and some people were looking for great hires. I worked hard, not to get out of my funk, but to help get those great people into new roles that would help fulfill them professionally and bring them balance personally. Those efforts helped to get me out of the lowest points of my year and continue building forward.

2. Growing Your Professional Network and Maintaining Mentor and Sponsor Relationships

Are you continuing to grow your professional network while being remote? How?

By the nature of changing to a role that was planned to be full-time remote, I was somewhat prepared that I would have to be building relationships with new people remotely. I have had experience with that before, from working with teams halfway around the globe to leading distributed teams in the USA. In both cases, the people I built relationships with were people who had already hired in, or I at least had the chance to go meet them in person during the hiring process. I also am an introvert who determined a decade ago to start improving my network. Since then I have maintained relationships with people I worked with as an early career engineer, mentors from my stint in venture capital and partners I worked with in the founding of my own startup.

My network helped me land a job during a pandemic. This new remote job brought on a new type of challenge. I had to recruit the most important person of my team, in a space where I have no background, for an organization that was yet to be announced, and I had to do it all remotely. I was fortunate to have a specific request for my limited network: "do you know of anyone that would like to be the policy director of my new commission that wants to upend how mobility policy is approached globally?"

From the network I have grown to date, I have a few friends that have strong networks in the mobility policy space, and I asked them to make introductions to people that might be interested in the role. Most of the individuals I was introduced to were ultimately not interested, but that did not end up being a setback. With the introductions from my friends, I would take the approach of "do you know of anyone, including yourself, that might be interested?" This took some pressure off the individuals as it no longer felt so much like a job interview and more of a conversation. I got to know some great thought leaders in mobility policy, which is a space that was new to me, and eventually met the person who would become my policy director as well.

I keep in touch with many of the people to whom I was introduced and know that we are valuable network nodes to have, even though there might not have been something for either of us in this first specific ask. However, by starting specific, it gave us some common ground from which to start our discussion, instead of just a generic "Hi, I would like to learn about what you know about mobility policy." We got to dive into areas like their background, interest, and other people in their network. It was a more bounded, and yet still open-ended, question that allowed us to kick off our relationship and allowed me to learn much more about my expanded network.

3. Personal Growth

Have you developed new behaviors (exercise, diet, meditation, hobbies, etc.) that help you get through this new stress?

I left a job as a co-founder of a fast-paced startup in January 2020 in the hopes that I could refocus my life and tackle the unhealthy side effects of so many years of high stress. At that point, I had stress-induced insomnia, weight gain, and zero emotional resilience. In February of 2020, I set out on what I thought would be a four- to six-week quest to rebalance myself, reduce my stress and then get back at it. The end of that timeline lined up precisely with the start of pandemic quarantine.

I will admit that I had not really made it far enough in the six weeks, including some "breaks" in my good habits, to be out of the woods. Quarantine was going to take what I had started as a brief aside and force me into adopting the changes full time. The changes were simple, but consistency was the key, and quarantine created the monotony that supported the consistency. I workout four times a week and eat a healthier, more balanced diet. Over the summer I switched my weight training sessions to online yoga. I know I should meditate more to help manage stress, but I am terrible at meditating on my own. My yoga studio tends to include meditation in their sessions, and I find this is a nice way of sneaking it in.

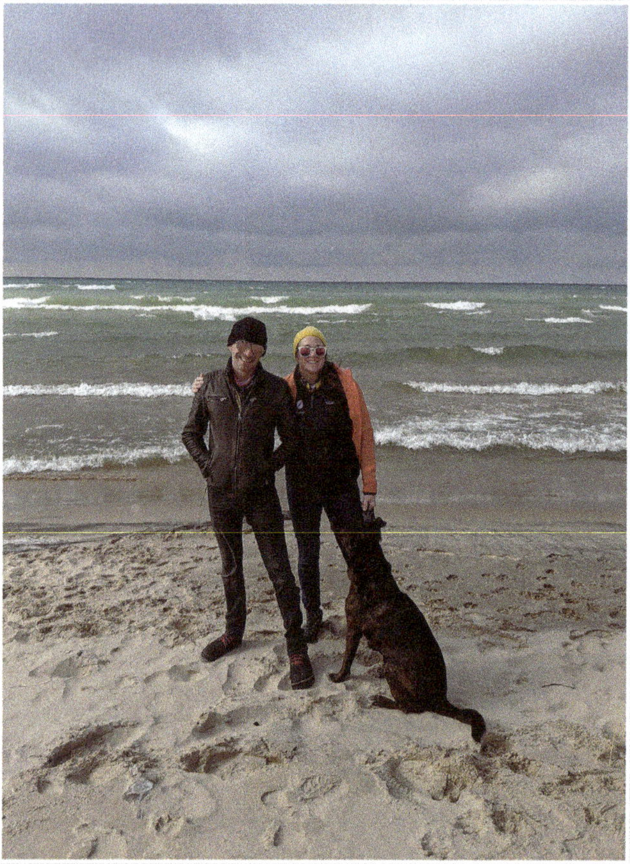

Alisyn Malek

Recently, I was talking to a therapist about meditation techniques, and I included how bad I was at making it a habit. I just can't force myself to sit and clear my mind for 15 minutes. She talked about studies that have shown that taking the time to free-form write, physically put pen to paper and write whatever comes to mind, for 20 minutes a day can be as effective as meditating. I was already the type of person to pick up a pen and paper when something was troubling me, to try to help get it out of my head, so this advice made sense. That has been the latest addition to my stress management technique set, and it has been incredibly helpful. From putting form to unformed concerns that would probably sneak up on me and get me very anxious in a few weeks to managing the emotion of a sudden suicide in the family, writing has helped me to make sense of my current stress and emotions and get out ahead of them instead of letting them get out ahead of me. One specific example was a vague sense of dread in bringing the new team member I had hired, even though I was very excited to work with them. As I wrote about my concerns, I realized I wasn't dreading the team member joining, I was worried that I had not been clear about what all we needed to be working on. This helped me to focus more clearly on setting a goal plan for 2021 instead of misdirecting my angst toward the action of growing my team.

4. Diversity, Equity, and Inclusion

There has been a lot of talk about diversity—and, in recent years, inclusion. Equity has entered the corporate conversation in a major way this year. What actions are you and your company taking? Are these methods aligned with company goals?

As a female who has worked in underrepresented fields like engineering and finance, I have a level of comfort in breaking molds and being "outside the norm." However, as a white female that was privileged enough to grow up in a comfortable suburb and attend a prestigious university, I also know that I have not had a lot of exposure to other types of molds to be broken. This is really important to the work I am doing currently, as I need to make sure that we have a diverse set of viewpoints helping to shape the policy recommendations that are going to impact people the world over.

It was with this awareness that I gladly attended a meeting for a program some of my colleagues had signed up for, which helps to bring more people of color into environmental advocacy. I had been working on some job descriptions, trying to keep the language open and welcoming, while still being expressive of the experience I would hope a candidate could bring. As we were talking with our coach, he brought up a simple point of something missing that could help broaden consideration from a more diverse candidate set. The job posting did not include a salary range or any details about benefits.

I was so busy worrying about what I was looking for, I had forgotten to think about what the candidates would be looking for, beyond an exciting-sounding job. For those looking to break the mold, they may not have fallback plans or insurance through a partner. Knowing not only that the job will be interesting but will provide for their basic needs is a real concern, one that I have too but was not able to boil down so succinctly. Especially for entry-level jobs in some spaces, the pay can be barely enough to make ends meet, and you might be lucky to get basic benefits like health insurance. For many candidates, this is make-or-break for deciding to apply for a job. Although the concern tends to fall away a bit as you get to an executive level, sharing that information still helps to level the playing field, so everyone knows what they can ask for. It was a very useful lesson that will stick with me on how I can make sure that I am growing diversity in my teams by growing the candidate pool that will consider the position. If I don't work to have diverse perspectives on my team, I know that I would not be able to provide appropriately focused research and subsequent conclusions that will help to shape policy decisions related to mobility for decades. This is why I think it is so important to start at recruiting and make sure that I can attract a broad array of candidates.

5. Sustainability

Sustainability trends (climate change, water availability, health, etc.) are some of the strongest drivers for future changes for companies and their strategies. What are you seeing within your company? Is your firm reading the trends and adapting strategies to survive and then thrive with new growth?

I have had the opportunity to work on sustainability issues since the start of my career. I have a passion for clean energy and had the opportunity to start my career working on electric vehicles. I then moved into strategy where I was working with an automaker to think about how they could bring autonomous vehicles (AVs) to market.

As we had our discussions about rideshare use cases and the sale of individual vehicles, the concept of vehicle miles traveled (VMT) came up often. This is the idea of essentially how many miles a vehicle travels in a given time, say a day or a year. We were talking about a brand-new technology that had the potential to fundamentally change the entire way everyone and everything moves around, and the team sitting around the table felt that they had no way to impact, positively or negatively, what VMT would be in this future. It was disappointing.

Recent reports were finding that rideshare companies like Uber and Lyft, were driving increases in VMT and heavy congestion and related slowing traffic in cities. With all of that in mind, I found it hard to believe that one of the largest corporations, at the dawn of a totally new approach to mobility, would sit back and take the approach of "well, we'll just have to wait and see what happens." So, I left. I co-founded an autonomous vehicle transportation company that would go about things differently. By working with communities from the start, we could work to avoid some of the unintended consequences of how people have historically approached transportation in the US.

It was a great experience, but as I got more involved in working with communities, I came to appreciate how separately all the issues of mobility are managed from a community's perspective. Economic development, the approach to creating jobs for people including finding the land and courting the new employers, was done with no regard to how people would get to those new jobs. Focus on preparing for electric AVs pulled attention in many communities away from current needs like providing better infrastructure for walking and biking, even those changes would ultimately help make AVs safer. EV advocates in communities saw their work as completely separate from carpooling or cycling initiatives, all which can help reduce the impact of mobility on our environment.

The more I was exposed to, the more I realized that no one, or at least very few people, was looking at the big picture. The big picture that considers all the factors together in how we build out our mobility system—from the vehicles to the services that provide the transportation and the infrastructure that we use. I left my startup with the intention to push the industry forward, to try to help more companies see this big picture and find ways to collaborate with each other and with the government, to help create a future with more positive environmental and social outcomes through mobility. I am doing this with my work at the Commission on the Future of Mobility. What I think has been so exciting is how many companies recognize this need and opportunity, are ready to think differently, and have signed on to join our work.

Debbie Manzano

Director of Manufacturing—Transmission, Driveline, and Powertrain Components
North America Vehicle Operations
Ford Motor Company

Background

Debbie Manzano is Director of Manufacturing of Transmission, Driveline, and Powertrain Components, serving in this role since January 2021.

In this role, she is responsible for five manufacturing plants in the US including Livonia Transmission, Van Dyke Transmission, Sharonville Transmission, Sterling Axle, and Rawsonville Components Plant.

Debbie Manzano

Previously, Manzano served as Plant Manager of the Dearborn Truck Plant, a role she held since 2018. She led the successful launch of the all-new 2021 F-150 and the groundbreaking of the Rouge Electric Vehicle Center. Prior to that, she was the plant manager of the Flat Rock Assembly Plant and Ohio Assembly Plant. Manzano began her career in manufacturing 26 years ago as a Quality Engineer at Dearborn Glass Plant. Debbie is a second-generation Ford employee and is proud to be part of the Ford Family. Manzano joined Ford in 1994. She holds a Bachelor of Science in Math and Statistics and a Master of Science in Industrial Engineering from the University of Michigan. Debbie's husband is also a Ford employee, and she has two stepchildren.

Debbie Manzano

Manzano is a Board Member of the Women of Ford. She loves being part of the collaborative and energetic Employee Resource Group.

Manzano recently earned honors in the *Automotive News* Top 100 Women in Leadership report.

Questions and Answers

1. Change Control, Resilience, and Work/Life Balance

How do you and your team continue to innovate and improve?

As Plant Manager of an automotive assembly plant, I have been back to work since April. Starting the factory back up in the middle of a pandemic created a challenge it took my whole team to accomplish. We had to learn how to operate under new COVID safety protocols. We had to consider the emotional toll it took on employees, and some people were scared, to say the least. Our key to success was communication, being present, and being accessible to let everyone know we were in this together.

During the short period of the lockdown, we all worked from home, we continued to hold daily meetings to plan for the resumption of production and stay connected. We worked as a team in the fast-changing environment. We learned together and looked out for one another while building America's best-selling truck! We had to learn how to safely operate a factory of approximately 4,500 people in the middle of a pandemic.

This had never been done before. We had an amazing team of people, a playbook to guide us, and a joint leadership team that made it happen. We developed and executed Ford's processes, which included social-distancing rules, cleaning protocols, PPE (personal protective equipment) requirements (i.e., masks), people flow, and temperature scans, to name a few. We held virtual town halls for all salaried employees so we could educate them on what to expect when they returned to work. We reviewed Ford's playbook and what everyone's role would be in keeping people safe. We had to overcome high absenteeism, become creative with the operating pattern, and establish extraordinary quality plans in a different way.

As the pandemic continued, we have improved at managing in this new way. We launched the new 2021 F-150 and all-new Hybrid version during this time. We have established a hybrid approach with our time and data management—using technology to make it happen. Webex Teams has become an enabler for sharing and communicating information to quickly solve problems at a distance. We have established efficiencies with our cleaning protocols and a daily layered audit for safety to ensure our employees stay safe. The pandemic will end, but as a result, we will be stronger and more flexible for future challenges.

2. Growing Your Professional Network and Maintaining Mentor and Sponsor Relationships

How do you keep your existing relationships in this remote world? Are you maintaining face time with other execs while being remote? How do your direct reports maintain their face time with you?

As mentioned earlier, as Plant Manager of an assembly plant, we have been back to work since April. We use our large conference room to hold meetings with everyone socially distanced. We always have a Webex available for anyone working from home or not comfortable joining a meeting in person. I am still mentoring several men and women. I schedule Webex meetings with anyone outside the plant or not able to meet in person. Even since COVID has begun, I am meeting with new employees via phone or Webex. As I am transitioning into my new role as Director of Manufacturing, I will be working out of multiple plants, which will give me an opportunity to interact with many new team members and develop new relationships, whether online or in person. There are team members that I no longer see as regularly due to the pandemic. For those team members, we have developed cadences to Zoom together to get some face time and share our stories and catch up. We know it is important to stay connected even while we have had to stay apart.

I have spent time talking with people from my past positions because of the pandemic. People have been calling to find out how things are going during this challenging time. I have also reached out to people to find out how they have been affected.

3. Personal Growth

Have you developed new behaviors (exercise, diet, meditation, hobbies, etc.) that help you get through this new stress?

I have been doing yoga practice for over 10 years and have never had to do it virtually—until now. Everything I was used to changed overnight. I was in lockdown with my husband due to the threat of the virus, and as a result, we were working from home and I was practicing yoga virtually. I knew it was better than not practicing but had to get used to this new way of doing yoga. It had its challenges: space, environment, technology, to name a few. Eventually, I was able to create my own yoga space at home and have recently added a reformer and elliptical. This new at-home "gym" was never in my plans, but plans change, and we learn to adapt.

About five years ago, I decided to deepen my yoga practice and registered for 200-hour yoga teacher training. I had no expectation to teach and really didn't even have a goal for the class when I signed up. I just knew yoga was good for me (physically and mentally) and wanted to learn more. After about seven weeks of staying home, it was time to go back to work and start the factory up. With the additional stress of work due to the pandemic challenges, I felt my yoga practice was not enough. During the pandemic, I took a yoga workshop (which was virtual due to the concerns with the virus). During the workshop, the host discussed the possibility of doing a 300-hour teacher training and asked if we would be interested in doing it virtually. It was a sign and I knew it was meant to be. I took the leap and made the commitment.

I signed up for a "virtual" 300-hour teacher training, which is a natural progression for yogis. Yoga is more than just the physical practice; it includes the breathing, the meditation, and the spiritual journey too. I am grateful that the pandemic has given me this opportunity to deepen my practice and continue my journey.

4. Diversity, Equity, and Inclusion

Are men engaged in the conversation around gender diversity and, if so, in what way?

I am on the board for Women of Ford, which is an employee resource group at Ford Motor Company. Our vision is to be the leading company for the empowerment and development of women with a mission to create an inclusive environment that fosters authenticity and equality. We have developed strategic imperatives to support and guide our work. Engaging men in the conversation around gender diversity is one of the imperatives I lead "Men As Advocates and Allies" for the Women of Ford. The team is a cross-functional group from leaders around the globe made up of both men and women. Our goal is to develop male advocates, using metrics, education, and leading by example. We have programs such as mentorship, a how-to for sponsorship, and tips for being an ally.

Men are stepping up and seeing that diversity and inclusion are good not only for the people and the culture but for the business. The commitment by men to sponsor, professionally develop and support women throughout the company and the communities we serve, is evident and continues to grow. It is impactful when men make the connection to their own daughters. This makes it personal, and they have an obligation to support gender diversity at work for the future of their own daughter's success. Engaging men in the conversation is important, and we are doing this at all levels of the company through dialogue sessions, shared experiences with co-workers on panels, and speed networking, not to mention numerous events to engage them. International Women's Day is also an outstanding way to get the word out and bring us together to learn and support one another.

5. Sustainability

Sustainability trends (climate change, water availability, health, etc.) are some of the strongest drivers for future changes for companies and their strategies. What are you seeing within your company? Is your firm reading the trends and adapting strategies to survive and then thrive with new growth?

Ford Motor Company has been an environmentally conscious company for a long time. The Dearborn Truck Plant (DTP), Ford's newest manufacturing facility which opened in 2004, was built with the environment in mind. DTP has a living roof created to attract birds and other wildlife. Skylights were installed for natural light. In addition, porous concrete was poured in our parking lots, which allows water to filter through it.

Ford is constantly changing when it comes to its product lineup. Ford has launched hybrid versions of many of its products and most recently launching the all-new electric Mach-E Mustang.

At DTP, the change is visible right outside my back door. We have broken ground for an all-new Rouge Electric Vehicle Center to manufacture the all-new F-150 electric truck. If this doesn't say Ford is changing, I don't know what does. Under our new CEO, "the Plan" is very clear, and our new truck is part of the change the company is making to adapt to the industry trends to provide more sustainable mobility solutions. In addition, we are using new technologies to make our factories smarter and helping our people work more efficiently, safer and effectively.

Ford was one of the large corporations that jumped in to help provide the much-needed PPE for our first responders and medical professionals during the COVID pandemic. Ford produced face masks, face shields, PAPRs, and respirators during the pandemic. Ford is still producing face masks that it provides to its employees and donates to those in need.

Ford Motor Company's continued investment in technology and the environment makes employees proud to say they work for the company.

Darci Marcum

Lansing Grand River Assembly Plant Director
General Motors

Background

Darci Marcum was named General Motors (GM) Lansing Grand River Assembly (LGR) Plant Director in January 2019.

In this role, she leads the operations for GM LGR. LGR has over 1,400 employees that produce the Chevrolet Camaro and Cadillac CT4 and CT5 that are all shipped globally.

Prior to becoming the LGR Plant Director, Darci was Assistant Plant Director of Arlington Assembly Plant in Texas. She successfully led plant operations for the global home of GM's award-winning, full-size SUVs—the Chevrolet Tahoe and Suburban, GMC Yukon and Yukon XL, as well as the Cadillac Escalade.

Darci joined GM as Production Supervisor at Moraine Assembly in 1994. Throughout her career, she has held positions in a variety of manufacturing operations with increasing responsibility within the U.S. and international assignments in Canada.

Darci holds a bachelor's degree in Industrial Management/Engineering from Purdue University and earned her MBA from the University of Dayton. Darci is a member of the Lansing Regional Chamber board and the Sparrow Hospital Foundation Board.

Darci and her husband, Josh, have one daughter, Lizzi.

Questions and Answers

1. Change Control, Resilience, and Work/Life Balance

Many have said that there is no separation of work and home these days—what do you do to manage this for your own work? What are you doing to increase the ability of your team to create and respect boundaries?

In manufacturing, we've been back in the workplace since the end of May 2020—after working remotely for just over two months. Some people have the impression that working from home is easier or preferable to working in the workplace. The answer is not the same for everyone, and not the same for everyone all the time. For me, I embraced the opportunity to work differently and find positives in all we do.

I don't often say no to meeting invites and requests for assistance from others, as they help me learn and grow. During my "work from home time" there were days with meetings starting at 6 am and 6 pm the same day. However, each day I would carve out time to spend with my daughter who was home with us. We'd go for a bike ride, visit the park, or play board games together each day. She taught me to play video games, I taught her to cook eggs (her favorite breakfast) and how to do long division. Although time together was not scheduled like we'd see in a normal day, we set expectations each day regarding when and how we'd enjoy it.

It is inspiring for me to see my daughter returning to school in a virtual environment. I hear some of the interactions that she has with her school peers, and I'm pleased to see her thriving in this new virtual environment so maturely for her young age. I'd like to think that her observation of my virtual interactions has shaped how she interrelates with her own team.

When it came to our work team, I asked their input regarding the best time of day for us to have our daily huddle and when is best to contact them, if needed. I feel that we were able to accommodate people while accomplishing our goal of preparing a safe workplace to which our team could return.

We did the same with our extended team. Before we left for quarantine, there were some employees who had not utilized virtual meeting tools. We provided the tools and coached them so we could interact virtually on a regular basis and gain their input as part of meeting scheduling decisions. As a result, our team gave us positive comments regarding the communication and connection to the business while out of the plant. Even though we are back in the office now, we continue to use virtual tools to connect with large teams simultaneously.

2. Growing Your Professional Network and Maintaining Mentor and Sponsor Relationships

Has your company maintained learning and leadership development opportunities, culture surveys, 360 surveys, etc. to grow skills and manage the emotional intelligence of the company? Has anything shifted? What have you learned?

GM focuses on creating the best environment for our entire team so that we all feel comfortable and confident in contributing in our workplace. We regularly survey our teams to understand how we are doing and use the results as fuel to continually improve. There is a full survey that is completed periodically and shorter surveys administered in between to give us a quick pulse of the organization.

In addition, twice each year I have the opportunity to give my leader feedback regarding how she is supporting me. My team uses the same process to provide me candid feedback; I am appreciative that GM offers this process. Although I have many examples of candid feedback my team provides to one another as a normal course of business, this is an excellent method to check in using data and examples of ways to further improve.

Feedback is a gift that I try never to squander. Sharing the results with the team has allowed us to open candid dialog about how to improve. Results from the 180 feedback reviews completed earlier this year as compared with later this year show an overall improvement, particularly in the areas that were specifically addressed. This only works when those surveyed are bold in providing feedback and leaders are humble enough to act upon that feedback. I value our team's ability to collaborate openly in this manner. They know I will act on the feedback that they provide, so they are more willing to share candidly.

I have also learned that one size does not fit all. It's rarely practical to survey everyone about everything. However, it is possible to check in with people to gain input quickly. I have a teammate who does this exceptionally well. After a brainstorming session, he will check in with the right stakeholders to get a pulse of the organization. These quick checks help guide our next steps. He's taught me how quickly we can enact change when we attain support regarding the best way to proceed.

3. Personal Growth

What is the most profound impact this pandemic has had the way you think about your job, company, family life? Will it be sticky or do you expect everything to return to the previous status quo?

In my career with GM, I have seen our teams transition plants from green fields and dirt mounds into working facilities, equipped with the latest technology, enabling us to build world-class vehicles. The processes in our plants enable us to build and test vehicles that are so advanced they can be considered moving computers with the highest safety and performance standards and capabilities.

Because of all the amazing things I have seen from the GM team, it is no surprise that we were able to partner with two different ventilator suppliers to help them manufacture thousands of ventilators for hospitals in need. I have so much pride in seeing our company develop processes to create and donate millions of masks for first line responders and address the problem of thousands of ventilators in disrepair, enabling them to be returned to service.

Although our facility was not directly involved in the activities above, I have several team members who were asked to take leadership roles in these new activities. Even though it meant leaving their homes and families during a time of extreme uncertainty, they accepted the challenge without hesitation. They had never built ventilators or even heard of our partner companies. They did it because they knew they could make a difference and could help our communities.

As we prepared our return-to-work plan, our entire manufacturing organization collaborated to create a safe work environment for our teams. Utilizing the CDC recommendations, coupled with key insight from GM's top medical director and safety professionals, GM developed a playbook to manufacture vehicles and vehicle components while in the middle of a global pandemic.

As teams returned to our new work environment, we shared the playbook in detail with them, including how we planned to ensure their safety and what we expected from each of them. Of course, people were nervous, we answered hundreds of questions. Yet once they understood the process and were provided with the data showing its success, they helped us comply, and many have personally thanked us for our leadership role in keeping them safe.

My two major learnings this year: 1) Nothing is impossible when we decide it is critical, dedicate key resources where they can be most effective, and quickly remove any roadblock that arises. 2) Our teams respond positively when we effectively explain why initiatives are important, how their role is key to our success, and that we will support them.

I will carry those two learnings with me as I see our teams consistently exceeding our expectations, and I will apply them again and again.

4. Diversity, Equity, and Inclusion

There has been a lot of talk about diversity—and, in recent years, inclusion. Equity has entered the corporate conversation in a major way this year. What actions are you and your company taking? Are these methods aligned with company goals?

I am proud to work for a company that values diversity and inclusion. On June 1, 2020, Mary Barra wrote a moving letter to our GM team exclaiming her expectations regarding how we work together to commit to inclusion, condemn intolerance, and stand up against racial injustice.

The events of 2020 have called on each of us to reexamine our personal feelings and personal bias. Much of my personal time I spend understanding how I can be a change agent for our team.

On Juneteenth, we observed an 8:46 period of silence for George Floyd. Shortly before and several times after that moment of silence, I have facilitated many conversations about race. These are different from past conversations as people are being more open in their thoughts and I am listening differently. I recognize now that phrases I have used before with good intention could be considered offensive or at least abrasive to people of color. Beliefs that I considered largely universal as "American" are not held by a significant part of the U.S. population. One of the best sources of learning came from our team and their willingness to share.

I also recognize my responsibility to proactively learn about race from the vast resources available. There is no shortage of studies, podcasts, and testimonials available online. When I can't fit in time to read, I find that downloading books allows me to concentrate on listening during long outdoor running sessions. There are some fantastic resources, both old and new, available for free through my local library.

Through all these inputs, I learned that making connections with individuals is key. The "golden" rule to "treat others as **you'd** want to be treated" is outdated.

Rather we can apply the "platinum" rule to "treat others as **they** want to be treated." For us to do this well, we must know what people want, and we learn that by connecting personally.

Under Mary Barra's leadership, GM has initiated an Inclusion Advisory Board composed of both internal and external members that Mary chairs. At our facility in Lansing, we have formed an Inclusion Leadership Team with volunteers willing to be change agents in our facility. This idea came from one of our listening sessions. We see them not as solely responsible for inclusion rather as key facilitators to help us increase our engagement throughout our facility as part of our journey in becoming the world's most inclusive company. I am excited to see our progress in 2021.

5. Sustainability

Sustainability trends (climate change, water availability, health, etc.) are some of the strongest drivers for future changes for companies and their strategies. What are you seeing within your company? Is your firm reading the trends and adapting strategies to survive and then thrive with new growth?

GM has boldly declared that we are committed to a future with Zero Crashes, Zero Emissions, and Zero Congestion. As we commit to an all-electric future, we are looking ahead to how we can reuse or recycle our electric vehicle batteries when they reach the end of their useful life. We are challenging ourselves to maximize the use of sustainable materials in building our vehicles and increasing the reuse or recycling vehicle content. We are challenging our facilities to be zero waste. In addition, we plan to fuel our plants with 100% renewable energy, domestically by 2030 and globally by 2040.

Other organizations are noticing our efforts and results. GM was recently awarded as the Leader in Sustainability by the Business Intelligence Group. We have received the 2020 Energy Star Partner of the Year Sustained Excellence Award for continued leadership and superior contributions to Energy Star, making this the ninth year GM has received an Energy Star award.

At our facility in Lansing, we challenge our teams to look for waste streams that we can either eliminate or convert to recycling. We reduced our energy and water usage on a per-unit basis this year as compared with last year, and we engage and empower our teams to eliminate waste in all they do.

Our teams are also encouraged to partner with the community. Recently, we sponsored a section of the Lansing River Trail, and our team has already made a positive impact on this treasure that is widely used by those in and around Lansing. Our facility received four Neighborhood Environmental Partner awards in 2020 for the nine activities we recently supported. The Neighborhood Environmental Partners recognizes environmental projects and partners who have worked together to improve the environment in their community. These are all events where we work with local community partners, elementary and middle schools to promote environmental education and stewardship.

Gail May

Division Manager
Honda of America Mfg., Inc.

Background

Gail May is the division manager for the Performance Manufacturing Center (PMC), the production location for the Acura NSX supercar and home to several exclusive "PMC Edition" Acura models. In her position, she provides leadership and direction for all production operations and is also responsible for strategic planning and implementation of initiatives to continuously exceed the expectations of Honda and Acura customers.

May joined Honda in 1993 with a BS in Mechanical Engineering from the Ohio State University. Her career started as an engineering staff associate in the product engineering development department at the Marysville Auto Plant. Here she served in a number of automotive quality and technical roles, each with increasing levels of responsibility, that led toward the successful deployment of several new models.

In 2005, May was promoted to operations manager where she had the opportunity to learn more deeply about the business side of the automotive world. In this role, May was responsible for staffing, managing the department budget, establishing business practices, and refining internal systems. Soon after, May was promoted to department manager, where she established and communicated the department vision, created strategic business plans, managed the daily activities and personnel to achieve defined targets and led the new model teams through multiple vehicle deployments including the Honda Accord, Acura RDX, and Acura TL.

In 2012, May was awarded the opportunity to join the Acura NSX new model development team which she credits as being one of the most exciting challenges of her career. Since being at the PMC, May has had responsibilities for the development of the facility, the systems and products. Through these roles as the NSX manufacturing quality project leader, the plant quality leader, and the technical leader for both new model and mass production activities, May's career in manufacturing leadership further advanced her to her current responsibility of running the only supercar manufacturing facility in North America.

Questions and Answers

1. Change Control, Resilience, and Work/Life Balance

How do you keep team spirit with your direct reports? Are you sensing any lack of trust or more trust? What factors/actions have the most effect on trust/lack of trust?

In all of my various roles at Honda, I've made it a point to get to know the other associates. Not only do I know their names, titles, and job responsibilities, but I also learn about their families and interests. Now more than ever, it is important to support one another personally and professionally. So transparency and leading by example have proven to be a successful combination, especially through the uncertain times we find ourselves in today.

As leaders, we need to ensure our teams know we are there for them. Throughout the pandemic, I have made it a priority to safely maintain a daily presence in the manufacturing plant. When the decision was made to allow many of our associates who typically work onsite to work remotely, I continued to make it a priority to connect virtually. Connecting via video conference meetings in the morning and at the end of the day helps reinforce the fact that even though we are not physically together in the plant, we are still a team.

Everyone talks about the importance of communication, and for me, that means it is important to share with my team not just what we are going to do but why we are doing it. My experience has been that once people understand the reasons behind the decisions that are being made, while they may not always like the direction, this level of information sharing builds trust in their leadership.

2. Growing Your Professional Network and Maintaining Mentor and Sponsor Relationships

How do you keep your existing relationships in this remote world? Are you maintaining face time with other execs while being remote? How do your direct reports maintain their face time with you?

It is important to me that associates always feel I'm approachable, no matter the topic. Oddly enough, during the pandemic, I feel I've had more time to interact with associates—either from six feet away or through a computer screen. With travel restrictions in place, I'm at the manufacturing plant more, which has allowed me to stay closer to home and closer to our associates in Ohio.

At the onset of the COVID pandemic, Honda worked quickly to put a good plan in place for many of our associates to work remotely. Even though the world seemed to come to a halt, the decision-making process for our team did not sit still. New safety protocols, masks, and social distancing became a part of our everyday conversations and quickly became key components for how we conducted business.

Despite our best efforts, like many other companies, we were challenged to find new and creative ways to engage outside of our normal production environment. When remote work hit its peak, my leadership team implemented a pyramid communication approach that involves a daily virtual meeting with our management group, and then those members hold virtual meetings with their teams.

The work and meetings continue, but with a completely new look and feel. Even when associates are working remotely, technology has provided us with the opportunity to keep our team members connected, engaged, and involved in our business.

3. Personal Growth

What is the most profound impact this pandemic has had on the way you think about your job, company, family life? Will it be sticky or do you expect everything to return to the previous status quo?

People are creatures of habit and do not like change. I soon realized that my own behaviors, attitudes, and words had a tremendous impact on the overall spirit and morale of the team. This is something I always knew; however, it was amplified, especially in the early days of the pandemic. In March when Honda halted production at all our automotive facilities in North America, my team looked to me for answers expecting that I would navigate them through this unknown situation, but it was unknown to me as well. We were receiving information daily about the virus and using that to create a safe working environment for our associates. This is where leadership prevailed. I continue to be proud of how we are navigating through these challenging times.

This COVID crisis involved Honda having to make a very difficult decision, as did the other automakers, when we suspended production across our operations. Given the health crisis our country faced, it was determined this was the best solution for our associates and the long-term health of the company. I am proud of how our associates and our company responded during this challenging time. I think we are a stronger company today because we were forced to reinvent ourselves and find new ways to do business.

I believe we also learned some valuable lessons along the way. First, nothing is a guarantee. Second, flexibility is key, and finally, we must remain agile, thinking outside the box.

4. Diversity, Equity, and Inclusion

Is the board of directors of your company diverse and representative of your workforce and/or customers? Is the leadership team? Is the workforce? If the workforce and customers aren't currently diverse, is there greater interest and commitment to making change in this regard?

As the auto industry and Honda evolve to meet the needs of our customers in the future, it is critical that we retain and nurture diverse leadership by providing opportunities for growth for all associates.

At Honda, we have formal activities like Business Resource Groups (BRG), ten of which are targeted to women at Honda across North America. We also have programs like our Leader Advancement Mentor Program (LAMP), which is a yearlong experience designed to accelerate the advancement of high-potential associates into executive leadership.

While Honda, as well as many other companies, have formal training and mentoring programs, I encourage everyone, but especially women, to be proactive and search on their own for mentors as well as sponsors. Mentors are very important because they help teach you how to think and how to navigate through your career, and sponsors are critical because they are your advocates, your voice in the room when you're not in it.

I am very grateful for the mentors I have had throughout my career, and most especially for my very first mentor who later became one of my sponsors, Clement D'Souza. He was the first leader of the Performance Manufacturing Center and has been a phenomenal support system to me. Being a present and active mentor, as well as a sponsor, is what great leadership is all about, as it is important that we never forget to pull the next generation up.

True and sustainable change requires action by senior leaders to hold themselves accountable to foster and advance diversity throughout all leadership ranks. And it is the responsibility of associates throughout the organization to be allies of diverse associates and to speak up in support of their colleagues to ensure they get the opportunities they deserve.

5. Sustainability

Sustainability trends (climate change, water availability, health, etc.) are some of the strongest drivers for future changes for companies and their strategies. What are you seeing within your company? Is your firm reading the trends and adapting strategies to survive and then thrive with new growth?

Protecting our environment is a top priority at Honda. I've seen firsthand the work being done, especially at my facility, the Performance Manufacturing Center (PMC). Our team is extremely proud of the Acura NSX, the world's first supercar to use hybrid electric motors to enhance and elevate every element of its dynamic performance, a proof point toward our ability to develop vehicles that incorporate Honda's environmental vision.

I am very familiar with this because my role over the past eight years has focused on NSX production at PMC, where the concept of sustainability was not just limited to the design of Acura's halo supercar. We have also created some unique production technologies and processes specifically designed for the NSX, keeping the importance of Honda's environmental objectives in mind. One such process involves the use of a zirconium pretreatment for the aluminum-intensive NSX space frame as part of the application of a corrosion-resistant primer. While instrumental for world-class quality, the use of zirconium also reduces environmental waste in the painting process.

Finally, in addition to the NSX design and the processes our team implemented, PMC itself reflects a sustainability initiative. I was a member of the original team that transformed this former warehouse space into a facility that would innovate both the means and the methods of producing low-volume specialty cars. The fact that we were able to bring this building back to life and create a state-of-the-art supercar facility really makes me proud. Together we are truly practicing what we preach when it comes to sustainable initiatives.

These initiatives will help us in our venture for carbon neutrality by 2050, with a strong focus on electrification based on our commitment to reduce global CO2 emissions. Working toward being carbon neutral by 2050, we are additionally targeting two-thirds of our global auto sales to be electrified by 2030.

Telva McGruder

Chief Diversity, Equity, and Inclusion Officer
General Motors

Background

Telva M. McGruder is Chief of Diversity, Equity, and Inclusion at General Motors (GM). Telva leads the development and execution of strategies that will ensure positive change toward a high-performing, inclusive culture. Prior to this role, Telva was Director of Workplace Engineering and Operations Solutions in the Sustainable Workplaces organization. She supported the global footprint for facility engineering, technologies, energy strategy, and multiple facility management strategies.

Earlier in her career, Telva held positions of increasing responsibility and influence within manufacturing engineering and at several manufacturing locations where she motivated teams to rethink the possible in project execution, maintenance, quality, operations, and labor negotiations. Telva earned her BS and MS degrees in Electrical Engineering from Purdue University.

Along with her professional accomplishments, Telva is dedicated to teaching and leading others inside and outside of General Motors. She is a member of the General Motors Inclusion Advisory Board. She is Chair of the Board of Directors for the Girl Scouts of Southeastern Michigan, Vice Chair of the advisory board for the Oakland University School of Health Sciences, a member of the advisory board for the University of Michigan School for Environment and Sustainability, and a member of the Board for Engineering Tomorrow.

Questions and Answers

1. Change Control, Resilience, and Work/Life Balance

How has your self-motivation been to excel, learn, reach out (virtually), and manage all aspects of your new work life?

Whether it's in the office or working remotely, I have a passion for uncovering new insights to solve complex challenges. That passion stems from my curiosity and my avid belief in cultivating the agility required to respond well to constant change. I stay agile by maintaining a diverse slate of topics I'm learning about at any given time. In recent months I have been very grateful that my years of persistence in staying out of my comfort zone and seeking to learn adequately prepared me for the tall challenges that have been thrust upon us. I have been even more motivated to jump in, build relationships, and help lead forward wherever I can, both inside and outside of work.

We have faced—and continue to face—extraordinary obstacles, but in many ways, they have also presented opportunities for us to reimagine who we are in the world, as a company and as individuals. In my new role as Chief of Diversity, Equity, and Inclusion, I am able to identify the key areas that are ripe for development and charge our global team with infusing the behaviors and actions that will create desired outcomes.

Our trajectory is ambitious—we aspire to become the most inclusive company in the world. We are cultivating a people-centered culture of high expectations while advocating for social, racial, and economic justice. In my current role, I combine my passion for solving complex challenges with my purpose to uplift people. Whatever happens, I remain eager and excited to apply the lessons I have learned and walk boldly into the future we're creating.

2. Growing Your Professional Network and Maintaining Mentor and Sponsor Relationships

Have your mentees been asking different questions than under usual working conditions? Have you needed to do more hand-holding? Do you see more mentees seeking career change or seeking educational opportunities? Something else?

Of course, the pandemic has shifted aspects of learning and communicating for many of us. Many of my mentees are eager to understand how they should be thinking about their respective career trajectories during this unprecedented time. They want to ensure they remain relevant, seen, and heard so they may continue their chosen career path in a virtual environment. I coach them on adapting the practices that we've discussed in the past to the virtual environment. There are very few bridges we cannot cross in this new environment. We just need to stay focused on the problem we're trying to solve—whether it be a technical issue or a career question—and adapt our communication patterns as needed in a virtual environment to complete the objective.

My mentees are certainly thinking differently about career options because our virtual environment has opened up new possibilities. I don't see career changes, but I am supporting them in navigating the new opportunities that have become apparent. Many people are struggling with working at work while their children are attending virtual classrooms or working at home with young children that need support in a virtual environment. We encourage our team members to speak up about these challenges, and through the awareness, we provide support mechanisms. We want to help them persevere, knowing that this virtual world is temporary.

Given my role, and the company's focus on diversity, equity, and inclusion (DEI), I have had many conversations with my protégés and many more in the company around racial justice and inclusion. People at all levels in the organization want to know how they can come together to make an impact right now, and they are creating change through their deeds. Overall, people are thinking more consciously about what they want, where they are headed, and how to be a better colleague and a better ally.

3. Personal Growth

Have you developed new behaviors (exercise, diet, meditation, hobbies, etc.) that help you get through this new stress?

2020 was especially challenging for personal growth. Many people were focused on just surviving the pandemic and the economic collapse that has come with it. While it can be a challenge to focus on improving yourself amid chaos, it's so important to continue learning, growing, and maturing in whatever ways you can. Every little bit helps elevate mental and physical energy.

I am fortunate that just before the pandemic hit, I started a yearlong class that requires I focus on a new area of personal growth and development each month. The class schedule and program has kept me on track to invest in evolving my relationships and improve myself physically, spiritually, mentally, and financially. I find that I do my best when I'm constantly striving to improve myself in all aspects of my life, not just professionally.

I've also been meditating a lot more often. Meditation is essential to ground me, maintain balance, and instill mental discipline. With consistent practice, meditation has many positive lasting impacts, including keeping my stress levels under control. I am an avid martial artist and have been for many years. My practice allows me to continually work on self-improvement, and it brings contentment through awareness and control of mind and body.

When handling complex problems like diversity, equity, inclusion, the impact of COVID, and more, I find it important to consciously focus on balancing the negative energy with some positive energy. I purposefully surround myself with positive energy whenever possible. I do that by connecting with my family and friends, staying faithful, reading good books, doing jigsaw puzzles, listening to music, and dancing around the house, just to name a few things. I also bring a healthy dose of optimism to everything that I do. We are good enough.

4. Diversity, Equity, and Inclusion

There has been a lot of talk about diversity—and, in recent years, inclusion. Equity has entered the corporate conversation in a major way this year. What actions are you and your company taking? Are these methods aligned with company goals?

At GM, we have demonstrated our commitment to diversity and inclusion for many years. We are boldly reaching farther than we ever have before as we aspire to be the most-inclusive company in the world. Galvanizing our team and business partners in trust and transparency will further enhance robust collaboration and increase the speed of innovation. These strengths will allow us to not only lead the industry but will allow us to more inclusively impact communities around the world as we transition to an all-electric future. Furthermore, our priorities of leading health and safety culture; supporting and investing in diversity, equity, and inclusion inside and outside of the company; and ensuring a sustainable future are integral to our corporate growth strategy.

Our action framework is based upon the ultimate goal of engaging our entire team in DEI while influencing change that will close gaps in our global communities. We work with our Inclusion Advisory Board to ensure consistent progress aligned with that goal. Some of the initiatives underway include

- We are building on current alliances and establishing new ones to advocate for and achieve equity in social justice, education, healthcare, and economic opportunities for Black and other marginalized groups.
- We are investing in organizations that are closing gaps in racial justice and inclusion.
- We believe our partners should reflect our values and expect them to demonstrate the same level of commitment to diversity, equity, and inclusion. We are engaging with our partners to align on expectations and support their growth in DEI.
- We have adopted enhanced diversity measures as well as talent acquisition and talent development approaches that will create a diversity pipeline that reflects the customers we serve and the communities in which we operate.
- We understand our employees are in different places along their individual journeys. We have developed and continue to develop and curate internal programming to promote inclusive leadership and behaviors throughout the team.
- We are reimagining workforce strategy and evaluating our systems to ensure that all GM employees have equitable, impactful experiences with positive moments that matter.
- We are exploring new pathways to onboard a broader array of talent that will strongly contribute to our outcomes. We believe that skills based hiring opens doors to talent that will thrive in our company, and we are active members of coalitions that will inform our strategies to that end. For example, we joined OneTen, a coalition of 30+ companies and leaders that aim to train and hire one million Black Americans over the next 10 years into family-sustaining jobs with opportunities for advancement.

5. Sustainability

Sustainability trends (climate change, water availability, health, etc.) are some of the strongest drivers for future changes for companies and their strategies. What are you seeing within your company? Is your firm reading the trends and adapting strategies to survive and then thrive with new growth?

At GM, we envision a world with zero crashes, zero emissions, and zero congestion. Now more than ever, sectors must come together to innovate and implement solutions to tackle climate change. We are seeing more businesses and companies step up efforts to reduce their environmental impact, and the need for greater cross-sector collaboration has never been greater. We understand the role the auto industry plays in contributing to climate change, and we embrace the responsibility of not only reducing our footprint but also working with our partners and suppliers to scale impact.

In our journey to realize an all-electric, zero-emissions future, we renamed our Detroit-Hamtramck facility in 2020 as Factory ZERO, the name aligning with our goal of a future with zero emissions. Factory ZERO will be entirely dedicated to manufacturing electric vehicles. The factory was also built with sustainability in mind: during the plant's physical transition, concrete waste and stormwater were repurposed, and the site features a 16.5-acre wildlife habitat and is home to species such as monarchs, foxes, and turkeys.

We also map our efforts and most material priorities to the 17 United Nations (UN) Sustainable Development Goals (SDG), which are forward-looking comprehensive goals meant to ensure peace and prosperity for people and the planet. To date, GM's strategic priorities are aligned with several UNSDG targets, including good health and well-being, industry innovation and infrastructure, energy efficiency, climate action, responsible consumption and production, and decent work and economic growth.

Lastly, we constantly seek opportunities to partner with organizations that share our vision for driving change. There are many pieces to this puzzle, and we cannot do this alone. As we continue to work towards creating a sustainable world, we want to share our resources and expertise, while also learning from others.

Amy Simms McLain

Head of Indirect Purchasing
Stellantis—North America

Background

Amy Simms McLain was named Head of Indirect Purchasing in December 2020. Prior to this role, McLain was Head of Global Supplier Relations and Risk Management responsible for improving supplier and industry relationships, supplier risk management and performance measurement, supplier labor relations, and supplier diversity.

Since first joining the company as a seating and leather buyer in 1996, McLain has garnered extensive experience across various departments, including business development, vehicle safety and regulatory compliance, purchasing, logistics, and supply chain management.

In addition to her core responsibilities, she serves on the board of the Stellantis Women's Alliance Business Resource Group and co-leads its Commerce Committee.

McLain holds a Bachelor of Science degree in Business from Miami University (1996) and a Master of Business Administration degree from Oakland University (2000).

She was born in Richmond, Indiana.

Questions and Answers

1. Change Control, Resilience, and Work/Life Balance

Many have said that there is no separation of work and home these days—what do you do to manage this for your own work? What are you doing to increase the ability of your team to create and respect boundaries?

I agree, there is no separation, and I don't fight it. I keep one calendar that includes both my professional and personal events. This works best for me and helps me carve out time to take care of myself. Throughout the pandemic, I completed my first ultramarathon. To prepare, I had to be very disciplined with my training runs and plan around any conflicts, so I blocked that time on my calendar.

Additionally, in my team, we try to keep Friday afternoons free of meetings. We started this as part of a summer hours' program that encouraged our teams to enjoy the summer weather. But as the summer ended, we decided to make it permanent. We find this allows people time to catch up. The implications of COVID have taught us all to become more accepting that people have personal priorities that may need to happen during the traditional work hours. Many of us had our children at home and were taking on more responsibilities there than we had before. I try to set examples by talking about it and encouraging our teams to open up if they are overwhelmed and take time to take care of themselves and their families.

Finally, I'm very fortunate to be part of a leadership team that has been extremely flexible in terms of who's doing what, and what priorities are most important between our respective teams. While the amount of work remains high, we are ensuring that the workload is dispersed evenly and reassessing it regularly.

2. Growing Your Professional Network and Maintaining Mentor and Sponsor Relationships

Have your mentees been asking different questions than under usual working conditions? Have you needed to do more hand-holding? Do you see more mentees seeking career change or seeking educational opportunities? Something else?

Certainly, the questions are a bit different, and my mentees have wanted to connect more frequently during the pandemic. The main themes that are different involve career development and networking in our virtual environment. Transitioning while remote is challenging, so some feel "stuck" and hesitant to consider developmental moves and instead await the return to normalcy. Others are dealing with the challenges of childcare and are actively seeking more flexible positions.

For other mentees that are very early in their career, the typical on-the-job and shadowing experiences that normally would come as one enters a company are now virtual. The "hands-on" training is limited given the travel restrictions and social distancing. It's a struggle and the learning curve widens. On the other hand, I am seeing others take advantage of this time by pursuing advanced online degrees sooner than they may have otherwise done. To put it bluntly, there is not a ton going on socially right now, and the mindset is that they might as well use this time to pursue an MBA. I remind them that we know there are obvious challenges with connecting, especially as a new employee, so the networking and engagement opportunities with our employee-run business resource groups are even more meaningful ways to get connected.

3. Personal Growth

What is the most profound impact this pandemic has had on the way you think about your job, company, family life? Will it be sticky or do you expect everything to return to the previous status quo?

As it relates to our industry, the pandemic has helped solidify the importance of proactive risk management and supply chain transparency. Stellantis is excellent at crisis management, and now we have the opportunity to experience the benefits of the advanced crisis planning we have enacted. Having a true understanding of the supply chain down to Tier N will continue to be a priority. Beyond this, we need to ensure we keep real-time communication channels open.

Amy Simms McLain

Personally, I used this opportunity to reinforce the importance of health with my team. We need to give attention to the critical actions that protect our health, such as regular exercise, sleep, and healthy eating. The stresses and pressures of work can tempt us to often forego these strategies and that can have a major impact on our well-being. When we as leaders communicate that it's okay and, in fact, are doing what's needed to protect our own health, it takes away those excuses—the guilt—that people might feel when putting their well-being first. During the summer, even while remote, we arranged "walking" meetings to ensure people were moving during the day.

4. Diversity, Equity, and Inclusion

The pandemic has hit hard for women in particular. Many are thinking about dialing back their careers or exiting altogether, which is very frightening for many companies. What should be done differently to retain women in the workplace?

Dealing with all the personal responsibilities during the pandemic has been a huge challenge for many, particularly women who traditionally take on more burden (and joy!) of children and household work, but it's also an enabler for new ways of working. There are some benefits to the forced remote work that many of us are experiencing. We see our kids more, we are much more engaged in what's going on with school, and we are getting insight into our team's lives outside of work. We have shown that it can work. We should build upon this and maintain these choices for our employees post-pandemic.

For those that are struggling, if we are to retain them, we must provide support and resources. For example, at Stellantis, we have the Working Parents Network that has been a huge help for many women and men navigating this new normal. We also have partnerships with childcare facilities and flexible spending accounts to offset the costs of these services.

5. Sustainability

What do you as a leader do to stay informed about sustainability trends that can impact the success of your company and its strategy?

As part of purchasing, we make a huge impact with respect to responsible sourcing and ensuring that our sourcing practices align with and integrate sustainable principles in all steps of our value chain. Electric vehicles and the conflict mineral focus for batteries is an area of focus for our entire industry. To stay informed, we are taking actions and expanding our partnerships with various global industry associations. We also continuously evaluate technology that will provide us enhanced transparency within our supply chain and have seen some really cool new developments in that space. Finally, we keep open lines of communication with our key supplier partners and work together to identify trends and find the areas where we can collaborate.

Deborah Mielewski

Technical Fellow of Sustainability
Ford Motor Company

Background

Dr. Deborah Mielewski is Technical Fellow of Sustainability at Ford Motor Company, the first female to hold the title of Fellow in the company's long history. She received her BSE (1986), MSE (1993), and PhD (1998) degrees in Chemical Engineering, from the University of Michigan and has been at Ford for 34 years. She initiated a biomaterials program at Ford Research in 2001. Her team was first to demonstrate soy-based foam that met all requirements for automotive seating, and it was launched on the 2008 Mustang. Since then, soy foam has been used on every Ford North American vehicle, reducing greenhouse gas emissions by over 250M lbs.

She continues to pioneer the development of sustainable materials that meet automotive requirements, including natural fiber composites and resins made from renewable feedstocks. Other successes include wheat straw-filled storage bins, rice hull wire channels, and tree-based consoles. Last year, Ford initiated making headlamp housings including coffee chaff through a partnership with McDonald's.

Dr. Mielewski is passionate about reducing Ford's environmental footprint through using sustainable materials. She has appeared in a Ford national commercial, the NOVA series "Making Things", TEDx, and Smithsonian's "The Age of Plastics" symposium and has been interviewed by media including *Wall Street Journal*, *Time Inc.*, Greenbiz, Cheddar, Fox Business, CNBC, and CNN. Her work has been acknowledged with over 60 journal publications, 20 patents, the Henry Ford Technology Award, R&D 100 Award, *Detroit Free Press* Automotive Leadership Award, Environmental Management Association Award, and 5 SPE Innovation Awards.

Questions and Answers

1. Change Control, Resilience, and Work/Life Balance

How do you and your team continue to innovate and improve?

Our group at Ford Motor Company Research is focused on developing new, more sustainable plastic materials. Some of our successes were launching soy-based foam on the Ford Mustang (2007), wheat straw-filled storage bins on the Ford Flex (2010), and tree-based composites (2012 and 2018) on consoles and armrests on our Lincoln products. We are a passionate and energetic group that believes in what we do and have implemented about a dozen industry-leading and innovative materials that reduce Ford's impact on the planet.

Unfortunately, sustainability is a topic that runs hot and cold in our society. As a result, our group has had to persevere through periods when "saving the planet" was not a popular or valued topic. We used those periods to focus in the lab and produce more results knowing that the importance of sustainability would rise again, and we would be ready. Flexibility in the portfolio of materials we research and keeping fixed on the goal of reducing Ford's impact on the planet has always kept us relevant and motivated.

It is this flexibility that came in handy when COVID pandemic restrictions shut down our laboratory in March. At first we wondered how a group that depended so heavily on working in the lab could continue to be productive. During the first few weeks, it became clear that there was a critical societal need for data on how long COVID survived on typical surfaces. Could one get sick from touching a surface contaminated with COVID and how long would it remain active? Additionally, when first responders were transporting infected individuals to hospitals, they needed ways to ensure that touch surfaces in the vehicle wouldn't make them sick.

As materials scientists, we immediately dug in and started investigating how we might help. Our Global External Alliances Network team discovered that the Ohio State University (OSU), Department of Microbiology could work with a surrogate COVID virus, and our team began collecting samples of typical automotive surface materials from high-touch surfaces like the steering wheel, seat fabric, carpet, door handles, and control buttons, each made from a different material. After some struggles to get the testing conditions just right, we were able to determine that heating the vehicle surfaces to 56°C for 15 minutes rendered the virus inactive.

This data was used to support a large project within the company to heat the interior of police vehicles (using the vehicle's own HVAC) to inactivate the coronavirus. During the project, our team also learned which materials are naturally less hospitable to viruses—an attribute we think customers may want in future vehicles. It was exciting to take our experience and expertise in materials to work on something new that had such high value to first responders. And even though much of the work was done through virtual meetings, we developed a close relationship with the OSU team. So strangely, the pandemic inspired us to work in a brand-new area in which we will continue to be active.

2. Growing Your Professional Network and Maintaining Mentor and Sponsor Relationships

How do you keep your existing relationships in this remote world? Are you maintaining face time with other execs while being remote? How do your direct reports maintain their face time with you?

I've been at Ford Motor Company for 34.5 years—all at our Research facility. My mentors taught me how to set up experiments, invent, and innovate and to produce solid scientific results. I get excited to share this knowledge with our new employees. Before COVID, my way of checking in with people was to stop by the labs and informally chat about work. It was a very effective way for me to be involved, and I looked forward to those impromptu interactions. When we shuttered the lab due to COVID in March, I was nervous about how our team would be able to remain productive.

At first, our team focused entirely on "catching up" at home. This meant reviewing data, writing reports, and invention disclosures that we hadn't gotten to and organizing plans for how to get back into the lab. This could easily be done remotely, and it felt like a luxury to finally have the time to focus on them. We began to establish a regular cadence of video calls, department meetings, and project reviews, but at first, we didn't get it all right. People walking through the room, children crying, and dogs barking were (and still sometimes are!) part of the work from home experience. We try to have fun with it. Since the summer, a fraction of our scientists have returned part-time to the lab, with procedures to do that safely. Replicating that "drop-in" experience has been partly maintained through regular phone and video calls. I was very concerned about the difficulty of on-boarding new group members without face-to-face contact with colleagues. Fortunately, the team has pulled together in "showing the ropes" to some new faces.

I think that maintaining contact with peers on the management side has been much easier. Before the pandemic, we met on a regular cadence, and we continue to do that, only virtually instead of in person. One of the real surprises for me was that technical conferences were able to proceed virtually and effectively. I delivered keynote talks and participated in panel discussions pretty much as before, but without the travel. I surely miss the social part of conferences—eating with colleagues, finding new topics to work on together, and catching up on personal lives. Even though in the big scheme of things, our team was able to be very productive in spite of the pandemic, I am anxious to return to a normal life.

3. Personal Growth

What is the most profound impact this pandemic has had the way you think about your job, company, family life? Will it be sticky or do you expect everything to return to the previous status quo?

I learned that I can do a lot more of my job from a distance than I would have ever thought possible. Also, that one can work effectively in very casual clothes! Being away from the laboratory with its daily hustle and bustle and lively engagements with colleagues is what I miss the most. It has been much more difficult to separate work from home since they have been occurring in the same space. When I used to commute

30 minutes each way to and from work, I realize now that I used that driving time to unwind from work and switch gears into home life. So that transition period is still missing from my life now.

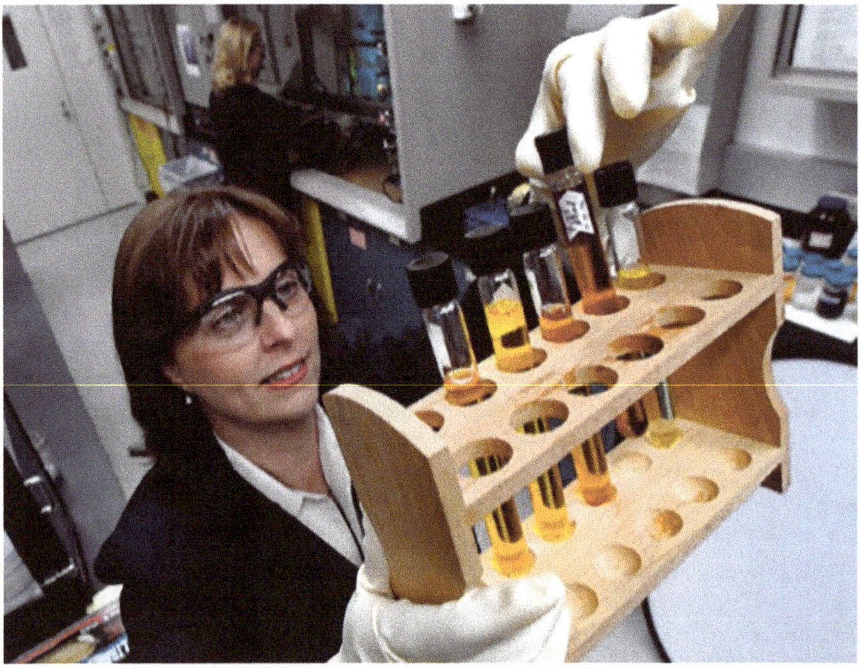

Deborah Mielewski

During the pandemic, I found myself scheduled to attend meetings without any breaks and late into the evening. This kind of crept up on me as there was really no reason to decline a meeting—I was at home and I could be flexible. At first, I would take a walk each day around noon, and I saw much more of the neighborhood than I ever had before. But over time that break disappeared, and some days I barely stood up from my desk all day. After a few months working exclusively from home, I was exhausted and wondered how I ever had time to commute! This was apparently an issue for many, and the company's leadership began to stress how important it was to balance work and home life and prioritize health. I have been trying hard to squeeze those walks back into my schedule.

Today, we have many of our scientists back at the lab at least part-time, collecting much-needed data and doing analysis and write up at home, and we have been able to do this with a very low incidence of COVID. But this requires constant vigilance—the reduced social engagement amongst staff and the wearing of facemasks certainly has certainly changed our collegial atmosphere. I hope that one day we can return to a more normal work cadence, as it can be isolating to work alone, even surrounded by family who is also online. As in most adversarial situations, there is a potential to learn something, and I think we learned that we are more resilient than we would have thought a year ago. I think that in the years to come, we will return to a more normal work life, but one thing that probably won't return is the culture of believing that reside at the office each day in order to effectively do your job.

My daughter had to stay home and complete her first semester of college virtually, which was heartbreaking considering that she also missed celebrating her senior year of high school. The silver lining there has been that her dad and I, both engineers, have been able to interact with her in many ways that would not have happened if she had moved away. We will always cherish the extra time we are having with her talking about chemical engineering "things"!

4. Diversity, Equity, and Inclusion

There has been a lot of talk about diversity—and, in recent years, inclusion. Equity has entered the corporate conversation in a major way this year. What actions are you and your company taking? Are these methods aligned with company goals?

When I came to the Ford Research Lab in 1986, there were only a few women in the entire 1,200 person facility. Although I always felt welcome, I also felt conspicuous. In STEM fields especially, it is very difficult to recruit and retain a diverse workforce, and therefore there must be an intentional effort to do so. Over the years, I was able to participate in Ford's intentional recruitment of many of the women that work in our lab today, and it was exciting to both be a part of and watch the lab transform. Early this year, Ford signed the United Nations (UN) Women's Empowerment Principles, part of the UN global contract, and was also acknowledged by the *Bloomberg* Gender-Equality Index. But we must "Go Further."

Over the past five years, our team has made deliberate efforts to mentor students and recruit interns from more diverse backgrounds and from areas with less opportunity. We've sought opportunities to coach kids of African-American and Hispanic descent with their science fair projects and provided them with tours and work in our lab. They have been nothing but brilliant and enthusiastic. We have also tried to make the laboratory a place where everyone feels welcome and included through extra social activities and daily "tea times" where we get to know one another better. And we also make sure that the interns get the opportunity to lead a project and present their work at a local conference. There is a marked difference in our students when they start working in the summer, and at the end—they have blossomed and found their passions and voice. It is an amazing process to watch.

This year, Ford contracted with Deloitte to perform an extensive audit and assessment of underrepresented employees' experiences as they relate to Diversity, Equity, and Inclusion (DEI). The audit included interviews, focus groups, listening sessions, and surveys. The results showed that the company has good intentions and some bright spots, but many opportunities for improvement. As a result, Ford leadership has vowed to accelerate lasting change for racial and ethnic equality through concrete steps such as a CEO-led diversity task force, DEI objectives for senior management, reverse mentoring for corporate officers, and people leader training. The company's leadership has shown a genuine desire to create a culture of belonging at Ford, where everyone is appreciated and respected. In this way, we can attract, retain, and develop people from all backgrounds, making our company stronger. I am proud to work for a company that has the desire to look within itself and make changes to improve.

Having a son with autism has made me acutely aware of the lack of work opportunities for disabled people. Ford has done an amazing job supporting programs to assist those with autism in learning to drive and has also initiated a work program. I have always been proud of Ford's efforts in helping the community.

5. Sustainability

Sustainability trends (climate change, water availability, health, etc.) are some of the strongest drivers for future changes for companies and their strategies. What are you seeing within your company? Is your firm reading the trends and adapting strategies to survive and then thrive with new growth?

Sustainability is not a trend at Ford but has always been part of the company's DNA. Ford's founder, Henry Ford was a pioneer in using plant-based materials and in reducing waste. During the 1940s, he demonstrated soy-based body panels and wheat straw-filled steering wheels. Ford believed that industry and agriculture should partner and utilize each other's products. He believed in zero waste—sometimes using shipping containers as floorboards in early vehicles.

Ford's great-grandson, Bill Ford has been both an inspiring leader and an avid environmentalist. He supported the 1980s Ford Recycling Action Team (or RAT patrol!) whose mission was to find and use recycled material sources. Bill also spearheaded the transformation of the Rouge Plant—turning one of the world's largest brownfield sites into one of the greenest assembly plants. The facility turns paint fumes into energy, has a sedum roof, utilizes natural light, and remediates the soil using grasses. In 2000, Bill Ford introduced our Corporate Sustainability Report, making us one of the first companies to track our environmental performance. And Ford committed to CO_2 reductions in support of the 2015 Paris Climate Agreement and held to them when the U.S. withdrew. The company recently announced a plan to use 100 percent locally sourced renewable energy (hydro, geothermal, wind, or solar) for all its manufacturing plants globally by 2035.

Recently our commitment to sustainability has intensified. In 2018, Ford committed $18B to develop 40 electrified platforms. We are currently launching the first all-electric Mustang, the Mach E, and our first electric F-150 will be launched in 2022. This year, Ford has committed to global carbon neutrality by 2050, and we were the only U.S. automaker to stand with California in voluntarily reducing vehicle emissions. Last week, Ford was awarded the Gold Medal for International Corporate Achievement in Sustainable Development by the World Environment Center (WEC), for the company's commitment to reduce CO_2 emissions through both vehicles and powering facilities with renewable energy.

Highlights within our lab include delivering several innovative and sustainable materials to Ford vehicles. In partnership with McDonald's, Ford is producing headlamp housings with 20% coffee chaff (the skin that comes off coffee beans during roasting) instead of talc. These headlamps have better mechanical properties, are over 20% lighter in weight, and have less impact on the planet—all while utilizing a material that is considered waste! We also partnered with Hewlett Packard to investigate the reuse of waste 3D printing powder into injection molded fuel clips on our trucks. The clips provide a seven percent weight reduction and an increase in chemical and moisture resistance. This was the fastest we've ever been able to implement a new sustainable material—less than one year—and during a global pandemic! Our company has for its entire existence played a leadership role in sustainability and it is something that many of our employees are proud of.

Barbara Pilarski

Global Head of Business Development
Stellantis

Background

Barbara J. Pilarski was named Global Head of Business Development, Stellantis in March 2021, responsible for identifying, negotiating, and executing strategic partnership arrangements with third parties. Pilarski previously served as Head of Business Development, FCA — North America and Head of Human Resources, FCA — North America.

She is the Executive Sponsor of the Stellantis Women's Alliance Business Resource Group, dedicated to pursuing the professional development and advancement of female employees.

Pilarski joined the company in 1985 as a financial analyst and has held various positions within the finance, human resources, and business development organizations.

Pilarski was twice named to the *Automotive News* list of the 100 Leading Women in the North American Auto Industry.

She serves on the Finance Committee of the Board of Directors for Beaumont Health, Michigan's largest healthcare system. She also serves as a board member for the Metro Detroit Youth Clubs, as well as a member of the Campaign Cabinet for United Way of Southeastern Michigan.

Pilarski earned a bachelor's degree in Finance from Wayne State University (1985) and holds a Master of Business Administration degree from the University of Michigan (1988).

Questions and Answers

1. Change Control, Resilience, and Work/Life Balance

What did you learn when you began to work from home or work in the office with a limited number of co-workers? What did you need to start doing and what did you need to stop?

I was never a strong advocate for work-from-home arrangements prior to the COVID pandemic. Of course, I did see the merit in working from home occasionally, especially when a work assignment required an exceptionally high level of focus and attention, and the environment at home was conducive to that type of activity. I viewed these nontraditional work arrangements as the exception, and not the rule, since I believed that my Business Development organization was most effective in solving problems and progressing our business transactions when we were working face-to-face with other Stellantis colleagues and business partners.

The pandemic changed all of that. Beginning in late March 2020, all FCA personnel in our corporate offices in Auburn Hills and elsewhere were required to carry out their day-to-day job responsibilities on a remote basis. In a flash, working from home became the rule at FCA and not the exception.

I learned some very important lessons while working remotely. First, I learned that I was wrong about work-from-home arrangements. Remote work did not create an impediment for my Business Development team; it was actually an enabler for us. We ended up closing more deals during the pandemic than we did during all of 2019. Second, I learned that while some people thrive in a remote work setting, others do not. For those who struggled due to a lack of structure, difficulty balancing work and home responsibilities, or other reasons, they needed special support and assistance to help them succeed, which I tried my best to provide. And third, I learned that I could trust my staff and colleagues to deliver good work on a timely basis, even if we weren't all together in the same building.

And so in the end, I needed to stop holding on to my outdated ideas about work-from-home arrangements and, instead, start to truly believe that a person's physical location has no real bearing on the capability of that person to provide significant value to the company.

2. Growing Your Professional Network and Maintaining Mentor and Sponsor Relationships

Have your mentees been asking different questions than under usual working conditions? Have you needed to do more hand-holding? Do you see more mentees seeking career change or seeking educational opportunities? Something else?

I mentor many Stellantis employees at various stages in their careers, some of which have expressed unique concerns as they try to navigate their professional development in this "new normal" world with COVID.

Working remotely has been exceptionally difficult for several of my mentees who are relatively new to Stellantis (i.e., employees with less than five years of work experience with the company). These mentees tend to be focused, to a greater extent than other employees, on building their professional network within the organization. They rely on face-to-face interactions to facilitate growth in these networks and have found the prolonged work-from-home arrangement, with no defined end date in sight, to be highly frustrating. In fact, one of my mentees chose to leave the company primarily because the new position he accepted required him to work in the office each day.

Many of these same mentees who are early in their careers also participate in rotational programs to broaden their experience base, meaning that they move to new positions within the company on a scheduled basis. I have a position within my own Business Development organization dedicated to this program, enabling an employee from the finance organization to rotate into my group every six months to gain exposure to my team and the work that we do. Some of my mentees who participate in these rotational programs have expressed concern that working remotely has not allowed them to receive a proper level of training and management exposure to effectively develop and carry out their work responsibilities. This has caused a heightened level of fear and anxiety among these employees, who are typically strong talents within the company and are motivated to overperform.

A few of my more seasoned mentees have expressed some level of mental fatigue as a result of extended remote work, as well as a desire to come into the office periodically to escape the complications of their home life and take advantage of some quiet time to get their work done.

Whatever the case, it's clear that the COVID pandemic has been challenging for many of my mentees. I have responded by making myself more available, being a good listener, and assuring my mentees that a return to normalcy is imminent. I have found that the best thing you can give to someone who is struggling is your own open heart and mind to help them work through their issues and gain a much-needed level of perspective and hope.

3. Personal Growth

Have you developed new behaviors (exercise, diet, meditation, hobbies, etc.) that help you get through this new stress?

During the first few months of working remotely due to the pandemic, each working day was like the last. I would wake up at 6:00 a.m. and then make my way to my laptop in my home office to start my day. I would take a quick break for lunch around noon, and before I knew it, it was 7:00 p.m. or later, and I was wondering where the day went. I spent nearly all of my time on conference calls with "camera off" since I often did not take the extra time in the morning to do my hair or makeup, which proved to be an unexpected benefit of working from home, but clearly limited my ability to really connect with my staff and colleagues during those early months.

At some point along the way, I decided to use my iPhone to check my level of physical activity and was shocked to learn that the total number of steps that I had taken during that particular day was less than 400, apparently all that was required to move to and from the different rooms in my home during a typical workday. I then mustered up the courage to get on the scale, only to be shocked once again at the weight that I had slowly but surely gained. If I was going to stay healthy during the lockdown so that I could reasonably manage any potential future COVID exposure, then something needed to change. And change it did.

With the warm months of summer now upon me, I decided to get up on my feet and start walking outside to improve my overall health. I live on 40 acres in Washington, Michigan, and so my daily walks started with my husband and me circling our fifteen-acre soybean field until we were both able to complete at least 10,000 steps. As the fall approached and the days became shorter, I moved to the treadmill in my basement to continue my daily walking regimen, the distance of which had now increased to between five and six miles per day. I even participated in a virtual marathon that required each participant to walk or run 26.2 miles over a month's time. I ended up walking nearly 185 miles over 33 days to help kids in Detroit gain access to laptops, the internet, and other tools and resources needed to be successful in a virtual learning environment.

They say that every dark cloud has a silver lining. While the pandemic was certainly that dark cloud, it eventually forced me to focus more time and attention on my own health and well-being. I am now at least ten pounds lighter, I get more sleep, and I look and feel a whole lot better than I did on that memorable day when I finally realized the toll that I was allowing the pandemic to take on me personally.

4. Diversity, Equity, and Inclusion

The pandemic has hit hard for women in particular. Many are thinking about dialing back their careers or exiting altogether, which is very frightening for many companies. What should be done differently to retain women in the workplace?

I'm not surprised that the pandemic is hitting women in the workplace particularly hard. In my own personal experience, I find that women tend to take on a disproportionate level of responsibility at home. When you couple that with the added requirement to carry out our work responsibilities from that same home, but then eliminate the support systems that we've come to rely on, such as childcare, you now have a potential recipe for disaster on your hands. Don't get me wrong. I am married to a really great guy and exceptional father who has always provided a significant level of support and assistance when it comes to managing our home life together. However, when push comes to shove, it is typically me who takes on the final responsibility for the kids and the house. And so therein lies the problem. This pandemic has forced many Stellantis women who are working from home to take on two full-time jobs concurrently: their job at Stellantis and their job at home.

Recognizing that this is a real problem is a first good step. At Stellantis, we have taken some important actions to address this issue. For example, we have established a process where employees are able to relocate on a temporary basis in order to be closer to family members, who can then provide much-needed childcare and other assistance. Our Purchasing organization has also negotiated reduced childcare rates with certain third-party providers for employees who feel comfortable using the service at this time. Further, some of our 11 business resource groups, such as the Women's Alliance, are also providing a platform for employees to seek advice and share best practices during this unprecedented time. And, as a last resort, Stellantis has also granted leaves of absence to employees to manage the complexities brought on by the pandemic.

We, as working women, also have a responsibility to take action to address this issue and prevent more of our female colleagues from leaving the workforce. As part of that action plan, we need to find the courage within ourselves to admit when we are struggling and to ask for help, and we should never view those two actions as signs of weakness. Oftentimes, organizations want to address the challenges faced by their employees, but either do not realize that those challenges exist or do not fully understand the underlying problems. Without raising our voices and making it clear that the status quo is not working, a permanent solution to this problem will continue to evade us. Suffering in silence is not the answer this time.

5. Sustainability

As part of employee development, does your company encourage and support employees volunteering for local nongovernmental organizations? Do you and your company consider this an opportunity for aligning company efforts, employee leadership development, and local progress on sustainability?

Stellantis considers volunteerism as an opportunity to align company efforts and employee leadership development, all focused on areas that are important to us from a sustainability perspective. My personal experience is definitely proof of that.

Stellantis has a long history of encouraging and supporting volunteerism by its employees, especially in areas that are critical to the success and sustainability of our communities. For example, Stellantis has partnered with United Way of Southeastern Michigan for over 70 years to enable our employees to donate their time, energy, and resources to support the important work of this organization. Stellantis also established its Motor Citizen's program as a platform for developing and offering volunteer opportunities to its employees. Salaried employees are encouraged to spend up to 18 hours of paid time off each year to volunteer for the organizations of their choice. As a further way to support employee engagement with local nonprofit organizations, Stellantis also supports employees who choose to serve on the boards of community nonprofit organizations.

With the support of Stellantis, I have leveraged volunteer opportunities to further develop my own leadership skills, while addressing matters of importance to the company. Stellantis actively supported my participation on United Way's Campaign Cabinet, along with 40 other community leaders, to oversee the organization's $60 million annual fundraising campaign, which is the primary source of funding for the critical services this organization provides. This experience allowed me to lead several large fundraising initiatives, while expanding my professional network in the process. I used the volunteer opportunities offered through the Motor Citizens program as an enabler to build a more cohesive team within my Business Development organization.

And, finally, my role representing Stellantis as a Board of Trustee member for the Metro Detroit Youth Clubs has allowed me to tap into my extensive network at Stellantis to bring important resources and programming to the deserving kids that this organization serves, including programming intended to address racial inequality issues.

Vickie Piner

Global Vice President of Quality of E-Systems
Lear

Background

Vickie Piner has been with Lear for 24 years, holding numerous roles centering on continuous improvement, product, and program execution. Her early experiences in engineering at Lear helped shape her passion for quality, which has led to increasing roles of responsibility.

In 2000, Piner was promoted to Director of North America JV Groups in Program Management, and in 2001, she was the first female African American to be named Vice President at Lear. Piner went on to be Global Vice President of Six Sigma, becoming known for her leadership in its deployment at Lear. She now serves as Global Vice President of Quality of E-Systems, managing global operational excellence to exceed customer expectations in product quality.

Piner holds a Master of Science in Industrial Management from Central Michigan University and attended GMI Engineering and Management Institute (now Kettering University), earning a bachelor's degree in Industrial Engineering. Throughout her career, she has been honored with industry awards, including *Diversity Journal*'s Women Worth Watching®, *Crain's Detroit Business* 40 under 40; Automotive Hall of Fame's Young Leadership and Excellence Award, and the GMI Distinguished Alumni Award.

Questions and Answers

1. Change Control, Resilience, and Work/Life Balance

How has your self-motivation been to excel, learn, reach out (virtually), and manage all aspects of your new work life?

I have found that I need to reach out to individuals in my team to do a "health check" on them since I can't get a read from them in person. I have also had to reach out to make sure that my team isn't burning out. This means talking to them not just about work but about their lives more than I ever have before. I think the personal touch is needed more to make sure they feel connected and appreciated.

How have you handled your mood swings or those of your co-workers or family?

I have handled my mood swings by giving myself a personal time-out. I force myself to go and do something else that gives me a sense of accomplishment beyond my work. I touch base with my son and sometimes have a conversation about what's going on with his friends, who has he talked to, and make sure that he is not distancing himself from his support structure just because he isn't seeing them. I also call other colleagues when I feel like I am shifting to a downward mood. Just check in, tell a couple of "I haven't worn make-up in five days" type of calls and send pics! We joke and talk about how we have to do better.

Many have said that there is no separation of work and home these days—what do you do to manage this for your own work?

I actually agree as I, too, am working more than I ever have just because I can, and don't have much competing with work. Setting times to have a sit-down dinner with your family or touching base with them or cleaning my house or walking outside for just a few minutes can clear the cobwebs away and help keep things in perspective. I also created a workspace in my home to remind me that I need to walk away from that space sometimes. It creates a visual clock for me on how much I am online.

How do you and your team continue to innovate and improve?

We are spending more time on talking about strategy and the makeup of our team. We talk about things going well and things not going well, and how we support our customers. We let our guards down and have more team discussions on improvements and weaknesses.

2. Growing Your Professional Network and Maintaining Mentor and Sponsor Relationships

How do you keep your existing relationships in this remote world? Are you maintaining face time with other execs while being remote? How do your direct reports maintain their face time with you?

Zoom is turning out to be a great tool! And I have never FaceTimed on cell calls more in my life. I send notes, and say, "Okay guys, my hair is combed and I am presentable! Can we face time today?" And I ask them to do the same. We get a joke out of it, but it sets a precedence that we are going to talk to each other.

I haven't spent much time growing my network, but I think I have put effort into strengthening the one I have. I was never good at "touch points" with no topic before. I am doing more of that, and each time, a topic normally develops that inspires me.

Have your mentees been asking different questions than under usual working conditions? Have you needed to do more hand-holding? Do you see more mentees seeking career change or seeking educational opportunities? Something else?

I am seeing that we need to reach out more and have "mental health" touch points. I am also seeing that more people are realizing that they can be successful working remotely, and some are starting to look at new opportunities that they had not considered before because for whatever reason, they were "landlocked" to their current locations. I think that we are going to see a lot of career churn after the COVID quarantine is over.

3. Personal Growth

What personal development opportunities have you taken advantage of now that you're not traveling?

I have had some diversity training and joined a cohort program that allows team members that would not normally have access to me to reach out for hour intervals to get to know each other. I love it. I have met employees in other countries and had personal one-on-one conversations that allow them to learn from me, and me to learn from them. It's a great initiative.

What is the most profound impact this pandemic has had the way you think about your job, company, family life? Will it be sticky or do you expect everything to return to the previous status quo?

The pandemic has taught me that people need personal connections. That does not have to be physical. We have senses that we have had to pull forward since we can't see body language and the nuances of behavior. I think that I have learned to really accept that individuals are different. I have some team members that have excelled in this environment and maybe it should be continued with them after the pandemic. I have some that really do need personal assurance and contact. I am hoping that all companies realize that we need to make our work environment work for all employees and not just the company model. It would be a mistake to return wholly to the status quo.

4. Diversity, Equity, and Inclusion

There has been a lot of talk about diversity—and, in recent years, inclusion. Equity has entered the corporate conversation in a major way this year. What actions are you and your company taking? Are these methods aligned with company goals?

At Lear, we have a long-standing commitment to a workplace that is diverse, inclusive, and free from bias and discrimination. We strive to ensure that Lear is consistently known as a great place to work. We have put added emphasis on fostering a culture where all employees feel engaged, accepted, and encouraged to bring their whole selves to work.

In 2020, we launched our *Together We Belong* diversity, equity, and inclusion (DEI) campaign to drive awareness, educate our employees, and fund organizations committed to change through a $1 million company donation. Our previous Chief Diversity Officer, Rashida Thomas, was promoted to Vice President of Global Talent Acquisition and is now leading our commitment to having a spectrum of diverse top talent at all levels of the organization. Rashida's replacement, Derrick Mitchell, is continuing to build the momentum of our global DEI program and our newly formed Executive Diversity Council to share, discuss, and celebrate diversity and inclusion efforts across our organization.

In 2019, Lear President and CEO Ray Scott signed the CEO Action for Diversity and Inclusion pledge, which reaffirmed our commitment to cultivating a workplace where diverse perspectives and experiences are welcomed and respected and where employees feel comfortable and empowered to discuss diversity and inclusion. We also hosted the interactive "Check Your Blind Spots" tour at our Southfield Headquarters campus and have expanded our Employee Resource Groups for women, people of color, and LGBTQ.

5. Sustainability

ESG (Environmental, Social, and Governance) expectations of investors is greatly accelerating for both equity and debt investments among the largest investment banks and pension funds. Is your company taking this investor trend seriously and adapting strategy to meet these expectations?

ESG has become an important factor in evaluating the long-term performance potential for companies around the world.

Employees, suppliers, potential and current investors, customers, and communities want to be assured that businesses are protecting the environment, treating their employees fairly, maintaining ethical practices, and supporting human rights. In fact, some strategic investors choose investments primarily based on ESG criteria.

Lear has been focused on these areas for many years, publishing an annual sustainability report, receiving very good scores from ESG ranking firms, and winning recognition from federal agencies and nongovernmental organizations in several countries. Lear views sustainability as another example of its commitment to its core value of *Getting Results the Right Way.*

To demonstrate senior management support and ensure greater cross-functional engagement, in 2020 Lear created a team of leaders focused on ESG.

With the new alignment, ESG is becoming more deeply integrated throughout Lear, from how products are manufactured, and work is conducted with our suppliers to how support is provided to local communities. From our outstanding response to COVID and the Safe Work Playbook to our employee engagement efforts and charitable activities, we have a compelling story to tell.

Environmental—Lear achieved climate change goals, originally set for 2018, several years ago and reestablished new goals for energy reduction and greenhouse gas emissions for 2020. Later this year, our company plans to announce a new set of long-term environmental goals

Social—Lear has a long-standing commitment to a harassment-free, discrimination-free workplace where everyone is welcome. This year, our company expanded our Employee Resource Groups, committed $1 million to support organizations addressing racial inequality, and joined the largest corporate sustainability initiative in the world, the UN Global Compact. In facilities around the globe, employees are supporting local communities by sharing their time and effort to worthy causes.

Governance—Lear has policies in place to promote sustainability. The Code of Business Conduct and Ethics covers compliance with local laws, conflicts of interest, accurate business and financial records, environmental health and safety, diversity, equal opportunity, and more. Guided by global reporting standards, violations of the Code can be reported to Lear by phone, email, and mail.

Mandy Rice

Vice President, Global Sales and E-Systems
Lear Corporation

Background

Mandy Rice is an automotive industry executive with 28 years of experience and a strong reputation for building talented teams, operational execution, and disciplined commercial and program management.

Rice started her career with Ford Motor Company in 1992, after earning a Bachelor of Science degree in Mechanical Engineering from Michigan State University. During her time with Ford, she gained extraordinary experience working in a variety of manufacturing facilities, sparking her passion for automotive and high-pressure, deadline-driven projects, and solidifying her strong work ethic.

She joined Lear Corporation in 1997 as a senior product engineer and quickly rose through the ranks to a Director of GM Division Interior Integration in 2000, where she led several successful product launches. While working at Lear, Rice completed a Master of Science degree in Industrial Operations from Lawrence Technological University. Rice was promoted to Vice President of Global Trim Sales in 2011, where she helped build the Surface Materials division through multiple roles in sales, program management, and engineering. She played a key role in the launch of Crafted by Lear and Intu™ Seating by leading product strategy and served as Vice President of Lear's Global FCA Seating business before being promoted to her current position of Vice President for Global Sales and E-Systems.

Questions and Answers

1. Change Control, Resilience, and Work/Life Balance

How have you handled your mood swings or those of your co-workers or family?

Given the unique situation we've been experiencing over the last year, I think it's understandable for everyone to have a range of emotions. Once we began to work remotely, I saw people reacting to their new work environment differently, and it became ven more important to be flexible and adapt to care for each other. I remember distinctly the day we discussed this as a management team and realized we needed to give our teams support. Within my team specifically, I offered an "off the grid day" for anyone who needed a break, no questions asked.

It was an extraordinary time of compassion and resilience. Everyone had different situations ranging from two parents working at home with young kids doing online school to people who were living alone. Some coworkers started exercise groups to work out together virtually; others did more Zoom calls with family. During meetings from home, we could hear a coworker's child playing in the background and got to know the names of people's pets—it gave us an opportunity to laugh and break the stress for a bit.

For me personally, when things got tense, I simply took a walk. I recognized how transformative walking outside for a few minutes could be. A mentor once told me "move your body, shift your mind," and I've found that really works. Because of this, I have continued to walk and now expanded that to hiking. I plan to continue this practice as we move forward into our new post-COVID normal.

2. Growing Your Professional Network and Maintaining Mentor and Sponsor Relationships

How do you keep your existing relationships in this remote world? Are you maintaining face time with other execs while being remote? How do your direct reports maintain their face time with you?

I had the unique experience of getting promoted into a new position in a new division during the pandemic. There were new customers, new team members, and a new executive team. Connecting was more important than ever, and it was all about frequent communication.

Our president of Lear's E-Systems Division, Carl Esposito, had brief daily staff meetings, which was very helpful. Our President and CEO, Ray Scott, also met with all global VPs weekly. Meetings were informal and short, but they allowed the team to connect and discuss the challenges we were facing. I had one-on-ones with each staff member weekly just to tune in. Sometimes we talked about what was going on at home and other times we worked together on the issues of the week. That dedicated time together created a bond as we forged together through difficult times.

Once we had implemented our Safe Work Playbook and it was allowed by local health orders, the executive team and other team members started back in the office, which was helpful. It was a big shot of energy for us—getting together again (socially-distanced), reconnecting on a daily basis, and having informal interactions—all helped us get back into the swing of things. Although we have proven that we can work remotely, there's something different about working together in person. For our international team members, we didn't use Zoom initially like other companies did. We maintained the same work practices we always used, which were Skype calls and conference calls. Frankly, whether we were in the office or at home didn't make a difference. With customers, we did use Microsoft Teams, Zoom, and FaceTime, in addition to getting on the phone regularly to stay in touch. We've done the best we can to maintain communication, but I am looking forward to the day we can travel again and get back to working face to face.

3. Personal Growth

What is the most profound impact this pandemic has had the way you think about your job, company, family life? Will it be sticky or do you expect everything to return to the previous status quo?

This pandemic has created a lot of shifts for me. Having family members get COVID, people I know pass away, friends and coworkers losing parents, and families pushed to their limits, it changes you. I love my job, but it is a job; it is not my life. The pandemic was a test for those of us who already had work-life balance issues. It was very easy to slip into a 24-hour work mode. It just never stopped, so you had to stop it. During the holidays, I made a handwritten sign for my desk at home that said, "Closed for Christmas." I kept that sign. It's a gentle reminder that work will always be there. There will always be new problems and challenges with each day, but our family and friends won't always be there. Time is so precious, and it's important that we take time to cherish those relationships while they are still here.

4. Diversity, Equity, and Inclusion

There has been a lot of talk about diversity—and, in recent years, inclusion. Equity has entered the corporate conversation in a major way this year. What actions are you and your company taking? Are these methods aligned with company goals?

The pandemic did not slow down our long-standing commitment to a workplace that is diverse, inclusive, and free from bias and discrimination.

In 2020, we launched our *Together We Belong* diversity, equity, and inclusion campaign to drive awareness, educate our employees, and fund organizations committed to change through a $1 million company donation.

We also conducted training that continued throughout the year, pairing employees with one another to continue to discuss DEI on a more personal, one-to-one basis. That's also helped build new relationships across the company with people who wouldn't have interacted before—which is great for broader organizational development and working together

Our previous Chief Diversity Officer, Rashida Thomas, was promoted to Vice President of Global Talent Acquisition and is now leading our commitment to having a spectrum of diverse top talent at all levels of the organization. Rashida's replacement Derrick Mitchell is continuing to build momentum of our global DEI program and our newly formed Executive Diversity Council to share, discuss, and celebrate diversity and inclusion efforts across our organization.

In 2019, Lear President and CEO Ray Scott signed the CEO Action for Diversity and Inclusion pledge, which reaffirmed our commitment to cultivating a workplace where diverse perspectives and experiences are welcomed and respected and where employees feel comfortable and empowered to discuss diversity and inclusion. We also hosted the interactive "Check Your Blind Spots" tour at our Southfield Headquarters campus and have expanded our Employee Resource Groups for women, people of color, and LGBTQ.

5. Sustainability

ESG (Environmental, Social, and Governance) expectations of investors is greatly accelerating for both equity and debt investments among the largest investment banks and pension funds. Is your company taking this investor trend seriously and adapting strategy to meet these expectations?

ESG has become an important factor in evaluating the long-term performance potential for companies around the world.

Employees, suppliers, potential and current investors, customers, and communities want to be assured that businesses are protecting the environment, treating their employees fairly, maintaining ethical practices, and supporting human rights. In fact, some strategic investors choose investments primarily based on ESG criteria.

Lear has been focused on these areas for many years, publishing an annual sustainability report, receiving very good scores from ESG ranking firms, and winning recognition from federal agencies and nongovernmental organizations in several countries. Lear views sustainability as another example of its commitment to its core value of *Getting Results the Right Way.*

We also report the status of our ESG efforts to our board of directors on a regular basis. This is also part of our messaging to our external investors and shareholders.

To demonstrate senior management support and ensure greater cross-functional engagement, in 2020 Lear created a team of leaders that focus on ESG.

With the new alignment, ESG is becoming more deeply integrated throughout Lear, including how products are manufactured, work is conducted with our suppliers, and support is provided to local communities. From our outstanding response to COVID and the Safe Work Playbook to our employee engagement efforts and charitable activities, we have a compelling story to tell.

Environmental—Lear achieved climate change goals originally set for 2018 several years ago and reestablished new goals for energy reduction and greenhouse gas emissions for 2020. Later this year, our company plans to announce a new set of long-term environmental goals.

Social—Lear has a long-standing commitment to a harassment-free, discrimination-free workplace where everyone is welcome. This year, our company expanded our Employee Resource Groups, committed $1 million to support organizations addressing racial inequality, and joined the largest corporate sustainability initiative in the world, the UN Global Compact. In facilities around the globe, employees are supporting local communities by sharing their time and effort to worthy causes.

Governance—Lear has policies in place to promote sustainability. The Code of Business Conduct and Ethics covers compliance with local laws, conflicts of interest, accurate business and financial records, environmental health and safety, diversity, equal opportunity, and more. Guided by global reporting standards, violations of the Code can be reported to Lear by phone, email, and mail.

Sonia Rief

Vice President, Vehicle Connected Services
and Program Management Office
Nissan Americas

Background

Sonia Rief is Vice President of Vehicle Connected Services and of the Program Management Office for Nissan Americas. She was appointed to this position in March 2019. In this role, Rief is responsible for managing vehicle line profitability and leading Nissan's Connected Services organization. Overseeing the Connected Service organization includes planning, delivery, marketing, and operations for internal and external customer content.

Previously, Rief was Director of the Program Management Office at the Nissan Technical Center North America (NTCNA) in Farmington Hills, Michigan and was responsible for vehicle line profit management of midsize sedans, and compact and midsize SUVs.

Rief joined Nissan in 2001, progressing through roles of increasing responsibility within the Research and Development function, including a one-year assignment in Japan supporting the Renault-Nissan Alliance.

Rief holds a bachelor's degree in Mechanical Engineering from North Carolina State University and an MBA from the University of Michigan.

Questions and Answers

1. Change Control, Resilience, and Work/Life Balance

What did you learn when you began to work from home or work in the office with a limited number of co-workers? What did you need to start doing and what did you need to stop?

In hindsight, the sink-or-swim approach to work from home was probably the best thing that could have happened to us. Without the chance to overthink and over-complicate the change, we learned and adjusted in the moment. We shared the common challenges of learning new technology, virtual communication, and the merging of personal and professional. At the same time, each of us had our personal challenges to face alone.

Due to the nature of our work, my teams were able to quickly transition to a work-from-home structure with minimal business disruption. The first challenge was to adjust to new technology and become Zoom experts. Almost immediately, we adopted best practice number 1, cameras always on. Virtual communication will never be as effective as in person, but often, it can be good enough. With cameras on and best practice number 2, active management of attendee engagement, many meetings were just as effective. This second practice, managing engagement, meant learning to speak into the camera, checking the body language of attendees, and directly asking for input from each. It also required a higher level of attention to and detail in the visuals being used for explanation.

Finally, the merging of professional and personal obligations became more complex as all the usual plans and schedules were upended. The biggest challenge of work from home in a global pandemic has been managing the changes in our own lives while accommodating the changes of others. Every person's situation has been unique. Maintaining motivation and output required a higher level of trust, communication, and flexibility than ever before. Despite this awareness and accommodation of others being the most challenging aspect of work from home, it was also the lesson I expect that will be most valuable once we return.

2. Growing Your Professional Network and Maintaining Mentor and Sponsor Relationships

Have your mentees been asking different questions than under usual working conditions? Have you needed to do more hand-holding? Do you see more mentees seeking career change or seeking educational opportunities? Something else?

The topics of mentor-to-mentee discussions have definitely changed during this period. There has been a shift away from long-term career planning to developing short-term coping strategies and analyzing the current state to learn for the future. In some cases, particularly for those with young families, short-term discussions are focused on navigating the personal and professional balance in a time when both must be managed simultaneously. This topic is relevant not only for those struggling with family priorities but almost universally as the separation between work life and home life has become nonexistent.

Others are questioning the best way to build or maintain business relationships in a virtual setting, especially when starting a new position. Other times, the discussion will turn to how we can translate this experience into a stronger business for the future. For example, the stability of supply chains and the robustness of processes to make fast assessments of risk were tested with varied results. These very recent and concrete results make for engaging conversations about past decisions and priorities for future change. At the same time, there has been for many of us an increased awareness of our own ability to react and adapt to change, leading to great conversations about self-development and personal strengths and weaknesses highlighted through this experience.

3. Personal Growth

What is the most profound impact this pandemic has had the way you think about your job, company, family life? Will it be sticky or do you expect everything to return to the previous status quo?

The pandemic has highlighted just how lucky I am in both my personal and professional life. My family made the most of our increased time together, and while the isolation was a challenge for my children, their resilience was amazing. This slowdown in the hectic pace of our lives has been a much-appreciated chance for each of us to be reminded of our priorities. I expect we'll return to post-pandemic life with a different view of how and with whom to spend our time.

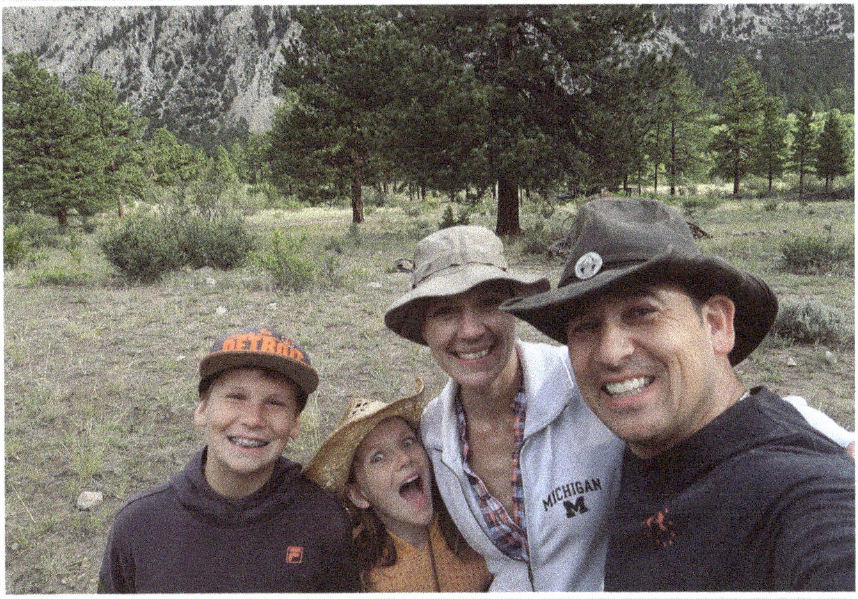

Sonia Rief

In my professional life, I was reassured to see the commitment of my team and my colleagues to making the most of a challenging situation. In fact, I think we all had a new appreciation for the benefits of remote work. With a team that works globally every day, the increased flexibility of schedules and locations allowed us to make the most of our day by eliminating commutes and downtime during the workday. Some of those breaks could now be used for personal activity without sacrificing any of our business priorities. I expect this learning will be one we carry forward. While the balance will shift back to more in-person activity, there's no doubt we'll adopt some of this flexibility as a permanent practice.

As our team adapted, so did our company. I had utmost confidence in Nissan's ability to adapt to a crisis quickly as we have in the past. The state of our business during this time made that more difficult than ever before. But we proved once again our ability to pull together in times of crisis as we powered through both the business recovery and the pandemic with absolute focus and collective commitment to our top priorities—the health and safety of our staff and the development and manufacturing of great products.

4. Diversity, Equity, and Inclusion

The pandemic has hit hard for women in particular. Many are thinking about dialing back their careers or exiting altogether, which is very frightening for many companies. What should be done differently to retain women in the workplace?

As many women face irreconcilable demands between their personal and professional lives, whether due to family responsibilities or the burnout that comes from blurring of the line between the two, it has become apparent that change is needed. Most companies are not well prepared to incorporate flexibility in time and location or to provide caregiver support services. Going forward, expectations of reasonably flexible schedules and/or locations will become the norm. The "norm" means programs which are applied without judgment or bias. They will be equally applied to and taken by both men and women and assumed to be the standard rather than the exception. At the same time, companies will likely need to provide support for men and women struggling with care for family members through providing services directly or, at least, support to find those services. As the maturity of flexibility and care support varies widely between companies, each will need to make a focused assessment of successes and failures in retention and productivity these last months and then engage all employees in making changes for the future.

Most critically, companies will need to be more competitive than the alternative, whether that be working for another company or not working at all. Women who are motivated, engaged in their jobs, and holistically supported by their companies are unlikely to consider leaving the workforce. More than ever, companies will be expected to invest in employee support and development and to continuously check in and address engagement across the workforce.

5. Sustainability

Sustainability trends (climate change, water availability, health, etc.) are some of the strongest drivers for future changes for companies and their strategies. What are you seeing within your company? Is your firm reading the trends and adapting strategies to survive and then thrive with new growth?

I expect all big companies are continuously gathering, studying, and adapting to market data on trends across multiple industries and regions. Most have teams dedicated to this external checking and internal translation of information. Certainly, Nissan is no different. From the beginning of the pandemic, we were reaching out to understand immediate impacts and long-term implications. While the pandemic was initially the main discussion topic, it was quickly broadened and then eclipsed by larger social issues around race, economics, and politics. Questions about future priorities now bring answers ranging from a new conservatism in spending to expectations of public companies to engage in social topics.

For some time now, automakers have understood the importance of climate change as a sustainability concern with huge implications on product strategy. Nissan has a long history of promoting electric vehicle (EV) technology and a commitment to mass market production. With the rapidly growing acceptance of EVs as a mainstream vehicle choice, we are reassured in our future vision which embraces this trend. To build on the current momentum, we are accelerating our activities to make EVs more widely accessible through better technology, lower costs, and increased infrastructure.

And while we continue to refine the future product portfolio given sustainability trends, the integration of changes to address larger social issues will take more discussion and time. I do believe that when we look back some years from now, this response to moral issues will be a key differentiator between companies that thrive and those that just survive.

Kiersten Robinson

Chief People and Employee Experiences Officer
Ford Motor Company

Background

As Chief People and Employee Experiences Officer, Kiersten Robinson has the responsibility to leverage Ford Motor Company's aligned and strategic enterprise capabilities through strong, diverse teams in support of the business, enterprise priorities, and progressive employee and workplace experiences.

Kiersten began her career at Ford in 1995 as a labor relations representative in Ford of Australia. In 1997 she served in the first of several international assignments with the Ford of Europe organization, based in Germany. Following two additional positions in Australia, Robinson moved to Ford's world headquarters in 2002 to hold a variety of roles of increasing responsibility, culminating in her appointment to Vice President of Human Resources for Ford Asia-Pacific in 2010, based in China. In 2016, Robinson was appointed to lead human resources for The Americas, and in the early 2017, her role was expanded to include Global Markets leading to her current role.

Questions and Answers

1. Change Control, Resilience, and Work/Life Balance

Many have said that there is no separation of work and home these days—what do you do to manage this for your own work? What are you doing to increase the ability of your team to create and respect boundaries?

Honestly, I have definitely struggled with the blurred line between work and home. Like many, my commute time has been converted to work time, and my days are significantly longer. This is okay for short bursts and is sometimes what is needed. It is not sustainable, however, as an ongoing work pattern. As such, I am focused on developing new habits—small, intentional, and repeatable habits—that will provide flexibility and establish a framework for both my team and me to better manage some of these boundaries.

Habit #1—Start the day right: Protect time on the calendar for exercise and have fun with it. This includes a weekly Peloton ride with members of my team. It's such a great way to connect and start the week.

Habit #2—It is okay to say "no": Time is our most precious resource and we need to protect it fiercely. This is hard for me because I want to say yes to everyone. To help with this, every Sunday, I review my calendar to ensure that I am spending my time in areas where the business or my team needs me the most. I use Microsoft Analytics to understand and improve my work patterns, review how I am spending my time, and to determine if my personal and professional commitments need adjusting.

Habit #3—The team: Be flexible, everyone's needs are different. I use check-ins to begin most of my meetings and to learn how everyone is doing. This has been a powerful way to connect and share the very "real" experiences of juggling competing demands during the pandemic. It creates a safe space to ask for help and flexibility. In addition, it provides an opportunity for us to share best practices in managing blurred boundaries and shared experiences, such as supporting our children through the challenges of remote schooling.

2. Growing Your Professional Network and Maintaining Mentor and Sponsor Relationships

Has your company maintained learning and leadership development opportunities, culture surveys, 360 surveys, etc. to grow skills and manage the emotional intelligence of the company? Has anything shifted? What have you learned?

Absolutely! The past year has redefined and reinforced what leadership skills and capabilities matter most in today's world. Emotional intelligence, empathy, compassion, trust, resilience, and optimism are foundational traits for leaders and almost agnostic of industry and company size. To support growth and development in these areas, we continue to invest in tools, curriculum, and learning experiences that build upon these important capabilities.

For example, when we were forced to shift our working norms earlier this year due to the pandemic, we recognized the importance for leaders to manage their energy while navigating constant change and the increasing uncertainty. Through our award-winning "next practice" sentiment strategy, we remain very connected to our workforce to understand how our leaders are living Our Truths—our shared values that govern how we live, act, and communicate. People leaders have the tools to develop personalized action plans that help their teams feel cared for, inspired, and empowered. Leaders are also able to get personalized and targeted feedback through the On-Demand Truths 360 Assessment that offers quantitative ratings for key behaviors and helps to foster greater communications, development, and productivity.

The way leaders show up is central to building **trust**—the cornerstone of Ford's winning aspiration. Other examples include our employee Culture Cabinet and Culture Street Team that, globally, are leading experiences specifically targeted to developing mindful leadership. One such effort was the "Soft Skills September" learning experience in which almost 10,000 North America employees participated. The most popular sessions of the event included Servant Leadership, Effective Listening, and EQ. Facilitated by leaders who are successfully demonstrating these skills, participants were energized and left committed to incorporating the practices in their daily interactions.

3. Personal Growth

Have you developed new behaviors (exercise, diet, meditation, hobbies, etc.) that help you get through this new stress?

Yes, and it is something I need to consistently focus on and be intentional about. I have practiced meditation and mindfulness for several years, and I find it a rejuvenating practice where I can be still and find perspective. One new habit I have really enjoyed is a two-hour virtual walk every Saturday with a friend. She lives in another state and walking and talking on the phone together has been a great way to decompress at the end of the week and stay connected. If it were not for the pandemic, I am not sure we would have considered exercising virtually together. It has been a great way to combat stress and create a healthy start to my weekend.

One of the greatest opportunities we have, collectively, is to talk more openly about stress and the importance of wellbeing and caring for each other. We have worked hard to destigmatize mental health, wellbeing, and coping with stress, and we have much more to do. At Ford, we have focused heavily on well-being, acknowledging the stress and strain of the pandemic on employees and their families. We talk about mental health and well-being in our weekly global town hall meetings and poll employees weekly—listening closely and asking how they are coping and what support they need. We try to provide the much-needed resources to help employees address some of the competing demands of work and home, including childcare support, flexible work arrangements, well-being programs, and learning options.

4. Diversity, Equity, and Inclusion

There has been a lot of talk about diversity—and, in recent years, inclusion. Equity has entered the corporate conversation in a major way this year. What actions are you and your company taking? Are these methods aligned with company goals?

In the wake of the tragic killing of George Floyd and other acts of social and racial injustice, Ford accelerated efforts to support a culture of belonging that puts the employee experience at the center of how we shape our culture. Inherent in those efforts is the recognition that "belonging" must include diversity, equity, and inclusion (DEI)—and that all three must be present for everyone to feel like part of the Ford family. In 2020, we embarked on the most comprehensive DEI assessment that the company has ever undertaken, which looked at the current state of the employee experience across race, ethnicity, and gender. The audit provided deeper insights into the challenges some of our employees face, which is guiding us in the actions to drive meaningful and lasting change for equality within Ford.

The audit revealed that we have several pride points as well as key opportunities to become more diverse, inclusive, and to place a greater focus on equity. The audit was a sober realization that we must go further to create a company where our differences are truly valued, and every team member can bring their whole selves to work. We defined a DEI North Star to ensure our actions are in service of an aspiration we all believe in and to harness the strong foundation already embedded in the Ford culture:

> "For more than a century, Ford has been a pioneer in providing opportunity to people regardless of race, gender, sexual orientation and background. We view this less with pride than the sober realization that we must go further to create a company where our differences are truly valued, and every team member can bring their whole selves to work. Creating a culture of belonging isn't just the right thing to do, it's also the smart thing. Diversity breeds innovation and the companies that attract the most talented and diverse workforce will succeed in our rapidly changing world.
>
> We are family. We celebrate our differences. We all belong."

Diversity breeds innovation, and the companies that attract the most talented and diverse workforce will succeed in our rapidly changing world. We believe our employees must have a voice in co-creating this better future and are working quickly to prioritize actions that will enable us to create sustainable long-term impact both inside and outside of Ford.

This is not a short-term commitment. Caring for each other and renewing our commitment to DEI is critical to our success.

5. Sustainability

As part of employee development, does your company encourage and support employees volunteering for local non-governmental organizations? Do you and your company consider this an opportunity for aligning company efforts, employee leadership development, and local progress on sustainability?

Corporate citizenship has been a top priority at Ford since our founding, with volunteerism long an integral part of our commitment to making a positive impact on society. We have a long-standing commitment to making a positive impact on society and build upon Henry Ford's legacy of helping create strong communities wherever Ford does business.

The Ford Volunteer Corps is on the front lines of our mission to strengthen communities. Since 2005, Ford employees have logged more than 1.7 million volunteer hours across six continents—building homes or gardens, renovating schools, feeding the hungry, installing clean water systems, and more. Every year, tens of thousands of employees volunteer in more than 1,500 community service projects around the world. Ford volunteers bring skill, enthusiasm, and teamwork to nonprofits, helping to get essential jobs done while the organizations focus on serving people in need.

Our "Thirty Under 30" program is an innovative philanthropic leadership course that matches young employees with nonprofits to address challenging social issues. Each class is made up of 30 diverse Ford employees under the age of 30. These fellows are selected from hundreds of competitive applicants from across the United States, Canada, and Mexico. Over the course of a year, the fellows learn how nonprofits operate, then work collaboratively to address major issues affecting people. The course introduces employees to design thinking—an increasingly popular process incorporating various mindsets, tools, and methods used to define and address complex problems. The fellows provide nonprofits with a different perspective on how to best engage new generations of donors and volunteers through technology, hands-on activities, and other means.

The Bill Ford Better World Challenge is a global grant program designed to inspire employees to brainstorm ideas for transforming daily life and solving problems in communities worldwide where Ford does business. Jointly funded by Bill Ford and Ford Fund, the program awards annual grants to employee-led projects that provide solutions to mobility challenges, meet basic needs such as food and shelter, or address water-related issues including access, hygiene, and sanitation. Projects are created, coordinated, and led by Ford employees in partnership with local nonprofit or nongovernmental organizations, giving employees a rare opportunity to serve with community activists and make a deep, lasting impact on the quality of life for people and families where they live and work.

While the pandemic has made life more difficult for all of us—especially our nonprofit partners and the people they serve—it has not dampened the spirit of giving among Ford employees who donated through virtual food drives, contactless food deliveries, in-kind donations, and holiday gifts.

Kimberly Rodriguez

Former Chief Executive Officer
Dura Automotive Systems

Background

Automotive industry veteran, Kimberly Rodriguez joined Dura Automotive Systems as Chief Executive Officer (CEO) and board member on September 1, 2020. Kimberly is an expert in transforming global organizations to maximize efficiencies in supply chain, manufacturing, and operational performance. During her 35-year career, she has assisted automakers and suppliers in driving value creation by leveraging the interface between finance, operational (plant floor) efficiency, and the effective use of technology.

Prior to joining Dura, Kimberly was CEO of Rush Trucking, guiding the reorganized company through the early days of the 2020 COVID automotive shutdown. She previously served as a principal of her own firm SCRM providing services to family/equity funds in transactions and restructurings. From 2010 to 2015, Kimberly was principal at KPMG, and from 2006 to 2010, she was a partner at Grant Thornton, where she brought on board her restructuring team and their industry-leading, proprietary financial and operational web-based analytical tool and its follow-on product to monitor extensive supply chains built during her time at Stout Risius Ross.

Kimberly sits on the Board of Directors for AMG Industries, LLC., and Romeo Rim. She is a founding member and the first female chair of the Private Director's Association.

Questions and Answers

1. Change Control, Resilience, and Work/Life Balance

How do you and your team continue to innovate and improve?

Ongoing innovation and improvement are a requirement, particularly in manufacturing. At Dura, we continuously raise the bar by establishing improvement goals at every level within the organization. Achieving self-imposed stretch goals drives ownership and engagement while necessitating fresh approaches. Innovation fostering, process focus, and agility all work in unison to arrive at effective value creation. And it is not just about solving today's problems. Much of the magic is anticipating future wants and needs, especially those that will give us a competitive advantage five to ten years from now. I try to create a balance of short-term and long-term thinking in our weekly agendas.

One area that I caution organizations to resist is a default reliance on throwing people or cash onto problems before really looking at what can be done to improve the processes at their core. A good rule is to evaluate whether processes are as efficient as possible before granting further expenditures.

Rewarding agility and accepting change assure that we do not restrict our vision to a narrow band of possible solutions. The COVID pandemic was a good lesson in agility. How can we run a global organization with limited travel? How can team members cross areas of expertise to support? How can I connect with a new organization without actually meeting most of them face to face? Setting aside time for creative problem solving, not accepting the notion that "it can't be done," is a core cultural mindset critical to making real innovation headway.

2. Growing Your Professional Network and Maintaining Mentor and Sponsor Relationships

How do you keep your existing relationships in this remote world? Are you maintaining face time with other execs while being remote? How do your direct reports maintain their face time with you?

It will be interesting to see how relationships evolve after the COVID required a move to remote connecting. I see potential positives and negatives from this evolution. On the positive side, people have accepted virtual connections, allowing the potential for a broader network base. It may also be an equalizer, as there is no physical barrier to cross between men and women, races, ages, cultures. Another positive has been the ability to see people in a more personal setting. In many cases, this has allowed business relationships to evolve into closer connections with a better understanding of the individuals we interact with.

However, some care has to be taken not to overuse email, i.e., not to send out corrections, irritations, disagreements over email versus a virtual face to face. The absence of face-to-face interaction can easily lead to misunderstanding and escalation through hostile email exchanges. There can also be a tendency not to reach out as much due to "Zoom exhaustion." Where possible, I have tried to alter the modes of communication and do more purposeful scheduling of calls than I might have done in a more person-to-person environment. More use of town halls, one-on-ones with all levels, and visiting in person where possible help keep the team together. In the manufacturing environment, on-site collaboration is a necessity to support launches and implement problem-solving activities. In this era of international travel restrictions, engaging with foreign ambassadors has helped administer access while adhering to regional safety protocols.

3. Personal Growth

Have you developed new behaviors (exercise, diet, meditation, hobbies, etc.) that help you get through this new stress?

I have spent a great deal of time on site with clients throughout my career, so I am not accustomed to spending a lot of time at my desk. To survive the daily video fest that I find myself in, I have taken to using a standing desk to move up and down. I also put a step under my desk so that if I am on a call (not video), where I do not have to use my keyboard, I can get in some movement. I have also taken to smiling heavily and waving as it is difficult to see if someone is smiling at you under a mask. In times of stress, it has been said that the CEO stands for the Chief Excitement Officer, and I believe that is true.

Stress relief is vital to sanity, and learning to let go is probably the hardest lesson. I have used yoga, tennis, reading material, and interaction with other people to stay focused in the present moment and to prompt clarity of thought. In a world that brings surprises and new challenges with every moment of every day, even the best-laid plans can end in a bust. As a sports coach's daughter, I am focusing on accepting my daily starting point, calling audibles when necessary, and always trying to move the ball forward toward the goal.

4. Diversity, Equity, and Inclusion

Is the board of directors of your company diverse and representative of your workforce and/or customers? Is the leadership team? Is the workforce? If the workforce and customers aren't currently diverse, is there greater interest and commitment to making change in this regard?

Dura is an international company with a significantly diverse workforce. Our business spans from seven countries across Europe to South America, China, Mexico, and the United States. We are focused on embracing diversity on all fronts, including diversity of thought, cultural background, race, and gender.

As Dura culture evolves under new ownership, diversity in our current and future leaders will be a strategic thrust. The addition of my role in the CEO position and diversity on our Board is a good start, but there is much work to be done. As a management team, it is our responsibility to cultivate individual thinking from all workforce levels. We are focused on bringing all views to the table. This approach has proven to result in a more stable, forward-thinking, and profitable company.

COVID has provided opportunities to adapt our approach to the recruitment of women. Given that the current at-home schooling situation is difficult for many women with children, we need to be more diligent in providing workplace solutions and flexibility that will allow us to attract and retain talent. There is support from our ownership group and Board to make headway on this issue. Our ownership group is a designated PRI (Principles in Responsible Investment) company, which is a public declaration as to their intent to focus on diversity, the environment, and community service.

5. Sustainability

ESG (Environmental, Social, and Governance) expectations of investors is greatly accelerating for both equity and debt investments among the largest investment banks and pension funds. Is your company taking this investor trend seriously and adapting strategy to meet these expectations?

ESG is accelerating across every aspect of our business environment. Our customers are demanding it, the retail customers are demanding it, investors and employees are demanding it; fundamentally, it is the right thing to do. Frankly, any organization that does not adapt its business to be a leader in ESG will not be around in the future. Dura is making significant investments to further our ESG initiatives through new programs, human capital, and financial commitments. It is a high-priority initiative driven by ownership and leadership that encompasses carbon footprint, diversity, equity and inclusion, energy usage, and community service. We follow the principles of responsible investment and incorporate ESG issues into our investment analysis and decision-making processes. In addition to embracing voluntary principles, it involves both internal and external third-party measurement to keep ourselves on track.

Strategic direction and management ownership is only the beginning. Manufacturers and employers similar to Dura must establish top-level and measurable metrics across the enterprise. Notably, the leading indicator KPI's must be a real-time topic of conversation and decision-making at every level and function of the organization. Our strategies include short-term and long-term initiatives to ensure Dura is a leader in ESG. It is a part of our strategic plan, and through our Hoshin planning system (a method for ensuring that the company's strategic goals drive progress and action at every level within that company), we can track our progress and continue setting new goals for improvement.

Sandra Phillips Rogers

Group Vice President, General Counsel and Chief Legal Officer and Chief Diverstity Officer
Toyota Motor North America, Inc.

Background

Sandra Phillips Rogers is Chief Legal Officer, Chief Diversity Officer, Board Director, Advisor, and ally. Her legal career and community leadership spans nearly 30 years, with extensive expertise in the private, oil and gas, pharmaceutical, and automotive sectors. Importantly, Phillips Rogers has been at the center of large-scale global transactions, complex litigation management, and strategy including issues/crisis management. Today, she oversees the vast legal services function for Toyota's North American operations, compliance and audit office, sustainability and regulatory affairs, and social innovation.

A graduate of the University of Texas at Austin, she is passionate and devoted to the success of women in the legal field and was a founding member of her alma matter's Center for Women in Law. In 2018, she received the University of Texas School of Law's Alumni Association's Outstanding Alumna Award. Phillips Rogers has been recognized by foundations, universities, and media organizations for her many contributions. Awards include *Automotive News*' 100 Leading Women and All Stars in 2020, *D-CEO*'s General Counsel Impact Player of the Year, *D-CEO*'s Dallas 500, and *Black Enterprise*'s Most Powerful Women in Business.

As a change agent, and Toyota's top D&I champion, Phillips Rogers is committed to driving unity, equity, and respect for *all* people through education, engagement, and action. Thanks in part to her vision and leadership, Toyota was recognized in *DiversityInc*'s Top 10 list in 2020.

- Public Boards: MSA Safety Incorporated (Law Committee Chair; Audit, Nominating, and Governance Committee Member) [NYSE: MSA]
- Nonprofit Boards: United Way of Metropolitan Dallas, UnidosUS, University of Texas Law School Foundation, Texas A&M Transportation Institute
- Membership: Executive Leadership Council

Questions and Answers

1. Change Control, Resilience, and Work/Life Balance

What did you learn when you began to work from home or work in the office with a limited number of co-workers? What did you need to start doing and what did you need to stop?

When I first began to work from home in mid-March 2020, I quickly learned that I would need a more consistent and effective way to communicate with my team and business colleagues. I set up daily calls with my leadership team to make sure we were touching base on the priorities the moment required, such as how to provide guidance so that our team members could be safe during the pandemic and how to interpret the myriad of local and state shelter-at-home or safer-at-home orders. I then needed to set up a schedule to make sure the non-pandemic priority matters were being addressed even while many courts around the country shuttered.

Our legal department made great use of digital charts and communication platforms that could be easily shared and updated in real time. I hold weekly meetings with my entire team ("Snacks with Sandra") as a casual check-in, which features important information but also light-hearted activities utilizing emerging gaming technologies like Kahoot. But perhaps most importantly, I make it a point to check in on team members to find out how they are doing personally.

Some of my team members live alone, others with children or elderly parents. The practice of *mendomi* (a Japanese word that means caring for family) became the norm. Part of *mendomi* also means trying to limit the duration/frequency of meetings and asking participants to open their video cameras so that we all can be seen as well as heard. As the pandemic wore on, I realized my team was not taking vacations. I encouraged my team to take time off, and in some instances, I strongly encouraged it! We have also had experts conduct workshops on meditation and wellness. To keep myself going, I take real lunch breaks and try to end the day early enough to get in some exercise.

2. Growing Your Professional Network and Maintaining Mentor and Sponsor Relationships

Are you continuing to grow your professional network while being remote? How?

One of the silver linings of the pandemic is that it has freed up more time to engage in professional development networking activity. Previously, I would limit myself to a certain number of networking activities, given the time it took to travel. I am actively involved in several executive and general counsel roundtable groups that not only have helped me maintain and grow my professional network but have also given me a wealth of information on how to navigate the challenges brought on by the pandemic and the social and racial justice issues that came to an inflection point in May 2020.

These virtual networking events also have given me a sense of calm and normalcy; I was not going through the year's challenges alone. I had a community I could draw upon and share wisdom and experiences. Even during the isolation of the pandemic, I feel more connected to my professional network than ever. And when the pandemic is over, I intend to keep growing my network, because this year has proven that we are stronger together.

3. Personal Growth

Have you developed new behaviors (exercise, diet, meditation, hobbies, etc.) that help you get through this new stress?

Once the pandemic settled in to stay for a while, I was determined to make this time count. While it's no excuse, my regular travel requirements made it very difficult to find an exercise and personal wellness routine that I could sustain. Now that I am not traveling, I am meditating each morning, and I find this helps me ease into the day with greater perspective. I also prepare breakfast every day rather than grabbing something on the fly. I think this also helps me get my day off to a more balanced start.

In addition, I regularly cook lunch and dinner. I am eating healthier, and this is something I plan to continue when our "new normal" takes hold. One thing I am most proud of is that I have taken up cycling. I started walking each day when the pandemic began, and it was a lifesaver in terms of getting outside my home office and seeing nature while getting a good workout. I had always wanted to cycle with my husband but had never really found the right way to get into the sport.

Sandra Phillips Rogers

In May 2020 my husband purchased an electric bicycle for me. Now instead of just seeing my neighborhood, I can bike eight miles down to White Rock Lake. Going to the lake makes me feel like I am at the beach, and I believe cycling has been a key component to weathering the pandemic mentally and physically. I still have yoga on my list to try!

4. Diversity, Equity, and Inclusion

There has been a lot of talk about diversity—and, in recent years, inclusion. Equity has entered the corporate conversation in a major way this year. What actions are you and your company taking? Are these methods aligned with company goals?

Toyota has been a leader in diversity and inclusion for many years, grounded in the company's core values of Respect for People and Continuous Improvement. We believe that it is important to have a workplace culture where team members can bring their full selves to work in order to unlock their highest potential and increase engagement and enrichment.

When George Floyd was killed in May 2020, Toyota, like many companies, realized that this moment required us to do even more for the cause of not only diversity, equity, and inclusion, but also social and racial justice. First, it was critical that Toyota speak out to denounce the racism, prejudice, and bigotry that led to Mr. Floyd's killing, and has unjustly impacted so many other Black Americans.

Second, we wanted to hear from our team members—how they were feeling and what they thought could be done to address racial injustice.

Third, drawing upon input from our team members, business partners, and external diversity advisory board, we developed a holistic approach that focused on (1) Advocacy, (2) Education, (3) Investment, (4) Business Partner Engagement, and (5) Team Member Development and Engagement.

Because our approach aligns with our core values and our overall approach to diversity and inclusion, we believe our efforts are sustainable and will make an impact to help address the cancer of racism that has existed for far too long in our society.

5. Sustainability

As part of employee development, does your company encourage and support employees volunteering for local nongovernmental organizations? Do you and your company consider this an opportunity for aligning company efforts, employee leadership development, and local progress on sustainability?

Toyota is proud to have Business Partnering Groups (BPGs)—13 different affinities and 100 chapters across North America—that are engaged in volunteer and community enhancement activities in the places where we live and work. Our BPGs are critical to cultivating an inclusive workforce, offering a voice and perspective for all team members, and providing support and advocacy for diverse communities. Each BPG has a leadership team comprised of team members and an executive sponsor.

Some of our larger BPGs, like the African American Collaborative (ACC) and the Women Influencing and Impacting Toyota (WIIT), host large development events at Toyota and partner with local organizations to provide much-needed resources to our communities and development opportunities for our team members. These partnerships and activities align with our core values and cultural priorities and have a 360-degree impact, which promotes sustainability.

This holistic approach resembles a hub and spokes, with our BPGs and team members at the core with arms extending to our community partners in the areas of workforce readiness, inclusive mobility, and community sustainability. This approach strengthens our internal operations and has served us very well during the pandemic and social injustice unrest of 2020.

Susan Sheffield

Executive Vice President and Chief Financial Officer
GM Financial

Background

Susan Sheffield currently serves as Executive Vice President and Chief Financial Officer, a position she's held since April 2018. Previously, she was the Executive Vice President and Treasurer, a role she assumed in June 2014. Prior to that, she served as Executive Vice President of Corporate Finance, from 2008 to 2014; Senior Vice President of Structured Finance, from 2004 to 2008; and Vice President of Structured Finance, from 2003 to 2004. Sheffield joined GM Financial, formerly known as AmeriCredit, in 2001 as Vice President in the Investor Relations group. Before joining the company, she worked in corporate and commercial banking for 13 years, primarily for JPMorgan and Wells Fargo Bank. Susan holds a bachelor's degree in Economics from the University of Illinois and a Master of Business Administration from Texas Christian University.

Questions and Answers

1. Change Control, Resilience, and Work/Life Balance

What did you learn when you began to work from home or work in the office with a limited number of co-workers? What did you need to start doing and what did you need to stop?

One key takeaway for me and other leaders I've spoken with during the shift to a work-from-home environment is the importance of extending grace to others. As leaders, our teams are comprised of diverse and unique people with diverse and unique needs and issues. And while that's always been the case, the COVID pandemic has brought this into focus in an entirely new and singular way, as employees have been forced to navigate unprecedented and sometimes very difficult family and health challenges. Ensuring our team members understand how much we care about them and their families' health and well-being remains paramount, and offering empathy and flexibility is integral to demonstrating that care.

I also believe the elevated conversations about mental health have been another positive byproduct of the changing workplace dynamics in the face of the pandemic. More people seem willing to speak openly and freely about their mental health struggles and triumphs, which in turn encourages and empowers others to do the same. This accelerated transparency and openness are healthy, not only for companies like ours but for our communities and society in general. As part of this, I've strived to become a better and more active listener, especially when someone is speaking from a place of vulnerability, to be present and authentic in these discussions, and to check in on my team and colleagues with more frequency and intention.

2. Growing Your Professional Network and Maintaining Mentor and Sponsor Relationships

Are you continuing to grow your professional network while being remote? How?

Networking is a skill I've long wished I'd developed and honed earlier in my career as it can have a significant impact on your professional path and trajectory. In the last decade, I've become much more diligent and consistent in my efforts to grow and maintain my network, including during the pandemic, although that has certainly evolved like all of our other interactions.

3. Personal Growth

What is the most profound impact this pandemic has had the way you think about your job, company, family life? Will it be sticky or do you expect everything to return to the previous status quo?

I believe one of the most profound impacts of the pandemic on leaders and companies will be how we learn and evolve from the "new normal" COVID has created. Before the pandemic, it wasn't uncommon to hear a leader express doubt that a strictly work-from-home structure could be successful. The resiliency and adaptability shown by our team members throughout the past ten months has answered this question and expanded our view on where and how people can work. We were really proud of the way our team pivoted so quickly and effectively to a remote working environment in the spring of 2020 (and throughout the crisis) to continue serving customers and dealers seamlessly. Most importantly, this paradigm shift allowed us to better safeguard our employees' and their families' health.

At the same time, not being together—spending hours on the phone or looking into a laptop camera or simply working in solitude—has also affirmed the unique value of togetherness. Many people I've talked with have expressed how much they miss seeing their colleagues and how lonely or overwhelming it can feel when work and home life are centered in the same physical space. Being together physically allows for more spontaneous collaboration and innovation. It is also important to preserving and communicating a strong culture. Developing talent and careers is critical for employee engagement, creating future leaders and overall company performance. The key will be how companies, leaders, and employees find the right balance and use the lessons and feedback from this grand experiment to come out on the other side better from it.

4. Diversity, Equity, and Inclusion

Are men engaged in the conversation around gender diversity and, if so, in what way?

At GM Financial, we believe men should be deeply and regularly engaged in conversations around gender diversity to affect meaningful and lasting change. At an executive level, the Diversity, Equity and Inclusion (DE&I) function reports directly to our President and CEO Dan Berce, who is and has always been a strong advocate for diversity and inclusion, including gender diversity, at the company. Kyle Birch, President of North America Operations, also serves as the executive sponsor of our DE&I program, which is a critically important role for him to embody, as the majority of our workforce reports into his organization.

From a programmatic perspective, our DE&I team, led by Global Vice President Shunda Robinson, has structured the discussions and resulting work streams on gender diversity to ensure men are engaged. The organization's first employee resource group, the Women's Inspiration Network, included an intentional focus on inviting and encouraging men to join their women colleagues in participating. We're proud of the strides the company has made since launching a formalized DE&I program in 2015, but we know there's certainly still much work left to do.

5. Sustainability

As part of employee development, does your company encourage and support employees volunteering for local nongovernmental organizations? Do you and your company consider this an opportunity for aligning company efforts, employee leadership development, and local progress on sustainability?

Facilitating and encouraging employee volunteerism is a cornerstone of our community investment footprint at GM Financial. Full-time employees are offered eight hours of paid time off each quarter to volunteer with a qualified 501(c)(3) organization, with part-time employees offered four hours. This means each year, thousands of employee volunteer hours are logged in service of communities across North America. Like our parent company, General Motors, GM Financial has also prioritized and invested in improving sustainability. This includes progress towards achieving "zero waste to landfill" status for all of our facilities, contributing toward the enterprise's efforts to reduce our carbon intensity, continuing to pursue a robust renewable energy strategy, and more. Paperless billing and e-contracting are other unique ways GM Financial is helping drive increased sustainability for the enterprise. These digital solutions for customers and dealers not only save money and reduce paper waste, they also lower our overall carbon footprint.

Christine Sitek

Executive Director, Global Purchasing and Supply Chain
General Motors

Background

Christine Sitek is a global leader with over 30 years' experience in the automotive industry with General Motors [NYSE:GM], a $137B auto manufacturer. Sitek's career at General Motors has been defined by bold cross-functional moves requiring extreme adaptability, change leadership, and turn-around capability. She has deep knowledge of new business model development, manufacturing and supply operations, purchasing, quality, customer experience, women's leadership, and crisis management.

In addition to her professional career, she currently serves on the Board for Inforum, a professional women's alliance, and the Detroit Institute of Arts (DIA). At the DIA she Chairs the Human Resources Management Committee and serves on the Executive Committee. At Inforum she serves on the Leadership Development Committee. She is also the executive sponsor for GM's women's employee resource group focused on attracting, retaining, engaging, and developing over 5,000 women globally.

In her current role as Executive Director for Interior and Exterior at GM Global Purchasing and Supply Chain (GPSC) she is responsible for managing tens of billions of dollars in global procurement spend of all interior and exterior vehicle commodities. She is developing and executing innovative sourcing strategies that maximize vehicle profitability and speed to market while improving supplier performance and relationships.

Sitek holds a Bachelor of Arts from Michigan State University and an MBA from the University of Detroit Mercy. She was three times named one of the "100 Leading Women in the North American Auto Industry" by *Automotive News*. In 2017, she was a Powered by Women honoree by *DBusiness Magazine*, Detroit's premier business journal.

Sitek resides in Michigan with her husband and two children.

Questions and Answers

1. Change Control, Resilience, and Work/Life Balance

Many have said that there is no separation of work and home these days—what do you do to manage this for your own work? What are you doing to increase the ability of your team to create and respect boundaries?

Having the flexibility to work from home during the pandemic has been incredible. General Motors has put the health and safety of its employees as a top priority. Energy and resources have been poured into the safety protocols for those employees that had to go into the office, labs, or manufacturing locations. If a job could be done from home, it is done from home. I personally have been working from home since March 13, 2019. The lack of separation between work and home can be very challenging. I learned very quickly that everyone's situation is unique. My husband, two adult children, and I are all working out of the same house. Internet bandwidth and overlapping conference calls is a daily battle. In addition, I found I had no sense of routine and often was skipping lunch and working well into the evenings. I realized very quickly that on my worst and stressful day; I had a less complicated environment than most of my employees. In addition to the demands of their jobs, many employees have young children ranging from infants to toddlers to school age. I knew if I was having a hard time separating work and home, my team was struggling even more. I did many empathy discussions with team members and conducted a pulse survey to obtain feedback.

We put a calendar entry on every employee's schedule from noon to 1:00 PM that simply says "Christine says take lunch." This was so simple, yet so effective. Team members called me right away and said because it is on my calendar and "you said it is ok," I have taken lunch or used the hour to focus on my family. We try very hard to end meetings ten minutes early so team members have time to transition, get something to drink, or check on their family before the next meeting. I have become much more disciplined in creating a routine for myself every day and setting a good example for my family and my team. I have made time to exercise every day. My family and I also eat dinner together every day. I have found that setting aside this time and purposefully blocking a calendar entry is very helpful. I work hard not to sweat the small stuff and simply be thankful for the health and safety of my friends, family, and team.

2. Growing Your Professional Network and Maintaining Mentor and Sponsor Relationships

How do you keep your existing relationships in this remote world? Are you maintaining face time with other execs while being remote? How do your direct reports maintain their face time with you?

I find that I need to be very intentional about maintaining relationships. When I was working in the office seeing people every day, connecting over a coffee, or even walking through the hallways was an everyday occurrence. I often had mentor/mentee meetings over lunch or dinner. Working from home has made networking difficult but not impossible. I have pushed myself and my team to turn our cameras on more often. I have a weekly "huddle" with my direct reports. We agreed to hold this meeting with the cameras turned on. Baseball caps are acceptable attire and the environment is casual. This meeting is incredibly valuable for us to connect with each other and to actually "see" each other. Seeing people's body language and facial expressions during discussions is so critically important to communication. I also hold virtual coffee chats with teams of employees called "Caffeine with Christine," where we turn cameras on as well. Virtual meetings with other executives both internally and externally have been instrumental in maintaining relationships and sharing best practices.

3. Personal Growth

Have you developed new behaviors (exercise, diet, meditation, hobbies, etc.) that help you get through this new stress?

The flexibility of working from home has allowed me to exercise almost daily. I have built time into my schedule every day for some time of activity. My husband and I try to walk together as often as we can. The time we spend together walking has been a bright spot during these difficult times. In addition to exercise, I am reading and streaming a bit more. I read and watch for the pure enjoyment, so this has been a great way to unplug and de-stress.

4. Diversity, Equity, and Inclusion

There has been a lot of talk about diversity—and, in recent years, inclusion. Equity has entered the corporate conversation in a major way this year. What actions are you and your company taking? Are these methods aligned with company goals?

An essential part of identifying solutions to the opportunities and challenges our industry faces is the importance of having a diversity of thoughts, ideas, and perspectives. This is even more critical given what's happening in the world today.

At General Motors, we aspire to be the most inclusive company in the world. In this moment, we each must decide what we can do—individually and collectively—to drive meaningful, deliberate change. To help make this happen, the company recently announced the Inclusion Advisory Board (IAB), which is made up of internal and external members and led by Mary Barra, our Chairman and CEO.

As a member of GM Global Purchasing and Supply Chain leadership team, we are proud that Dennis Archer Jr., the CEO of Ignition Media Group and founding partner of Archer Corporate Services (ACS) has volunteered to serve on the Board.

We are confident that GM, with our key stakeholders and supplier partners, will be industry leaders for the imperative purpose. We have proven that we can lead the way.

- GM was the first automaker to establish a supplier diversity program in 1968.
- African-American suppliers represented 32% of our total diverse spend in 2019, and GM's 8-year average for total tier-1 diverse spend is $3.6 billion.
- The company's African-American supplier spend has consistently accounted for over $1 billion with nearly 60 of the 360 total tier-1 suppliers, and four of our 17 Supplier Council members are black suppliers.

Our focus areas moving into 2021 will continue to be on supplier diversity health checks, which are comprehensive assessments that account for both GM and supplier feedback relative to six key performance indicators to measure both short- and mid-term supply chain inclusion. We will also continue to emphasize our diverse supplier development efforts, including maintaining support of our strategic partnership with Dartmouth's Tuck Diverse Business Executive Education, which awards 20 to 25 scholarships annually.

Our supplier diversity vision remains to serve as an economic engine that drives empowerment, equity, and inclusion within our supply chain and community. We are proud of our history at GM—but more importantly—excited about the future.

5. Sustainability

Sustainability trends (climate change, water availability, health, etc.) are some of the strongest drivers for future changes for companies and their strategies. What are you seeing within your company? Is your firm reading the trends and adapting strategies to survive and then thrive with new growth?

We are acutely aware of the responsibility and opportunity to use GM's scale and resources to drive a better, more sustainable, and inclusive future for all. GM's vision is one with Zero Crashes, Zero Emissions, and Zero Congestion. In this pivotal moment in time, our sights are set on the many ways we can drive sustainable value for each and every one of our stakeholders.

We recognize building a more sustainable future is something that will require engagement from all of us, and GM's Global Purchasing and Supply Chain (GPSC) organization is uniquely positioned to play a key leadership role within the company. We are committed to forming and nurturing exemplary supplier relationships built on integrity and shared values. Early in 2020, we launched the GPSC Sustainability team, which includes a diverse team of nearly 60 members from all areas of the organization and outside the function.

This team has already made an impact, including the addition of a sustainability metric to our supplier scorecard. In addition, the team held three symposiums with suppliers in 2020, including the Sustainability Through Innovation Symposium in the fall. This engagement had over 650 participants from 18 countries including GPSC employees, tier-1 suppliers, industry leaders, and academic thought-leaders sharing insights around innovation and sustainability.

In 2020, we also established the GM Supplier Sustainability Sub-Council, which was created to foster an environment of idea sharing, goal setting, and accountability among GM and the ten global suppliers.

With our pillars of sustainable suppliers, sustainable materials, green logistics, and sustainable packaging, our goal is nothing less than to positively change the world and help establish GM as a leader in sustainability.

Anna Stefanopoulou

William Clay Ford Professor of Technology
University of Michigan

Background

Prof. Anna Stefanopoulou is the William Clay Ford Professor of Technology at the University of Michigan. Stefanopoulou joined the Department of Mechanical Engineering in 2000 after working in the automotive industry. She is in the fellow rank of three engineering societies (IEEE, SAE, ASME). Her innovation in powertrain control technology has been recognized by multiple awards and has been documented in a book, 21 U.S. patents, 340 publications (8 of which have received awards) on estimation and control of internal combustion engines and electrochemical processes such as fuel cells and batteries. Stefanopoulou also has co-authored influential reports on the cost-effectiveness of fuel-efficient technologies for light-duty vehicles, sponsored by the National Academies, to help inform policymakers.

Questions and Answers

1. Change Control, Resilience, and Work/Life Balance

Many have said that there is no separation of work and home these days—what do you do to manage this for your own work? What are you doing to increase the ability of your team to create and respect boundaries?

I am not very good about managing this separation myself. In fact, there was no such separation in my life before. Even before the pandemic, my work and non-work life were mixed and seamlessly integrated in my day, having frequently meetings and even lab work after dinner. Finding time to exercise and go for long walks with my family in nature was an important goal for me, so I was always organizing everything around these few milestones. Throughout the pandemic, we tried to communicate and define better similar constraints for all of us. In some sense, we flipped the notion that these are constraints or boundaries, and we treated them more as values that we should not only respect but celebrate.

2. Growing Your Professional Network and Maintaining Mentor and Sponsor Relationships

Have your mentees been asking different questions than under usual working conditions? Have you needed to do more hand-holding? Do you see more mentees seeking career change or seeking educational opportunities? Something else?

The physical-distancing restrictions in the lab have many challenges. Most of our experiments require new instrumentation that is always safer to perform with others in presence. Experiments are a teamwork. More importantly, our students learn from shadowing and assisting more senior students. There were a lot more meetings and a concentrated effort to compensate for the missing opportunities for such lab interactions and experience.

Obviously, many of our students were nervous about launching their career in the middle of the pandemic, but most of them saw it as an opportunity to take extra responsibilities and courses. We created certificates, Journal/book clubs, and projects for extra credit especially in data analytics and simulation tools.

3. Personal Growth

Have you developed new behaviors (exercise, diet, meditation, hobbies, etc.) that help you get through this new stress?

I started cooking with my 15-year-old daughter and eating a regular lunch, followed by a walk. That midday break helped me with all the conference calls that often start at 7 am and continue at 9 pm. I will miss this precious break when we both go back to school.

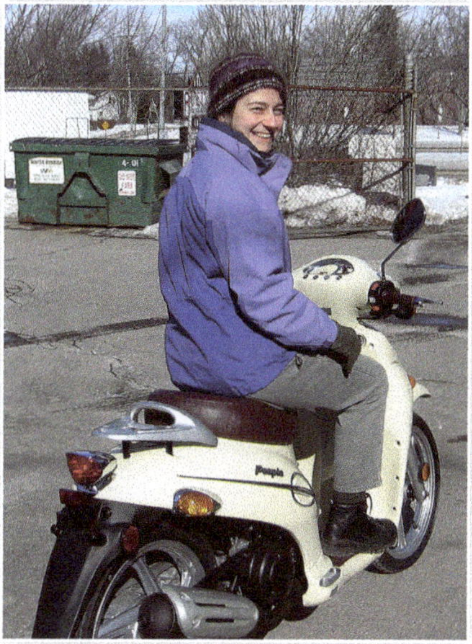

Anna Stefanopoulou

We were also very lucky to create a pod with two other families, so we started sharing shopping chores, cooking recipes, movies, and stories when it was feasible in our patios. It was a great connection and a fun activity that kept us all engaged, yet healthy and happy. I will try to maintain this friendship and share more delicious dishes and hikes together.

4. Diversity, Equity, and Inclusion

The pandemic has hit hard for women in particular. Many are thinking about dialing back their careers or exiting altogether, which is very frightening for many companies. What should be done differently to retain women in the workplace?

For those of us fortunate to stay healthy and stable financially, the pandemic made us more alert of important long-term career goals and life values. Companies and institutions that cared about diverse talent recognize the need to retain the best. For this, they embraced flexibility, trust, communication, and openness along with daycare support for young children and/or elderly parents. Schedule flexibility and remote work is important even for the ones that felt the need to start a hobby, or devoted to a community cause, or started a philanthropic activity. So balancing flexibilities across a team is important and can only happen if diversity is respected and celebrated.

5. Sustainability

What do you as a leader do to stay informed about sustainability trends that can impact the success of your company and its strategy?

Our students demand our attention and action to avert and manage the climate crisis. I participate in the University of Michigan Commission on Carbon Neutrality, where we provided recommendation on how to decarbonize the three UM campuses in Ann Arbor, Flint, and Dearborn. This can only happen in collaboration and in coordination with the communities around the campuses and specifically the city of Ann Arbor. To this end, I also participate in various community groups that are thinking of barriers, needs, and proposing comprehensive policies for adopting electric vehicles (EVs), electric heating and cooling for buildings, and other efficiency improvements along with energy storage for renewables. One such example is the EV readiness ordinance to support and accelerate Ann Arbor's effort (A2Zero) that set an ambitious strategy for reaching community-wide carbon neutrality by 2030.

Sandy Stojkovski

Chief Executive Officer, North America
Vitesco Technologies, LLC

Background

Sandy Stojkovski was appointed Chief Executive Officer (CEO) for Vitesco Technologies North America (VT NA, formerly Continental Powertrain division), effective October 2019. In this role, she oversees all the North American activities for the company.

Stojkovski has collected broad business experience with corporations ranging in size from start-ups to Fortune 500 companies during her distinguished 25-year career. Prior to joining Vitesco Technologies in 2017 as Senior Vice President of the Global Injectors Product Line, Stojkovski held numerous executive leadership positions including North American Powertrain President and General Manager of Magneti Marelli, Vice President of Global Engineering at TRW Automotive, and more than 10 years as an automotive technology consultant. In this area, Stojkovski founded her own advanced technology planning firm, which was later acquired by AVL.

Stojkovski earned an MBA, a master's degree in Industrial and Systems Engineering, and a bachelor's degree in Mechanical Engineering from the University of Michigan. She serves on SAE's North American International Powertrain Leadership Committee, is a board member of Inforum, an executive steering committee member for Inforum's AutomotiveNEXT, and a CTI Symposium USA Advisory Board member. Stojkovski was recently honored as one of the 2020 *Automotive News* 100 Leading Women.

Stojkovski and her family currently reside in Northville, Michigan.

Questions and Answers

1. Change Control, Resilience, and Work/Life Balance

What did you learn when you began to work from home or work in the office with a limited number of co-workers? What did you need to start doing and what did you need to stop?

With the experience of having navigated the 2008-2009 financial crisis, our management team and I quickly recognized the crisis the COVID pandemic presented. What took a little more time was to assess all the ways a global pandemic was likely to be much more severe (health, financial, civil rights, and political). We, like the rest of the industry, didn't have a roadmap for how to navigate a pandemic. Furthermore, as a relatively new CEO for North America leading a team deep into the process of readying for our pending spin-off from Continental, it was an unanticipated test for us. So a big crisis, no roadmap, and a new leader and team that hadn't worked together much before...sounds great, right? Actually, in many ways it was. Upon reflection, what was vital to our success was the clarity of our strategic goals for 2030 and a determination to navigate the crisis in a way that we would come out better for having gone through it.

I believe that you can't overcommunicate in a crisis. Open communication drives problem solving, alignment, and, most importantly, trust. But it's precisely in a crisis where a leader finds sometimes more questions than answers. Some leaders wait to meet with their teams until they have all the answers. Instead, we put in place a scaffolding set of digital internal communication meetings in North America for the leadership team, the management team, for all-employee meetings, and many "let's talk, coffee chats." Supported by a clear value placed on using "radical truth" borrowed from Ray Dalio, anyone could ask anything and expect either an answer on the spot or an answer once one was available. This more vulnerable approach to communications showed me just how powerful it is to hold the meetings, to answer what you can, and get comfortable not having all the answers.

I continue to get feedback through various channels that this approach to communications is and was highly appreciated. It required investing in the time and tools to make it possible. It also required taking the risk to be open to receive any question. But, as I reflect on 2020, I believe we proved that you really can turn a crisis into a positive, transformative event.

2. Growing Your Professional Network and Maintaining Mentor and Sponsor Relationships

Are you continuing to grow your professional network while being remote? How?

This is definitely not the time to retreat and stop networking. I have always been intentional and deliberate in communicating and building relationships especially externally. I have really missed the benefit of the normal rotation of industry conferences, dinners, and other face-to-face venues where relationships are built and fostered. I can't wait until those events are back to normal, but in the meantime, I have put in place a rotation of digital meetings to ensure priority relationships are nurtured.

I have further spoken at various external venues such as the Center for Automotive Research (CAR) Management Briefing Seminars or the Car Training Institute (CTI) Symposium USA to remain visible and accessible within the industry.

I also serve on several external boards, some of which are outside of automotive. Serving in these ways enables me to continue to grow my professional network and gain experiences. Working with others across diverse organizations has offered an excellent opportunity to form strong bonds with very talented people, learn from a diversity of perspectives, and witness effective leadership styles.

3. Personal Growth

What personal development opportunities have you taken advantage of now that you're not traveling?

I've always loved team sports—the competition and camaraderie is great. But along the way, I've learned that my race is not in competition with others. My race is against "yesterday me." I am on a journey to fulfill my purpose which I have defined as being the kind of leader I would want to have. One who creates the kind of environment where all talent can fulfill their fullest potential. This is not about one skill in particular—it's a journey of ongoing personal development, and with another 20 years or so to go in my career, I'm probably halfway there, but I'm always working to improve upon yesterday me. Therefore, I have always been disciplined about daily personal growth and development and physical activity. While not new, the suspension of travel has given me more time for both—often at the same time. Extra walks while listening to inspiring podcasts have replaced commute times while evenings and weekends are filled with martial arts, service on external boards, and reading up on our industry. All of this helps me to be resourceful and to be of greater service to my team—because you can't give what you don't have.

4. Diversity, Equity, and Inclusion

There has been a lot of talk about diversity—and, in recent years, inclusion. Equity has entered the corporate conversation in a major way this year. What actions are you and your company taking? Are these methods aligned with company goals?

There has been a lot of talk, indeed. As an engineer, I've never been satisfied with the talk, as I didn't believe the actions taken were appropriately connected to a clear understanding of the underlying root causes. This disconnect between the two is something I vowed to reconcile.

I've long believed that it is the **leader's mission to create an environment where all talent can thrive** so that there is diversity of expressed thoughts. I admit, this leader's mission idea started for me out of my personal frustration in some of the obstacles I faced as a minority in a male-dominated industry. But this initial frustration motivated me to ensure that in each leadership role I've held, to work to create that environment within my sphere of influence.

When I took over as CEO VT NA in the fall of 2019, I realized that I now had the span of responsibility where I could establish systemic solutions for diversity and inclusion (D&I). There was no "they" to look to establish this environment—that "they" for North America was me. Within our annual strategy-setting process in February, we identified an action in support of employee satisfaction as establishing a diversity and inclusion program. Our D&I project stalled during the early months of COVID, but in May/June, with the killing of George Floyd and the global calls for social justice and equal rights, it was painfully obvious that our previous well-intentioned approaches weren't sufficient. But every crisis is an opportunity, and for DE&I, this was a catalyzing moment for us.

And so, we the leadership team at Vitesco Technologies North America, launched our own DE&I strategy development for the region, elevating DE&I on par with our overall business strategy. The goal is to establish DE&I by addressing systemic root causes and thereby transforming our culture as a company, as opposed to some lesser form of compliance training that checks a box once a year. A journey to create a culture where all talent can thrive to their fullest potential...because it's the right thing to do, and it's best for the company.

During the past months, we have actively engaged in programs with Inforum, pledged our support through the PwC CEO Action pledge, and joined the Center for Automotive Diversity, Inclusion, and Advancement (CADIA) CEO Roundtable. We conducted in depth workshops with my extended leadership team to develop a regional strategy for DE&I. This strategy includes many actions, some of which are already in place including establishing a Women's Employee Resource Group (Women of Vitesco Technologies) and employee advisory councils in all three countries in our region. We also held our own employee "Courageous Conversations" for sharing and listening to experiences of diverse and minority employees.

While this strategy and these actions are an important beginning to our journey, they are also only a beginning. I am, however, confident that we will make sustainable progress on this regional journey especially now that we expand its scope worldwide for Vitesco Technologies.

5. Sustainability

Sustainability trends (climate change, water availability, health, etc.) are some of the strongest drivers for future changes for companies and their strategies. What are you seeing within your company? Is your firm reading the trends and adapting strategies to survive and then thrive with new growth?

Vitesco Technologies is, by definition, linked with sustainability. We are a leading international developer and manufacturer of modern powertrain technologies specifically targeting sustainable mobility. We are focused on intelligent and reliable system solutions and components for electric, hybrid, and combustion powertrains. Our goal at Vitesco Technologies is to make mobility clean, efficient, and affordable globally. One of the underlying principles of our business is the reduction of emissions in transportation.

As previously announced, our parent company Continental intends to spin off its automotive powertrain business as Vitesco Technologies in 2021. In our preparations, we are transforming Vitesco Technologies to fully support the emerging era of electrification in the automotive industry. Our core business contains our

Electrification Technology portfolio, our highly electronics-focused business of Electronic Controls as well as our Sensing and Actuation technologies. As Vitesco Technologies, we have undergone a review of strategic options, which include the exit or phaseout of certain product lines associated with legacy internal combustion engines.

The result is a clear focus on our electronics expertise and electrification growth opportunities.

Maximiliane Straub

President, Global Business Services
Bosch

Background

Maximiliane (Max) Straub is President and Chair of the Board of Management of Global Business Services for Robert Bosch GmbH, a position she has held since January 2020. In addition, she serves as CFO for Robert Bosch LLC and as Chair of the Board of Directors for the Bosch Community Fund, the company's U.S.-based foundation.

Prior to assuming this role, she served as Executive Vice President of Finance, Administration, and Controlling of Robert Bosch LLC from 2010 to 2019. In this position, she shaped Bosch's North American strategy for diversity and inclusion, corporate social responsibility, and innovation. Straub is passionate about technology and innovation, having guided internal startups through the Bosch Startup Platform and regularly mentoring external startups.

Straub currently serves on the Board of Directors of Inforum, a professional organization focused on creating strategic connections to help advance professional women in Michigan and the Midwest. In 2010, 2015 and 2020, Straub was recognized by *Automotive News* as one of the "Top 100 Women in the Auto Industry." She is a guest lecturer for the University of Michigan Ross School of Business program, "Ascending to the C-Suite: From Theory to Practice." Straub currently serves on the Board of Directors for SMART Global Holdings (NASDAQ: SGH). Her prior board service includes Horizon Global Corporation (NYSE: HZN) and MTS Systems Corporation (NASDAQ: MTSC).

Questions and Answers

1. Change Control, Resilience, and Work/Life Balance

How has your self-motivation been to excel, learn, reach out (virtually), and manage all aspects of your new work life?

It might sound strange, but I have the feeling that my entire career has prepared me for facing change, including how to work through a global pandemic. I love people and technology and learned early how to carefully juggle work life and home life. Being self-motivated has created opportunities to learn different skills, tinker in new areas, and work through incredible challenges.

The pandemic created an urgency to learn many new things, mainly new tools for communication and collaboration, and skills to provide effective leadership and feedback in a completely remote and global work environment. While the transition to virtual communication tools was already underway, virtual collaboration tools were more difficult to gain acceptance. For me, feedback in a virtual world was one of the most difficult endeavors. While we have many new tools to gauge associate well-being, I struggled with the lack of personal, face-to-face dialogue with our teams. The pandemic stole our chance for regular alignment and discussion in a trusted space. I quickly had to adapt and make a conscious effort to build that same trust over video tools where people are naturally more reluctant. I invested significant time in asking associates about their personal situation, fears, workload, and needs until they were comfortable sharing on their terms.

While adapting to new virtual tools and working from home, I needed to quickly learn how to set boundaries on working time. I could have been stationed at my computer all day and night throughout 2020. Between working across global time zones, networking across the industry, and staying connected to family and friends across the world, I made sure to take time for one of my personal passions—reading. One of the bright spots of the pandemic was reading a comprehensive biography of Leonardo Da Vinci, one of the greatest inventors with a mind far ahead of his time.

Being curious, I also used my newfound "non-travel" time to learn as much as I could about COVID, which helped me make informed decisions. This research also helped me realize the impact of inequalities in such a time. I wanted to learn everything about how COVID exacerbated societal inequity—why it happened, what decisions in history were made, and what impact they continue to have. The knowledge of "why" is always extremely important to me because it highly influences the solutions and the timeframe to change things.

2. Growing Your Professional Network and Maintaining Mentor and Sponsor Relationships

Has your company maintained learning and leadership development opportunities, culture surveys, 360 surveys, etc. to grow skills and manage the emotional intelligence of the company? Has anything shifted? What have you learned?

I had just taken a new position two months before the pandemic—leading a massive transformation of our Global Services business encompassing more than 10,000 associates around the world. Our new leadership team did not have time to get to know each other before we all went into the home office across three different continents. The transformation of this business will result in a completely new organization, including end-to-end process definitions, global collaboration models, and many other changes. A daunting task in a "regular" environment and outrageous in the face of a completely virtual world. Our leadership team had to find new ways to develop trust with our associates and engage them in the change management process.

From the beginning of our tenure, we committed to transparent and two-way communication. For example, we implemented leadership dialogues which not only provided information to associates but secured associate feedback through polls and open Q&A. We shifted our communication strategy to a digital-first mindset, using blogs and virtual workshops to maintain cooperation, virtual content learning to continue training possibilities, and on-demand education tools for associates to utilize when it was convenient for them. One key learning was the need to change how we provided information in a digital setting compared to in person—we significantly shortened individual modules, added more opportunities for small-group interaction, and created more downtime for associates to step away from their screens. Together, these changes helped to keep people engaged.

Despite the challenges of the pandemic, we managed to achieve the learning and development milestones we had planned, but it was very tough for people. After some months we had to think more about incorporating learning opportunities for mental and physical well-being, as the pandemic had added quite some additional stress on all our associates. For example, we provided hints to not send e-mails at any time so that associates do not feel pressure to reciprocate, and we actively followed up with associates to gauge their ability to balance work and home time.

3. Personal Growth

Have you developed new behaviors (exercise, diet, meditation, hobbies, etc.) that help you get through this new stress?

Leading myself during the pandemic was quite difficult, and I have to admit that I am still working on it. Before the pandemic, my global position meant a lot of travel to properly meet with teams around the world. Now from my home office outside of Detroit, I needed to find a way to be accessible to teams across multiple time zones, resulting in a working day that could easily be around the clock. Some months into the pandemic, I had to self-regulate my daily schedule—I went into a two shift operation for myself, working very early in the morning until about noon, taking a two- to three-hour break to refresh my mind, and starting my second shift later in the afternoon through the evening. Most of the time I use this break to spend time with my boys, going on long walks, and connecting with family and friends. Walking with friends helped my mind to recharge.

One of my favorite relaxation tools is actually to work with my hands. This includes everything from cooking and gardening to renovating houses. We were fortunate this summer and found a dream property for tinkerers—my partner is also very handy around the house! Three cabins dating from 1937 to 1970, the oldest being a log home. We gutted the cabins and are now rebuilding them. People around me are often surprised that I know how to tile, paint, lay floors, and many more things, but I have been doing that all my life. My parents were quite poor when they got married, and my mom has always done everything herself, from sewing our clothes to painting the walls. She taught both my brother and I to not only do the same things but to honor the work with our hands. These lifelong skills also helped us in our journey to independence, something she always pushed us to be. I truly enjoy being able to see the results of my work immediately and see how something can transform from shambles to a dream. Seeing these accomplishments of my hard work have always given me tremendous energy. A positive side effect of renovating is that I can think about anything and everything while working and have come up with many solutions, tactics, and new things to try while doing so.

I still have to continue to push myself to think about my mental and physical health—I spend way too many hours at my desk! To force myself to engage in more physical activity, I installed a Pedometer App on my phone with clear goals of steps to take every day. In addition, I have installed a certain routine to stay in touch with people I care about; I just cannot do more virtual meetings after long workdays.

Despite these efforts, it is still incredibly hard when I can't be there to support loved ones who have experienced tragedy during the pandemic. Not being able to say goodbye to loved ones, not being able to embrace those grieving, and not being there to share in the physical support in the wake of loss has been incredibly difficult for me to accept. I have learned during this pandemic that these little gestures have way more importance than we previously realized, and the healing process will take a long time due to the fact that we could not see each other, touch each other, and help each other through difficult times.

4. Diversity, Equity, and Inclusion

The pandemic has hit hard for women in particular. Many are thinking about dialing back their careers or exiting altogether, which is very frightening for many companies. What should be done differently to retain women in the workplace?

Inequalities were placed under a microscope in 2020, as we saw the consequences of COVID on working women. Not only are women more in service industries than men—where they also had to struggle between jobs where they were overproportionally exposed to getting infected—but women are commonly the primary caregiver for children and bore the impact of homeschooling and childcare during the pandemic. According to a 2020 survey from Brookings*, one out of four women who became unemployed during the pandemic reported the job loss was due to a lack of childcare, twice the rate of men surveyed.

The good news is that for companies like Bosch, the workplace has become more accepting of the concept of virtual work. It has become the norm, not the exception, to hear children playing or dogs barking in the background of a meeting. Company culture has evolved more in the past year than in the past decade to accept that people may work at different hours of the day to balance their family and work responsibilities. The pandemic fast-tracked efforts to digitally transform our workplace with new tools and cultural norms, including video. In a short period of time, we learned that a productive culture is far more impactful than a presence culture. Most importantly, I believe we rediscovered empathy through the pandemic. Across all levels of the organization, COVID served as a reminder that we all face personal struggles that must be balanced with workplace responsibilities.

The bad news is that these accomplishments are generally limited to those positions that are able to be performed from home and have limited impact on women in the healthcare and service industries. But I'm encouraged by solutions developed to support women—and men—working in service industries and caring for families during the pandemic. For example, the creation of low-cost childcare options specifically for frontline workers. In some countries, individuals can apply for income replacement when needing to stay home due to caretaking. It is unacceptable that highly developed countries like the United States have struggled to support working women during this pandemic. Changing this situation will not happen overnight, but we must learn from 2020, continue to identify the inequalities, and jointly work on solutions across industries.

* https://www.brookings.edu/essay/why-has-covid-19-been-especially-harmful-for-working-women/

5. Sustainability

As part of employee development, does your company encourage and support employees volunteering for local nongovernmental organizations? Do you and your company consider this an opportunity for aligning company efforts, employee leadership development, and local progress on sustainability?

One of the reasons I work for Bosch is that the company has been thinking about sustainability for many years. This longstanding approach is also clear in our mission—"Invented for life"—meaning that we want our products to spark enthusiasm, improve the quality of life, and help conserve natural resources. While sustainability has been part of our DNA for more than 135 years, we achieved a new level of commitment in 2020 by becoming the first global industrial enterprise to achieve net-zero carbon emissions with respect to the energy we produce and source. All 400 Bosch locations worldwide have been carbon neutral since 2020.

In addition to this global commitment to sustainability, it is also part of our DNA to encourage our associates to contribute to our mission through the support of local communities. In North America, we realize this commitment primarily through two avenues. I'm proud that we launched our regional foundation, the Bosch Community Fund, in 2012. Through the foundation, we directly support nonprofit partners in and around Bosch communities with more than $5 million in annual grants focused on the areas of STEM education and sustainability. Balancing the foundation, we also maintain a strong associate engagement strategy to support our regional corporate social responsibility (CSR) goals. While we have many programs, one of my favorites is an associate volunteer effort we call "Bosch Builds." The program was developed by my mentee, Alissa Cleland, about eight years ago and provides associates working time to volunteer in the local community, directly engaging with our nonprofit partners. Bosch Builds has become a signature program for our headquarter sites, and the framework is available for other locations to adapt to their specific needs. The program has been an impactful tool for team building, as well as creating joint volunteer opportunities with our customers.

The impact of COVID in 2020 required us to reflect on how our community engagement could adapt to the pandemic. The Bosch Community Fund was able to swiftly amend grant criteria to include COVID relief provisions. In total, the Bosch Community Fund invested $1 million through 55 grants to nonprofits responding to COVID, supporting direct and indirect needs for immediate and long-term community assistance. As in-person volunteering was not possible during the pandemic, our CSR strategy shifted to provide virtual support across the region. For example, the first Bosch Cares month occurred in October, with 30 days of our regional locations coming together to support local nonprofits where our associates are most passionate and engaged. Our goal was to show our associates, and communities, that Bosch continues to pay it forward and live the values of our founder, even in difficult times. More than 8,400 associates from 15 Bosch locations in the region participated in our virtual Bosch Cares events, with more than $43,000 donated to local nonprofits that are important to our team members.

Kristen Tabar

Group Vice President of Vehicle Development and Engineering
Toyota Motor North America Research and Development

Background

Kristen Tabar is Group Vice President of Vehicle Development and Engineering at Toyota Motor North American Research and Development (TMNA R&D) in York Township, Michigan, responsible for vehicle development design engineering teams for Toyota's North American operations. In this role, Tabar directs the vehicle development strategy, introducing new technology and systems, working with North American manufacturing centers and local suppliers to deliver vehicles matching customer expectations and Toyota's high level of quality.

Previously, Tabar was Vice President of Corporate Quality at TMNA headquarters in Plano, Texas. Prior to that role, Tabar served as Vice President of the Technical Strategy Planning Office at TMNA R&D in York Township, Michigan. She also served as Vice President of Electrical Systems Engineering. Tabar joined Toyota in 1992 as an electronics engineer.

Passionate about women's leadership, Tabar supports a range of outreach and continuing development initiatives related to STEM education for women. Currently, she serves on Toyota's Diversity Advisory Board, Audit Committee, and Investment Council.

Tabar earned a bachelor's degree in Electrical Engineering from the University of Michigan. She is married to her husband Dan for 25 years and has three future engineering daughters: Andrea, Danielle, and Natalie.

Questions and Answers

1. Change Control, Resilience, and Work/Life Balance

What did you learn when you began to work from home or work in the office with a limited number of co-workers? What did you need to start doing and what did you need to stop?

The COVID pandemic had a profound impact on work-style philosophies. Prior to the outbreak, our work culture was dominated by face-to-face interactions, large cross-functional status meetings, multiple rounds of reviews and "red-pen" checks, and a foundation of Genchi Genbutsu or "Go and See." COVID shutdowns and travel restrictions forced companies and leaders to think differently.

Immediately, we had to convert in-office workforces to remote/work-at-home workforces. The most critical needs were communication. While most companies had some form of remote/virtual meetings, many members didn't use the technology regularly. Learning curves, operation logistics, and confidentiality issues dominated our daily work. Although the technical shift went exceedingly fast, the mindset lagged. At first, it was treated as "temporary" accommodations, things we could "work around" for "a few weeks." We implemented crisis management teams for urgent supply chain issues, held daily executive meetings to confirm critical items, and keep work moving as much as possible. We created COVID Safe@Work and Safe@nywhere protocols for our members to follow and converted facility operations to meet strict cleaning and distancing requirements.

As the days of COVID lockdown continued with no clear end in sight, we changed tactics. Our crisis management focused on restarting production and supply chain logistics. This enormous task was complicated by COVID. We had to ensure our essential workers had a safe work environment by implementing additional cleaning and social-distancing protocols. We also supported our partners ensuring our "extended family" was safe as well. Supply chains were the work of everyone, and shortfalls or delays were reviewed multiple times per day. COVID also proved unpredictable from a labor force perspective, unable to know when someone may be exposed and the subsequent quarantine impact. We spent much more time reinforcing safety protocols, contact tracing, and checking in on team members, a process called mendomi (meaning taking care of our workers like they were family).

Although nonessential, nonmanufacturing work transitioned to virtual, we were able to move forward on some systems improvements including normalizing paperless drawing/specification releases, conversion to simulation rather than multiple physical evaluations, adoption of a global virtual communication platform, and various new automated tools enabling shorter, more productive essential in-office time. These enhancements helped us realize effective productivity, team member balance, and peace of mind.

2. Growing Your Professional Network and Maintaining Mentor and Sponsor Relationships

Have your mentees been asking different questions than under usual working conditions? Have you needed to do more hand-holding? Do you see more mentees seeking career change or seeking educational opportunities? Something else?

COVID shifted the process of mentorship. The format became mostly virtual; however, when most work was virtual, a little more "casual" or "normal" discussion was a welcome part of the day. The virtual format also "normalized" the longer-distance mentorship, opening this activity across a wider geography or parts of the company. There were also more challenges such as identifying stress, mood, or anxiety without the face-to-face interaction. The format changed, but the purpose and need remained as strong as ever.

We continued to encourage a "board of directors" approach to mentors. This philosophy seeks mentors for skill-specific improvements as well as career guidance and overall leadership. We also recommend mentors that are more senior to your position, equivalent or peer to your position, and reverse or below your position. These recommendations give mentees a broad perspective and allow for feedback from many different sources.

While mentees continued this process during the pandemic, they needed more support finding mentors. I was impressed by their persistence and thoughtfulness to move forward; however, it seemed strange and perhaps more intimidating to initiate new mentors—the coffee or lunch meeting was a little more complicated in a virtual environment. Nevertheless, my mentees seemed keen to maintain and grow their personal networks, deepen their self-reflection, and pursue their career path and goals.

Many of my mentees also looked to our Business Partnering Groups for relationship building. These teams bring together members that may not interact based on roles or business responsibilities. Meetings and activities gave members a chance to build new relationships across broader parts of the organization. Mentees seemed to use these groups to build peer mentoring and learn leadership and project management skills outside their core role.

Regarding career path and goals, many mentees used this time to retrain in new skill sets including programming, business financials, or management skills. These took various forms including self-taught, mini-seminars, internal training, and formal education/classroom courses. The mentor discussions seem to be focused on new mid- to long-term opportunities. Mentees were more open and interested in opportunities outside their comfort zone. They were less focused on tactically "what's next" and more strategically on "where can I learn and build skills."

3. Personal Growth

What is the most profound impact this pandemic has had the way you think about your job, company, family life? Will it be sticky or do you expect everything to return to the previous status quo?

One of the key tenants of my work is "Safety First." Under a global pandemic touching all parts of business, culture, and personal life, I realized the importance and deeper meaning of that philosophy. My work culture provided strong structure and guidance during the COVID pandemic. But "Safety First" took on a broader and more personal meaning.

Under normal conditions, we thought about safe products for our customers and safe work environments for our team members. With the pandemic, maintaining a safe work environment became much more complicated. We had to re-evaluate our workspaces, cleaning protocols, personal protective equipment, and ability to maintain social distancing. We created and implemented new safety protocols for use on and off our sites. Although maintaining safety, health, and well-being were always a priority for my job and my company, the pandemic brought real focus on the importance.

Our members and their families became part of our safety umbrella. We spent more time connecting with our members virtually. Checking on their physical health, stress, and overall well-being. We offered support from health professionals for COVID and all the related side effects. Despite all the planning and protocols, we also recognized the need for flexibility.

We managed sudden, unplanned absenteeism due to COVID, public orders, exposure quarantining, and family commitments. Our members and their families were struggling with the new normal and taking care of those who were ill or exposed, supporting children in remote learning and elderly who may have existing health concerns and needs. It reminded us that people are our greatest asset and we could not underestimate the need to protect our members and their families, following our long practice of mendomi.

4. Diversity, Equity, and Inclusion

The pandemic has hit hard for women. Many are thinking about dialing back their careers or exiting altogether, which is very frightening for many companies. What should be done differently to retain women in the workplace?

The pandemic has stressed the workforce in many ways. Caring for children when other family members or daycare options were eliminated became quite a challenge. While many women had the flexibility to work from home or use sick child days, longer-term supervision and education support was a completely different situation. Families were faced with the need to support and/or supervise their children's school time or even in some cases revert to homeschooling to maintain academics.

While remote work/work from home did offer more scheduling flexibility, it also forced more complexity and the need to "juggle" or "wear more hats." Families had to prioritize basic health and safety of their families over their careers, and in many cases, women seem to have taken the lion's share of these added pandemic responsibilities.

Companies need to understand this condition and continue to allow for work flexibility. Daily work hours may need more flexibility or be split to early morning and later afternoon to allow for school support during core hours. Temporary part-time or leaves of absence also need to be utilized.

Most importantly, companies need to show respect and empathy for workers struggling with the effects of the pandemic. Mentors and sponsors need to reassure members of their value and the company's commitment to work together during these unprecedented times. Policies should be adapted to prioritize workplace stability and empower or incentivize management towards the retention of high-performing talent.

5. Sustainability

Sustainability trends (climate change, water availability, health, etc.) are some of the strongest drivers for future changes for companies and their strategies. What are you seeing within your company? Is your firm reading the trends and adapting strategies to survive and then thrive with new growth?

We have a strong sustainability strategy towards 2050. It includes products, prioritized areas of research and innovation, new manufacturing and operating standards, and focus on environmental and health standards (reference: Toyota Environmental Challenge 2050). This is a global strategy and aligns all teams towards the same basic goal—Moving toward a sustainable relationship with our planet.

Each of the six sections sets the environmental vision and explains some specific measures towards achievement. While the focus is on eliminating or minimizing any potential negative environmental impacts from our products or operations, the driving force is to improve the environment for the health and well-being of all people.

Progress is reviewed regularly, and specific measures are adjusted per our planning cycles. A great example is our fuel cell commercial truck project. Repurposing the fuel cells from a traditional vehicle project for use in a commercial truck cuts air pollution in heavily congested port areas. This improves the environment and health of workers at the port and residents in the surrounding communities.

While we always keep close watch of public policy and ensure we are meeting requirements, there are still many changes on how to define appropriate sustainability and targets. Having an internal strategy and tuning it to meet any new public policy keeps us on track long term. The critical point is to "normalize" the changes and show how each low-/zero-emission vehicle or carbon-neutral facility impacts the environment or local community. We need to share our plan and progress and gain support to make these strategies successful.

Lynn Antipas Tyson

Executive Director, Investor Relations
Ford Motor Company

Background

Lynn's career spans over 25 years of leadership roles in treasury, international corporate finance, corporate communications, and investor relations serving in senior-level positions at Ford, PepsiCo, Dell, and other leading companies. Lynn has also provided strategic communications consulting services to companies looking to enhance the effectiveness of their investor relations programs. Specialty areas include leveraging investor relations as a competitive advantage, strategic communications, IPOs, and crisis communications. Lynn's capabilities have been recognized by the equity market across several sectors for building and leading world-class investor relations functions, and she is also a recipient of the Silver Anvil Award for excellence in crisis communications from the Public Relations Society of America.

As Head of Investor Relations for Ford, Lynn is responsible for leading all of Ford's investor relations initiatives, including representing the company to equity and fixed income investors and rating agencies, and providing strategic counsel to support value creation and risk mitigation. Lynn's career includes 14 years of finance and strategic communications experience with PepsiCo, where she ultimately served as Senior Vice President for Investor Relations, and 10 years at Dell, where she led Investor Relations and Global Corporate Communications. Prior to Dell, Lynn led Investor Relations for YUM! Brands, where she was involved in its spin-off from PepsiCo in 1997.

Lynn holds a bachelor's degree in Psychology from the City College of New York and an MBA in Finance and International Business from the Stern School of Business at New York University.

Lynn lives in New York with her husband, son, mother, three horses, and two dogs.

Questions and Answers

1. Change Control, Resilience, and Work/Life Balance

How do you keep team spirit with your direct reports? Are you sensing any lack of trust or more trust? What factors/actions have the most effect on trust/lack of trust?

The quality of relationships, including trust and feeling connected, is predicated on communication. This is especially true as we grapple with the effects of a global pandemic—massive ambiguity, feelings of isolation, juggling work and home, and even profound loss. In this environment, it falls to leaders to make sure our team members are engaged and valued.

That means "speaking" often—by video, by phone, in texts, with short emails—including about things that aren't task related. Asking people how they and their friends and family are doing—then listening to and following up on what's said. Showing through your words and actions that you really do care. Allowing them to selectively see you as human, too. Interestingly, I've heard lots of people—on my team and others—say they feel more connected now even though we are all working remotely. Video conferencing can be a powerful communications tool. It allows you to quickly pull people together to talk about emerging topics, or just to check in—to replace that relationship time that normally happens in the hallway or someone's office doorway.

I've been in meetings that kick off with energizing music videos—and before we talk business, we end up sharing things about our musical tastes. With real-time word clouds, we check in anonymously with each other. During virtual "Happy Hours," we play online games like Skribbl.io. We keep track of people's video backgrounds—are they real? Have you changed rooms? Who is the person in the photo behind you? Children wander in, sit on their parent's lap, and join calls, some sit in the background doing homework. Dogs bark, noise from lawnmowers disrupts calls. By default, we have cracked the door open to who we really are—bringing people closer and fostering trust through a different, higher level of connection.

2. Growing Your Professional Network and Maintaining Mentor and Sponsor Relationships

Are you continuing to grow your professional network while being remote? How?

The short answer is, "Yes!" This global shock has forced us—no matter the profession or sector—to look outward to learn from and depend on others. I reach out more frequently to my existing network while also branching out as connections grow because the tools to do that are the same ones we're using all day, every day in our teams. With video conferencing now ubiquitous, I've participated in far more panel discussions than I ever could have physically attended—from how my profession is adapting to the new normal to how we're keeping our teams engaged to topics and issue unrelated to the pandemic, like how companies are now addressing diversity, equity, and inclusion in the face of social unrest. After these discussions, participants are more inclined to use social platforms to continue the dialogues. The last year has been a profound shared experience which, in many ways, has shrunk our worlds even though we're physically farther apart.

3. Personal Growth

Have you developed new behaviors (exercise, diet, meditation, hobbies, etc.) that help you get through this new stress?

For years, it's been hard for me to prioritize time for myself and focus on self-care. For many years, I have been a member of a "sandwich" generation, with a child still at home and elderly parents who live with us. Tending for my family—being present for them—while working full time takes its toll. Working from home, with no commute, gives me more time and the chance to manage it more efficiently. An offsetting risk is finding myself still sitting in my home office at 8 or 9 at night. So I bought a Peloton and put it in my office. All day, it lurks behind me, reminding me to move, meditate, and stretch. No excuses! I also make sure to spend time with my horses. I walk outside a few times a day to interact with them—and, when the weather is nice, I will even work from my barn. I live in an equestrian community, so with all of us stuck at home, we now schedule group rides early in the morning and even late in the evening on weekdays—not just on weekends, as we used to. The personal breaks can be 10 minutes, 30 minutes, or more, depending on the day. But the key is every day I have to do things to take care of myself. It took several months to develop these new habits; the test will be to sustain them when things return to whatever the new normal looks like.

4. Diversity, Equity, and Inclusion

The pandemic has hit hard for women in particular. Many are thinking about dialing back their careers or exiting altogether, which is very frightening for many companies. What should be done differently to retain women in the workplace?

For as long as I can remember—so that's more than 30 years—working from home has had negative connotations. Early in my career, in the late 1980s, a manager I knew asked if she could work from home a few days a week after the birth of her child. This was unheard of at the time, but the then-recent advent of the personal computer made it possible. The company agreed—and, amazingly, managed to survive!

Over time, the manager continued to move up the corporate ladder and remained a loyal and productive employee until her retirement a few years ago. I learned three powerful lessons from watching this play out, long before anyone heard of a coronavirus:

1. When parts of your personal life are in conflict with your profession, don't suffer in silence. For more than 40 years, it's been illegal to treat pregnant women differently from other people. There are ways to accommodate different needs, and winning organizations recognize and apply them.
2. If you require something outside the norm to be effective, ask for it. And,

3. Leaders remove barriers to people doing what's best for themselves and the company. The past year has shown that the range of what's possible to accommodate people is much wider than most of us imagined.

Remember, we earn trust when we show trust in people's positive intentions. It's a "human" thing.

5. Sustainability

ESG (Environmental, Social, and Governance) expectations of investors is greatly accelerating for both equity and debt investments among the largest investment banks and pension funds. Is your company taking this investor trend seriously and adapting strategy to meet these expectations?

There has always been interest in ESG from a subset of investors. The idea isn't new, though the number and variety embracing these principles continue to grow. Early in my career at PepsiCo, investors pushed for things like deposit laws; recycling; more environmentally friendly packaging, including less content; and treatment of wastewater, providing clean water (which is vital to bottling beverages) in developing countries and communities. More recently, investors have pushed for consumer product companies to manufacture healthier products as a way to help combat the obesity epidemic in young people.

While there are altruistic aspects to it, at its core, ESG is really about how public companies interact with the world around them and the associated risks. Managing risk is essential for money-management firms. They are charged with protecting a person's or an institution's investments while also generating an appropriate financial return. This spans a company's geographic footprint, labor conditions, DEI, mark on the environment, effect on communities where it operates, and political contributions. At Ford, ESG is deeply woven into the company and everything we do. As a result, we have constructive and transparent ongoing conversations with investors about ESG. We influence their thinking and they influence ours.

Bonnie Van Etten

Group Chief Accounting Officer
Stellantis N.V.

Background

Bonnie Van Etten is the Group Chief Accounting Officer for Stellantis N.V. and is responsible for overseeing the company's accounting, reporting, and internal controls. She was named to the position in February 2021 and is based in Auburn Hills, Michigan.

Prior to her current role, she was Vice President Group Chief Accounting Officer for Fiat Chrysler Automobiles.

Bonnie has handled a number of increasing financial responsibilities within the company including serving as Head of Global Technical Accounting and Accounting Research for FCA US.

She joined the Company in December 2010 from American Express, where she last served as Vice President for Regulatory Reporting and previously worked for PwC in various capacities in Indianapolis, Indiana; Amsterdam, The Netherlands and Duesseldorf, Germany. She received her bachelor degree in Finance from Anderson University, Indiana (USA). Bonnie was a member of the Interpretations Committee of the International Accounting Standards Board from 2014 to 2020. Bonnie is a Board Member of InForum. She is married to Mark and they have a daughter.

Questions and Answers

1. Change Control, Resilience, and Work/Life Balance

What did you learn when you began to work from home or work in the office with a limited number of co-workers? What did you need to start doing and what did you need to stop?

At first, we all thought working from home was temporary and that we would all be back together soon. As I started to realize that wasn't going to be the case and that it could be a long time before I was able to travel and see my entire team in person again, I made some changes. For virtual meetings, I make sure to turn my camera on, even if others choose not to, as I think seeing faces fosters more interaction between people. Another change is scheduling regular meetings and touch points. I made a significant effort not to cancel or reschedule staff or one-to-one meetings. I also changed the way I approached meetings to allow for time to just chat. You can get a real sense of how people are doing this way. While I met with my direct reports regularly prior to working from home, I made sure that we had time to talk about how they were doing and how their teams were doing. I asked what I could do to help support them and/or their teams. I feel like our teams are much more connected (ironically) now than in the past. Since we are all virtual, there are less barriers to reaching out, to scheduling video calls, and to be able to talk to someone "screen to screen," which has helped us to work through problems and issues together real time using video instead of over the phone.

The technology that we have in place allows for a very quick way to add people to conversations, to start a video conference quickly, and to also use the chat function with a group of individuals. Our technology solutions have been and continue to be crucial to our continued success. For example, using video conferencing, we review, edit and finalize documents together even though we were in different countries. In addition, this shift to virtual working significantly benefited my teams outside the US. They now have the flexibility to work from home, which wasn't possible before the pandemic. I continue to encourage my teams to seek out and implement efficient ways to do our normal work and to think of ways to streamline what we do. We have been forced to prioritize, which we have used to critically evaluate the ways in which we work and the scope of what we do. I've been so proud and amazed at all the ideas that the teams have come up with and implemented to work better together, to manage with less, and to accomplish our targets despite all the challenges.

2. Growing Your Professional Network and Maintaining Mentor and Sponsor Relationships

How do you keep your existing relationships in this remote world? Are you maintaining face time with other execs while being remote? How do your direct reports maintain their face time with you?

I have found this to be particularly difficult as the hallway conversations or being in the right place at the right time to participate in important conversations just doesn't happen organically in a remote environment. It has to be much more intentional and that has been a challenge for me personally. With the boundaries of work and life blending, this aspect usually takes a back seat to the day-to-day work and fitting in of family life. For my team, I have been intentional about including team members in meetings that I haven't had exposure to recently. I also ask my team to bring their staff members to meetings and have them present so that I can continue to have interactions with my broader global team.

Have your mentees been asking different questions than under usual working conditions? Have you needed to do more hand-holding? Do you see more mentees seeking career change or seeking educational opportunities? Something else?

We were in a bit of a unique position in that we were managing the uncertainty of a pending merger along with the ongoing impact of the COVD pandemic that has changed nearly all facets of our work and life. Exacerbating the situation is the heightened level of social unrest, a tumultuous election year in the U.S. and rapidly changing circumstances individuals and families must continue to navigate. I talk with my direct reports about what their career aspirations are and what roles or areas they might be interested in. I also discuss with my team the need to ensure our employees have opportunities to move into different positions. Even with the uncertainty, it is always good for employees to know they have opportunities they can pursue. Timing for rotations is never ideal, and it's our job as leaders to pave the way for our employees to be able to take advantage of rotational opportunities. From my experience, one's next role may not even exist today. This is certainly true during a merger. We have to be ready for those opportunities by focusing on the work to be done now and ensuring that we are performing to the best of our abilities with what we have been given responsibility for now. For me, it is exciting to think about being part of the formation and transformation of the newly merged Stellantis.

3. Personal Growth

What personal development opportunities have you taken advantage of now that you're not traveling?

I have spent more time with my personal coach focusing on how to be a better "me," and I have also had more time to focus on my family. With no travel and no commute, I have been at nearly every bedtime and haven't missed any birthdays! This has been such a blessing as these are all things that I missed before. I also took part in the virtual Detroit marathon. While I have done half marathons and triathlons a long time ago, I no longer run and wouldn't have thought of participating in a marathon. However, as it was virtual and could be done over time, it was the perfect opportunity to challenge myself to fit in more physical activity. I found this time to be particularly refreshing as it forced me to focus on nature, my surroundings and take a break from work. I scheduled meetings with myself for these walks to ensure that I made the time.

What is the most profound impact this pandemic has had the way you think about your job, company, family life? Will it be sticky or do you expect everything to return to the previous status quo?

It is easy to say "There is more to life than work," but this has certainly caused me to focus more on that now.

4. Diversity, Equity, and Inclusion

The pandemic has hit hard for women in particular. Many are thinking about dialing back their careers or exiting altogether, which is very frightening for many companies. What should be done differently to retain women in the workplace?

This is indeed a reality. Particularly in the early days of the pandemic, the lack of childcare/school contributed to a lot of stress for families. With not having family nearby, we leaned on our support network to continue to support us as parents. My husband and I both work, and we needed help to ensure our daughter was taken care of. Despite this additional support, the stress of the pandemic, the isolation of virtual school, and complete change in our everyday routines impacted our daughter significantly, which made parenting even more challenging. We have learned a lot as parents and as a family through this time, and we are working to keep the positive changes we've made that have benefited our family.

If we want women to have the opportunities to fully participate in the workplace, then the network supporting women must be maintained. Most working mothers I know outsource portions of the household management. Without that support, working parents, mothers especially, are forced to make choices, which usually involve pulling back from, or quitting entirely, the workforce, or overstretch themselves. Areas to focus on making improvements, in my view, are to normalize flexible working arrangements (alternative hours and remote working) and provision of quality, reliable, and affordable options for childcare and schooling.

In addition, open and transparent communication with women to understand their career and family interests and then working with them to support those choices in a win-win way. For example, if a woman wants to take a career break, pause, or take on less responsibility for a period of time to focus on family/other matters, then don't count her out completely but rather support that decision and continue to find meaningful ways for her to contribute and grow her career, even if it is at a different pace than considered "normal." In addition, companies can support job sharing, which provides a way for women (or anyone) to continue to contribute meaningfully yet balance other family or personal needs. If implemented, all of these will benefit the entire workforce, not just women. Companies and leaders should not assume women do not want to advance their careers at the same time as focusing on family; talk to women and find out what they want and find a mutually beneficial way to support them.

5. Sustainability

Sustainability trends (climate change, water availability, health, etc.) are some of the strongest drivers for future changes for companies and their strategies. What are you seeing within your company? Is your firm reading the trends and adapting strategies to survive and then thrive with new growth?

Not only is it good business, but it is also being a responsible citizen in the many locations in which we live and work around the globe. Among other initiatives regarding sustainability, we are finding alternative ways to power our vehicles to meet increasingly stringent compliance requirements. This drives exciting innovation in our products. From a finance perspective, it is very interesting to support the business and operations as they work to address these changes in a profitable way.

Sylvia Veitia

Ford Credit Executive Vice President for Operations and Customer Experience
Ford Motor Company

Background

Sylvia Veitia joined Ford Motor Credit Company in January 2019. Ford Credit is Ford Motor Company's global financial services provider, with $141 billion in managed receivables. Today, as Ford Credit Executive Vice President for Operations and Customer Experience, she leads a global team of 4,000 and oversees Ford Credit's business and call centers, dealer and customer experiences, and operations to deliver world-class service and predictable portfolio performance. Veitia has transformed global process efficiency by redesigning and optimizing operations. She serves as President and Chair of the Global Ford Hispanic Network employee resource group.

As a direct report of the Ford Credit President and CEO, she has led the development of a global strategy for a client contact center designed to meet the long-term needs of an evolving business; developed a strategic direction for global business center operations, including originations, account servicing, customer service, and collections; developed a strategy and oversees global quality and process management; and developed the strategic direction of customer service.

Veitia previously led transformational initiatives at Barclays, serving as Managing Director and Global Head of Business Architecture, Lean and Automation, and Customer Experience, optimizing and managing services touching 35 million customers. Previously, she was Head of Customer Experience Management for Citi Cards, whose portfolio represented $80 billion in managed receivables.

Veitia also had 21 years with the American Automobile Association (AAA) Mid-Atlantic, serving as Vice President overseeing member experience, brand and membership, e-business, driver education, club publication, corporate communications, financial services, and public and government relations for automotive, insurance, travel, and membership products.

Veitia is married and has three children, with whom she enjoys music, cooking, and travel. Born and raised in Puerto Rico, it was there where her interest in the automotive industry was sparked working at her father's car dealership. As a teen, she visited an automotive plant where she realized her passion for engineering and the automotive industry. Veitia holds a bachelor's degree in Sociology and a master's degree in Human Services Administration, both from Rider University in New Jersey, and completed the Columbia Business School Senior Executive program.

Questions and Answers

1. Change Control, Resilience, and Work/Life Balance

What did you learn when you began to work from home or work in the office with a limited number of co-workers? What did you need to start doing, and what did you need to stop?

While working from home, I learned to lead in an undefined professional space. My team and I needed to adapt to a rapidly changing situation and devise new methods to handle unplanned circumstances. In addition, the pandemic impacted different global regions in disparate ways, including varying regulatory responses, requiring us to address each country's needs individually. A crisis can force individuals and teams to re-examine and move past their resistance to necessary change and progress.

I also learned that shifting all work to remote proved to be a great equalizer with respect to global meetings. In the past, those dialing in remotely—particularly from another country—often felt at a disadvantage to those attending in person. Fully remote meetings have leveled the playing field, and all attendees feel equally engaged and heard. When we return to in-person meetings, it will be important to make extra effort to ensure that remote attendees engage as much as in-person participants. Through these meetings, as each country's team began to experience the effects of the pandemic, they were able to learn from those in countries that had already suffered the initial brunt of the pandemic.

For the teams to feel a sense of accomplishment in an uncertain environment, I started to break our work into smaller increments. Even if circumstances changed, the teams could see and appreciate their accomplishments and feel that they served an integral role in the organizational effort.

Overall, regardless of the particular challenges, relying on our organization's core values and caring for each member of each team allowed us the flexibility to adapt to the rapidly changing environment.

Finally, I stopped the counterproductive extended focus on troubling issues that were outside our control, including regulatory delays and inconsistencies and the spread of the pandemic generally. I instead encouraged the team to accept the situation at hand and focus all our efforts on how we could support our customers. While so much of what was happening was outside our control, work not only helped serve as a distraction for some, but workplace accomplishments also helped our team members feel they were helping in a difficult time.

2. Growing Your Professional Network and Maintaining Mentor and Sponsor Relationships

Have your mentees been asking different questions than under usual working conditions? Have you needed to do more hand-holding? Do you see more mentees seeking career change or seeking educational opportunities? Something else?

My mentees and team have asked very different questions since the pandemic began—questions about the virus, the economy, and the impact of the pandemic on consumers. They have sought guidance and certainty that I could not provide beyond the immediate future. I have had to provide more direct individual support since the pandemic began. I have encouraged mentees and team members to take business risks to support our customers and make assumptions in an environment where mistakes were permissible, so long as the team remained action driven, rather than paralyzed by fear of the unknown. I also encouraged team members to rely on each other and provide support where more work was required, including supporting completely different teams and team members at a lower level who might be overwhelmed with work responsibilities.

I have encouraged mentees and team members to provide space to colleagues where personal issues arose, such as illness or caregiving needs. I also developed informal ways to connect, such as virtual happy hours, and spent more time checking in with individuals on a personal level, including sharing my own struggles during long days and personal loss. We have to empathize with one another because you don't know what people are going through in their personal lives.

3. Personal Growth

What is the most profound impact this pandemic has had on the way you think about your job, company, family life? Will it be sticky or do you expect everything to return to the previous status quo?

The pandemic has most profoundly impacted the way I think about Ford by giving me the opportunity to see the company's core principles in action. Having arrived at Ford a year before the pandemic hit, I saw that Ford is first and foremost dedicated to helping people. For example, when the production lines shut down, Ford immediately pivoted to producing personal protective equipment (PPE) and ventilators. A century ago, Henry Ford espoused the principle that business exists for service. Ford has embodied that principle by building, financing, and servicing trailblazing, iconic vehicles. When that was suddenly made impossible, Ford, hearkening back to its efforts during WWII, found other ways to utilize its talents to serve.

Today, Ford's overarching truth is "Put people first." Through these team efforts, I saw that the organization's priorities directly align with my personal values. "Ford Proud" is more than a campaign, it is the essence of our work. I was particularly proud to arrange for the shipment of thousands of pieces of PPE to Puerto Rico, including some distributed to the hospital where I was born. Receiving thanks from medical professionals who benefited from our collective efforts reinforced my pride in participating in this work.

As far as family life, working from home helped make nightly family dinners the rule rather than the exception. It allowed me to have some additional time that otherwise would have been spent traveling or commuting with the people who mean the most to me and help sustain me.

Sylvia Veitia

I believe that professionally and personally, we have the opportunity to continue with the best of what we have learned from our experience, yet return to those aspects of in-person work that contribute to the vitality of the organization and that many are now missing.

4. Diversity and Inclusion

There has been a lot of talk about diversity—and, in recent years, inclusion. Equity has entered the corporate conversation in a major way this year. What actions are you and your company taking? Are these methods aligned with company goals?

Diversity, equity, and inclusion (DEI) are part and parcel of our company goals, and they are especially important to me personally. Many of our activities center on celebrating the diversity of our employees and working to understand others' viewpoints.

We regularly hold "Speedialogues." These employee-led discussions provide employees the opportunity to discuss topics openly, as a team and as individuals, to understand our unconscious biases and reinforce and foster an environment that supports inclusive behaviors. Employees break into small groups and talk with the goal of building a culture of empathy and belonging. Speedialogues are offered globally and are held virtually when we cannot physically be in the office.

We also participate in Day of Understanding, which is an annual event filled with presentations by internal and external speakers and interactive sessions for employees designed to foster a culture of inclusion and understanding. Company leaders like myself hold listening sessions, in partnership with our diverse employee resource groups (ERGs), with small groups of employees who share their personal DEI experiences in the company. In the session I joined, I was honored that employees shared their feelings so openly. It was a humbling experience.

Additionally, as chair of the Ford Hispanic Network, I'm proud of all the events our employees organize such as volunteering and mentoring in local high schools, Spanish language instruction and Hispanic Heritage Month. Ultimately, our DEI goal is to go beyond inclusion and provide an environment where everyone's unique attributes are valued and leveraged in all we do.

We have accelerated our actions around career progression. Mentoring circles match managers with a group of employees to mentor. We've also begun posting more of our open jobs internally, giving everyone an equal opportunity to see and apply for these positions.

5. Sustainability

Sustainability trends (climate change, water availability, health, etc.) are some of the strongest drivers for future changes for companies and their strategies. What are you seeing within your company? Is your firm reading the trends and adapting strategies to survive and then thrive with new growth?

I am incredibly proud to work for a company that does as much as Ford does to make the world a better place. We have a goal to reach carbon neutrality by 2050, strengthening our commitment to the Paris Agreement, and have identified steps to get us there. I believe we can excite our customers by offering some of our most popular vehicles as electrified models.

We support the global community with charitable contributions and initiatives designed to give back when a natural disaster hits. When Hurricane Maria devastated Puerto Rico in 2017, Ford Motor Company Fund donated $1.5 million in aid and donated vehicles. We also helped provide mental health workshops and counseling for residents.

We mean it when we say we want to become the most inclusive and diverse global company, and we celebrate our successes. For example, Ford became the first auto company and Ford Credit Argentina became the first auto finance company to sign the United Nations Women's Empowerment Principles. These are a series of commitments to promote gender equality in the workplace and society.

Marianne Vidershain

Vice President and Treasurer
Lear Corporation

Background

Marianne Vidershain is Vice President and Treasurer at Lear Corporation, a $20 billion Fortune 150 global automotive technology leader in Seating and E-Systems. In this role, she is responsible for providing liquidity to navigate economic cycles, support the company's growth strategy, and deliver a competitive return to shareholders. Ms. Vidershain leads a global organization in charge of capital structure strategy and execution, bank and rating agency relationships, cash management operations, and financial risk management, including foreign exchange and insurance, across 38 different countries and regulatory regimes.

During her 16-year career at Lear, Ms. Vidershain has progressed through increasing roles of responsibility within corporate treasury and operational finance. Most recently, she served as Vice President and Assistant Treasurer from 2018 to 2021, Director of Global Financial Planning and Analysis from 2015 to 2018, and Director of Finance-Global Purchasing from 2014 to 2015.

Before joining Lear, Ms. Vidershain held positions at Ford Motor Co. and Visteon Corp. in product development finance and commercial finance in the Interior Systems and Climate Control divisions, as well as financial planning and treasury, where she drove improvement and visibility of profitability metrics for each of the key product segments.

Ms. Vidershain earned a Bachelor of Science in Finance and Master of Business Administration from the University of Michigan. She is currently a member of the Inforum Finance Committee and a member of the Philanthropist Program for United Way for Southeastern Michigan.

Questions and Answers

1. Change Control, Resilience, and Work/Life Balance

What did you learn when you began to work from home or work in the office with a limited number of co-workers? What did you need to start doing and what did you need to stop?

I learned to communicate differently and connect with my team more often. I learned that the more time I take to emotionally bond with my team the more they feel like I truly care about them. I think, during these times, you have to go beyond the generic "How are you?" The COVID pandemic has been a true test of leadership, trust, transparency, and empathy. During this time, I learned more about my team's families and personal situations, their kids, parents, and various issues that they have been going through. I have learned that every person has different concerns and may react differently to the same message. I also learned that communication and messages sometimes can get lost over the phone when you don't see each other in person.

I needed to become more flexible and open to new ways of working. My team members may not have always been available or immediately reachable as they were in the office, due to homeschooling kids or caring for family members. I needed to get adjusted to the new time constraints and be respectful of other responsibilities my team had.

I also learned to stop being plan-driven and to become purpose-driven. A lot of plans and projects had to be cut short or "repurposed." Very little leadership training or development prepares leaders to handle a crisis. I needed to get comfortable with uncertainty, which is not an easy thing to do as the Treasurer because my main objective is to make sure the company has enough liquidity to run the business. I am used to being able to plan ahead, to run a financial model; instead, we were running many different scenarios with vastly different outcomes. We didn't know what to expect, we didn't know when automotive production would be up and running again. All we knew is that we needed to be prepared for any scenario, even the worst outcome.

I needed to listen, trust, and empower my team more than ever. In times of crisis, you find out who your real leaders are. People who demonstrate that they are committed and willing to go an extra mile, even if they are not asked to step up or it's not in their job description. Those who are willing to carry extra weight and add value to a company in crisis are always remembered.

2. Growing Your Professional Network and Maintaining Mentor and Sponsor Relationships

Have your mentees been asking different questions than under usual working conditions? Have you needed to do more hand-holding? Do you see more mentees seeking career change or seeking educational opportunities? Something else?

The art of mentoring can be challenging even in normal times. It takes commitment and it's not easy putting yourself out there. During the pandemic in a remote work environment, mentoring is needed more than ever. COVID has changed all aspects of our lives. A mentor can provide some time and space for the mentee to catch their breath and vent some of the pent-up anxiety caused by COVID.

I found that it's not as important to give my mentees advice about how to solve a specific technical problem or learn new technical skills. Emotional support became more important. You ask questions like "What is your biggest challenge right now? Is it still okay in your world?" Sometimes I feel pressured to immediately give them advice, but I realized that understanding what motivates my mentees and what is important to them is what I should be doing instead.

Leading with empathy in my mentee interactions has always been important, but never more so than during the pandemic. I started checking in with my mentees more frequently. I think if someone is struggling with the demands placed on them or with the uncertainty of the situation, reaching out to a mentor may be the last thing on their mind. Or they may just hesitate to reach out thinking that a mentor is too busy for a call.

Young people may be impacted differently. You need to understand your emotions and the emotions of your mentee. As a mentor, I can play a critical role, providing them with a stabilizing force. I can be someone who can help talk them down when they are scared, burned out, or confused—off the record.

They are exploring and launching their careers in difficult circumstances. They require more hand-holding. They are asking themselves and their mentors what will stick and how they can differentiate themselves and succeed in this new environment. Has there been a permanent change? What is going to work going forward? My mentees have asked me if there are new skills they need to gain to be successful in their career. Just like everyone else, they are wondering how to respond and reset in whatever the new norm may be.

I also learned that the relationship with my mentees is not one way. I found that I was also learning from my mentees. Reverse mentoring can pay big dividends, both emotionally and practically, especially in this changing world. When I voice my appreciation, it helps to build an even stronger mentor/mentee relationship.

3. Personal Growth

Have you developed new behaviors (exercise, diet, meditation, hobbies, etc.) that help you get through this new stress?

The pandemic has tested everyone's resilience qualities. We learned not to take anything for granted. Resilience is earned and learned. I moved from the Ukraine to the U.S. in my last year of high school without my mom, leaving behind my two sisters and friends, knowing only the basics of English. As a teenager, I had to learn and succeed in a completely unfamiliar environment—without the support system I was used to by my side.

Family is the most important thing in my life. As a mom of three young kids (oldest is 13 and youngest is 3), I don't have much time for hobbies. The time I don't work, I spend with my family.

Marianne Vidershain

I enjoy traveling, spending time on the beach, and going out to restaurants to have fun. These activities became a lot more challenging or nonexistent during COVID. I also had to step up in my role and work more hours to manage liquidity during the crisis.

My husband has been working remotely, and my kids have been learning virtually from home since the beginning of the COVID outbreak, so there are a lot of people stuck in the house at the same time. It occasionally gets loud and crazy.

Have I been stressed out during these times? Sure, more than once. What makes it harder is that sometimes you can't really see the light at the end of the tunnel.

I have been managing stress by learning to enjoy the small things in life. We have been taking a lot more walks. I find that getting out of the house to walk around even for 15-20 minutes makes a big difference to my day. I try to walk almost every day, even if it's 30 degrees outside.

I'm not an exerciser, but I do enjoy pilates. I used to take classes twice a week with my instructor before COVID. I can't do it in person now, so it is replaced with Zoom. My 13-year-old daughter and I take a Zoom pilates class every Sunday morning. It feels great, and it is something that I can do together with my daughter.

We have been playing a lot of board games. It's a fun family activity that everyone can participate in. We can get really competitive too!

The past year has been a struggle for everyone. I think you need to find what works for you to unplug and relax. It's something different for everyone. I believe we will all come out of this stronger and start appreciating things more… simple things that we took for granted before the pandemic.

4. Diversity, Equity, and Inclusion

There has been a lot of talk about—and, in recent years, inclusion. Equity has entered the corporate conversation in a major way this year. What actions are you and your company taking? Are these methods aligned with company goals?

Diversity, Equity, and Inclusion (DEI) has been a critical part of my company's culture and success for many years. As a diverse team, we are more innovative, make better decisions, and achieve faster results. This is what makes us a better company.

Our company's strength comes from our employees and their ability to bring their whole selves to work. "Be Inclusive" is one of our core values. We take pride in being a business where all of our employees, no matter their race, gender, or sexual orientation, are valued and can be themselves.

We formed an Executive Diversity Council to develop and share a comprehensive DEI strategy, prioritize activities, and drive accountability and results across the organization. My company believes that embracing DEI throughout the global organization enables our people and our business to succeed in every region where we operate.

In 2019, our CEO Ray Scott signed the CEO Action for Diversity and Inclusion pledge, and our headquarters campus hosted the Check Your Blind Spots tour bus. In 2020, our previous Chief Diversity Officer Rashida Thomas was named Vice President of Global Talent Acquisition, and she is committed to furthering diversity throughout the company. Additionally, we announced a new campaign called "Together We Belong," with actions to drive awareness and engagement, educate our team, and fund organizations committed to racial justice. We formed Employee Resource Groups (ERGs) that have worked to create a more inclusive environment at Lear.

I recently participated in virtual DEI "Together We Belong" training. In phase two of the training, I've had an opportunity to be paired with a colleague from a different background and have guided conversations over the course of multiple weeks. I'm finding this very impactful. It is more than a training, it is a fantastic experience.

We can all do more to drive change both inside and outside of the company. We need to be actively involved in diversity efforts and engage our teams in a meaningful dialogue. On my team, I spend time making sure that all ideas are welcome and heard.

It is critical to continue our efforts to empower and promote diverse talent to leadership roles and ensure all genders, races, and ethnicities are represented across every level of the organization. The DEI program needs to be measurable to be impactful.

The only way to create change is to keep pushing forward!

5. Sustainability

ESG (Environmental, Social, and Governance) expectations of investors are greatly accelerating for both equity and debt investments among the largest investment banks and pension funds. Is your company taking this investor trend seriously and adapting strategy to meet these expectations?

Sustainability has become increasingly relevant in all areas of our lives as well as affecting companies worldwide in their financial and business decisions. ESG principles have turned into key criteria for decisions made by employees, customers, investors, and communities about who they want to work for or do business with. They are also becoming increasingly prominent factors as part of both equity and debt investment mandates. For instance, BlackRock, the world's largest asset manager, is putting sustainability at the center of its investment strategy.

My company has been committed to a sustainable future for our environment, our community, and our business for many years, publishing a sustainability report each year and receiving recognition from ESG ranking firms, nongovernmental organizations, and federal agencies for our efforts. To us, it's more than just a corporate social responsibility strategy, it's part of our culture and one of our core values—Getting Results the Right Way.

COVID reminded us that companies with strong ESG principles are better prepared to face unexpected challenges. For example, my company created the Safe Work Playbook and made it available to all organizations to help us and other businesses safely resume operations. In 2020, Lear also created a team of company leaders to further the integration of ESG initiatives throughout Lear, from how we work with suppliers and support local communities to how we manufacture products.

As a Fortune 500 company with 161,000 employees around the world, every employee can make an impact through improving economic well-being in their communities, fostering educational preparedness to help people around us to thrive in their daily lives, and protecting the environment we all share. We believe in giving back. Working together with our customers, suppliers, employees, and communities, we think of ourselves as one family dedicated to protecting the environment, supporting our communities, and sustaining economic prosperity for everyone's benefit.

Earlier this year, we expanded our sustainability efforts by announcing several new environmental goals, including aspiring to achieve net-zero emissions by 2050. We are planning to increase renewable energy use, improve energy efficiency at facilities, expand engineering efforts for vehicle electrification and lighter weight products, and heighten sustainability requirements for our suppliers.

There are still a lot of challenges as well as opportunities that lie ahead of the sustainability trends. The auto industry is changing as the result of innovation in the areas of electrification, autonomous driving, and shared mobility, therefore creating a lot of opportunities for OEMs and suppliers. Meanwhile, high uncertainty remains around which emergent technologies will become industry standards, how uptake will vary across regions, and how regulations will shape the market.

Corporate vision and leadership will be key in navigating this uncharted territory. ESG is a long-term business strategy. As the traditional business model is changing, the auto industry needs to consider innovative approaches, build agility, and be open to different viewpoints to address these challenges.

Marlo Vitous

Head of Supply Chain Management Planning,
Stellantis–North America
Global Head of Inner-Regional Flow

Background

Marlo Vitous was named Head of Supply Chain Management Planning of Stellantis–North America, and Global Head of Inner-Regional Flow in June 2019, responsible for the optimization of the supply chain and operational activities.

Prior to this, Vitous was Director of the Interior and Electrical Purchasing, responsible for leading a global team.

Vitous has been with the company for over 20 years working in various roles in purchasing, manufacturing, supply chain, and supplier quality.

Vitous is Co-chair of AutomotiveNEXT at Inforum and a member of the Women's Alliance at Stellantis. She was recognized as one of *Automotive News* "100 Leading Women in the Auto Industry" in 2015 and featured in the book "*The Road to the Top Is Not on the Map: Conversations with Top Women of the Automotive Industry*" in 2019, sponsored by SAE and Inforum.

Vitous earned a bachelor's degree in Science and Business Administration from Central Michigan University (1998) and a Master of Business Administration from Wayne State University (2001).

Vitous was born in Norfolk, Virginia.

Questions and Answers

1. Change Control, Resilience, and Work/Life Balance

What did you learn when you began to work from home or work in the office with a limited number of co-workers? What did you need to start doing and what did you need to stop?

Given my global responsibilities, leading from a distance was not new to me, but having to live it every day has shown me how effective we can be. My team delivered extraordinary results within a challenging environment. I saw their resilience and commitment to Stellantis. I also saw them grow and persevere through it. Resilience is important during this time period since we live in a world of constant change and adversity. It also made me realize how human we are, and we miss that human interaction by not being together. So as work-from-home became the "new normal," I quickly realized that we needed to take the time for small talk and camaraderie versus clicking from meeting to meeting and jumping into the business topics. We also needed to give people time between meetings to stretch their legs since they are more confined to one space. We needed to rethink work schedules and understand that all employees have different needs. My touch points with the organization started to center around important company milestones that connected the teams with the latest product announcements, but also how the company was adjusting to support their needs. For me, I focused on taking care of myself both mentally and physically while ensuring to find unique moments with my family.

2. Growing Your Professional Network and Maintaining Mentor and Sponsor Relationships

How do you keep your existing relationships in this remote world? Are you maintaining face time with other execs while being remote? How do your direct reports maintain their face time with you?

Technology has truly been an enabler here. While I certainly miss seeing everyone face to face, I purposefully find ways to connect on a personal level. For example, a simple, private text message to a colleague to say hello and ask how they are doing helps keep our connection. And, while we encourage our team members to turn on their video during meetings to "see" each other, I am flexible and using other more traditional technologies, like a text message or phone call, to ensure we are keeping an open line of communication. In this time of isolation, I try to remember the quote from Helen Keller, "Alone we can do so little, together we can do so much." This is one reason I am also still very active in other organizations, whether it be internal mentorship roles or external networking opportunities. I have many peer mentors that I respect very much in this industry, and they have provided welcomed advice, benchmarking, and more. In regards to connecting with my leadership, this has not been an issue as we have a full suite of collaborative tools that have enabled our digital transformation seamlessly and effectively.

3. Personal Growth

What is the most profound impact this pandemic has had on the way you think about your job, company, family life? Will it be sticky or do you expect everything to return to the previous status quo?

Serving as a global supply chain leader during the COVID pandemic has been one of the most challenging moments in my career. My mental and physical health is now a top priority to me. I think about how well my team performed, how we survived, and how I have grown as a leader through this. I learned that people, including myself, are very adaptable and will rise to any occasion, and I learned the importance of work-life integration. I do believe this will change how we work and live moving forward, and I am constantly reminded of my blessings. Whenever we find ourselves doubting how far we can go, we should remember how far we have come. As the saying goes, "Tough times don't last, tough people do." With this in mind, I stayed focused on the fact that my family, my friends, and my team are all in this together. That we may not be able to control every situation, but we can control our attitude and how we deal with it.

4. Diversity, Equity, and Inclusion

There has been a lot of talk about diversity—and, in recent years, inclusion. Equity has entered the corporate conversation in a major way this year. What actions are you and your company taking? Are these methods aligned with company goals?

Our culture is centered on a work environment that is one of mutual respect and integrity. This includes flexible work options, demonstrating our appreciation and gratitude for each other, and making diversity and inclusion part of the fabric of our business. Our senior executive management supports diversity and inclusion efforts with both their words and actions within our global workplace. For example, in global town halls, diversity and inclusion efforts are a key topic, especially as we shine a light on the 10 employee-run business resource groups that are working tirelessly to support our diverse talent pool. As an executive leader, I take it upon myself to also drive this change and encourage inclusion on all levels. I encourage everyone to do the same—be the change and lead by example. I continue to mentor many diverse employees, which is a real passion of mine. I also discuss specific goals and actions with the leaders inside my organization. We have also had "courageous conversations" in our department at every level where team members are encouraged to share their perspectives, pose tough questions, and have a continuous dialogue about the world around us. Change starts when people start talking, and this leads to understanding and commitment. I have found the better you know someone the more understanding you have of their perspectives, and this helps break down barriers and allows people to find common ground. Discussions, when done with openness and understanding, are the key to having a truly inclusive organization. These conversations must continue for lasting change. When we talk about change, we bring about the change.

5. Sustainability

As part of employee development, does your company encourage and support employees volunteering for local nongovernmental organizations? Do you and your company consider this an opportunity for aligning company efforts, employee leadership development, and local progress on sustainability?

The employee culture at Stellantis has always had a strong focus on giving back to our communities. Motor Citizens is our company-wide volunteer program that provides employees paid time each year to make a difference through service in their community, and we know many people volunteer much more on their personal time. For example, this year I participated in a virtual marathon to support United Way's efforts to close the digital divide in Detroit by providing students with laptops and other technology they needed to learn virtually. As a "non-runner," the goal seemed impossible, but I was motivated by the more than 300 Stellantis employees, families, and friends that led Team Jeep to do more for our community. Together, Team Jeep was able to raise over $150,000 to support our community in a sustainable and effective way. Without the leadership across Stellantis encouraging us to keep going, I could not have done it. Looking back, it was just another one of those challenges I did not know how I was going to achieve, but one step at a time, I did it.

Julia Wada

Group Vice President
Strategy, Innovation, and Transformation
Toyota Financial Services

Background

Julia Wada is Group Vice President, Strategy, Innovation, and Transformation at Toyota Financial Services (TFS). Wada serves on the Executive Management Committee and reports to Mark Templin, President and CEO.

Wada leads strategic transformation initiatives and efforts while building diverse, inclusive, and engaged teams. She is a team builder and champion of One Toyota initiatives including TFS' high-performing culture and capabilities. She led the successful transition of TFS' headquarters move to Plano, Texas as part of the One Toyota leadership team.

Wada joined Toyota Motor Sales (TMS) in 1991 as part of the Graduate Management Associate program. At both TMS and TFS, her career has spanned a variety of leadership responsibilities including product planning, pricing, sales planning, strategic planning, human resources, real estate and facilities, diversity and inclusion, information technology, and indirect procurement shared services.

Prior to her Toyota career, Wada worked as a program manager and engineer for Lockheed Missiles and Space Company. She earned her Bachelor of Science degree in Mechanical Engineering at the University of California at Berkeley and her Master of Science degree in Management from the MIT Sloan School of Management.

Wada serves on the board of directors for the Toyota Foundation, a $100 million endowment to support STEM education. She also serves on the boards of the Japan-America Society of Dallas/Fort Worth and the Dallas Holocaust and Human Rights Museum.

Questions and Answers

1. Change Control, Resilience, and Work/Life Balance

What did you learn when you began to work from home or work in the office with a limited number of co-workers? What did you need to start doing and what did you need to stop?

My team and nearly all my co-workers at Toyota Financial Services (TFS) have been able to work remotely and did so beginning March 2020 to current. It's been incredible to see everyone pull together to figure out how to execute and deliver to our customers. We've been able to exceed expectations across the board. What I've relearned is the critical role of our culture and core values and how they serve as guideposts in times of crisis. Toyota's "start your impossible" mindset sets the tone for what's expected, and our values of "respect for people" and "continuous improvement" guide our focus and decision-making every day. A crisis exposes who one really is, whether at the company level or personally.

From the very top of our company, the vision was set that we will strive to come out of this stronger than ever, and we challenged our team members to "stop things that need to be stopped," "change the way of doing," and "do things we must do." With this simple directive, our team focused on what was truly important and knew they were trusted to identify these things and make them happen. We have stopped many things, big and small, that were no longer adding value. For example, surveys that had very limited usage were stopped. Pilots were stopped that no longer made sense because customer behaviors had changed. We've also changed many things to be more effective or efficient because they could be done differently. With new digital capabilities, we were able to fully automate processes that were very manual in the past and better serve our customers. Finally, we continue to do new things, responding to the immediate needs of our customers, as well as starting projects or initiatives that are important to our long-term success, such as new business development and system implementations.

2. Growing Your Professional Network and Maintaining Mentor and Sponsor Relationships

Has your company maintained learning and leadership development opportunities, culture surveys, 360 surveys, etc. to grow skills and manage the emotional intelligence of the company? Has anything shifted? What have you learned?

Learning and continued development is something that we believe is critical to our long-term success as a company. So yes, we have maintained our focus in these areas as well as surveys and connection points so that we have a pulse on how our team members are feeling. In some ways, we have increased our focus. For example, with nearly all our office-based team members working from home, we shifted to virtual learning and now have very robust online resources to support what we call the 3E's of development: Education, Exposure, and Experience. In addition, extensive resources were developed to support remote work, and we continue to develop these as we are planning for a future hybrid work environment.

Our people leaders are the lynchpin to our ability to be successful as a company. Think about the saying "people don't leave companies; they leave their managers." When you have a great manager, a person who knows and cares about you, who listens to you, who supports your development, and puts you in positions to shine, it makes coming to work so much more rewarding. Managers have always had to be intentional, but what I've learned through this crisis is that we must be intentional in different ways. The way we normally connect with our teams has changed, and we have needed to find different ways to connect. At Toyota, one of the things we have broadened is our practice of the Japanese concept of "mendomi," or taking care of our workers like they are family. During this period, this has meant "checking in," getting to know people more personally, taking time to listen, and being fully present. They seem like little things, but it's the little things that can make a real difference. We've become more flexible and more comfortable sharing who we are, and we've had to be more resilient. The definition of "professional" has moved away from "what's appropriate" and perfectionism. Nobody has time or energy to waste, and getting things done is more important than getting things perfect.

I love quotes and one of my favorites is from Benjamin Franklin. He said, "When you're finished changing, you're finished." My top Gallup strength is "learner," and when I came across this quote early in my Toyota career, it really resonated with me so I actually cut it out (that was way back when I read things hard copy!) and had it on my desk for many years. One of my favorite books is *Mindset: The New Psychology of Success* by Carol Dweck, which was recommended to me years ago by someone I met at a communications training course. The basic concept is that one can become "smarter" through effort, and it's become well known. In our school district in Frisco, Texas, they are now incorporating these concepts into their teaching model. If you haven't read it, I highly recommend it. Continuous learning, applying a growth mindset, has been key to my success professionally and personally.

3. Personal Growth

Have you developed new behaviors (exercise, diet, meditation, hobbies, etc.) that help you get through this new stress?

Yes, I have developed new behaviors, and I've increased behaviors I recognized were more important to me at this time. Like the "stop, change, start" approach that we took at work; upon reflection, I took a similar approach personally. With the health and security of my family and my work family being a top priority, I felt I had to do a better job taking care of myself to be able to do show up how I wanted to. For me, that meant putting my own "structure" on my day. I adopted a more regular morning routine that includes exercise, reading, and meditation. While I had a routine before, the added hour to my day that I got from no longer having a commute went to more exercise and family time. I also had to exercise differently.

Julia Wada

No longer going to a gym, I discovered YouTube exercise videos courtesy of my daughter, who is a 2020 high school graduate. I really like the options, which cover all kinds of workouts from cardio and pilates to strength training and from as short as five minutes. I have also tried to be more consistent about when I end my workday. It's been nice to be able to just walk over to the kitchen and share more in dinner preparation than I have been for many years by "being home" just 30 minutes earlier than usual.

I have been practicing mindfulness for a couple of years now, and it has helped me to quiet that inner voice, be more "in the moment," and be more objective. It is also very helpful in managing stress. I can feel the stress relief in my body from meditation. I'm proud to be with a company that is now providing mindfulness resources as a benefit for our team members this year as a result of the efforts of two terrific female leaders who brought their personal mindfulness stories to Toyota and championed the benefits it could bring.

4. Diversity, Equity, and Inclusion

Are men engaged in the conversation around gender diversity and, if so, in what way?

Absolutely. My experience, personally and professionally, has been one where certain men are engaged in the conversation through their everyday actions, as leaders, whether through involvement in education/training, coaching, mentoring, sponsoring or advocating, and championing for change. Of course, this doesn't mean that there isn't more to be done. Plenty of others are not actively engaged. Men, and white men, are still the majority in most decision-making roles in nearly all industries, government, and social organizations, and while there has been progress, it has been very slow. In addition, now pandemic-driven issues risk taking much, if not all, of that progress backward. Men must be a bigger, more proactive part of the change.

The most meaningful action men can take is to "walk the talk." Male leaders who clearly value diversity of thought and intentionally create an inclusive and open environment to cultivate that diversity of thought stand out as exceptional leaders. One of my role models is a prior CEO of TFS who was way ahead of his time when it came to this and still stands out as exceptional. He used to say to his management committee (in the early 2000s) that if you have the same opinion as everyone else here, then I don't need you at this table. And the key is that he truly meant it. He surrounded himself with people who didn't look like him or think like him or each other, and he listened to them. It didn't make the conversations easier, because we didn't agree, and we were passionate about our ideas, but it pushed our thinking, made for better decisions, and ultimately made us better as leaders. He created an environment where we thought differently, made different decisions, and took actions that were different than if we didn't have that diversity of thought to inform us. He was the role model and he held us accountable. It's as simple as that. Just imagine if most male leaders did this. What a tidal wave of change it would produce.

5. Sustainability

What do you as a leader do to stay informed about sustainability trends that can impact the success of your company and its strategy?

One of my favorite places in the world is Yosemite, and I am someone who loves being outdoors. Thank goodness that is something we've still been able to do during the pandemic! One "benefit" or "silver lining" of this pandemic is the fact that as humankind, we are going through this together. There has been a growth in understanding how small our world is and how quickly things can change. Remember seeing how smog was virtually eliminated when we were all under "quarantine" in the Spring of 2020? It's up to each of us and all of us to take care of our planet. This is reflected in the way customers and investors are increasingly considering ESG (environmental, social, and governance) in how they evaluate companies.

I do a lot of reading to stay informed, supplemented more recently by podcasts, videos, and other opportunities from my network, social media or streaming forum-based learning. These issues have been important to me and areas of focus for my company for a long time, and I have been able to be directly involved in several efforts.

I've learned from what we've done as a company and the activities we're involved with, whether that is our Diversity, Equity, and Inclusion work or our Toyota Environmental Challenge 2050 in support of UN Sustainable Developmental Goals, to make the world better, safer, and healthier.

Like so many others, it hit me hard this year that progress in social justice can never be taken for granted and that there was so much I didn't understand, despite many years of responsibility for diversity and inclusion in my work and my own lived experience as an ethnic minority. I have intentionally expanded my sources of information and my personal and professional network this year to be more diverse, especially including more Black and Brown voices, and I commit to continuing to learn and act in this arena. I'm grateful to be part of Toyota's Social Justice Advocacy Committee, which was presciently created by our Chief Diversity Officer toward the beginning of 2020.

One of the reasons I have stayed with Toyota for 30 years is that it is a company whose founders were clear that the reason the company exists is to make lives better and contribute to society. We can only do this if we take care of what we have.

Deborah Wahl

Global Chief Marketing Officer
General Motors

Background

Deborah Wahl was appointed General Motors (GM) Global Chief Marketing Officer (CMO) on September 1, 2019. She previously served as the Global CMO of Cadillac, where she redefined the brand's strategy and implemented new creative, analytics, and positioning to drive growth for the brand. Deborah played a role in the leadership team that broke a global sales record in 2018.

Rooted firmly in the school of performance marketing, she believes in using data to change how the teams seek insights and engage with consumers. As General Motors Global CMO, Deborah will help the General Motors marketing organization build on its success and accelerate growth by ensuring alignment. Growth will come through a key focus on customer value creation with more creative, effective, and agile customer engagement.

Prior to joining General Motors, Deborah served as Senior Vice President and CMO for McDonald's from 2014 to 2017, where she played a key role in the brand's turnaround, proudly bringing All Day Breakfast to McDonald's consumers. In addition to McDonald's, Deborah has held a number of CMO and marketing leadership positions, including at PulteGroup, Chrysler, and Lexus.

Deborah earned a bachelor's degree in Economics from Wellesley College and an MBA from the Wharton School. She also has a master's degree from the Lauder Institute, University of Pennsylvania.

Deborah is an active business leader who serves on the board of Groupon and as the Chair of the MMA Board, as well as on the Board of Trustees of Cranbrook Educational Community.

Questions and Answers

1. Change Control, Resilience, and Work/Life Balance

Many have said that there is no separation of work and home these days—what do you do to manage this for your own work? What are you doing to increase the ability of your team to create and respect boundaries?

I think what's true is the natural and clear separation between work and home started blurring with laptop computers and smartphones, and now the pandemic has further eroded that divide for those of us who were used to heading to an office each day. If you're now at home, your day doesn't have the very tangible bookends of a commute where you may listen to a podcast or music and have a moment of calm. What that means is it's now much more important to force that separation, making it a personal priority, and lead by example.

For me, that means shutting down my computer and cooking dinner with my family, something I hadn't done in ages. And it means setting up an out-of-office message, even if during the pandemic there isn't a literal office. For others, it may mean protecting a few hours of time with kids doing homework, or pursuing a hobby, or putting exercise time on the calendar and protecting those personal needs. When leaders set those boundaries and talk about the steps they've taken, it empowers teams to do the same. It's so important to humanize the challenge and communicate using personal examples.

2. Growing Your Professional Network and Maintaining Mentor and Sponsor Relationships

Are you continuing to grow your professional network while being remote? How?

Professional and personal networking during a pandemic poses unique challenges. We spend most of our days in virtual meetings, during our normal working hours - it's also become the only way to connect with those who are not in your immediate household. These personal and professional connections are so important to maintain, even a quick call just to see how someone's day is going could mean the world of difference for them and for yourself. We're all going through so many new experiences right now, figuring out new ways forward and efficient ways to work. On May 25th our country was faced with the murder of George Floyd, which brought a renewed and unprecedented need for social change. Change that will last and create a more inclusive world with more diverse workplaces. The time for action is now.

With that mindset, I've taken on the role of Global Chair for the MMA, and leveraged our board membership with the Association of National Advertisers, to push for new safety protocols, take hate speech head-on, and push for diversity and inclusion measures within the industry and within General Motors. We need to be aligned and thinking of solutions together across companies and across industries. When General Motors can align with companies like P&G, Mastercard, and Unilever on important topics, we can accomplish so much and do it with a greater sense of urgency.

I would say that during the pandemic and the social movement for racial justice have brought out the best from organizations and peers and the willingness to share as a community has improved. Just as GM learned how to build ventilators to support the common good during COVID, I've seen firsthand that when marketers focus on a cause, we move the world forward.

3. Personal Growth

What personal development opportunities have you taken advantage of now that you're not traveling?

I've taken this time to truly delve deep into the social injustice happening in our country and around the world. I want to, need to, understand and advance the personal role I have as well as the societal obligation we all share to work toward a goal of eliminating social injustice and racism in our communities. In the days and weeks following George Floyd's murder, our company took steps including a stated aspiration to be the most inclusive company in the world. We formed an Inclusion Advisory Board to help us get there in a real, honest, and authentic way. I've found those moves so empowering and have used those initial steps to not only develop goals for my own organization but to guide the marketing and advertising messages we bring to our audiences.

At a personal level, my journey started with learning—building my reading list and reaching out to colleagues, experts, and groups for information that would help me, as well as asking others what they've read and what they think to get input and grow personally. We've had a lot of conversations inside my team, a lot of hard but important conversations, and that dialogue is ongoing in groups I'm a part of, like the International Women's Forum.

In terms of change for my organization, those early conversations have grown into action and changes in how we act. We've brought in new partners and created new pathways to solutions. We have an agency, Robot, that's helping us on that journey; along with partners like Ozy, and influencers we're building relationships with. Our team developed an action plan that will help us grow diversity with urgency. We can't do that without open dialogue, so I've expanded the use of diagonal slices at our company so I'm hearing all perspectives regularly.

4. Diversity, Equity, and Inclusion

The pandemic has hit hard for women in particular. Many are thinking about dialing back their careers or exiting altogether, which is very frightening for many companies. What should be done differently to retain women in the workplace?

At GM we've had a focus on women in the workforce, growing women in STEM fields in particular, and helping women reenter the workforce after leaving for family care needs. We have a program called Take 2 that starts with a 12-week training course and is aimed at bringing women back into careers as well as advancing them. I think that program's going to be so important as we look at the world beyond the pandemic.

This time continues to put such a strain on families, and for those who have stepped away, we have to be able to welcome them back.

During this time we've also introduced a new and flexible 12-week family leave option for those who simply need a temporary relief to support children or parents. This is for everyone, we know society's pressures heavily lean on women, so this is another tool our mothers and daughters have available.

Challenges women encounter at work are encountered by men as well, but they're perceived differently, and we have to be aware of that and be empathetic. I and other leaders in our company have been listening, we have groups thinking about these new or amplified challenges. We're empowering team members who have young kids to help lead the conversation and bring ideas to address these stressful times and have enabled support groups to share frustrations.

The solutions have to start with showing empathy—thinking about not only the parents who get more of the attention but also those single employees. People who are going through this pandemic alone with no one to talk to. We have to make sure that while we're all remote, no one feels alone. A big learning from recent months has been how to empower employees to ask for what they need, showing employees they're valued, by creating a culture of transparency and care. We can't make assumptions drawing from the pre-COVID era. We're learning to be nimble and agile, I think a lot of what we learn will carry on for lifetimes.

5. Sustainability

As part of employee development, does your company encourage and support employees volunteering for local nongovernmental organizations? Do you and your company consider this an opportunity for aligning company efforts, employee leadership development, and local progress on sustainability?

While General Motors has always had great volunteerism among its employees and within its communities—especially in Southeast Michigan—I would consider the COVID response our employees led to be the most heroic act of mass volunteering I've ever witnessed. From the earliest days of March 2020, our people were putting in long hours, solving new problems, like building ventilators and masks and other PPE. These inspired a new wave of people stepping up to deliver those materials to the frontline workers in need.

We've continued making masks throughout 2020, and many of the employees making them have done so on a volunteer basis, creating millions of masks that have gone out into the world. It's been so inspiring to watch and so rewarding to be part of an organization that is excited and willing to do right in the world. And it's inspired our daily work as well. We're more focused than ever on creating an all-electric future and a safer world for all.

What's more, we've done all of that while not missing a beat on our ongoing volunteer initiatives and programs—our GM Student Corps, our STEM commitments, we even worked with the Girl Scouts to create a new set of badges around automotive engineering and STEM careers. And we've created new projects to help those impacted by the economic challenges of 2020, including a food bank we hosted in Orlando, Florida for the furloughed employees of Disney's parks.

Jennifer Wahnschaff

Head of Continental Intelligent Transportation Systems (ITS)
Interior Division
Continental AG

Background

Jennifer Wahnschaff is Senior Vice President of ITS Segment Mobility Services globally, a position she has held since March 2018. In this role, Ms. Wahnschaff is responsible for building Continental's cloud-based services and solutions for OEMs, fleets, and aftermarket customers by utilizing the company's deep knowledge and expertise as a leading technology company.

Prior to this position, Ms. Wahnschaff was Vice President of Instrumentation and Driver HMI for the Americas, following an international delegation with Continental in Babenhausen, Germany. In this role, she was responsible for guiding the product development, technology roadmap, and overall organization for the Business Unit for the North and South American markets.

Ms. Wahnschaff joined the company in April 2001 as Senior Mechanical Engineer in the Interior Division, Instrumentation, and Displays Business Unit. Since then she has held numerous leadership positions within Quality, Project, and General Management.

Ms. Wahnschaff began her distinguished career in the automotive sector with GM/Delphi as a technical student in 1989. She was later promoted to Senior Mechanical Engineer in the Interior Division with GM/Delphi. In 1998, she joined Irvin division of Takata as Senior Mechanical Engineer and Team Leader for Interior Seating and Sun Visors.

Ms. Wahnschaff was recognized by *DBusiness Magazine* as one of Metro Detroit's Most Powerful Women in 2016. She earned a Bachelor of Science in Mechanical Engineering degree from Michigan State University.

Ms. Wahnschaff currently resides in San Jose, California with her husband, Olaf, and has two children.

Questions and Answers

1. Change Control, Resilience, and Work/Life Balance

What did you learn when you began to work from home or work in the office with a limited number of co-workers? What did you need to start doing and what did you need to stop?

We started in mid-March to close down the offices due to the shelter-in-place order issued in Santa Clara County, in San Jose, CA. Initially, we thought that it would only last a few weeks, but we quickly realized it was going to be much longer and that we needed to educate ourselves. Thru town halls, stand-up meetings, and small group planning meetings, we discussed COVID facts and safety measures and dedicated the time to communicate and reassure our teams. We very quickly decided that both more and open communication was necessary to keep everyone informed and reduce anxiety. Each meeting had at least half of the meeting dedicated to open forum questions. All in all, with MS Teams video conferences, cloud document sharing, and our great IT team, we were able to continue work on several critical projects virtually. We had a very small core team who had access to the building to receive critical shipments or run test equipment using PPE and multiple other safety measures. We immediately stopped all noncritical travel, which ended up being over 90%. Customers were very supportive to move to virtual reviews or status demonstrations.

We had to be sensitive to the personal situation of each team member and adapt schedules as needed. Several team members had to juggle between caring for children or workspace to allow time for their spouse or other family members. The most difficult part has been to keep the personal, informal connections with the team. We used virtual coffee hours, pizza parties, and favorite work-from-home pictures to try to keep this connection going. The team has had to find new ways to connect, and I'm pleased with how we continue to link with each other in new ways.

2. Growing Your Professional Network and Maintaining Mentor and Sponsor Relationships

How do you keep your existing relationships in this remote world? Are you maintaining face time with other execs while being remote? How do your direct reports maintain their face time with you?

With most conventions and workshops cancelled, it has been more challenging to maintain and grow a professional network. I have attended several virtual conventions because it is still so very important to stay connected with changes in the market. LinkedIn is also a great space for sharing and connecting with others. I personally really appreciate the link thru online communities in the automotive and IOT space. This has helped to both reconnect with old connections and establish new ones. Due to the pandemic, I have found that it is sometimes easier to reconnect by scheduling virtual meetings. You can get a face-to-face easier via video, and it doesn't require a flight.

3. Personal Growth

What is the most profound impact this pandemic has had the way you think about your job, company, family life? Will it be sticky or do you expect everything to return to the previous status quo?

I have found that I really enjoy working from home. When I reflect on what my life was like before—always on a plane and often spending weekends and evenings away from home—I realized how much I missed. I realized I gained a huge efficiency by eliminating travel and a commute. We still have to stay connected and often with global colleagues and customers, so as a compromise, I have moved to "virtual travel" weeks. For one full week, I shift my working hours to either Asia or Europe and schedule all the meetings I would have had with a full day. It may sound difficult, but it ends up being the same time shift I would have done if I flew to a new time zone but without the need for a flight. This works for most office meetings, but if I had to go to the manufacturing floor, it may not work. I don't think I will travel as much in the future since I have learned so many different ways to conduct business virtually.

4. Diversity, Equity, and Inclusion

The pandemic has hit hard for women in particular. Many are thinking about dialing back their careers or exiting altogether, which is very frightening for many companies. What should be done differently to retain women in the workplace?

We have some really great families who take an active role in discussing with their partners how to manage work-life balance in the household. We need to continue to encourage this progressive way of thinking. You have to really listen to the needs of your partner and make sure you each take turns adapting to life's challenges. No one should take their partner for granted and assume that they will just step in to fill in the gaps.

Our culture has not completely shifted away from the stereotype of then 50's family. I strongly believe that sustainable gender diversity starts at home. Each family unit should decide how to split roles for work or chores without gender bias. Children learn from example from what they see at home and at their friends' homes.

This will take time, so in the meantime, we should continue to provide resources and flexibility to both men and women caring for their families. As long as resources are offered, bias doesn't restrict taking them, we can encourage a balanced approach in the home.

5. Sustainability

As part of employee development, does your company encourage and support employees volunteering for local nongovernmental organizations? Do you and your company consider this an opportunity for aligning company efforts, employee leadership development, and local progress on sustainability?

Pre-COVID volunteering was a strong part of the company culture and supported thru sponsored events and paid time off. We consider this as a part of our company values to give back to the community and to drive employee engagement. Over the last year, it has been more difficult to donate time and effort to local nonprofit organizations. We have shifted our focus to support local groups by donating masks or face protectors to frontline workers. We had a virtual innovation workshop to encourage our team members to come up with ideas to support immediate needs, and several great ideas were generated to support gig workers, frontline workers, and return to office sanitization. We want to continue to show we are engaged with local events and continue to make a positive impact in our community.

Judy Wheeler

Division Vice President, Nissan Sales and Regional Operations
Nissan U.S.

Background

Judy Wheeler is Division Vice President for Nissan Sales and Regional Operations, Nissan U.S. She was appointed to this position in November 2020. In this role, Wheeler is responsible for the field sales organization and leading sales operations, distribution, fleet, and certified pre-owned sales.

Most recently, Wheeler was Division Vice President for Dealer Network Development and Customer Quality at Nissan North America, Inc. She was responsible for all Dealer Network Development (DND) operations for Nissan and Infiniti brands (the US and Canada) and optimizing revenue streams to increase brand strength. She was also responsible for all training for the dealers and the field organization, customer quality activities, and the oversight of call centers in the U.S. and Canada.

Previously, beginning in April 2018, Wheeler was Division Vice President for U.S. and Canada Dealer Network Strategy at Nissan North America, Inc. and was responsible for DND in the U.S. and Canada.

Prior to that, Wheeler was Division Vice President for Sales Operations and North/West Regions. She led the Nissan division sales operations, vehicle operations, fleet, and remarketing functions and was accountable for all facets of Nissan's U.S. domestic sales activities with a focus on increasing revenue and profit generation for the Nissan brand and dealer network, as well as driving sales performance in the Nissan West, Northwest, Midwest, and Northeast Regions.

Before this, Wheeler was Vice President for Sales at Nissan Division U.S. She also served as Vice President of Nissan Southeast Region, where she was responsible for regional sales and marketing activities in Nissan's Southeast Region. Before that, she was Director of Marketing for Nissan Canada, Inc., where she was responsible for all planning and implementation of marketing communications and media for national, retail, digital, customer relationship management, social sponsorships, and auto shows. Wheeler was also responsible for product planning, day-to-day marketing actions, and intelligence gathering, plus overseeing Nissan and Infiniti incentives.

Wheeler holds a bachelor's degree in Business Administration from the University of Wisconsin and an MBA from St. Mary's College, and she has successfully completed the Harvard Business School Executive Management Program as well as the Executive Leadership Program at the Wharton School of Business. She is also the Executive Sponsor of the Women's Business Synergy Team at Nissan North America. In 2020, she was recognized by *Automotive News* as one of the Top 100 Leading Women in the Automotive Industry.

Questions and Answers

1. Change Control, Resilience, and Work/Life Balance

How do you and your team continue to innovate and improve?

When COVID started, I was writing daily emails to my team of 900+ employees with updates on staying safe and caring for their families as well as Nissan's plan for taking care of employees and the strategy for handling business in this new environment. We quickly moved into Zoom meetings, keeping our protocol for boundaries on personal and professional balance. One of the things we quickly developed within my direct report team was a strategy to feature a daily "Working From Home Hero." We had set questions that employees voluntarily responded to with pictures that outlined how they were working in this new environment. To keep it engaging, the questions changed every few weeks. As time moved on, this profile feature moved from a daily to weekly update and eventually to an "All Employee Newsletter" completed by a committee. This has been a great way to learn tips from the group and to have fun.

2. Growing Your Professional Network and Maintaining Mentor and Sponsor Relationships

How do you keep your existing relationships in this remote world? Are you maintaining face time with other execs while being remote? How do your direct reports maintain their face time with you?

I keep my existing relationships with continuous open communication. As an executive team, we meet weekly via Zoom. To maintain constant communication with direct staff while working virtually, I've implemented a weekly meeting, personal one-on-one touchpoints, as well as an All-Employee Monthly Meeting. Additionally, every few weeks the team has a social celebration via Zoom to further drive engagement and to maintain high employee morale.

3. Personal Growth

Have you developed new behaviors (exercise, diet, meditation, hobbies, etc.) that help you get through this new stress?

Absolutely! On work-from-home days, I take an hour-long walk with my husband over lunch. I also purchased a Peloton early on during quarantine and now bike or take classes every other day at a minimum to keep on the right track for health and mental well-being. I also picked up hobbies and started to do things that I hadn't done for years, but I enjoy, such as a vegetable and herb gardening, oil painting, feeding the birds, taking time during the summer to work from my lake home, and Zooming with friends and family members weekly. I also had daily updates with my daughter, sister, and nieces using the MarcoPolo app, which was a very personal way to stay connected. I also continued to read every day before bed since I'm an avid reader.

4. Diversity, Equity, and Inclusion

Is the board of directors of your company diverse and representative of your workforce and/or customers? Is the leadership team? Is the workforce? If the workforce and customers aren't currently diverse, is there greater interest and commitment to making change in this regard?

Nissan has both a diverse workforce and customer base. The senior leadership team is taking intentional actions focused on improving diversity, equity, and inclusion efforts. Recently, the U.S. launched a regional board of directors that is diverse and established a cross-functional Diversity Council. The Diversity Council is focused on creating greater awareness throughout the organization, implementing training courses and developing a new action plan for college and intern recruitment programs. Also we created and launched a program to assist in increasing the diversity of our dealer network.

5. Sustainability

What do you as a leader do to stay informed about sustainability trends that can impact the success of your company and its strategy?

Daily, I'm keeping informed on industry trends through media pertaining to our business. I discuss with the executive team, my peers, and my direct reports potential opportunities where we can build our business in areas that align with the Nissan brand. We also discuss with our dealers' future opportunities to gauge their interest to ensure support and alignment.

Kate S. Whitefoot

Assistant Professor
Mechanical Engineering and Engineering and Public Policy
Carnegie Mellon University

Background

Kate S. Whitefoot is an assistant professor in the Department of Engineering and Public Policy and the Department of Mechanical Engineering at Carnegie Mellon University. She is a thrust leader of Technology Commercialization for the NextManufacturing Center and a Faculty Affiliate at the Carnegie Mellon Scott Institute for Energy Innovation. Prior to her current position, she served as Senior Program Officer and the Robert A. Pritzker Fellow at the National Academies of Sciences, Engineering, and Medicine where she directed the Academies' Manufacturing, Design, and Innovation program.

Professor Whitefoot's research bridges engineering design theory and analysis with that of economics to study the design and manufacture of energy and environmental technologies and their adoption in the marketplace. She currently serves on the National Academies Committee on Assessment of Technologies for Improving Fuel Economy of Light-Duty Vehicles as well as the World Economic Forum's Global Futures Council for Clean Air. Her research is published in *Science*, the *Proceedings of the National Academy of Sciences of the United States of America*, and *Environmental Science and Technology* among others. She has worked with several companies in the automotive, aerospace, and high-tech industries and has been invited to present briefings at the White House, Capitol Hill, the Department of Commerce, and the Environmental Protection Agency.

Dr. Whitefoot earned three degrees from the University of Michigan: a Bachelor of Science and Master of Science in Mechanical Engineering and a PhD in Design

Science—a multidisciplinary program where she concentrated in Mechanical Engineering and Economics.

Questions and Answers

1. Change, Resilience, and Work/Life Balance

What did you learn when you began to work from home or work in the office with a limited number of co-workers?

One of the challenges and opportunities with shifting work online has been how to take advantage of online platforms to continue to improve how we do things and how we interact with each other. We redesigned courses, research meetings, and conferences to be online. Very quickly, it was clear there were concerns about how we could mimic in-person teaching and interactions online. But it would be a shame to focus all this effort on redesigning these activities, only to "go back" to the way they were run in the past. I wanted instead to focus on what we could do online that would improve our courses and work that we could learn from and incorporate what worked into in-person activities once they resumed. One example is adding interactive online brainstorming and sketching platforms into a team-project engineering design course. The students can collaborate live with each other, applying the concepts taught in the lecture that day. And as an instructor, I can check in on their work and correct any misconceptions as necessary. Another example is in reviewing code with my PhD students. Debugging code together online has been very successful, and we spot and solve issues faster than was possible in person. We'll keep using these tools even after in-person instruction resumes.

2. Growing Your Professional Network and Maintaining Mentor and Sponsor Relationships

Have your mentees been asking different questions than under usual working conditions? Have you needed to do more hand-holding? Do you see more mentees seeking career change or seeking educational opportunities? Something else?

In the first few months of the pandemic, over half of my students needed to move for various reasons. Some had signed a lease to be close to campus and then found themselves confined to a small space with no need to be on campus. Others had family circumstances that required them to move. And moving in the middle of the pandemic and lockdown restrictions was quite an undertaking. It has been important to me to have more personal conversations with my students under these circumstances to check in on what is happening in their lives and how they are affected, directly or indirectly, by the pandemic. My goals for mentorship during this time have been to adjust expectations and timelines—understanding the inevitable hit to productivity that the changing circumstances of the pandemic will have—condense projects down to what is most essential and make contingency plans to absorb the impact on my students.

3. Personal Growth

Have you developed new behaviors (exercise, diet, meditation, hobbies, etc.) that help you get through this new stress?

I have really seen a coming together during the pandemic that has strengthened many relationships and has been an unexpected blessing in these times. I have become closer with many of my friends and colleagues as we commiserate over the various trials, sorrow, relief, and uncertainties of the past year. These relationships will continue to be a source of joy and strength into the future.

4. Diversity, Equity, and Inclusion

There has been a lot of talk about diversity—and, in recent years, inclusion. Equity has entered the corporate conversation in a major way this year. What actions are you and your organization taking?

The tragic deaths of George Floyd, Breonna Taylor, and so many others this past year have pushed the long-standing issues of systemic racism and bias to the forefront of the agenda within academia. I have not seen this level of commitment to make meaningful change within academia to advance diversity, equity, and inclusion (DEI) before in my career, and I would like to see it continue. An important way to do this is with institutional reforms. At Carnegie Mellon University, an example is that many departments require DEI statements from faculty and student candidates. It is now becoming the norm that these statements do not only provide a commitment to DEI but specific plans for how the candidate will lead activities once on campus to contribute to meaningful institutional change. Another example is having DEI-specific objectives within strategic plans at every level of the organization so that specific outcomes are planned to provide focus and accountability.

5. Sustainability

Human capital—employee talent—is one ultimate driver of business and company success. Aligning talent to sustainability trends has proven to be a winning approach for recruiting, retaining, and developing top talent because employees want to do more with their careers ... and do good while also doing well. Have you and your company moved to incorporate sustainability into your strategies for attracting, retaining, and developing your human capital?

So many engineering students have chosen to pursue the discipline because they want to make the world a better place. I see this all of the time. Some of the most driven young engineers are personally motivated by using technology for sustainability, both environmental and social, including addressing climate change, reducing emissions, the development of sustainable mobility, and empowering the workforce. It is certainly important for recruitment to show these candidates how they can improve sustainability through engineering. But it is not just recruiting. It is also aligning the mission of the work with the values of the people who conduct that work. My goal is that the passions for sustainability of incoming engineers are reflective in their work and influence the direction of future research in my group.

Cynthia Williams

Global Director, Sustainability, Homologation, and Compliance
Ford Motor Company

Background

Cynthia Williams is Ford Motor Company's Global Director for Sustainability, Homologation, and Compliance. She assumed this position in December 2019. In this role, Cynthia is responsible for sustainable business plans and policies, environmental negotiations with regulatory bodies around the world, reporting on the company's environmental and social performance, and engaging with nongovernment organizations and other external stakeholders.

Since joining Ford in 1992, as part of the Ford College Graduate Program in the Automotive Emissions and Fuel Economy Office, Cynthia has held several positions, which include Ford's Sustainability, Environment, and Safety Director in Asia Pacific, Automotive Safety Assistant Director, Ford's Environmental Policy Manager, and On-Board Diagnostics Compliance Manager.

She was the Executive Champion for the Professional Women's Network and the Gay, Lesbian, Bisexual, or Transgender Employee Resource Groups in Asia Pacific. Cynthia held numerous positions in the Ford African Ancestry Network and is committed to mentoring young engineers, students, and peers.

Cynthia is currently on the Board of Directors for CALSTART and VELOZ, nonprofit organizations working to develop and promote clean, efficient transportation solutions. Cynthia will serve on Governor Whitmer's Council on Climate Solutions which will identify and recommend the emissions-reduction strategies.

A native of Flint, MI, Cynthia earned a Bachelor of Science degree in Mechanical Engineering from Michigan State University and a master's degree in Business Administration from the University of Detroit Mercy.

Questions and Answers

1. Change Control, Resilience, and Work/Life Balance

Many have said that there is no separation of work and home these days—what do you do to manage this for your own work? What are you doing to increase the ability of your team to create and respect boundaries? How do you keep the team spirit with your direct reports? Are you sensing any lack of trust or more trust? What factors/actions have the most effect on trust/lack of trust?

COMMUNICATION AND ENGAGEMENT, I believe, are the key components to keep the team motivated. When the pandemic started, we literally left the office on Friday and began working from home on Monday without skipping a beat. The team quickly mobilized to understand first and foremost what was needed to make sure that our employees and customers were safe. It was very important to keep employees up to date with corporate plans regarding working from home and potential return-to-work information. The leadership team maintained touchpoints with the employees to provide the confidence that the company had a plan.

Before leaving the office, folks understood that I had an open-door policy. If you needed to talk, one could always stop by and schedule time to see me. Under the new normal, that quickly shifted to a virtual open-door policy. In-person meetings immediately became WebEx or Zoom calls with cameras on. I made it a priority to maintain 1:1 meetings as well as quarterly skip level meetings with employees. As part of my management style, I have always been flexible and willing to change. One of the most underutilized tools is to listen to employees and to work together to develop actionable plans. Whether it is related to employee well-being, development, a corporate goal, or social unrest, we were able to continue to discuss these items in a virtual environment. As we developed innovative strategies to meet and exceed our day-to-day activities and deliver long-term goals, I was even more amazed at how the team demonstrated flexibility and resiliency.

2. Growing Your Professional Network and Maintaining Mentor and Sponsor Relationships

Are you continuing to grow your professional network while being remote? How?

Working remotely most definitely has its benefits. I have had the opportunity to participate in multiple webinars, panels, leadership forums, employee resource group meetings, and recruiting events without the added costs of travel. The webinar and panel sessions typically bring together key stakeholders, often with different viewpoints regarding a subject matter. Staying engaged is a great way to share knowledge and learn from others. It can provide a means to connect with a smaller team to hone in on a specific topic with key experts and work together toward a common goal.

It is also a great way to recruit new talent for the workplace. Virtual career fairs are something that I would have not imagined but is a powerful mechanism to connect with students.

Virtual professional networking has given me an opportunity to connect, extend my reach, and engage with more people globally via Zoom calls and social media outlets.

3. Personal Growth

Have you developed new behaviors (exercise, diet, meditation, hobbies, etc.) that help you get through this new stress?

The coronavirus has definitely changed the lives of nearly everyone around the world. Working from home can be convenient but also can be stressful at times with everyone relying on "Mom"—cooking, cleaning, homework, etc. I was inspired by a colleague in India to start a new hobby to relieve stress through painting. To get started, I ordered a painting with a twist starter kit. In a normal world, I would be traveling, shopping, or relaxing on a beach. Given that, my first painting was a beach scene. This hobby has allowed me to disconnect from both work and family for a few hours a month and focus on my well-being.

Cynthia Williams

My new hobby is not only fun, it's therapeutic. It provides an opportunity to have time for myself or time to connect with female friends through social media. Similar to a book club, it provides an avenue for open dialogue to discuss non-work-related things. I have found it to be very relaxing and a great way to wind down. This has been an excellent release valve for me, and ultimately in the long-term, I believe it will have a positive impact on my health and mental well-being.

4. Diversity, Equity, and Inclusion

Is the board of directors of your company diverse and representative of your workforce and/or customers? Is the leadership team? Is the workforce? If the workforce and customers aren't currently diverse, is there greater interest and commitment to making change in this regard?

Ford understands that leveraging the diversity of our people makes our business stronger and helps us reflect the communities in which we live and work. We have embedded diversity and inclusion in our People Strategy to create a culture that enables us to attract, retain, and develop top talent. We have many teams and Employee

Resource Groups focused on inclusion, supported by partnerships fostering diversity among suppliers, communities, and customers.

For more than a century, Ford has been a pioneer in providing opportunity to people regardless of race, gender, ability, sexual orientation, and background. We view this less with pride than the sober realization that we must go further to create a company where our differences are truly valued and every team member can bring their whole selves to work. Creating a culture of belonging isn't just the right thing to do, it's also the smart thing. Diversity breeds innovation, and the companies that attract the most talented and diverse workforce will succeed in our rapidly changing world.

Ford committed to the CEO Action for Diversity and Inclusion pledge in 2018, and in early 2020 we became a signatory to the United Nations Women's Empowerment Principles. For the third year in a row, Ford was included in the 2021 GEI in recognition of its commitment to transparent gender reporting and workplace equality. To engage employees, we launched a global day of understanding in March 2020, a virtual lunch and learn series centered around belonging, and conducted a diversity, equity and inclusion audit. The audit identified positive findings, as well as opportunities for improvement. We are working together to improve the employee experience.

5. Sustainability

Sustainability trends (climate change, water availability, health, etc.) are some of the strongest drivers for future changes for companies and their strategies. What are you seeing within your company? Is your firm reading the trends and adapting strategies to survive and then thrive with new growth?

Sustainability is one of my greatest passions and one of the biggest issues facing businesses today. Sustainability has been one of Ford's priorities for more than 20 years. Our annual sustainability report highlights our sustainability leadership in the industry and the progress we have made in reducing our impact on the planet while maintaining a strong business and producing vehicles that customers love. We have set the following ambitious goals to help us make a positive impact on the communities where we live and work:

- **Carbon neutrality:** Achieve carbon neutrality by 2050.
- **Human rights:** Source only raw materials that are responsibly produced.
- **Diversity:** Create a truly diverse culture where everyone feels like they belong.
- **Energy:** Use 100 percent locally sourced renewable electricity for all manufacturing plants globally by 2035.
- **Waste:** Achieve true zero waste to landfill across our operations; Eliminate single-use plastics from our operations by 2030.
- **Access:** Drive human progress by providing mobility and accessibility for all.
- **Water:** Make zero water withdrawals for manufacturing processes; Use freshwater for human consumption only.

- **Air:** Achieve zero air emissions from our vehicles and facilities.
- **Materials:** Utilize only recycled or renewable content in vehicle plastic.
- **Safety:** Work toward a future that is free from vehicle crashes and workplace injuries.

The world is constantly changing, so Ford conducts a formal materiality assessment to help us identify and prioritize the sustainability issues that matter most to our business and are of most concern to our stakeholders. The process we undertake enables us to focus our sustainability strategy, resources, and reporting on these issues. We conduct materiality assessments every two years. The analysis identified our most material issues as

- Electrification and alternative fuels/batteries
- Vehicle product safety and quality
- Economic performance
- Climate change, air quality and renewable energy/energy future

We consider human capital, human rights, health and safety, and diversity and inclusion as issues of great importance for social and economic progress. We also acknowledge other emerging trends and assess them for inclusion as they arise. COVID has reinforced the importance of putting people first and embracing disruption to evolve.

Allyson Witherspoon

Chief Marketing Officer
Nissan U.S.

Background

Allyson Witherspoon is the U.S. Chief Marketing Officer for Nissan. Prior to this, Allyson was Vice President, Marketing Communications and Media, after returning to the U.S. from a global position in Yokohama, Japan, where she was the general manager for Nissan global brand engagement.

Interested in cars and design at an early age, Allyson has spent her entire career in the automotive sector. A female senior executive in a male-dominated industry, Allyson's mission has been to champion other women in their quest for unconventional career paths.

Prior to her roles at Nissan and Infiniti, Allyson served as the global business director for Volvo in Amsterdam, Netherlands, adding to her marketing agency experience that included leading accounts for BMW North America and Mercedes-Benz USA in New York City.

One of the pivotal experiences in her career was being in Saudi Arabia in 2018 on behalf of Nissan on the week that women there won the right to drive.

Previously named a "Top 40 under 40" by *Automotive News*, Allyson was recognized in 2020 as a Female Frontier for breaking brand barriers by *Campaign US* and was also named one of the "100 Leading Women in North American Auto Industry" by *Automotive News*.

Questions and Answers

1. Change Control, Resilience, and Work/Life Balance

What did you learn when you began to work from home or work in the office with a limited number of co-workers? What did you need to start doing and what did you need to stop?

I've learned so much over the last 10 months of this pandemic and adapting to working from home as well as being in the office with a limited number of co-workers.

The biggest lesson is making sure you adapt as things evolve. From a work and project standpoint, it was about being able to pivot as consumer behavior changed so rapidly and dramatically. I had to throw away plans that had been in place for months and create new ones from scratch to be implemented in a matter of hours.

From a people management standpoint, it was all about creating connections over Zoom and a constant stream of communication about what was happening with the industry, our company, and how we were adapting. Over time, the Zoom fatigue set in and I had to adjust by creating connections over the phone (so retro!), messenger apps, or even in person, but socially distanced.

The ability to take the time to understand the situation, listen to feedback from employees and consumers, and then be able to adapt isn't new, but we are now having to do all of this in the moment and in a very short amount of time. The biggest change is not being so tied to existing plans that you miss or ignore the opportunity to connect with consumers or your employees in an even more meaningful way based on what's going on around them. I believe and hope this behavior will be something that stays with me personally and professionally after the pandemic is over.

2. Growing Your Professional Network and Maintaining Mentor and Sponsor Relationships

How do you keep your existing relationships in this remote world? Are you maintaining face time with other execs while being remote? How do your direct reports maintain their face time with you?

It's definitely a challenge to maintain existing relationships in a remote world. Zoom has helped, but it has also become a burden and unhealthy to sit in front of a screen for 14 hours a day. Since June, a small group of our executive team has been going to the office, so we've been having some socially distanced face time for a while at an executive level. You don't realize how much you miss this until you're there and seeing people. We're all wearing masks and staying apart and still doing almost all meetings via Zoom, but it's the in-between time to catch up with colleagues that I find very valuable.

For my direct reports, it's been important to have an established cadence of 1:1s and leadership team meetings. In March, I held daily standups with my directors and bi-weekly all-staff meetings as things were changing so quickly and we were all adjusting to remote working. That cadence of meetings became too much for the team, my directors, and even myself, so I adjusted to weekly director meetings, weekly or bi-weekly 1:1s, and then a monthly all-staff meeting. I've been trying to adjust based on the needs of the team members. At first, I thought it was important to do everything via Zoom and see each other on screen, but we all have been struggling with Zoom fatigue (myself included), so I try to do 1:1s over the phone or check in with people through individual messages, texts, etc. It's also nice to connect with team members via social media and get to know people on a more personal level.

3. Personal Growth

What personal development opportunities have you taken advantage of now that you're not traveling?

It's been so strange not to travel every week—I was on an airplane so much over the last 15 years that my personal hashtag was #onaplane! I've lived almost half of the last decade overseas in Europe and then in Japan and was constantly traveling. My lifestyle was a bit bohemian so being at home was nice, and nesting for the first time in my adult life was comforting. Making my home a relaxing but also productive place to be has also been key.

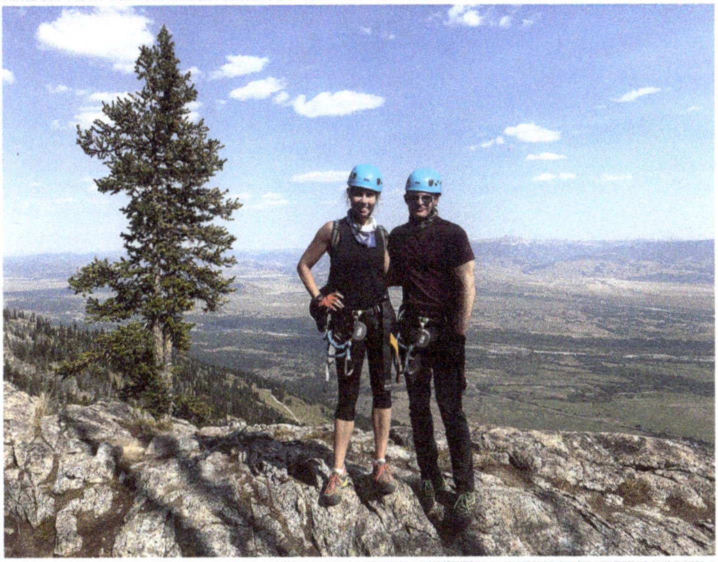

Allyson Witherspoon

Focusing on keeping myself healthy became a priority. I've been a runner for many years but had some injuries recently, so I started doing yoga regularly as well as meditating. This has helped to balance out all of the running I was doing but also to take time to breathe and calm my mind and body. I've also started to spend much more time outside and in nature. I took a few small trips and learned how to rock and mountain climb, which I really love now. It's been a great way to push myself athletically, it's out in nature in the elements, and you can do it in a healthy and socially distanced way.

4. Diversity, Equity, and Inclusion

Is the board of directors of your company diverse and representative of your workforce and/or customers? Is the leadership team? Is the workforce? If the workforce and customers aren't currently diverse, is there greater interest and commitment to making change in this regard?

Nissan has a diverse workforce and customer base and is committed to finding solutions when it comes to equitable access. In the U.S., we have established a new regional board of directors that is more diverse than in the past. Our leadership team is focused on making intentional change. Our chairman is a huge advocate for diversity and inclusion, and this is now a regular part of his communications. It's important for everyone at all levels to see that commitment, so it's appreciated that he constantly reinforces this message. This has translated into commitment at all levels.

For my marketing and customer experience department, I have committed to addressing equality, inclusion, and systematic change as a marketing organization, which includes both in front of the camera as well as behind the camera. We have made changes to achieve representation in communications that better reflects our country's demographics, increase our spending in multicultural marketing, achieve an equitable creative supply chain through creative productions, and double down on cross-industry partnerships to enable a higher degree of engagement with an understanding of diverse communities.

5. Sustainability

Sustainability trends (climate change, water availability, health, etc.) are some of the strongest drivers for future changes for companies and their strategies. What are you seeing within your company? Is your firm reading the trends and adapting strategies to survive and then thrive with new growth?

Nissan is definitely a company that reads the trends and adapts strategies to address the rapidly changing needs of consumers. Brands have needed to become more purposeful in order to connect with consumers.

Our brand purpose is driving innovation to enrich people's lives. This focus is to build a truly sustainable and mobile society. And this purpose will be reflected in everything we do. From a product standpoint, we have a legacy of being pioneers in electric vehicles—we created the first electric vehicle in 1947 named the Tama and then the first mass-produced electric vehicle with the Nissan LEAF in 2010. We will launch the all-electric Nissan Ariya crossover in 2021, which will add to our existing product line up.

Our commitment to a sustainable future is more than just building efficient vehicles. In every aspect of our business—from our headquarters in Japan to our offices worldwide to our dealerships in the community—we are actively working towards reducing both our energy consumption and environmental impact.

Nissan has manufacturing facilities in 20 countries, and in every one of them, we are always looking for ways to increase efficiency and decrease energy use. Renewable energy generated by the sun, wind, water, and biogas are helping to power our plants in Asia, Africa, Europe, and North and South America. The Nissan Energy Savings Collaboration (NESCO) monitors energy loss at our plants and proposes effective countermeasures designed to reduce our CO2 emissions by 30,000 tons annually.

Also, most recently, we announced our commitment to achieve carbon neutrality across the company's operations and the life cycle of our products by 2050. And, as part of this effort, by the early 2030s every all-new Nissan vehicle offering in key markets will be electrified.

Rekha Wunnava

Global Director, Automotive Design and Build IT
Ford Motor Company

Background

Rekha Wunnava is an executive in Information Technology at Ford, currently in the role of Global Director for Automotive Design and Build Information Technology (IT). In this role, she is helping shape the future of Ford's core automotive domain through digital transformation.

Rekha has contributed to Ford IT's growth and transformation during her 18 years with the company (25+ years in the IT industry) with roles as the IT Director for Manufacturing and leading the IT Strategy, Learning, and Change Management. Having lived and worked in India, UK, China, and the USA, she has a unique perspective on global cultures and is the executive champion for Ford IT's culture transformation. She enjoys combining that with her technical experiences to create winning strategies and a vibrant culture that energizes a multigenerational workforce. She is passionate about empowering women and developing leaders at all levels and is the executive sponsor for Ford's Women of Ford, Technology employee resource group. In 2020, she was selected by *Automotive News* as one of the 100 Leading Women in the North American Auto Industry.

Rekha studied in India focusing on accounting, finance, and computer science. She resides in Michigan with her husband and two golden retrievers.

Questions and Answers

1. Change Control, Resilience, and Work/Life Balance

What did you learn when you began to work from home or work in the office with a limited number of co-workers? What did you need to start doing and what did you need to stop?

The decision to work from home was made almost overnight, and it was one of the biggest challenges to be placed in front of any IT team, let alone one that supports hundreds of thousands of workers globally.

The resiliency, creativity, and innovation of the team shone through in quickly responding to the needs of the enterprise. From assessing the types of equipment needed by various groups to work remotely to ensuring that those who needed to work onsite were able to do so safely by leveraging technology to enable those needs was no small feat. It was a great learning experience to observe firsthand that nothing unites a team like having a common purpose, especially one that is for the greater good of humanity.

As we started to settle into the reality of working from home, we went through phases of getting comfortable with working remotely. Saving a couple of hours of commute each day was quickly taken over by longer work hours and more meetings. Sitting in one place all day without breaks was becoming the norm. Even basic workplace activities like a walk across the hallway or cafeteria visits no longer existed. We were now in charge of creating those activities on our own, in our homes. I needed to make a conscious effort to give myself stretch breaks and quiet time to ensure I would be able to perform at my best. My assistant and I made a conscious effort to place calendar holds for breaks and lunch, and limited meeting hours.

The next realization was that lack of face-to-face interaction was creating a mental distance and impacting my holistic well-being. Our leadership team underwent training on Thriving in a Crisis. This couldn't have come at a better time as it reinforced some basic principles of taking care of yourself, looking after each other, and delivering what matters, in that order. That was the perfect learning and reminder to start focusing on what I needed to do to take care of myself. I turned to mindfulness and yoga and incorporated those into my daily routine.

Next, I turned my attention to my teams and established weekly check-in meetings with my leadership team, as well as a series of "Reflections with Rekha" meetings with my global employees. These forums were designed to have no agenda so we could just chat and check in on each other. This gave us space to learn and share what was going on in our lives, our fears, hopes, and coping mechanisms we had developed. Having re-established that connection through virtual touchpoints has had a positive impact on me, and I have received overwhelmingly positive feedback from my teams.

As I reflect on the months gone by and how we have evolved and adjusted to a new normal, my key reflections are (1) the importance of human interaction, (2) how resilient and innovative we can be when we unite behind a cause, and (3) being grateful for what we have.

2. Growing Your Professional Network and Maintaining Mentor and Sponsor Relationships

Has your company maintained learning and leadership development opportunities, culture surveys, 360 surveys, etc. to grow skills and manage the emotional intelligence of the company? Has anything shifted? What have you learned?

I am fortunate to work for a company whose core value is to **Put People First**. In addition to the leadership program for Thriving in a Crisis that I mentioned above, there were several additional shifts that were made in response to the needs of our people and their development.

- Global town hall meetings every other week with the CEO and executive leadership—These meetings were instantiated for sharing information with employees transparently so everyone is informed on what was going on, what was known, and what was yet unknown. It helped greatly with emotional resilience as employees were not left guessing what to expect. These have now continued to provide an ongoing forum for information sharing and Q&A.
- Weekly surveys to sense the instant pulse of how employees were feeling, as well as the more formal pulse and culture surveys were continued. The results of these were shared during these town hall meetings for everyone to be able to see how the mood of the organization was shifting and see where they fit in with the rest of the company in terms of their own personal feelings.
- Mentoring programs continued to be executed virtually, with remote collaboration. These continue to provide opportunities for employees to connect with their mentors to broaden their professional exposure.
- Guild (communities of interest) events, focused on leadership development, provide employees opportunities to interact with senior leaders on various themes of essential (behavioral) skills.
- Various activities and events in the IT organization aimed at creating a vibrant workplace culture such as culture camps, power-up learning sessions, and other structured learning modules for creating a culture of accountability continue to be offered to team members, most of them with video-on-demand capability to be able to watch at a time that's convenient to people's schedules
- Internal and external speaking events on various technical topics have continued to be held virtually to develop and showcase technical talent in the organization.
- Learning and listening events designed to help further the awareness and understanding of Diversity, Equity, and Inclusion with external benchmarking to develop action plans for each function in the company.

These are just a few examples of the emphasis we continue to place, even when working remotely, on developing our talent on technical and leadership skills and continue to build and nurture professional relationships and networking.

3. Personal Growth

Have you developed new behaviors (exercise, diet, meditation, hobbies, etc.) that help you get through this new stress?

Once I got through the initial slump of inactivity and sitting in front of a laptop all day, I quickly realized that was not healthy and started to incorporate some simple disciplines into my daily routines:

- Replaced caffeine with green tea in the mornings
- Watching the portions of my meals
- Reduced intake of sugary treats (except when I cheat :))
- Meditating for at least a few breaths most days
- In-home yoga practice, a walk outdoors when the weather is decent and other fitness routines (a few times a week)
- Making time to connect with family and friends on a regular basis via group chats or video calls
- Virtual happy hour or coffee/tea break with colleagues
- And the occasional online retail therapy ;)

I have good weeks and bad weeks, but overall my physical and mental fitness is at least moving in the right direction, and the weighing scale is also starting to show some kindness. Although none of these shifts are dramatic in nature and neither is the result, the key is to recognize that it takes effort to form these habits—and the need to prioritize yourself and your well-being. It's like the safety instructions you get on an airplane to put on your own mask (no pun intended) before helping others.

4. Diversity, Equity, and Inclusion

The pandemic has hit hard for women in particular. Many are thinking about dialing back their careers or exiting altogether, which is very frightening for many companies. What should be done differently to retain women in the workplace?

Studies have shown that the pandemic has hit certain minority groups disproportionately. Additionally, women who have multiple responsibilities of balancing a career with other priorities like family, elder care, etc. are struggling to cope and faced with slowing down or having to choose. This could cause a long-term impact on diversity in the workplace if nothing is done about it. There are various measures that companies can take, and many are taking, to address this situation.

One of the most basic things that can be done is to create a safe environment for candid conversations. People leaders need to listen with empathy to understand the challenges their employees and women, in particular, are facing. Having that kind of a caring and nurturing environment provides the psychological safety and can reduce stress. This might be easier said than done because listening and empathy don't come naturally to everyone and needs to be consciously developed.

A few examples of support that our company provided during the peak of the pandemic included:

- Short-term sabbatical programs at reduced compensation to provide relief to handle some specific issues or challenges, following which the employee resumes a normal schedule.
- Parental support such as online tutoring was another great option for families that are balancing multiple priorities.
- Additionally, employee resource groups focused on development and networking for women play a huge role in building a sense of community. They provide opportunities for women to find their support system and develop not just their technical and leadership talent but also coping mechanisms by learning from others who are/were in a similar situation.

Recognizing the challenges that women face and providing options for them to be able to contribute, to whatever extent they can, will help retain them in the workforce. Investing in targeted development programs and ensuring they are providing opportunities to demonstrate their capabilities will create the right long-term impact for improving and sustaining gender diversity.

5. Sustainability

Sustainability trends (climate change, water availability, health, etc.) are some of the strongest drivers for future changes for companies and their strategies. What are you seeing within your company? Is your firm reading the trends and adapting strategies to survive and then thrive with new growth?

This is an easy one for me as I am fortunate to work for a company that is a world leader in sustainability measures. Just recently, Ford was awarded the 2020 Gold Medal for International Corporate Achievement in Sustainable Development by the World Environment Center (WEC). Despite a challenging business environment, Ford has doubled down on its sustainability commitment because what's good for the planet is good for business. From signing a voluntary agreement with the state of California for greenhouse gas emissions to our commitment to reduce emissions in line with the Paris Climate Agreement, Ford continues to lead the way among global automakers. What makes Ford stand out is our sustained commitment to this cause with Bill Ford leading the industry by publishing the first sustainability report in 1999 and continuing to make consistent progress since then. We also lead the way in the research and implementation of bio-based products in our vehicles.

Congresswoman Debbie Dingell, who presented the award to Ford, summarizes it well in her message, "To my dear friend, Bill Ford, Jim Farley, and the entire Ford Motor Company and its employees, congratulations on this well-earned award and recognition. When it comes to existential threats like climate change, we need companies like Ford who aren't afraid to lead and do what's right. We need corporations that see sustainability not just as a moral imperative but an economic opportunity to shape our future. I am so honored to present the Gold Medal Award from the

World Environment Center to Bill Ford, Jim Farley, and the Ford Motor Company today."

Source: https://media.ford.com/content/fordmedia/fna/us/en/news/2020/12/17/ford-world-environment-center-award.html

This is also a matter of personal pride for me based on the work that my global team does to provide technology solutions to help deliver on our environment and sustainability commitments including meeting various regional regulatory requirements.

For more on Ford's commitment to ESG (Environmental, Social, and Governance), see the link below:

https://corporate.ford.com/microsites/sustainability-report-2020/esg-reporting-hub.html

Angela Zepeda

Chief Marketing Officer
Hyundai Motor America

Background

Angela Zepeda is the chief marketing officer for Hyundai Motor America. She is responsible for all of Hyundai's marketing and advertising activities in the U.S. and is an expert in developing consumer-centric campaigns that build brands and drive business results.

At Hyundai, Angela led the development of Hyundai's 2020 Super Bowl commercial, "Smaht Pahk," which finished second in the *USA TODAY* Ad Meter and was the highest performing commercial overall in Ace Metrix. During the COVID-19 pandemic, she helped spearhead the company's response, including the expansion of digital retailing and communicating about Hyundai's corporate social responsibility efforts.

Angela was most recently at Hyundai's agency of record Innocean USA. Previous to Innocean, Angela was CEO of Quigley-Simpson and CMO of Campbell Ewald–Los Angeles. She also worked at some of Los Angeles' best-known agencies, including TBWA\Chiat\Day, Team One, Rapp, Doner, and FCB, providing counsel to clients in the automotive, healthcare, financial services, and packaged goods industries.

Angela is a member of ThinkLA, the American Association of Advertising Agencies, and the American Advertising Federation and has held board positions with the Susan G. Komen organization and the LAGRANT Foundation.

Questions and Answers

1. Change Control, Resilience, and Work/Life Balance

Many have said that there is no separation of work and home these days—what do you do to manage this for your own work? What are you doing to increase the ability of your team to create and respect boundaries?

For years I've said that I did not lead a balanced life, but rather an integrated life. As technology made it easier for us to work remotely and at any time of the day, the lines between personal life and work life continued to blur.

With my position and level of responsibility, I took this new way of working as liberating, as it allowed me to be more efficient and productive. It's something that works for me, and I'm able to successfully manage business and personal life together. However, I know this doesn't work well for everyone, especially those with families and children.

Boundaries for home life are different when it comes to families, and it requires respect for those who are raising children as well as managing full-time jobs. I think leadership starts at the top, and while I was fine working during "off hours," I don't expect anyone on my team to work in the same way. The focus is always on the quality of the work and getting work done on time, and less on how the work gets done.

This also oftentimes requires a cultural shift within the company to adapt to how technology has changed the traditional work structure. At Hyundai, we've definitely had more of a traditional mindset, but I'm proud that our entire leadership team and parent company in Korea are recognizing the benefits of flexibility. It's helping our business performance and allowing us to retain and attract top talent.

Today's options for working remotely forces all of us to be flexible and understanding, and respect that one-size-does-not-fit-all in today's new world of working.

2. Growing Your Professional Network and Maintaining Mentor and Sponsor Relationships

How do you keep your existing relationships in this remote world? Are you maintaining face time with other execs while being remote? How do your direct reports maintain their face time with you?

Face time with other executives interestingly increased with COVID-19 by using technology to connect. In the past, I may have tried to set in-person meetings or appointments to see partners or other colleagues. That was often impossible to figure out on a busy calendar. With less travel and in-person commitments, people tend to have more availability to connect. Video conference has allowed us a new accepted way of connecting, creating more "in-person" meetings than ever before.

I encourage my direct reports to communicate frequently and provide more updates than when we were all together. Despite an often hectic schedule, I try to always be available for my team. I welcome things like even short text messages to keep me apprised of critical projects.

It's true that screen time and Zoom fatigue is real, but it has helped bring out the best in people's creativity. I've been invited to several gatherings with female executives for a shared experience event, from wine tasting to a virtual spa. It's been fun and it's allowed all of us to show our personalities outside of work more. I think it has brought us closer together with a greater understanding and empathy for who we are as real people.

3. Personal Growth

What personal development opportunities have you taken advantage of now that you're not traveling?

Have you developed new behaviors (exercise, diet, meditation, hobbies, etc.) that help you get through this new stress?

In the early days of COVID, when we went to a work-from-home schedule, I didn't like it. I thrive on structure and a fast-paced schedule, which I had done for years and hadn't fully realized what a hamster wheel I had been on. A few weeks into working at home, I started to take a deep breath and enjoy not commuting and jumping on and off airplanes, landing in a new city every few days. With COVID-19, I did "slow down," taking time to exercise regularly and take a daily Spanish class, something that I had wanted to do for a long time.

Angela Zepeda

These two extra activities were great, and it felt good to accomplish something else beyond work. It had been years since I had done that, and I realized I was burning myself out. COVID-19 allowed me to reset and not feel like I had to work every minute of the day. Carving time away from work was critical, and this time gave me the permission to do it. While I am looking forward to getting back to some sort of normal work life in the office and on the road, I am hoping to bring a little of this new-found reset forward.

4. Diversity, Equity, and Inclusion

There has been a lot of talk about diversity—and, in recent years, inclusion. Equity has entered the corporate conversation in a major way this year. What actions are you and your company taking? Are these methods aligned with company goals?

Over the summer with the racial injustice protests, we took immediate action as a company to look at ways to improve our own diversity and inclusion efforts. We first looked internally to ensure all of our employees felt supported and to understand what they felt we needed to do better as a company. At Hyundai, we are fortunate to have several active employee resource groups, including one for Black employees, and we immediately engaged with them to determine our best way forward.

We then took action to create an external diversity council that reports to the Office of the President and CEO of Hyundai, with a charge to take a look at our business to improve diversity representation. As part of that initiative, we also set up an internal mentoring program to develop diverse talent and prepare them for senior- or executive-level positions. In marketing, we committed to a 15% diversity spend across our business activities by 2022, including the hiring of African-American and Hispanic agencies to implement a more inclusive marketing strategy that includes creative, talent, staffing, production, and media buys.

Lastly, we revised our executive performance metrics to include diversity and inclusion in our business results, putting diversity and inclusion as an external metric to hold Hyundai and its executives accountable to deliver.

5. Sustainability

Sustainability trends (climate change, water availability, health, etc.) are some of the strongest drivers for future changes for companies and their strategies. What are you seeing within your company? Is your firm reading the trends and adapting strategies to survive and then thrive with new growth?

At the center of Hyundai Motor Company's management philosophy is "Progress for Humanity." Hyundai has actively sought to improve the conditions of life for all humankind by making continuous efforts to reduce its ecological footprint, which means producing eco-friendly vehicles and operating its business sites in an eco-friendly manner.

We will accomplish this through the following areas: improved vehicle fuel efficiency, next-generation weight reduction technology advancements, renewable energy technologies, hazardous substances waste reduction, and recycling waste resources.

On the vehicle front, in Hyundai's global 2025 strategic plan, securing electrification leadership is one of the main pillars. By 2025, we aim to become the world's third-largest automaker of eco-friendly vehicles by selling 670,000 electric vehicles annually, comprising 560,000 battery-electric vehicles and 110,000 fuel-cell electric vehicles. The goal is to electrify most new models by 2030 in key markets such as Korea, the USA, China, and Europe.

We recently launched the Ioniq brand of vehicles that will open a new chapter of electrified mobility at Hyundai. Under Ioniq, we will offer customer-centric EV experiences centered on connected lifestyle solutions in line with our vision of "Progress for Humanity." Ioniq will also serve as a platform for our broader sustainability initiatives. For example, we recently partnered with thought leaders—fashion designer Maria Cornejo and British adventurer David de Rothschild—on a commitment to sustainable living and inviting eco-conscious consumers everywhere to take action in the global fight against climate change.

Index

www.ingramcontent.com/pod-product-compliance
Lightning Source LLC
Chambersburg PA
CBHW041206220326
41597CB00030BA/5065
* 9 7 8 1 4 6 8 6 0 2 9 9 9 *